LSAT
LOGICAL
REASONING
BIBLE

POWERSCORE
TEST PREPARATION

CONTENTS

CHAPTER ONE: INTRODUCTION

CHAPTER TWO: THE BASICS OF LOGICAL REASONING

CHAPTER THREE: THE QUESTION STEM AND ANSWER CHOICES

CHAPTER FOUR: MUST BE TRUE QUESTIONS

CHAPTER FIVE: MAIN POINT QUESTIONS

CHAPTER SIX: CONDITIONAL REASONING

Chapter Seven: Weaken Questions

Chapter Eight: Cause and Effect Reasoning

Chapter Nine: Strengthen, Justify the conclusion, and Assumption Questions

Chapter Ten: Resolve the Paradox Questions

Chapter Eleven: Formal Logic

Chapter Twelve: Method of Reasoning Questions

Chapter Thirteen: Flaw in the Reasoning Questions

Chapter Fourteen: Parallel Reasoning Questions

CHAPTER FIFTEEN: NUMBERS AND PERCENTAGES

CHAPTER SIXTEEN: EVALUATE THE ARGUMENT QUESTIONS

CHAPTER SEVENTEEN: CANNOT BE TRUE QUESTIONS

CHAPTER EIGHTEEN: POINT AT ISSUE QUESTIONS

CHAPTER NINETEEN: PRINCIPLE QUESTIONS

CHAPTER TWENTY: SECTION STRATEGY AND TIME MANAGEMENT

CHAPTER ANSWER KEY AND QUESTION USE TRACKER

MORE INFORMATION

About PowerScore

PowerScore is one of the nation's fastest growing test preparation companies. Headquartered on Hilton Head Island in South Carolina, PowerScore offers LSAT, GMAT, GRE, and SAT preparation classes in over 75 locations in the U.S. and abroad. For more information, please visit our website at www.powerscore.com.

CHAPTER ONE: INTRODUCTION

Introduction

Welcome to the *PowerScore LSAT Logical Reasoning Bible*. We congratulate you on your savvy purchase—you have bought the most advanced book ever published for the LSAT Logical Reasoning section. The purpose of this book is to provide you with a powerful and comprehensive system for attacking the Logical Reasoning section of the Law School Admission Test (LSAT), and by thoroughly studying and correctly applying this system we are confident you will increase your Logical Reasoning score.

This book has been carefully designed to reinforce your understanding of the concepts behind the Logical Reasoning section. The concepts and techniques discussed herein are drawn from our live LSAT courses, which we feel are the most effective in the world. As we progress through the chapters, we will prove how well the PowerScore methodology works by applying the techniques to real LSAT questions. Throughout the book you will encounter real questions drawn from actual LSATs, and all questions are used with the permission of Law Services, the producers of the LSAT. The use of real questions is essential to your success on the LSAT, and no question in this book has been modified from its original form.

In order to apply our methods effectively and efficiently, we strongly recommend that you carefully read and re-read each of the discussions regarding arguments, concepts, and question types. We also suggest that as you finish each question you look at both the explanation for the correct answer choice and the explanations for the incorrect answer choices. Closely examine each problem and determine which elements led to the correct answer, and then study the analyses provided in the book and check them against your own work. By doing so you will greatly increase your chances of recognizing the patterns present in all Logical Reasoning sections.

This book also contains a variety of drills and exercises that supplement the discussion of techniques and question analysis. The drills help strengthen specific skills that are critical for LSAT excellence, and for this reason they are as important as the LSAT questions. In the answer keys to these drills we will often introduce and discuss important LSAT points, so we strongly advise you to read through all explanations.

On page 525 there is a complete quick-reference answer key to all problems in this book. The answer key contains a legend of question identifiers, as well as chapter-by-chapter answer keys and a unique reverse lookup that lists all question used in this book sorted by the LSAT administration date and

PrepTest number.

If you are looking to further improve your LSAT score, we also recommend that you pick up a copy of the renowned *PowerScore LSAT Logic Games Bible*. The *Logic Games Bible* contains our system for attacking the Analytical Reasoning section of the LSAT. When combined with the *Logical Reasoning Bible*, you will have a formidable methodology for attacking the test. The *LSAT Logic Games Bible* is available through our website at www.powerscore.com and at fine retailers everywhere.

Because new LSATs appear every several months, and access to accurate and up-to-date information is critical, we have devoted a section of our website to *Logical Reasoning Bible* students. This free online resource area offers supplements to the book material, answers questions posed by students, and provides updates as needed. There is also an official book evaluation form that we strongly encourage you to use. The exclusive *LSAT Logical Reasoning Bible* online area can be accessed at:

www.powerscore.com/lrbible

If we can assist you in your LSAT preparation in any way, or if you have any questions or comments, please do not hesitate to contact us via email at lrbible@powerscore.com. Additional contact information is provided at the end of this book. We look forward to hearing from you!

A Brief Overview of the LSAT

The Law School Admission Test is administered four times a year: in February, June, September/October, and December. This standardized test is required for admission to any American Bar Association-approved law school. According to Law Services, the producers of the test, the LSAT is designed "to measure skills that are considered essential for success in law school: the reading and comprehension of complete texts with accuracy and insight; the organization and management of information and the ability to draw reasonable inferences from it; the ability to reason critically; and the analysis and evaluation of the reasoning and argument of others." The LSAT consists of the following five sections:

- 2 Sections of Logical Reasoning (short arguments, 24-26 total questions)
- 1 Section of Reading Comprehension (4 long reading passages, 26-28 total questions)
- 1 Section of Analytical Reasoning (4 logic games, 22-24 total questions)
- 1 Experimental Section of one of the above three section types.

You are given 35 minutes to complete each section. The experimental section is unscored and is not returned to the test taker. A break of 10 to 15 minutes is given between the 3rd and 4th sections.

The five-section test is followed by a 30 minute writing sample.

The Logical Reasoning Section

Each Logical Reasoning Section is composed of approximately 24 to 26 short arguments. Every short argument is followed by a question such as: "Which one of the following weakens the argument?" "Which one of the following parallels the argument?" or "Which one of the following must be true according to the argument?" The key to this section is time management and an understanding of the reasoning types and question types that frequently appear.

Since there are two scored sections of Logical Reasoning on every LSAT, this section accounts for approximately 50% of your score.

The Analytical Reasoning Section

This section, also known as Logic Games, is probably the most difficult for students taking the LSAT for the first time. The section consists of four games or puzzles, each followed by a series of five to eight questions. The questions are designed to test your ability to evaluate a set of relationships and to make inferences about those relationships. To perform well on this section you must understand the major types of games that frequently appear and develop the ability to properly diagram the rules and make inferences.

When you take an actual LSAT, they take your thumbprint at the testing site. This is done in case of test security problems.

At the conclusion of the LSAT, and for five business days after the LSAT, you have the option to cancel your score. Unfortunately, there is no way to determine exactly what your score would be before cancelling.

The Reading Comprehension Section

This section is composed of four reading passages, each approximately 450 words in length. The passage topics are drawn from a variety of subjects, and each passage is followed by a series of five to eight questions that ask you to determine viewpoints in the passage, analyze organizational traits, and evaluate specific sections of the passage. The key to this section is to read quickly with understanding and to carefully analyze the passage structure.

The Experimental Section

Each LSAT contains one experimental section, which does not count towards your score. The experimental can be any of the three section types described above, and the purpose of the section is to test and evaluate questions that will be used on *future* LSATs. By pretesting questions before their use in a scored section, the experimental helps the makers of the test determine the test scale. To learn more about the experimental section, we suggest you visit the PowerScore website, where you can find an extensive discussion of the experimental section, including how to identify the section and how to approach the section.

The Writing Sample

For many years the Writing Sample was administered before the LSAT.

A 30-minute Writing Sample is given at the conclusion of the LSAT. The Writing Sample is not scored, but a copy is sent to each of the law schools to which you apply. In the Writing Sample you are asked to defend one of two possible courses of action. Each course of action is described in a short paragraph and you are given two primary criteria to consider in making your decision. You must write a short essay supporting your choice. Do not agonize over the Writing Sample; in law school admissions, the Writing Sample is not a primary element for three reasons: the admissions committee is aware that the essay is given after a grueling three hour test and is about a subject you have no personal interest in; they already have a better sample of your writing ability in the personal statement; and the committee has a limited amount of time to evaluate applications.

You must attempt the Writing Sample! If you do not, Law Services reserves the right not to score your test.

The LSAT Scoring Scale

Each administered LSAT contains approximately 101 questions, and your LSAT score is based on the total number of questions you answer correctly, a total known as the raw score. After the raw score is determined, a unique Score Conversion Chart is used for each LSAT to convert the raw score into a scaled LSAT score. Since June 1991, the LSAT has utilized a 120 to 180 scoring scale, with 120 being the lowest possible score and 180 being the highest possible score. Notably, this 120 to 180 scale is just a renumbered version of the 200 to 800 scale most test takers are familiar with from the SAT, GRE, and GMAT. Just drop the "1" and add a "0" to the 120 and 180.

Since the LSAT has 61 possible scores, why didn't the test makers change the scale to 0 to 60? Probably for merciful reasons. How would you tell your friends that you scored a 3 on the LSAT? 123 sounds so much better.

Although the number of questions per test has remained relatively constant over the last eight years, the overall logical difficulty of each test has varied. This is not surprising since the test is made by humans and there is no precise way to completely predetermine logical difficulty. To account for these variances in test "toughness," the test makers adjust the Scoring Conversion Chart for each LSAT in order to make similar LSAT scores from different tests mean the same thing. For example, the LSAT given in June may be logically more difficult than the LSAT given in December, but by making the June LSAT scale "looser" than the December scale, a 160 on each test would represent the same level of performance. This scale adjustment, known as equating, is extremely important to law school admissions offices around the country. Imagine the difficulties that would be posed by unequated tests: admissions officers would have to not only examine individual LSAT scores, but also take into account which LSAT each score came from. This would present an information nightmare.

The LSAT Percentile Table

It is important not to lose sight of what LSAT scaled scores actually represent. The 120 to 180 test scale contains 61 different possible scores. Each score places a student in a certain relative position compared to other test takers. These relative positions are represented through a percentile that correlates to each score. The percentile indicates where the test taker ranks in the overall pool of test takers. For example, a score of 163 represents the 90th percentile, meaning a student with a score of 163 scored better than 90 percent of the people who have taken the test in the last three years. The percentile is critical since it is a true indicator of your positioning relative to other test takers, and thus law school applicants.

There is no penalty for answering incorrectly on the LSAT. Therefore, you should guess on any questions you cannot complete.

Charting out the entire percentage table yields a rough "bell curve." The number of test takers in the 120s and 170s is very low (only 1.6% of all test takers receive a score in the 170s), and most test takers are bunched in the middle, comprising the "top" of the bell. In fact, approximately 40% of all test takers score between 145 and 155 inclusive, and about 70% of all test takers score between 140 and 160 inclusive.

The median score on the LSAT scale is approximately 151. The median, or middle, score is the score at which approximately 50% of test takers have a lower score and 50% of test takers have a higher score. Typically, to achieve a score of 151, you must answer between 55 and 59 questions correctly from a total of 101 questions. In other words, to achieve a score that is perfectly average, you can miss between 42 and 46 questions. Thus, it is important to remember that you do not have to answer every question correctly in order to receive an excellent LSAT score. There is room for error, and accordingly you should never let any single question occupy an inordinate amount of your time.

The Use of the LSAT

The use of the LSAT in law school admissions is not without controversy. Experts agree that your LSAT score is one of the most important determinants of the type of school you can attend. At many law schools a multiplier made up of your LSAT score and your undergraduate grade point average is used to help determine the relative standing of applicants, and at some schools a sufficiently high multiplier guarantees your admission.

For all the importance of the LSAT, the exam is not without flaws. As a standardized test currently given in the paper-and-pencil format, there are a number of skills that the LSAT cannot measure, including listening skills, note-taking ability, perseverance, etc. Law Services is aware of these limitations and on an annual basis they warn all law school admission offices about overemphasizing LSAT results. Still, because the test ultimately returns a number for each student, the tendency to rank applicants is high. Fortunately, once you get to law school the LSAT is forgotten. For the time being consider the test a temporary hurdle you must leap in order to reach the ultimate goal.

For more information on the LSAT, or to register for the test, contact Law Services at (215) 968-1001 or at their website at www.lsac.org.

CHAPTER TWO: THE BASICS OF LOGICAL REASONING

The Logical Reasoning Section

The focus of this book is on the Logical Reasoning section of the LSAT, and each Logical Reasoning section contains a total of 24 to 26 questions. Since you have thirty-five minutes to complete the section, you have an average of approximately one minute and twenty-five seconds to complete each question. Of course, the amount of time you spend on each question will vary with the difficulty of each question and the total number of questions per section. For virtually all students the time constraint is a major obstacle, and as we progress through this book we will discuss time management techniques as well as time-saving techniques that you can employ within the section.

On average, you have 1 minute and 25 seconds to complete each question.

The Section Directions

Each Logical Reasoning section is prefaced by the following directions:

> "The questions in this section are based on the reasoning contained in brief statements or passages. For some questions, more than one of the choices could conceivably answer the question. However, you are to choose the <u>best</u> answer; that is, the response that most accurately and completely answers the question. You should not make assumptions that are by commonsense standards implausible, superfluous, or incompatible with the passage. After you have chosen the best answer, blacken the corresponding space on your answer sheet."

Because these directions precede every Logical Reasoning section, you should familiarize yourself with them now. Once the LSAT begins, *never* waste time reading the directions for any section.

Let's examine these directions more closely. Consider the following sentences: "For some questions, more than one of the choices could conceivably answer the question. However, you are to choose the <u>best</u> answer; that is, the response that most accurately and completely answers the question." By stating up front that more than one answer choice could suffice to answer the question, the makers of the test compel you to read every single answer choice before making a selection. If you read only one or two answer choices and then decide you have the correct one, you could end up choosing an answer that has some merit but is not as good as a later answer. One of the test makers' favorite tricks is to place a highly attractive wrong answer choice immediately before the correct answer choice in the hopes that you will pick the wrong answer choice and then move to the next question without reading any of the other answers.

Always read each of the five answer choices before deciding which answer is correct.

Assumptions are a critical part of LSAT Logical Reasoning, and we will talk about assumptions in more detail in a later chapter.

Here's a good example of what they expect you to assume: when "television" is introduced in a stimulus, they expect you to know, among other things, what a TV show is, that TV can portray the make-believe or real, what actors do, and that TV is shown by beaming signals into TV sets in homes and elsewhere.

The question to the right, from the October 2003 LSAT, is presented for demonstration purposes only. The problem contains Formal Logic, which we will examine in great detail in a later chapter. For those of you who wish to try the problem now, the correct answer is listed in the first sidebar on the next page.

The other part of the directions that is interesting is the sentence that states, "You should not make assumptions that are by commonsense standards implausible, superfluous, or incompatible with the passage." The implication here is that you can make some assumptions when working with questions, but not other assumptions. Of course, Law Services does not hand out a list of what constitutes a commensense assumption! Even outside of the LSAT, the test makers do not clearly state what assumptions are acceptable or unacceptable for you to make, mainly because such a list would be almost infinite. For LSAT purposes, approaching each question you can take as true any statement or idea that the average American would be expected to believe on the basis of generally known and accepted facts. For example, in a question you can assume that the sky sometimes becomes cloudy, but you cannot assume that the sky is always cloudy (unless stated explicitly by the question). LSAT questions will *not* require you to make assumptions based on extreme ideas (such as that it always rains in Seattle) or ideas not in the general domain of knowledge (such as the per capita income of residents of France). Please note that this does not mean that the LSAT cannot set up scenarios where they discuss ideas that are extreme or outside the bounds of common knowledge. Within a Logical Reasoning question, the test makers can and do discuss complex or extreme ideas; in these cases, they will give you context for the situation by providing additional information. However, be careful about assuming something to be true (unless you believe it is a widely accepted fact or the test makers indicate you should believe it to be true). This last idea is one we will discuss in much more detail as we look at individual question types.

The Parts of a Logical Reasoning Question

Every Logical Reasoning question contains three separate parts: the stimulus, the question stem, and the five answer choices. The following diagram identifies each part:

1. Most serious students are happy students, and most serious students go to graduate school. Furthermore, all students who go to graduate school are overworked. ——— Stimulus

Which one of the following can be properly inferred from the statements above? ——— Question Stem

(A) Most overworked students are happy students.
(B) Some happy students are overworked.
(C) All overworked students are serious students. ——— Answer Choices
(D) Some unhappy students go to graduate school.
(E) All serious students are overworked.

Approaching the Questions

When examining the three parts, students sometimes wonder about the best strategy for attacking a question: should I read the question stem first? Should I preview the five answer choices? The answer is *Read the parts in the order given*. That is, first read the stimulus, then read the question stem, and finally read each of the five answer choices. Although this may seem like a reasonable, even obvious, approach we mention it here because some LSAT texts advocate reading the question stem before reading the stimulus. We are certain that these texts are seriously mistaken, and here are a few reasons why:

The correct answer to the problem on the previous page is answer choice (B). This is not an easy problem, but after you read through our chapter on Formal Logic this question will seem very reasonable.

1. Understanding the stimulus is the key to answering any question, and reading the question stem first tends to undermine the ability of students to fully comprehend the information in the stimulus. On easy questions this distraction tends not to have a significant negative impact, but on more difficult questions the student often is forced to read the stimulus twice in order to get full comprehension, thus wasting valuable time. Literally, by reading the question stem first, students are forced to juggle two things at once: the question stem and the information in the stimulus. That is a difficult task when under time pressure. The bottom line is that any viable strategy must be effective for questions at all difficulty levels, but when you read the question stem first you cannot perform optimally. True, the approach works with the easy questions, but those questions could have been answered correctly regardless of the approach used.

2. Reading the question stem first often wastes valuable time since the typical student will read the stem, then read the stimulus, and then read the stem again. Unfortunately, there simply is not enough time to read every question stem twice.

3. Some question stems refer to information given in the stimulus, or add new conditions to the stimulus information. Thus, reading the stem first is of little value and often confuses or distracts the student when he or she goes to read the stimulus.

4. On stimuli with two questions, reading one stem biases the reader to look for that specific information, possibly causing problems while doing the second question, and reading both stems before reading the stimulus wastes entirely too much time and leads to confusion.

5. For truly knowledgeable test takers there are situations that arise where the question stem is fairly predictable. One example—and there are others—is with a question type called Resolve the Paradox. Usually, when you read the stimulus that accompanies these questions, an obvious paradox or discrepancy is presented. Reading the question stem beforehand does not add anything to what you would have known just from reading the stimulus. In later chapters we will discuss this situation and others where you can predict the question stem with some success.

In our experience, the vast majority of high-scoring LSAT takers read the stimulus first.

6. Finally, we believe that one of the main principles underlying the read-the-question-stem-first approach is flawed. Many advocates of the approach claim that it helps the test taker avoid the "harder" questions, such as Parallel Reasoning or Method of Reasoning. However, test data show that questions of any type can be hard or easy. Some Method of Reasoning questions are phenomenally easy whereas some Method of Reasoning questions are extremely difficult. In short, the question stem is a poor indicator of difficulty because question difficulty is more directly related to the complexity of the stimulus and the corresponding answer choices.

Understandably, reading the question stem before the stimulus sounds like a good idea at first, but for the majority of students (especially those trying to score in the 160s and above), the approach is a hindrance, not a help. Solid test performance depends on your ability to quickly comprehend complex argumentation; do not make your task harder by reading the question stem first.

Analyzing the Stimulus

As you read the stimulus, initially focus on making a quick analysis of the topic under discussion. What area has the author chosen to write about? You will be more familiar with some topics than with others, but do not assume that everything you know "outside" of the stimulus regarding the topic is true and applies to the stimulus. For example, say you work in a real estate office and you come across an LSAT question about property sales. You can use your work experience and knowledge of real estate to help you better understand what the author is discussing, but do not assume that things will operate in the stimulus exactly as they do at your workplace. Perhaps property transactions in your state are different from those in other states, or perhaps protocols followed in your office differ from those elsewhere. In an LSAT question, look carefully at what the author says about the topic at hand; statements presented as facts on the LSAT can and do vary from what occurs in the "real world." This discrepancy between the "LSAT world" and the "real world" is one you must always be aware of: although the two worlds overlap, things in the LSAT world are often very different from what you expect. From our earlier discussion of commonsense assumptions we know that you can assume that basic, widely-held facts will hold true in the LSAT world, but by the same token, you cannot assume that specialized information that you have learned in the real world will hold true on the LSAT. We will discuss "outside information" in more detail when we discuss LSAT question types.

Next, make sure to read the entire stimulus very carefully. The makers of the LSAT have extraordinarily high expectations about the level of detail you should retain when you read a stimulus. Many questions will test your knowledge of small, seemingly nitpicky variations in phrasing, and reading carelessly is LSAT suicide. In many respects, the requirement forced upon you

Reading closely is a critical LSAT skill.

to read carefully is what makes the time constraint so difficult to handle. Every test taker is placed at the nexus of two competing elements: the need for speed (caused by the timed element) and the need for patience (caused by the detailed reading requirement). How well you manage these two elements strongly determines how well you perform. Later in this chapter we will discuss how to practice using time elements, and near the end of the book we will discuss section management techniques.

Finally, analyze the structure of the stimulus: what pieces are present and how do those pieces relate to each other? In short, you are tasked with knowing as much as possible about the statements made by the author, and in order to do so, you must understand how the makers create LSAT arguments. We will discuss argumentation in more detail in a moment.

LSAT argumentation is one of the main topics of this book, and will be discussed in every chapter.

Stimulus Topics

The spectrum of topics covered by Logical Reasoning stimuli is quite broad. Previous stimuli topics have ranged from art to economics to medicine and science. According to the makers of the test, "the arguments are contained in short passages taken from a variety of sources, including letters to the editor, speeches, advertisements, newspaper articles and editorials, informal discussions and conversations, as well as articles in the humanities, the social sciences, and the natural sciences." Further, LSAT question topics "reflect a broad range of academic disciplines and are intended to give no advantage to candidates from a particular background."

Despite the previous statement, many LSAT students come from a humanities background and these test takers often worry about stimuli containing scientific or medical topics. Remember, the topic of a stimulus does not affect the underlying logical relationship of the argument parts. And, the LSAT will not assume that you know anything about advanced technical or scientific ideas. For example, while the LSAT may discuss mathematicians or the existence of a difficult problem in math, you will not be asked to make calculations nor will you be assumed to understand esoteric terminology. Any element beyond the domain of general public knowledge will be explained for you, as in the following example from the December 2003 LSAT:

Some specific topics do recur, and we will note those in future chapters.

> Scientist: Isaac Newton's *Principia*, the seventeenth-century work that served as the cornerstone of physics for over two centuries, could at first be understood by only a handful of people, but a basic understanding of Newton's ideas eventually spread throughout the world. This shows that the barriers to communication between scientists...

The stimulus above, although reproduced only in part, is a good example of how the test makers will supply information they feel is essential to understanding the question. In this case, the reader is not expected to understand either the content or historical importance of *Principia*, and so the test makers conveniently furnish that information. Thus, although on occasion you will see a stimulus that references an ominous looking word or idea (recent examples include *superheated plasma* and *toxaphene*), you will not need to know or be assumed to know anything more about those elements than what you are told by the test makers. When you read a science-based stimulus, focus on understanding the relationship of the ideas and do not be intimidated by the terminology used by the author. As we will ultimately find, reading an LSAT stimulus is about seeing past the topic to analyze the structural relationships present in the stimulus. Once you are able to see these relationships, the topic will become less important.

Arguments versus Fact Sets

LSAT stimuli fall into two distinct categories: those containing an argument and those that are just a set of facts. Logically speaking, an argument can be defined as a set of statements wherein one statement is claimed to follow from or be derived from the others. Consider the following short example of an argument:

> All professors are ethical. Mason is a professor. So Mason is ethical.

The first two statements in this argument give the reasons (or "premises") for accepting the third statement, which is the conclusion of the argument.

Fact sets, on the other hand, are a collection of statements without a conclusion, as in the following example:

> "The Jacksonville area has just over one million residents. The Cincinnati area has almost two million residents. The New York area has almost twenty million residents."

The three sentences above do *not* constitute an argument because no conclusion is present and an argument, by definition, requires a conclusion. The three sentences merely make a series of assertions without making a judgment. Notice that reading these sentences does not cause much of a reaction in most readers. Really, who cares about the city sizes? This lack of a strong reaction is often an indication that you are not reading an argument and are instead reading just a set of facts.

When reading Logical Reasoning stimuli, you should seek to make several key determinations, which we call the Logical Reasoning Primary Objectives™. Your first task is to determine if you are reading an argument or a fact set.

Primary Objective #1: Determine whether the stimulus contains an argument or if it is only a set of factual statements.

To achieve this objective, you must recognize whether a conclusion is present. Let us talk about how to do this next.

Identifying Premises and Conclusions

For LSAT purposes, a premise can be defined as:

"A fact, proposition, or statement from which a conclusion is made."

Premises support and explain the conclusion. Literally, the premises give the reasons why the conclusion should be accepted. To identify premises, ask yourself, "*What reasons has the author used to persuade me? Why should I believe this argument? What evidence exists?*"

A conclusion can be defined as:

"A statement or judgment that follows from one or more reasons."

Conclusions, as summary statements, are supposed to be drawn from and rest on the premises. To identify conclusions, ask yourself, "*What is the author driving at? What does the author want me to believe? What point follows from the others?*"

Because language is the test maker's weapon of choice, you must learn to recognize the words that indicate when a premise or conclusion is present. In expressing arguments, authors often use the following words or phrases to introduce premises and conclusions:

Premise Indicators	Conclusion Indicators
because	thus
since	therefore
for	hence
for example	consequently
for the reason that	as a result
in that	so
given that	accordingly
as indicated by	clearly
due to	must be that
owing to	shows that
this can be seen from	conclude that
we know this by	follows that
	for this reason

Because there are so many variations in the English language, these lists cannot be comprehensive, but they do capture many of the premise and conclusion indicators used by LSAT authors. As for frequency of appearance, the top two words in each list are used more than any of the other words in the list.

When you are reading, always be aware of the presence of the words listed

A premise gives a reason why something should be believed.

A conclusion is the point the author tries to prove by using another statement.

Make sure to memorize these word lists. Recognizing argument elements is critical!

Arguments can contain more than one premise and more than one conclusion.

above. These words are like road signs; they tell you what is coming next. Consider the following example:

> Humans cannot live on Venus because the surface temperature is too high.

As you read the first portion of the sentence, "Humans cannot live on Venus," you cannot be sure if you are reading a premise or conclusion. But, as soon as you see the word "because"—a premise indicator—you know that a premise will follow, and at that point you know that the first portion of the sentence is a conclusion. In the argument above, the author wants you to believe that humans cannot live on Venus, and the reason is that the surface temperature is too high.

About 75% of LSAT stimuli contain arguments. The remainder are fact sets.

In our daily lives, we make and hear many arguments. However, unlike on the LSAT, the majority of these arguments occur in the form of conversations (and when we say "argument," we do not mean a fight!). Any LSAT argument can be seen as an artificial conversation, even the basic example above:

> Author: "Humans cannot live on Venus."
> Respondent: "Really? Why is that?"
> Author: "The surface temperature of Venus is too high."

If at first you struggle to identify the pieces of an argument, you can always resort to thinking about the argument as an artificial conversation and that may assist you in locating the conclusion.

Here are more examples of premise and conclusion indicators in use:

1. "The economy is in tatters. Therefore, we must end this war."

   "Therefore" introduces a conclusion; the first sentence is a premise.

2. "We must reduce our budget due to the significant cost overruns we experienced during production."

   "due to" introduces a premise; "We must reduce our budget" is the conclusion.

Important note: premises and conclusions can be constructed without indicator words present.

3. "Fraud has cost the insurance industry millions of dollars in lost revenue. Thus, congress will pass a stricter fraud control bill since the insurance industry has one of the most powerful lobbies."

   This argument contains two premises: the first premise is the first sentence and the second premise follows the word "since" in the second sentence; the conclusion is "congress will pass a stricter fraud control bill."

Notice that premises and conclusions can be presented in any order—the conclusion can be first or last, and the relationship between the premises and the conclusion remains the same regardless of the order of presentation. For example, if the order of the premise(s) and conclusion was switched in any of the examples above, the logical structure of the argument would not change.

Order of presentation has no effect on the logical structure of the argument. The conclusion can appear at the beginning, the middle, or the end of the argument.

Also notable is that the premises and the conclusion can appear in the same sentence, or be separated out into multiple sentences. Whether the ideas are together or separated has no effect on the logical structure of the argument.

If a conclusion is present, you *must* identify the conclusion prior to proceeding on to the question stem. Often, the reason students miss questions is because they have failed to fully and accurately identify the conclusion of the argument.

Primary Objective #2: If the stimulus contains an argument, identify the conclusion of the argument. If the stimulus contains a fact set, examine each fact.

Remember, a fact set does *not* contain a conclusion; an argument must contain a conclusion.

One Confusing Form

Because the job of the test makers is to determine how well you can interpret information, they will sometimes arrange premise and conclusion indicators in a way that is designed to be confusing. One of their favorite forms places a conclusion indicator and premise indicator back-to-back, separated by a comma, as in the following examples:

> "Therefore, since..."
> "Thus, because..."
> "Hence, due to..."

This form is called the "conclusion/ premise indicator form."

A quick glance would seemingly indicate that what will follow is both a premise and a conclusion. In this instance, however, the presence of the comma creates a clause that, due to the premise indicator, contains a premise. The end of that premise clause will be closed with a second comma, and then what follows will be the conclusion, as in the following:

> "Therefore, since higher debt has forced consumers to lower their savings, banks now have less money to loan."

"Higher debt has forced consumers to lower their savings" is the premise; "banks now have less money to loan" is the conclusion. So, in this instance "therefore" still introduces a conclusion, but the appearance of the conclusion is interrupted by a clause that contains a premise.

Premise and Conclusion Recognition Mini-Drill

Each of the following problems contains a short argument. For each argument, identify the conclusion and the premise(s). Answers on the next page.

1. "Given that the price of steel is rising, we will no longer be able to offer discounts on our car parts."

2. "The political situation in Somalia is unstable owing to the ability of individual warlords to maintain powerful armed forces."

3. "Since we need to have many different interests to sustain us, the scientists' belief must be incorrect."

4. "So, as indicated by the newly released data, we should push forward with our efforts to recolonize the forest with snowy tree crickets."

5. "Television has a harmful effect on society. This can be seen from the poor school performance of children who watch significant amounts of television and from the fact that children who watch more than six hours of television a day tend to read less than non-television watching children."

6. "The rapid diminishment of the ecosystem of the Amazon threatens the entire planet. Consequently, we must take immediate steps to convince the Brazilian government that planned development projects need to be curtailed for the simple reason that these development projects will greatly accelerate the loss of currently protected land."

Premise and Conclusion Recognition Mini-Drill Answer Key

1. Features the premise indicator "given that."
   Premise: "Given that the price of steel is rising,"
   Conclusion: "we will no longer be able to offer discounts on our car parts."

2. Features the premise indicator "owing to."
   Premise: "owing to the ability of individual warlords to maintain powerful armed forces."
   Conclusion: "The political situation in Somalia is unstable"

3. Features the premise indicator "since."
   Premise: "Since we need to have many different interests to sustain us,"
   Conclusion: "the scientists' belief must be incorrect."

4. Features the conclusion/premise form indicator "So, as indicated by."
   Premise: "as indicated by the newly released data"
   Conclusion: "we should push forward with our efforts to recolonize the forest with snowy tree crickets."

5. Features the premise indicator "this can be seen from." The second sentence contains two premises.
   Premise 1: "This can be seen from the poor school performance of children who watch significant amounts of television"
   Premise 2: "and from fact that children who watch more than six hours of television a day tend to read less than non-television watching children."
   Conclusion: "Television has a harmful effect on society." Note how this sentence does not contain a conclusion indicator. Yet, we can determine that this is the conclusion because the other sentence contains two premises.

6. Features the conclusion indicator "consequently" and the premise indicator "for the simple reason that." There are also two premises present.
   Premise 1: "The rapid diminishment of the ecosystem of the Amazon threatens the entire planet."
   Premise 2: "for the simple reason that these development projects will greatly accelerate the loss of currently protected land."
   Conclusion: "we must take immediate steps to convince the Brazilian government that planned development projects need to be curtailed"

Additional Premise Indicators

Additional premises are still, of course, premises. They may be central to the argument or they may be secondary. To determine the importance of the premise, examine the remainder of the argument.

Aside from previously listed premise and conclusions indicators, there are other argument indicator words you should learn to recognize. First, in argument forms, sometimes the author will make an argument and then for good measure add another premise that supports the conclusion but is sometimes non-essential to the conclusion. These are known as additional premises:

<u>Additional Premise Indicators</u>

Furthermore
Moreover
Besides
In addition
What's more

Following are two examples of additional premise indicators in use:

1. "Every professor at Fillmore University teaches exactly one class per semester. Fillmore's Professor Jackson, therefore, is teaching exactly one class this semester. Moreover, I heard Professor Jackson say she was teaching only a single class."

    The first sentence is a premise. The second sentence contains the conclusion indicator "therefore" and is the conclusion of the argument. The first sentence is the main proof offered by the author for the conclusion. The third sentence begins with the additional premise indicator "moreover." The premise in this sentence is non-essential to the argument, but provides additional proof for the conclusion and could be, if needed, used to help prove the conclusion separately (this would occur if an objection was raised to the first premise).

2. "The city council ought to ease restrictions on outdoor advertising because the city's economy is currently in a slump. Furthermore, the city should not place restrictions on forms of speech such as advertising."

    The first sentence contains both the conclusion of the argument and the main premise of the argument (introduced by the premise indicator "because"). The last sentence contains the additional premise indicator "furthermore." As with the previous example, the additional premise in this sentence is non-essential to the argument but provides additional proof for the conclusion.

Counter-premise Indicators

When creating an argument, an author will sometimes bring up a counter-premise—a premise that actually contains an idea that is counter to the argument. At first glance, this might seem like an odd thing for an author to do. But by raising the counter-premise and then addressing the complaint in a direct fashion, the author can minimize the damage that would be done by the objection if it were raised elsewhere.

Counter-premises can also be ideas that compare and contrast with the argument, or work against a previously raised point. In this sense, the general counter-premise concept discusses an idea that is in some way different from another part of the argument.

Counter-premises, also called adversatives, bring up points of opposition or comparison.

Counter-premise Indicators

But
Yet
However
On the other hand
Admittedly
In contrast
Although
Even though
Still
Whereas
In spite of
Despite
After all

Following is an example of a counter-premise indicator in use:

1. "The United States prison population is the world's largest and consequently we must take steps to reduce crime in this country. Although other countries have higher rates of incarceration, their statistics have no bearing on the dilemma we currently face."

   The first sentence contains a premise and the conclusion (which is introduced by the conclusion indicator "consequently"). The third sentence offers up a counter-premise as indicated by the word "although."

Each of the following problems contains a short argument. For each argument, identify the conclusion, the premise(s), and any additional premises or counter-premises. Answers on the next page.

1.   Wine is made by crushing grapes and eventually separating the juice from the grape skins. However, the separated juice contains impurities and many wineries do not filter the juice. These wineries claim the unfiltered juice ultimately produces a more flavorful and intense wine. Since these wine makers are experts, we should trust their judgment and not shy away from unfiltered wine.

2.   Phenylketonurics are people who cannot metabolize the amino acid phenylalanine. There are dangers associated with phenylketonuria, and products containing phenylalanine must carry a warning label that states, "Phenylketonurics: contains phenylalanine." In addition, all children in developed societies receive a phenylketonuria test at birth. Hence, at the moment, we are doing as much as possible to protect against this condition.

3.   During last night's robbery, the thief was unable to open the safe. Thus, last night's robbery was unsuccessful despite the fact that the thief stole several documents. After all, nothing in those documents was as valuable as the money in the safe.

Additional Premise and Counter-Premise Recognition Mini-Drill Answer Key

1. Features the counter-premise indicator "however" and the premise indicator "since."

> Premise: "Wine is made by crushing grapes and eventually separating the juice from the grape skins."
>
> Counter-premise: "However, the separated juice contains impurities and many wineries do not filter the juice."
>
> Premise: "These wineries claim the unfiltered juice ultimately produces a more flavorful and intense wine."
>
> Premise: "Since these wine makers are experts,"
>
> Conclusion: "we should trust their judgment and not shy away from unfiltered wine."

2. Features the additional premise indicator "in addition" and the conclusion indicator "hence." In this problem the additional premise is central to supporting the conclusion.

> Premise: "Phenylketonurics are people who cannot metabolize the amino acid phenylalanine."
>
> Premise: "There are dangers associated with phenylketonuria, and products containing phenylalanine must carry a warning label that states, 'Phenylketonurics: contains phenylalanine.' "
>
> Additional Premise: "In addition, all children in developed societies received a phenylketonuria test at birth."
>
> Conclusion: "Hence, at the moment, we are doing as much as possible to protect against this condition."

3. Features the counter-premise indicator "despite"; the additional premise indicator "after all"; and the conclusion indicator "thus." The additional premise serves to downplay the counter-premise.

> Premise: "During last night's robbery, the thief was unable to open the safe."
>
> Counter-premise: "despite the fact that the thief stole several documents."
>
> Additional Premise: "After all, nothing in those documents was as valuable as the money in the safe."
>
> Conclusion: "Thus, last night's robbery was unsuccessful "

Recognizing Conclusions Without Indicators

Many of the arguments we have encountered up until this point have had conclusion indicators to help you recognize the conclusion. And, many of the arguments you will see on the LSAT will also have conclusion indicators. But you will encounter arguments that do not contain conclusion indicators. Following is an example:

> The best way of eliminating traffic congestion will not be easily found. There are so many competing possibilities that it will take millions of dollars to study every option, and implementation of most options carries an exorbitant price tag.

An argument such as the above can be difficult to analyze because no indicator words are present. How then, would you go about determining if a conclusion is present, and if so, how would you identify that conclusion? Fortunately, there is a fairly simple trick that can be used to handle this situation, and any situation where you are uncertain of the conclusion (even those with multiple conclusions, as will be discussed next).

Law Services says you are expected to possess, in their words, "a college-level understanding of widely used concepts such as argument, premise, assumption, and conclusion."

Aside from the questions you can use to identify premises and conclusions (described earlier in this chapter), the easiest way to determine the conclusion in an argument is to use the Conclusion Identification Method™:

> Take the statements under consideration for the conclusion and place them in an arrangement that forces one to be the conclusion and the other(s) to be the premise(s). Use premise and conclusion indicators to achieve this end. Once the pieces are arranged, determine if the arrangement makes logical sense. If so, you have made the correct identification. If not, reverse the arrangement and examine the relationship again. Continue until you find an arrangement that is logical.

Let us apply this method to the argument at the top of this page. For our first arrangement we will make the first sentence the premise and the second sentence the conclusion, and supply indicators (in italics):

> *Because* the best way of eliminating traffic congestion will not be easily found, *we can conclude that* there are so many competing possibilities that it will take millions of dollars to study every option, and implementation of most options carries an exorbitant price tag.

Does that sound right? No. Let us try again, this time making the first sentence the conclusion and the second sentence the premise:

> *Because* there are so many competing possibilities that it will take millions of dollars to study every option, and implementation of most options carries an exorbitant price tag, *we can conclude that* the best

way of eliminating traffic congestion will not be easily found.

Clearly, the second arrangement is far superior because it makes sense. In most cases when you have the conclusion and premise backward, the arrangement will be confusing. The correct arrangement always sounds more logical.

Complex Arguments

Up until this point, we have only discussed simple arguments. Simple arguments contain a single conclusion. While many of the arguments that appear on the LSAT are simple arguments, there are also a fair number of complex arguments. Complex arguments contain more than one conclusion. In these instances, one of the conclusions is the main conclusion, and the other conclusions are subsidiary conclusions (also known as sub-conclusions).

While complex argumentation may sound daunting at first, you make and encounter complex argumentation every day in your life. In basic terms, a complex argument makes an initial conclusion based on a premise. The author then uses that conclusion as the foundation (or premise) for another conclusion, thus building a chain with several levels. Let us take a look at the two types of arguments in diagram form:

In abstract terms, a simple argument appears as follows:

Conclusion

↑

Premise

As discussed previously, the premise supports the conclusion, hence the arrow from the premise to the conclusion. By comparison, a complex argument takes an initial conclusion and then uses it as a premise for another conclusion:

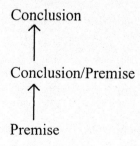

Conclusion

↑

Conclusion/Premise

↑

Premise

Thus, a statement can be both a conclusion for one argument and a premise for another. In this sense, a complex argument can appear somewhat like a ladder, where each level or "rung" is used to build the next level. Given enough time you could build an argument with hundreds of levels. On the LSAT, however,

A simple argument does not mean that the argument is easy to understand! Simple in this context means that the argument contains only a single conclusion.

there are typically three or four levels at most. Let us look at an example of a complex argument:

> Because the Vikings have the best wide receiver in football, they therefore have the best offense in football. Because they have the best offense in football, they will win the Super Bowl next year.

The makers of the LSAT love to use complex argumentation because the presence of multiple conclusions tends to confuse students, making attractive wrong answer choices easier to create.

In this argument, the first sentence contains a premise followed by a conclusion. This initial conclusion is then used in the second sentence as a premise to make a larger conclusion:

> Premise: "Because the Vikings have the best wide receiver in football,"
> Sub-Conclusion (conclusion of the previous premise/Premise for the following conclusion): "they therefore have the best offense in football."
> Main Conclusion: "they will win the Super Bowl next year."

As we will see in Chapter Twelve while discussing Method of Reasoning questions, one of the most commonly used complex argument forms is to place the main conclusion in the first sentence of the argument, and then to place the sub-conclusion in the last sentence of the argument, preceded by a conclusion indicator. This form is quite useful since it tends to trick students into thinking the last sentence is the main conclusion.

Another form of complex argumentation occurs with two-speaker stimuli. In these questions, two separate speakers are identified, and each presents his or her own argument or comment. Here is an example from the June 2003 LSAT:

> Anne: Halley's Comet, now in a part of its orbit relatively far from the Sun, recently flared brightly enough to be seen by telescope. No comet has ever been observed to flare so far from the Sun before, so such a flare must be highly unusual.
>
> Sue: Nonsense. Usually no one bothers to try to observe comets when they are so far from the Sun. This flare was observed only because an observatory was tracking Halley's Comet very carefully.

In the argument above, each speaker presents premises and a conclusion. As often occurs with this form of question, the two speakers disagree.

One of the benefits of a two-speaker stimulus is that the test makers can introduce multiple viewpoints on the same subject. As you might imagine, the presence of multiple viewpoints tends to be confusing, and the extra viewpoints offer the test makers the opportunity to ask a wider variety of questions.

A Commonly Used Construction

Even within a single-speaker stimulus the test makers can raise alternate viewpoints. One of the most frequently used constructions is to raise a viewpoint at the beginning of the stimulus and then disagree with it immediately thereafter. This efficiently raises two opposing views in a very short paragraph. These stimuli are recognizable because they often begin with the phrase, "Some people claim..." or one of the many variations on this theme, including but not limited to the following:

"Some people propose..."
"Many people believe..."
"Some argue that..." or "Some people argue that..."
"Some critics claim..."
"Some critics maintain..."
"Some scientists believe..."

The structure of this opening sentence is remarkably consistent in form, and adheres to the following formula:

A *number* (some, many, etc.) of *people* (critics, students, teachers, legislators, vegetarians, psychologists etc.) *believe* (claim, propose, argue, etc.) that...

Of course, there are exceptions, as with these opening sentences from previous LSATs:

"Although some people claim..."   (starts with "although")
"It has been claimed that..."   (drops the *number* and *people*)
"Cigarette companies claim that..."   (drops the *number*)

The author can also break up the idea, by inserting contextual information, as in the following example:

"*Some critics* of space exploration programs *claim* that..."

The use of this device to begin a stimulus almost always leads to the introduction of the opposing view, as in the following partial stimulus from the October 2003 LSAT:

Editorialist: Some people propose that, to raise revenues and encourage conservation, our country's taxes on oil, gasoline, and coal should be increased. Such a tax, however, would do more harm than good.

The editorialist uses the "Some people propose" device to introduce one opinion of taxes and then in the following sentence counters the idea with the view that turns out to be the editorialist's main point ("Such a tax, however..."). The remainder of the problem went on to explain the reasoning behind the editorialist's view.

Given the frequency with which this construction appears at the beginning of stimuli, you should learn to begin recognizing it now. We will again discuss this device in the Main Point section.

Truth versus Validity

So far, we have only identified the parts that are used to construct arguments. We have not made an analysis of the reasonableness or soundness of an argument. But, before moving on to argument analysis, you must be able to distinguish between two commonly confused concepts: validity and truth.

When we evaluate LSAT arguments, we are primarily concerned with validity. That is, what is the logical relationship of the pieces of the argument and how well do the premises, if accepted, prove the conclusion? We are less concerned with the absolute, real world truthfulness of either the premises or the conclusion. Some students will at first try to analyze every single LSAT statement on the basis of whether it is an absolutely true statement (does it happen as stated in the real world). For the most part, that is wasted effort. LSAT Logical Reasoning is primarily focused on whether the conclusion follows logically from a set of given premises. In many cases, the LSAT makers will let you work under a framework where the premises are simply accepted as factually accurate, and then you must focus solely on the method used to reach the conclusion. In a sense this could be called relative truthfulness—you are only concerned about whether the conclusion is true relative to the premises, not whether the conclusion is true in an absolute, real world sense. This is obviously a critical point, and one we will analyze later as we discuss different question types.

Argument Analysis

Once you have determined that an argument is present and you have identified the conclusion, you must determine if the argument is a good one or a bad one. This leads to the third Primary Objective:

Primary Objective #3: If the stimulus contains an argument, determine whether the argument is strong or weak.

To determine the strength of the argument, consider the relationship between the premises and the conclusion—do the premises strongly suggest that the conclusion would be true? Does the conclusion feel like an inevitable result of

Logicians spend a great deal of time discussing validity and truth, even going so far as to create complex truth tables that analyze the validity of arguments. We are not concerned with such methods because they do not apply to the LSAT.

In logic, the terms "strong/ weak," "good/ bad," "valid/ invalid," and "sound/unsound" are used to evaluate arguments. For our purposes, "strong," "good," "valid," and "sound" will be interchangeable and all terms refer to the logical structure of the argument. The same holds true for "weak," "bad," "invalid," and "unsound."

the premises? Or does the conclusion seem to go beyond the scope of the information in the premises? How persuasive does the argument seem to you? When evaluating argument validity, the question you must always ask yourself is: Do the given facts support the conclusion?

To better understand this concept we will examine two sample arguments. The following argument uses the fact set we used before, with the addition of a conclusion:

> "The Jacksonville area has just over one million residents. Cincinnati has almost two million residents. The New York area has almost twenty million residents. Therefore, we should move to Jacksonville."

The last sentence contains the conclusion, and makes this an argument. Notice how the presence of the conclusion causes you to react more strongly to the stimulus. Now, instead of just reading a set of cold facts, you are forced to consider whether the premises have proven the given conclusion. In this case the author asks you to accept that a move to Jacksonville is in order based on the population of the city. Do you think the author has proven this point?

When considering the above argument, most people simply accept the premises as factually accurate. There is nothing wrong with this (and indeed in the real world they are true). As mentioned moments ago, in LSAT argumentation the makers of the test largely allow authors to put forth their premises unchallenged. The test makers are far more concerned about whether those premises lead to the conclusion presented. In the argument above, there is no reason to doubt the accuracy of the premises, but even if we accept the premises as accurate, we still do not have to accept the conclusion.

Most people reading the argument above would agree that the reasoning is weak. Even though the premises are perfectly acceptable, by themselves they do not prove that "we should move to Jacksonville." The typical reader will experience a host of reactions to the conclusion: Why Jacksonville—why not a city that is even smaller? What is so important about population? What about considerations other than population size? Because questions of this nature point to flaws in the argument, we would classify the argument as a poor one. That is, the premises do not prove the conclusion. As shown by this example, the acceptability of the premises does not automatically make the conclusion acceptable. The reverse is also true—the acceptability of the conclusion does not automatically make the premises acceptable.

The following is an example of a strong argument:

> "Trees that shed their foliage annually are deciduous trees. Black Oak trees shed their leaves every year. Therefore, Black Oak trees are deciduous."

An argument can be valid without being true. For example, the following has a valid argument structure but is not "true" in a real world sense:

"All birds can fly. An ostrich is a bird. Therefore, an ostrich can fly."

Questions such as the ones posed in this paragraph suggest that the author has made unwarranted assumptions while constructing the argument. We will discuss assumptions in more detail later.

In this argument, the two premises lead directly to the conclusion. Unlike the previous argument, the author's conclusion seems reasonable and inevitable based on the two premises. Note that the strength of this argument is based solely on the degree to which the premises prove the conclusion. The truth of the premises themselves is not an issue in determining whether the argument is valid or invalid.

Inferences and Assumptions

When glancing through LSAT questions, you will frequently see the words *inference* and *assumption*. Let us take a moment to define the meaning of each term in the context of LSAT argumentation.

Most people have come to believe that the word *inference* means probably true or likely to be true. Indeed, in common usage *infer* is often used in the same manner as *imply*. On the LSAT these uses are incorrect. In logic, an inference can be defined as something that *must be true*. Thus, if you are asked to identify an inference of the argument, you must find an item that must be true based on the information presented in the argument.

Earlier we discussed assumptions in the context of commonsense assumptions that you can bring into each problem. In argumentation, an assumption is simply the same as an *unstated* premise—what must be true in order for the argument to be true. Assumptions can often have a great effect on the validity of the argument.

Assumptions are a part of every argument, and we will discuss them in detail in Chapter Nine.

Separating an inference from an assumption can be difficult because the definition of each refers to what "must be true." The difference is simple: an inference is what follows from an argument (in other words, a conclusion) whereas an assumption is what is taken for granted while making an argument. In one sense, an assumption occurs "before" the argument, that is, while the argument is being made. An inference is made "after" the argument is complete, and follows from the argument. Both concepts will be discussed in more detail in later chapters, but for the time being you should note that all authors make assumptions when creating their arguments, and all arguments have inferences that can be derived from the argument.

The Mind of an LSAT Author

Actually, Law Services now calls themselves the "producers of the LSAT." This signifies that some important test-making functions are now outsourced.

Let us take a moment to differentiate the makers of the test from the author of each stimulus. The maker of the test is Law Services, the organization that oversees the protocols under which the LSAT is constructed, administers the test, and processes and distributes the results. The stated purpose of the test makers is to examine your ability to analyze arguments, in an attempt to assess your suitability for law school. The author of the stimulus is the person from whose point of view each piece is written or the source from which the piece is drawn. Sometimes the persona of the author is made abundantly clear to you because the stimulus is prefaced by a short identifier, such as *Politician* or *Professor*, or even a proper name such as *Fran* or *Inez*. The source of a stimulus can also be made clear by similar identifiers, such as *Advertisement* or *Editorial*.

LSAT students sometimes confuse the aim of the test makers with the way those aims are executed. We know that Law Services has an active interest in testing your ability to discern reasoning, both good and bad. The makers of the exam intentionally present flawed arguments because they want to test whether you are easily confused or prone to be swayed by illogical arguments. This often raises situations where you are presented with arguments that are false or seemingly deceptive in nature. This does not mean that the *author* of the piece is part of the deception. The role of an LSAT author is simply to present an argument or fact set. LSAT authors (as separated from the test makers) do *not* try to deceive you with lies. Although LSAT authors may end up making claims that are incorrect, this is not done out of a willful intention to deceive. Deception on the *author's* part is too sophisticated for the LSAT— it is beyond the scope of LSAT stimuli, which are too short to have the level of complexity necessary for you to detect deception if it was intended. So, you need not feel as if the author is attempting to trick you in the making of the argument. This is especially true when premises are created. For example, when an LSAT author makes a premise statement such as, "19 percent of all research projects are privately funded," this statement is likely to be accurate. An LSAT author would not *knowingly* create a false premise, and so, when examining arguments the likelihood is that the premises are not going to be in error and you should not look at them as a likely source of weakness in the argument. This does not mean that authors are infallible. LSAT authors make plenty of errors, but most of those errors are errors of reasoning that occur in the process of making the conclusion. In later chapters we will examine these flawed reasoning methods in detail.

Not only do LSAT authors not attempt to deceive you, they believe (in their LSAT-world way) that the arguments they make are reasonable and solid. *When you read an LSAT argument from the perspective of the author, he or she believes that their argument is sound.* In other words, they do not knowingly make errors of reasoning. This is a fascinating point because it means that LSAT authors, as part of the LSAT world, function as if the points they raise and the conclusions they make have been well-considered and are airtight. This point will be immensely useful when we begin to look at certain forms of reasoning.

Consider the following argument: "My mail was delivered yesterday, so it will also be delivered today."

Although this argument is flawed (it could be Sunday and the mail will not be delivered), the author has not intentionally made this error. Rather, the author has made the conclusion without realizing that an error has occurred.

Read the Fine Print

One of the purposes of the LSAT is to test how closely you read. This is obviously an important skill for lawyers (who wants a lawyer who makes a critical mistake on a big contract?). One of the ways the LSAT tests whether you have this skill is to probe your knowledge of exactly what the author said. Because of this, you must read all parts of a problem incredibly closely, and you must pay special attention to words that describe the relationships under discussion. For example, if an author concludes, "Therefore, the refinery can achieve a greater operating efficiency," do not make the mistake of thinking the author implied that greater operating efficiency *will* or *must* be achieved. The LSAT makers love to examine your comprehension of the exact words used by the author, and that leads to the fourth Primary Objective:

Primary Objective #4: Read closely and know precisely what the author said. Do not generalize!

When it comes to relationships, the makers of the LSAT have a wide variety of modifiers in their arsenal. The following are two lists of words that should be noted when they appear, regardless of whether they appear in the premises or conclusion.

These word lists do not require memorization. They are presented to give you a broad idea of the type of words that can take on an added importance in LSAT questions.

Quantity Indicators	Probability Indicators
all	must
every	will
most	always
many	not always
some	probably
several	likely
few	should
sole	would
only	not necessarily
not all	could
none	rarely
	never

Quantity indicators refer to the amount or quantity in the relationship, such as "some people" or "many of the laws." Probability indicators refer to the likelihood of occurrence, or the obligation present, as in "The Mayor should resign" or "The law will never pass." Many of the terms fit with negatives to form an opposing idea, for example, "some are not" or "would not."

Words such as the Quantity and Probability Indicators are critical because they are a ripe area for the LSAT makers to exploit. There are numerous examples of incorrect answer choices that attempted to capitalize on the meaning of a single word in the stimulus and thus you must commit yourself to carefully examining every word on the test.

Scope

One topic you often hear mentioned in relation to argumentation is scope. The scope of an argument is the range to which the premises and conclusion encompass certain ideas. For example, consider an argument discussing a new surgical technique. The ideas of surgery and medicine are within the scope of the argument. The idea of federal monetary policy, on the other hand, would not be within the scope of the argument.

Arguments are sometimes described as having a narrow (or limited) scope or a wide (or broad) scope. An argument with a narrow scope is definite in its statements, whereas a wide scope argument is less definite and allows for a greater range of possibility. When we begin to examine individual questions, we will return to this idea and show how it can be used to help consider answer choices in certain situations.

Scope can be a useful idea to consider when examining answer choices, because some answer choices go beyond the bounds of what the author has established in the argument. However, scope is also a concept that is overused in modern LSAT preparation. One test preparation company used to tell instructors that if they could not answer a student's question, they should just say that the answer was out of the scope of the argument! As we will see, there are always definite, identifiable reasons that can be used to eliminate incorrect answer choices.

Notating Arguments

When first studying Logical Reasoning, many students ask if they should make notations on or next to each question. The answer depends on the student. Some people feel very comfortable making notes in the margin and marking important words or phrases; other students feel these notes waste time and are distracting. In our experience, either approach can be successful—it is simply a matter of personal preference.

In general, because so many people get used to note-taking and highlighting text in college, we feel that you should make notes unless you find them bothersome. Although most students develop their own personal system, here are a few symbolizations that you might find useful:

Basic Underlining or Circling

This is the simplest and most common technique of all: attempt to pick out words or phrases that give decisive information or indicate a turning point in the stimulus. One or two quick underlines can help crystallize the information, allowing you to more easily handle the information. Some students prefer to circle key words instead of underlining, and that works equally well. Here is an example of underlining:

Notations made to the stimulus are different from diagramming in response to a form of reasoning. In the chapter on sufficient and necessary conditions we will discuss the diagramming of conditional statements, and most people will find that making those diagrams is extremely helpful.

LSAT rules do allow the use of a highlighter pen, and some students use that instead of underlining. In our experience, switching between your pencil and the highlighter pen uses up too much time so try to underline instead of highlighting. Conversely, highlighting on the Reading Comprehension section works well because the passages are so much longer.

Scientist: Isaac Newton's *Principia*, the seventeenth-century work that served as the cornerstone of physics for over two centuries, <u>could at first</u> be understood by only a handful of people, but a basic understanding of Newton's ideas <u>eventually spread</u> throughout the world. This shows that the barriers to communication between scientists and the public are <u>not impermeable</u>. Thus recent scientific research, <u>most</u> of which also can be described <u>only</u> in language that seems esoteric to most contemporary readers, may also become part of everyone's intellectual heritage.

Bracketing Text

This technique is best for denoting the conclusion. Example:

> In his book, published in 1892, Grey used the same metaphor that Jordan used in her book, which was published in 1885. The metaphor is so unusual that there is little chance that two different people independently created it. Therefore, it is highly likely that Grey read Jordan's book.] C

The "C" stands for "conclusion."

With many test takers, notating becomes so habitual as to be second nature. When this occurs, the amount of time used by notating is minimal.

Remember, notation systems are simply a helpful tool to keep track of the information in each stimulus. Although it will help you organize and quickly locate information, you are still responsible for identifying the conclusion and overall structure of the passage. Most importantly, be consistent in your notations! By always notating the same elements in the same way, you can move through the test as fast as possible with maximum accuracy.

Final Chapter Note

The discussion of argumentation in this chapter is, by design, not comprehensive. The purpose of this chapter is to give you a broad overview of the theory underlying LSAT arguments. In future chapters we will apply those theories to specific questions and continue to expand upon the discussion in this chapter. The vast majority of students learn best by examining the application of ideas, and we believe the great bulk of your learning will come by seeing these ideas in action.

Premise and Conclusion Analysis Drill

For each stimulus, identify the conclusion(s) and supporting premise(s), if any. The answer key will identify the conclusion and premises of each argument, the logical validity of each argument, and also comment on how to identify argument structure. Each stimulus comes from a real LSAT question. *Answers on Page 38*

1. Every year, new reports appear concerning the health risks posed by certain substances, such as coffee and sugar. One year an article claimed that coffee is dangerous to one's health. The next year, another article argued that coffee has some benefits for one's health. P From these contradictory opinions, we see that experts are useless for guiding one's decisions about one's health.

    A. What is the conclusion of the argument, if any?

    B. What premises are given in support of this conclusion?

    C. Is the argument strong or weak? If you think that the argument is weak, please explain why.

2. Some teachers claim that students would not learn
    curricular content without the incentive of grades. But
    students with intense interest in the material would learn
    it without this incentive, while the behavior of students
    lacking all interest in the material is unaffected by such an
    incentive. The incentive of grades, therefore, serves no
    essential academic purpose.

    A. What is the conclusion of the argument, if any?

    B. What premises are given in support of this conclusion?

    C. Is the argument strong or weak? If you think that the argument is weak, please explain why.

3. Damming the Merv River would provide irrigation for the
    dry land in its upstream areas; unfortunately, a dam would
    reduce agricultural productivity in the fertile land
    downstream by reducing the availability and quality of
    water there. The productivity loss in the downstream area
    would be greater than the productivity gain upstream, so
    building a dam would yield no overall gain in agricultural
    productivity in the region as a whole.

    A. What is the conclusion of the argument, if any?

    B. What premises are given in support of this conclusion?

    C. Is the argument strong or weak? If you think that the argument is weak, please explain why.

4. In a study, infant monkeys given a choice between two surrogate mothers—a bare wire structure equipped with a milk bottle, or a soft, suede-covered wire structure equipped with a milk bottle—unhesitatingly chose the latter. When given a choice between a bare wire structure equipped with a milk bottle and a soft, suede-covered wire structure lacking a milk bottle, they unhesitatingly chose the former.

A. What is the conclusion of the argument, if any?

B. What premises are given in support of this conclusion?

C. Is the argument strong or weak? If you think that the argument is weak, please explain why.

5. While it was once believed that the sort of psychotherapy appropriate for the treatment of neuroses caused by environmental factors is also appropriate for schizophrenia and other psychoses, it is now known that these latter, more serious forms of mental disturbance are best treated by biochemical—that is, medicinal—means. This is conclusive evidence that psychoses, unlike neuroses, have nothing to do with environmental factors but rather are caused by some sort of purely organic condition, such as abnormal brain chemistry or brain malformations.

A. What is the conclusion of the argument, if any?

B. What premises are given in support of this conclusion?

C. Is the argument strong or weak? If you think that the argument is weak, please explain why.

Premise and Conclusion Analysis Drill

6. If relativity theory is correct, no object can travel forward in time at a speed greater than the speed of light. Yet quantum mechanics predicts that the tachyon, a hypothetical subatomic particle, travels faster than light. Thus, if relativity theory is correct, either quantum mechanics' prediction about tachyons is erroneous or tachyons travel backwards in time.

A. What is the conclusion of the argument, if any?

B. What premises are given in support of this conclusion?

C. Is the argument strong or weak? If you think that the argument is weak, please explain why.

7. Any course that teaches students how to write is one that will serve them well later in life. Therefore, since some philosophy courses teach students how to write, any student, whatever his or her major, will be served well in later life by taking any philosophy course.

A. What is the conclusion of the argument, if any?

B. What premises are given in support of this conclusion?

C. Is the argument strong or weak? If you think that the argument is weak, please explain why.

Premise and Conclusion Analysis Drill

8. It is well known that many species adapt to their environment, but it is usually assumed that only the most highly evolved species alter their environment in ways that aid their own survival. However, this characteristic is actually quite common. Certain species of plankton, for example, generate a gas that is converted in the atmosphere into particles of sulfate. These particles cause water vapor to condense, thus forming clouds. Indeed, the formation of clouds over the ocean largely depends on the presence of these particles. More cloud cover means more sunlight is reflected, and so the Earth absorbs less heat. Thus plankton cause the surface of the Earth to be cooler and this benefits the plankton.

A. What is the conclusion of the argument, if any?

B. What premises are given in support of this conclusion?

C. Is the argument strong or weak? If you think that the argument is weak, please explain why.

Premise and Conclusion Analysis Drill Answer Key

Question #1. Stimulus drawn from the October 2002 LSAT.

> Conclusion: From these contradictory opinions, we see that experts are useless for guiding one's decisions about one's health.
>
> Premise: Every year, new reports appear concerning the health risks posed by certain substances, such as coffee and sugar.
>
> Premise: One year an article claimed that coffee is dangerous to one's health.
>
> Premise: The next year, another article argued that coffee has some benefits for one's health.

The conclusion is introduced by the phrase "we see that."

The argument is weak. The conclusion is far too strong in saying that "experts are useless." Just because the different articles about substances disagree does not prove that experts cannot help you with your *health* (a much broader field than the substances cover). In addition, the articles about coffee could have covered differing aspects of coffee, some of which are beneficial and some of which are detrimental.

Question #2. Stimulus drawn from the October 2002 LSAT.

> Conclusion: The incentive of grades, therefore, serves no essential academic purpose.
>
> Premise: Some teachers claim that students would not learn curricular content without the incentive of grades.
>
> Premise: But students with intense interest in the material would learn it without this incentive, while the behavior of students lacking all interest in the material is unaffected by such an incentive.

The conclusion contains the conclusion indicator, "therefore." Note also the use of the "Some teachers claim..." device discussed earlier in the chapter. This construction raises a viewpoint that the author eventually argues against.

The argument is weak. When discussing the students, the author makes the mistake of discussing only the extremes—those with intense interest and those lacking all interest. No effort is made to address the students who fall between these extremes.

Premise and Conclusion Analysis Drill Answer Key

<u>Question #3</u>. Stimulus drawn from the October 2002 LSAT.

> Conclusion: Building a dam would yield no overall gain in agricultural productivity in the region as a whole.

> Premise: Damming the Merv River would provide irrigation for the dry land in its upstream areas.

> Premise: Unfortunately, a dam would reduce agricultural productivity in the fertile land downstream by reducing the availability and quality of water there.

> Premise: The productivity loss in the downstream area would be greater than the productivity gain upstream.

The conclusion is introduced in the last sentence by the indicator "so."

The argument is strong. The author discusses both the upstream and downstream areas, showing that the gain from the dam in the upstream area would not offset the loss of productivity in the downstream area. In fact, it appears an even stronger conclusion would be warranted, such as "building a dam would yield an overall loss of productivity. Since the author directly addresses overall productivity, possible objections about acreage and volume produced are rendered moot. The author even goes so far as to indicate that the downstream land is fertile, deflecting another possible objection about the work involved in making the land productive.

Note that this is a good example of a fantasy stimulus, one that is based on a scenario that does not exist in the real world. There is no "Merv River" anywhere in the world (although there was an ancient city of Merv in Turkmenistan). Stimuli like this one are often created to portray a certain reasoning form or situation. While fantasy stimuli are often obvious (containing fake countries, etc.), you should not approach them any differently than real-world, fact-based stimuli because Logical Reasoning is about argumentation, and argumentation can be portrayed equally well in real world or fantasy stimuli.

<u>Question #4</u>. Stimulus drawn from the June 2002 LSAT.

> Premise: In a study, infant monkeys given a choice between two surrogate mothers—a bare wire structure equipped with a milk bottle, or a soft, suede-covered wire structure equipped with a milk bottle—unhesitatingly chose the latter.

> Premise: When given a choice between a bare wire structure equipped with a milk bottle and a soft, suede-covered wire structure lacking a milk bottle, they unhesitatingly chose the former.

Careful! The stimulus is only a fact set and does not contain a conclusion. Therefore, there is no argument present and no evaluation of argument validity can be made.

Question #5. Stimulus drawn from the December 2001 LSAT.

> Conclusion: This is conclusive evidence that psychoses, unlike neuroses, have nothing to do with environmental factors but rather are caused by some sort of purely organic condition, such as abnormal brain chemistry or brain malformations.

> Premise: While it was once believed that the sort of psychotherapy appropriate for the treatment of neuroses caused by environmental factors is also appropriate for schizophrenia and other psychoses, it is now known that these latter, more serious forms of mental disturbance are best treated by biochemical—that is, medicinal—means.

The conclusion is introduced by the phrase "this is conclusive evidence that."

The argument is weak. Again, the language used by the author is too strong—"nothing to do with environmental factors"—for the evidence provided by the premises. Nowhere in the argument has the author proven beyond a shadow of doubt that environmental factors do not play a role in neuroses.

Question #6. Stimulus drawn from the December 2000 LSAT.

> Conclusion: Thus, if relativity theory is correct, either quantum mechanics' prediction about tachyons is erroneous or tachyons travel backwards in time.

> Premise: If relativity theory is correct, no object can travel forward in time at a speed greater than the speed of light.

> Premise: Yet quantum mechanics predicts that the tachyon, a hypothetical subatomic particle, travels faster than light.

The conclusion is introduced by the indicator "thus." The second premise is actually a counter-premise introduced by the indicator "yet."

The argument is strong. Note how the author qualifies the conclusion, using the phrase "if relativity theory is correct." This qualifying phase makes the argument easier to defend because it protects against the possibility that relativity theory is wrong (if relativity theory is wrong, the author's conclusion does not apply). Note the conclusion concerning travelling backwards in time as the other possibility is set up by the fact that quantum theory predicts that no object can travel forward in time at a speed greater than the speed of light. If an object cannot travel forward in time, then it must travel backwards (time does not stop, of course, so those are the only two options).

Premise and Conclusion Analysis Drill Answer Key

Question #7. Stimulus drawn from the December 2002 LSAT.

> Conclusion: Any student, whatever his or her major, will be served well in later life by taking any philosophy course.

> Premise: Any course that teaches students how to write is one that will serve them well later in life.

> Premise: Some philosophy courses teach students how to write.

The conclusion is introduced by the device "therefore, since" and in this case the inserted premise is quite lengthy.

The argument is weak. Although the premise indicates that *some* philosophy courses teach students how to write, the conclusion goes too far in saying students will be served well in later life by taking *any* philosophy course.

Question #8. Stimulus drawn from the October 1999 LSAT.

> Conclusion: This characteristic [altering the environment] is actually quite common

> Premise: It is well known that many species adapt to their environment, but it is usually assumed that only the most highly evolved species alter their environment in ways that aid their own survival.

> Premise: Certain species of plankton, for example, generate a gas that is converted in the atmosphere into particles of sulfate.

> Premise: These particles cause water vapor to condense, thus forming clouds.

> Premise: Indeed, the formation of clouds over the ocean largely depends on the presence of these particles.

> Premise: More cloud cover means more sunlight is reflected, and so the Earth absorbs less heat.

> Premise: Thus plankton cause the surface of the Earth to be cooler and this benefits the plankton.

This argument is hard to absorb because the subject matter is challenging and the structure is complex. The main conclusion is actually the second sentence. There is another conclusion in the argument, in the last sentence, but this is a sub-conclusion. This sub-conclusion appears in the plankton example, and like all examples, it is used to illustrate the main conclusion.

The argument is strong. A viewpoint is presented (that it is thought that only highly evolved species alter their environment) and then this viewpoint is disputed with the example of a simple organism that changes its environment. Although the author has not proven undeniably that the characteristic is "quite common" (this would require more examples), the author has successfully shown that non-highly evolved species exhibit that characteristic, making it likely that the characteristic appears in other species.

CHAPTER THREE: THE QUESTION STEM AND ANSWER CHOICES

The Question Stem

The question stem follows the stimulus and poses a question directed at the stimulus. In some ways the question stem is the most important part of each problem because it specifies the task you must perform in order to get credit for the problem.

LSAT question stems cover a wide range of tasks, and will variously ask you to:

- identify details of the stimulus

- describe the structure of the argument

- strengthen or weaken the argument

- identify inferences, main points, and assumptions

- recognize errors of reasoning

- reconcile conflicts

- find arguments that are identical in structure

On average, you have 1 minute and 25 seconds to complete each question.

Analyzing the Question Stem

When examining a typical Logical Reasoning section, you may come to the conclusion that there are dozens of different types of question stems. The test makers create this impression by varying the words used in each question stem. As we will see shortly, even though they use different words, many of these question stems are identical in terms what they ask you to do.

In order to easily handle the different questions, we categorize the question stems that appear on the LSAT. Fortunately, every question stem can be defined as a certain type, and the more familiar you are with the question types, the faster you can respond when faced with individual questions. Thus, one of your tasks is to learn each question type and become familiar with the characteristics that define each type. We will help you accomplish this goal by including a variety of question type identification drills, and by examining each type of question in detail. This leads to the fifth Primary Objective:

Primary Objective #5: Carefully read and identify the question stem. Do not assume that certain words are automatically associated with certain question types.

Make sure to read the question stem very carefully. Some stems direct you to focus on certain aspects of the stimulus and if you miss these clues you make the problem much more difficult.

You must correctly analyze and classify every question stem because the question stem ultimately determines the nature of the correct answer choice. A mistake in analyzing the question stem invariably leads to a missed question. As we will see, the test makers love to use certain words—such as "support"—in different ways because they know some test takers will automatically assume these words imply a certain type of question. Properly identifying the question stem type will allow you to proceed quickly and with confidence, and in some cases it will help you determine the correct answer before you read any of the five answer choices.

The Thirteen Logical Reasoning Question Types

Each question stem that appears in the Logical Reasoning section of the LSAT can be classified into one of thirteen different types:

1. Must Be True/Most Supported
2. Main Point
3. Point at Issue
4. Assumption
5. Justify the Conclusion
6. Strengthen/Support
7. Resolve the Paradox
8. Weaken
9. Method of Reasoning
10. Flaw in the Reasoning
11. Parallel Reasoning
12. Evaluate the Argument
13. Cannot Be True

Occasionally, students ask if we refer to the question types by number or by name. We always refer to the questions by name as that is an easier and more efficient approach. Numerical question type classification systems force you to add two unnecessary levels of abstraction to your thinking process. For example, consider a question that asks you to "weaken" the argument. In a numerical question classification system, you must first recognize that the question asks you to weaken the argument, then you must classify that question into a numerical category (say, Type 10), and then you must translate Type 10 to mean "Weaken." Literally, numerical classification systems force you to perform an abstract, circular translation of the meaning of the question, and the translation process is both time-consuming and valueless.

Question stems contain criteria that must be met. This criteria could be to weaken the argument, find the method of reasoning, etc.

In the following pages we will discuss each question type in brief. Later we will examine each question type in its own chapter.

1. Must Be True/Most Supported

    This category is simply known as "Must Be True." Must Be True
    questions ask you to identify the answer choice that is best proven by
    the information in the stimulus. Question stem examples:

    "If the statements above are true, which one of the following must also
    be true?"

    "Which one of the following can be properly inferred from the
    passage?"

2. Main Point

    Main Point questions are a variant of Must Be True questions. As you
    might expect, a Main Point question asks you to find the primary
    conclusion made by the author. Question stem example:

    "The main point of the argument is that"

3. Point at Issue

    Point at Issue questions require you to identify a point of contention
    between two speakers, and thus these questions appear almost
    exclusively with two-speaker stimuli. Question stem example:

    "Larew and Mendota disagree about whether"

4. Assumption

    These questions ask you to identify an assumption of the author's
    argument. Question stem example:

    "Which one of the following is an assumption required by the
    argument above?"

5. Justify the Conclusion

    Justify the Conclusion questions ask you to supply a piece of
    information that, when added to the premises, proves the conclusion.
    Question stem example:

    "Which one of the following, if assumed, allows the conclusion above
    to be properly drawn?"

6.   Strengthen/Support

These questions ask you to select the answer choice that provides support for the author's argument or strengthens it in some way. Question stem examples:

"Which one of the following, if true, most strengthens the argument?"

"Which one of the following, if true, most strongly supports the statement above?"

7.   Resolve the Paradox

Every Resolve the Paradox stimulus contains a discrepancy or seeming contradiction. You must find the answer choice that best resolves the situation. Question stem example:

"Which one of the following, if true, would most effectively resolve the apparent paradox above?"

In the answer key to this book, all questions are classified as one of these thirteen types. There are also additional indicators designating reasoning type, etc.

8.   Weaken

Weaken questions ask you to attack or undermine the author's argument. Question stem example:

"Which one of the following, if true, most seriously weakens the argument?"

9.   Method of Reasoning

Method of Reasoning questions ask you to describe, in abstract terms, the way in which the author made his or her argument. Question stem example:

"Which one of the following describes the technique of reasoning used above?"

10.   Flaw in the Reasoning

Flaw in the Reasoning questions ask you to describe, in abstract terms, the error of reasoning committed by the author. Question stem example:

"The reasoning in the astronomer's argument is flawed because this argument"

11. Parallel Reasoning

Parallel Reasoning questions ask you to identify the answer choice that contains reasoning most similar in structure to the reasoning presented in the stimulus. Question stem example:

"Which one of the following arguments is most similar in its pattern of reasoning to the argument above?"

12. Evaluate the Argument

With Evaluate the Argument questions you must decide which answer choice will allow you to determine the logical validity of the argument. Question stem example:

"The answer to which one of the following questions would contribute most to an evaluation of the argument?"

13. Cannot Be True

Cannot Be True questions ask you to identify the answer choice that cannot be true or is most weakened based on the information in the stimulus. Question stem example:

"If the statements above are true, which one of the following CANNOT be true?"

Other question type elements will be discussed, most notably question variants (such as Argument Part questions) and overlays (such as Principle questions). Those will be discussed in later chapters.

Although each of these question types is distinct, they are related in terms of the root function you are asked to perform. Questions that appear dissimilar, such as Must Be True and Method of Reasoning, are actually quite similar when considered in terms of how you work with the question. All question types are variations of four main question "families," and each family is comprised of question types that are similar to each other.

On the next page, we delineate the four families using box-and-arrow diagrams that reflect the flow of information between the stimulus and the answer choices.

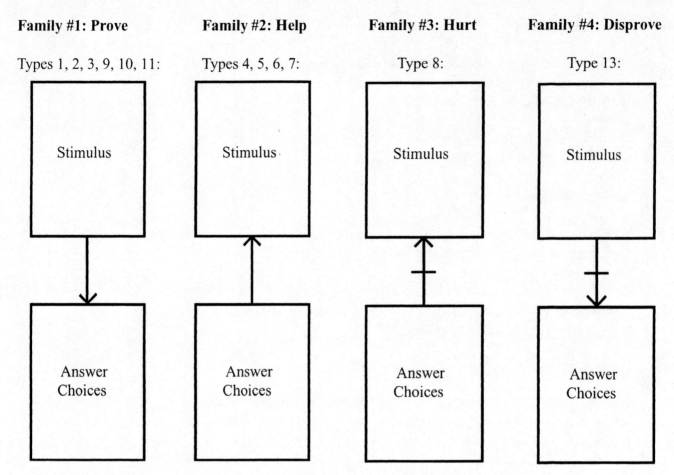

Family #1: Prove   **Family #2: Help**   **Family #3: Hurt**   **Family #4: Disprove**

Types 1, 2, 3, 9, 10, 11:   Types 4, 5, 6, 7:   Type 8:   Type 13:

Family #1, also known as the Must Be or Prove Family, consists of the following question types:

> (1) Must Be True
> (2) Main Point
> (3) Point at Issue
> (9) Method of Reasoning
> (10) Flaw in the Reasoning
> (11) Parallel Reasoning

Family #2, also known as the Help Family, consists of the following question types:

> (4) Assumption
> (5) Justify the Conclusion
> (6) Strengthen/Support
> (7) Resolve the Paradox

Family #3, also known as the Hurt Family, consists of the following question type:

> (8) Weaken

Family #4, also known as the Disprove Family, consists of the following question type:

> (13) Cannot Be True

The boxes on the preceding page represent the stimulus and answer choices for any given Logical Reasoning question. The arrows represent the flow of information; one part of the problem is simply accepted and the other part is affected. There are two basic rules to follow when analyzing the diagrams:

1. The part (stimulus or answer choices) at the start of the arrow is accepted as is, and no additional information (aside from general domain assumptions) can be brought in.

2. The part (stimulus or answer choices) at the end of the arrow is what is affected or determined (for example, are you asked to Weaken the argument or determine which answer Must Be True?).

One of the signature features of the four question families is that they define the parameters of what you can do with the information in each question.

In very rough terms, the part at the start of the arrow is taken for granted and the part at the end of the arrow is under suspicion. While this characterization may sound a bit vague, this occurs because there are four different types of relationships, and the details vary from type to type.

Part of the purpose of classifying questions into these four categories is to understand the fundamental structure of Logical Reasoning problems. Many students ask the following two questions upon seeing Logical Reasoning questions for the first time:

1. Should I simply accept every statement in the stimulus as true?

2. Can the answer choices bring in information that is off-the-page, that is, ideas and concepts not stated in the stimulus?

The answer to both questions depends on the question stem and corresponding question family. Let us examine each question family and address these questions in more detail.

The First Question Family

The First Question Family is based on the principle of using the information in the stimulus to prove that one of the answer choices must be true.

In the First Family diagram, the arrow points downward from the stimulus to the answer choices. Hence, the stimulus is at the start of the arrow, and the answer choices are at the end of the arrow. According to the rules above, whatever is stated in the stimulus is simply accepted as given, with no additional information being added. And, because the arrow points to the answer choices, the answer choices are "under suspicion," and the information in the stimulus is used to prove one of the answer choices correct.

Because the stimulus is accepted as stated (even if it contains an error of reasoning), you cannot bring in additional information off the page—you can only use what is stated in the stimulus. Thus, in a Must Be True question, only what the author states in the stimulus can be used to prove one of the answer choices. This reveals the way the arrow works: you start at the stimulus and then use only that information to separate the answers. If an answer choice references something that is not included or encompassed by the stimulus, it will be incorrect. In a Method of Reasoning question, for example, the process works the same. If one of the answers references some method of argumentation that did not occur in the stimulus, then the answer is automatically incorrect. The test makers do not hide this relationship. Most question stems in this family (especially Must Be True) will contain a phrase similar to, "The information *above, if true...*" (italics added). In this way the test makers are able to indicate that you should accept the statements in the stimulus as given and then use them to prove one of the answer choices.

The following rules apply to the First Question Family:

1. You must accept the stimulus information—even if it contains an error of reasoning—and use it to prove that one of the answer choices must be true.

2. Any information in an answer choice that does not appear either directly in the stimulus or as a combination of items in the stimulus will be incorrect.

These rules will be revisited in more detail once we begin analyzing individual Logical Reasoning questions.

The Second Question Family

The Second Question Family is based on the principle of assisting or helping the author's argument or statement in some way, whether by revealing an assumption of the argument, by resolving a paradox, or in some other fashion.

As opposed to the First Family, in this family the arrow points upward to the stimulus. This reverses the flow of information: the answer choices are at the start of the arrow, and the stimulus is at the end of the arrow. Functionally, this means you must accept the answer choices as given, and the stimulus is under suspicion. Accepting the answer choices as given means you cannot dispute their factual basis, even if they include elements not mentioned in the stimulus (we often call this "new" or "outside" information). The test makers make this principle clear because most question stems in this family contain a phrase similar to, "Which one of the *following, if true,*..." (italics added). By including this phrase, the test makers indicate that they wish you to treat each answer choice as factually correct. Your task is to examine each answer choice and see which one best fits the exact criteria stated in the question stem (justify, strengthen, etc.).

In this question grouping, the stimulus is under suspicion. Often there are errors of reasoning present, or leaps in logic, and you are asked to find an answer choice that closes the hole. When you encounter a question of this category, immediately consider the stimulus—were there any obvious holes or gaps in the argument that could be filled by one of the answer choices? Often you will find that the author has made an error of reasoning and you will be asked to eliminate that error.

The following rules apply to the Second Question Family:

1. The information in the stimulus is suspect. There are often reasoning errors present, and depending on the question, you will help shore up the argument in some way.

2. The answer choices are accepted as given, even if they include "new" information. Your task is to determine which answer choice best meets the question posed in the stem.

The Third Question Family

The Third Question Family consists of only one question type—Weaken. Accordingly, you are asked to attack the author's argument.

Compared to the Second Question Family, the only difference between the diagrams is that the third family diagram has a bar across the arrow. This bar signifies a negative: instead of strengthening or helping the argument, you attack or hurt the argument. In this sense the third family is the polar opposite of the second family; otherwise the two question families are identical.

For the Third Question Family, the following rules apply:

1. The information in the stimulus is suspect. There are often reasoning errors present, and you will further weaken the argument in some way.

2. The answer choices are accepted as given, even if they include "new" information. Your task is to determine which answer choice best attacks the argument in the stimulus.

The Fourth Question Family

The Fourth Question Family also consists of only one question type—Cannot Be True. As such, this question family is based on the principle that you must use the information in the stimulus to prove that one of the answer choices cannot occur.

Compared to the First Question Family, the only difference in the diagram is that the Fourth Family diagram has a bar across the arrow. Again, this bar signifies a negative; instead of using the information in the stimulus to prove one of the answer choices must be true, you instead prove that one of the answer choices cannot occur or that it disagrees with the information in the stimulus. In this sense the fourth family is the polar opposite of the first family; otherwise the two question families are identical.

For the Fourth Question Family, the following rules apply:

1. You must accept the stimulus information—even if it contains an error of reasoning—and use it to prove that one of the answer choices cannot occur.

2. Any information in an answer choice that does not appear either directly in the stimulus or as a combination of items in the stimulus will be incorrect. The correct answer choice will directly disagree with the stimulus or a consequence of the stimulus.

As you might expect, there are deeper relationships between the individual question types and the question families. As we discuss the mechanics of individual questions we will further explore these relationships.

Those of you reading closely may have noticed that one of the question types was not listed among the Families. Evaluate the Argument questions are a combination of the second and third question families, and we will explain those questions in more detail in Chapter Sixteen.

Question Type Notes

The following is a collection of notes regarding the Thirteen Question Types. These notes help clear up some questions that typically arise when students are learning to identify the question types. In the chapters that discuss each question type we will reintroduce each of these points.

- Must Be True, Cannot Be True, and Resolve the Paradox questions are generally connected to stimuli that do *not* contain conclusions. All remaining question types must be connected to stimuli with conclusions (unless a conclusion is added by the question stem, as sometimes occurs). Hence, when a stimulus without a conclusion appears on the LSAT, only three types of questions can be posed to you: Must Be True, Cannot Be True, or Resolve the Paradox. Question types such Weaken or Method of Reasoning do not generally appear because no argument or reasoning is present, and those question types ask you to address reasoning. Generally, Resolve the Paradox questions are easy to spot because they contain a paradox or discrepancy. In addition, Must Be True questions appear far more frequently than Cannot Be True questions. Thus, if you encounter a stimulus without a conclusion and without a paradox, you are most likely about to see a Must Be True question stem.

- Weaken and Strengthen are polar opposite question types, and both are often based on flawed or weak arguments that contain holes that must be closed or opened further.

- Method of Reasoning and Flaw in the Reasoning questions are a brother/sister pair. The only difference between the two is that Flaw in the Reasoning question stems explicitly note that the stimulus contains an error of reasoning. In a Method of Reasoning question the stimulus contains valid or invalid reasoning.

- Parallel Reasoning questions are a one-step extension of Method of Reasoning questions in that you must first identify the type of reasoning used and then parallel it. Method of Reasoning and Parallel Reasoning questions both have a strong Must Be True element.

- Main Point, Evaluate the Argument, and Cannot be True appear the least frequently on the LSAT.

Question Type Variety

One of the aims of the test makers is to keep you off-balance. An unsettled, frustrated test taker is prone to making mistakes. By mixing up the type of questions you face, the makers of the test can keep you from getting into a rhythm. Imagine how much easier the Logical Reasoning section would be if you faced twenty-five consecutive Must Be True questions. For this reason, you will always see a spread of questions within each section, and you will rarely see the same question type twice in a row. Since this situation is a fact of the LSAT, before the test begins prepare yourself mentally for the quick shifting of mental gears that is required to move from question to question.

"Most" in Question Stems

Many question stems—especially Strengthen and Weaken stems—contain the qualifier "most." For example, a typical question stem will state, "Which one of the following, if true, most weakens the argument above?" Astute test takers realize that the presence of "most" opens up a Pandora's box of sorts: by including "most," there is a possibility that other answer choices will also meet the criteria of the question stem (Strengthen, Weaken, etc.), albeit to a lesser extent. In other words, if a question stem says "most weakens," the possibility is that every answer choice weakens the argument and you would be in the unenviable task of having to choose the best of a bunch of good answer choices. *Fortunately, this is not how it works.* Even though "most" will appear in many stems, you can rest assured that only one answer choice will meet the

Of course, every once in a while two answer choices achieve the desired goal; in those cases you simply choose the better of the two answers. Normally, the difference between the two answers is significant enough for you to make a clear distinction as to which one is superior.

criteria. So, if you see a "most weakens" question stem, only one of the answers will weaken the argument. So, then, why does "most" appear in so many question stems? Because in order to maintain test integrity the test makers need to make sure their credited answer choice is as airtight and defensible as possible. Imagine what would occur if a question stem, let us say a Weaken question, did not include a "most" qualifier: any answer choice that weakened the argument, even if only just very slightly, could then be argued to meet the criteria of the question stem. A situation like this would make constructing the test exceedingly difficult because any given problem might have multiple correct answer choices. To eliminate this predicament, the test makers insert "most" into the question stem, and then they can always claim there is one and only one correct answer choice.

Identify the Question Stem Drill

Each of the following items contains a question stem from a recent LSAT problem. In the space provided, categorize each stem into one of the thirteen Logical Reasoning Question Types: Must Be True, Main Point, Point at Issue, Assumption, Justify the Conclusion, Strengthen, Resolve the Paradox, Weaken, Method of Reasoning, Flaw in the Reasoning, Parallel Reasoning, Evaluate the Argument, or Cannot be True. While we realize that you have not yet worked directly with each question type, by considering the relationships now you will have an advantage as you attack future questions. In later chapters we will present more Identify the Question Stem drills to further strengthen your abilities. *Answers on Page 57*

1. Question Stem: "Which one of the following, if true, most helps to explain the viewpoint of the historians described above?"

   Question Type: _____

2. Question Stem: "Which one of the following can be properly inferred from Rosen's statement?"

   Question Type: _____

3. Question Stem: "Which one of the following, if true, most seriously weakens the reasoning above?"

   Question Type: _____

4. Question Stem: "Which one of the following is an assumption required by the argument above?"

   Question Type: _____

5. Question Stem: "Which one of the following arguments is most similar in its pattern of reasoning to the argument above?"

   Question Type: _____

6. Question Stem: "Of the following, which one most accurately expresses the main point of the argument?"

   Question Type: _____

7. Question Stem: "Which one of the following, if true, would provide the most support for the economists' assertion?"

   Question Type: _____

8. Question Stem: "The argument is flawed because it"

   Question Type: _____

9. Question Stem: "The dialogue most supports the claim that Tony and Raoul disagree about whether"

   Question Type: _____

10. Question Stem: "If the statements above are true, which one of the following must be false?"

    Question Type: _____

11. Question Stem: "The advertisement proceeds by"

    Question Type: _____

12. Question Stem: "Which one of the following, if assumed, would allow the conclusion to be properly drawn?"

    Question Type: _____

13. Question Stem: "The answer to which one of the following questions would most help in evaluating the columnist's argument?"

    Question Type: _____

14. Question Stem: "Sue challenges Anne's reasoning by"

    Question Type: _____

15. Question Stem: "The statements above, if true, most strongly support which one of the following?"

    Question Type: _____

Identify the Question Stem Drill Answer Key

The typical student misses about half of the questions in this drill. Do not worry about how many you miss; the point of this drill is to acquaint you with the different question stems. As you see more examples of each type of question, your ability to correctly identify each stem will improve.

1. Question Type: Resolve the Paradox
Stem drawn from the June 2003 LSAT. The presence of the phrase "Which one of the following, if true," indicates that this question stem must be from either the second or third question family. Because the third family is Weaken, and the question stem asks you to "explain," the question cannot be from the third family. Thus, the question must be from the second family and can only be an Assumption, Justify, Strengthen, or Resolve question. The idea of explaining is most closely aligned with Resolving the Paradox.

2. Question Type: Must Be True
Stem drawn from the June 2002 LSAT. The word "inferred" means "must be true," hence that is the classification of this question.

3. Question Type: Weaken
Stem drawn from the October 2002 LSAT. The presence of the phrase "Which one of the following, if true," indicates that this question stem must be from either the second or third question family. The presence of the word "weakens" indicates that this is a Weaken question.

4. Question Type: Assumption
Stem drawn from the December 2003 LSAT. The key words in this stem are "required" and "assumption," making this an Assumption question. You must be careful when you see the word "assumption" because that word can also be used in Justify the Conclusion questions. That usage will be discussed in more detail in Chapter Nine.

5. Question Type: Parallel
Stem drawn from the October 2003 LSAT. The key phrases in this stem are "most similar" and "to the argument above." Because the argument in the stimulus is used as a model for one of the answers, this is a Parallel Reasoning question.

6. Question Type: Main Point
Stem drawn from the December 2001 LSAT. Because the stem asks you to find the main point, this question is categorized as Main Point.

7. Question Type: Strengthen
Stem drawn from the December 2003 LSAT. The presence of the phrase "Which one of the following, if true," indicates that this question stem must be from either the second or third question family. Because the third family is Weaken, and the question stem asks you to "support," the question cannot be from the third family. Thus, the question must be from the second family and can only be an Assumption, Justify, Strengthen, or Resolve question. The idea of supporting is the same as Strengthening.

8. Question Type: Flaw

Stem drawn from the June 2002 LSAT. The presence of the word "flawed" could indicate either a Weaken question or a Flaw in the Reasoning question. In this case, the stem requests you to identify the flaw in the argument (or reasoning), hence this question is a Flaw in the Reasoning question.

9. Question Type: Point at Issue

Stem drawn from the October 2002 LSAT. The presence of two speakers—Tony and Raoul—and the phrase "disagree about" indicates that this is a Point at Issue question.

10. Question Type: Cannot Be True

Stem drawn from the December 2003 LSAT. The phrase "must be false" is equivalent to "cannot be true." Thus, this question is properly classified as Cannot Be True. Note that the phrase "If the statements above are true" indicates that this question stem must come from either the first or fourth question family.

11. Question Type: Method

Stem drawn from the June 2003 LSAT. By asking how the advertisement "proceeds," the test makers wish to know the way in which the argument is made, in other words, the method of the reasoning.

12. Question Type: Justify

Stem drawn from the October 2003 LSAT. In some ways, this is an unfair question to ask so early in the book (sorry!). On the surface this appears to be an Assumption question, so if you listed that as your answer, do not feel badly. As we will discuss in Chapter Nine, the presence of the words "if" and "properly drawn" along with "assumed" normally indicate a Justify question, as they do here.

13. Question Type: Evaluate

Stem drawn from the December 2001 LSAT. The key phrase is "evaluating the columnists's argument," which indicates that the test makers require you to find the question that would best help in evaluating the author's argument. Thus, the question is classified as Evaluate the Argument.

14. Question Type: Method

Stem drawn from the June 2003 LSAT. Although the question stem uses the word "challenges," this is not a Weaken question because the stem asks for a description of the way Anne's reasoning was challenged. Thus, you are asked to identify Sue's method of reasoning.

15. Question Type: Must Be True

Stem drawn from the October 2003 LSAT. The phrase "The statements above, if true," indicates that this question must come from either the first or fourth question family. In this case, the "most strongly support" is used with the intent of proving one of the answers as correct. Hence, this is a Must Be True question. Note how the use of the word "support" in this question stem differs from the usage in problem #7.

"Except" and "Least" in Question Stems

The word "except" has a dramatic impact when it appears in a question stem. Because "except" means "other than," when "except" is placed in a question it negates the logical quality of the answer choice you seek. Literally, it turns the intent of the question stem upside down. For example, if a question asks you to weaken the argument, the one correct answer weakens the argument and the other four answers do not weaken the argument. If "except" is added to the question stem, as in "Each of the following weakens the argument EXCEPT," the stem is turned around and instead of the correct answer weakening the argument, the four incorrect answers weaken the argument and the one correct answer does not weaken the argument.

Many students, upon encountering "except" in a question stem, make the mistake of assuming that the "except" charges you with seeking the polar opposite. For example, if a question stem asks you to weaken the argument, some students believe that a "Weaken EXCEPT" question stem actually asks you to strengthen the argument. This is incorrect. Although weaken and strengthen are polar opposites, because except means "other than," when a "Weaken EXCEPT" question stem appears, you are asked to find any answer choice other than Weaken. While this could include a strengthening answer choice, it could also include an answer choice that has no effect on the argument. Thus, in a "Weaken EXCEPT" question, the four incorrect answers Weaken the argument and the one correct answer does not weaken the argument (could strengthen or have no effect). Here are some other examples:

The true effect of "except" is to logically negate the question stem. We will discuss Logical Negation in more detail in the Assumption question chapter.

1.   "Which one of the following, if true, strengthens the argument above?"

        One correct answer: Strengthen
        Four incorrect answers: Do not Strengthen

"Each of the following, if true, strengthens the argument above EXCEPT:"

        One correct answer: Does not Strengthen
        Four incorrect answers: Strengthen

2.   "Which one of the following, if true, would help to resolve the apparent discrepancy above?"

> One correct answer: Resolves the Paradox
> Four incorrect answers: Do not Resolve the Paradox

"Each of the following, if true, would help to resolve the apparent discrepancy above EXCEPT:"

> One correct answer: Does not Resolve the Paradox
> Four incorrect answers: Resolve the Paradox

As you can see from the two examples, the presence of except has a profound impact upon the meaning of the question stem. Because "except" has this powerful effect, it always appears in all capital letters whenever it is used in an LSAT question stem.

The word "least" has a similar effect to "except" when it appears in a question stem. Although "least" and "except" do not generally have the same meaning, when "least" appears in a question stem you should treat it *exactly the same* as "except." Note: this advice holds true only when this word appears in the question stem! If you see the word "least" elsewhere on the LSAT, consider it to have its usual meaning of "in the lowest or smallest degree."

Let us look more closely at how and why "least" functions identically to "except." Compare the following two question stems:

"Which one of the following, if true, would help to resolve the apparent discrepancy above?"

> One correct answer: Resolves the Paradox
> Four incorrect answers: Do not Resolve the Paradox

"Which one of the following, if true, helps LEAST to resolve the apparent discrepancy described above?"

> One correct answer: Does not Resolve the Paradox
> Four incorrect answers: Resolve the Paradox

By asking for the question stem that "least" helps resolve the paradox, the test makers indicate that the four incorrect answers will more strongly help resolve the paradox. But, in practice, when "least" is used, all five answer choices do *not* resolve the paradox to varying degrees. Instead, four answers resolve the paradox and the one correct answer does *not* resolve the paradox. Why do the test makers do this? Because the test makers cannot afford to introduce uncertainty into the correctness of the answers. If all five answer choices resolve the paradox, then reasonable minds could come to a disagreement about which one "least" resolves the paradox. In order to avoid this type of controversy, the test makers simply make sure that exactly one answer choice does not resolve the paradox (and, because that answer choice does not resolve the paradox it automatically has the "least" effect possible). In this way, the test makers can present a seemingly difficult and confusing task while at the same time avoiding a test construction problem. Because of this situation, any time you encounter "least" in a question stem, simply recognize that four of the answers will meet the stated criteria (weaken, strengthen, resolve, etc.) and the one correct answer will not. Thus, you will not have to make an assessment based on degree of correctness.

Here is another example comparing the use of the word "least:"

"Which one of the following, if true, would most strengthen the argument above?"

One correct answer: Strengthen
Four incorrect answers: Do not Strengthen

"Which one of the following, if true, LEAST strengthens the argument above?"

One correct answer: Does not Strengthen
Four incorrect answers: Strengthen

Because "least," like "except," has such a strong impact on the meaning of a question stem, the test makers kindly place "least" in all capital letters when it appears in a question stem.

In the answer keys to this book, we will designate questions that contain "except" or "least" by placing an "X" at the end of the question stem classification. For example, a "Weaken EXCEPT" question stem would be classified as "WeakenX." A "Strengthen EXCEPT" question stem would be classified as "StrengthenX" and so on. The only exception to this rule will be a question that states, "Each of the following could be true EXCEPT." Those questions will be designated "Cannot Be True," and we will discuss this in more detail in Chapter Seventeen.

Each of the following items contains a question stem from a recent LSAT question. In the space provided, categorize each stem into one of the thirteen Logical Reasoning Question Types: Must Be True, Main Point, Point at Issue, Assumption, Justify the Conclusion, Strengthen, Resolve the Paradox, Weaken, Method of Reasoning, Flaw in the Reasoning, Parallel Reasoning, Evaluate the Argument, or Cannot be True, and notate any Except (X) identifier you see. *Answers on Page 63*

1. Question Stem: "Each of the following, if true, supports the claim above EXCEPT:"

   Question Type: _____

2. Question Stem: "Each of the following, if true, weakens the argument EXCEPT:"

   Question Type: _____

3. Question Stem: "Which one of the following, if all of them are true, is LEAST helpful in establishing that the conclusion above is properly drawn?"

   Question Type: _____

4. Question Stem: "Each of the following describes a flaw in the psychologist's reasoning EXCEPT:"

   Question Type: _____

5. Question Stem: "Which one of the following, if true, does NOT help to resolve the apparent discrepancy between the safety report and the city's public safety record?"

   Question Type: _____

6. Question Stem: "If the statements above are true, each of the following could be true EXCEPT:"

   Question Type: _____

Except and *Least* Identify The Question Stem Mini-Drill Answer Key

1. Question Type: StrengthenX
Stem drawn from the October 2003 LSAT. The four incorrect answer choices Strengthen the argument; the correct answer choice does not Strengthen the argument.

2. Question Type: WeakenX
Stem drawn from the December 2002 LSAT. The four incorrect answer choices Weaken the argument; the correct answer choice does not Weaken the argument.

3. Question Type: StrengthenX
Stem drawn from the December 2003 LSAT. The four incorrect answer choices Strengthen the argument ("helpful in establishing the conclusion" is the same as Strengthen); the correct answer choice does not Strengthen the argument. The "LEAST" in the stem functions in the same fashion as "EXCEPT."

4. Question Type: FlawX
Stem drawn from the October 2000 LSAT. The four incorrect answer choices describe a Flaw in the Reasoning; the correct answer choice does not describe a Flaw in the Reasoning.

5. Question Type: ResolveX
Stem drawn from the June 2002 LSAT. Although this question stem uses neither "except" nor "least," the use of the word "NOT" indicates that the four incorrect answer choices Resolve the Paradox and the correct answer choice does not Resolve the Paradox. Hence, this question is classified ResolveX.

6. Question Type: Cannot Be True
Stem drawn from the October 2003 LSAT. As noted earlier, when the "could be true EXCEPT" construction appears, the question will be classified as Cannot Be True. This is because the four incorrect answers are Could Be True, and the remaining answer choice is the opposite—Cannot Be True.

Prephrasing Answers

Prephrasing is the LSAT version of the old adage, "An ounce of prevention is worth a pound of cure."

Most students tend to simply read the question stem and then move on to the answer choices without further thought. This is disadvantageous because these students run a greater risk of being tempted by the expertly constructed incorrect answer choices. One of the most effective techniques for quickly finding correct answer choices and avoiding incorrect answer choices is prephrasing. Prephrasing an answer involves quickly speculating on what you expect the correct answer will be based on the information in the stimulus.

All high-scoring test takers are active and aggressive. Passive test takers tend to be less involved in the exam and therefore more prone to make errors.

Although every answer you prephrase may not be correct, there is great value in considering for a moment what elements could appear in the correct answer choice. Students who regularly prephrase find that they are more readily able to eliminate incorrect answer choices, and of course, many times their prephrased answer is correct. And, as we will see in later chapters, there are certain stimulus and question stem combinations on the LSAT that yield predictable answers, making prephrasing even more valuable. In part, prephrasing puts you in an attacking mindset: if you look ahead and considering a possible answer choice, you are forced to involve yourself in the problem. This process helps keep you alert and in touch with the elements of the problem.

Primary Objective #6: Prephrase: after reading the question stem, take a moment to mentally formulate your answer to the question stem.

Keep in mind that prephrasing is directly related to attacking the stimulus; typically, students who closely analyze the stimulus well can more easily prephrase an answer.

The Answer Choices

All LSAT questions have five lettered answer choices and each question has only one correct, or "credited," response. As with other sections, the correct answer in a Logical Reasoning question must meet the Uniqueness Rule of Answer Choices™, which states that "Every correct answer has a unique logical quality that meets the criteria in the question stem. Every incorrect answer has the opposite logical quality." The correctness of the answer choices themselves conforms to this rule: there is one correct answer choice; the other four answer choices are the opposite of correct, or incorrect. Consider the following specific examples:

1.   Logical Quality of the Correct Answer: Must Be True
     Logical Quality of the Four Incorrect Answers:
          the opposite of Must Be True = Not Necessarily True (could be not necessarily the case or never the case)

2.   Logical Quality of the Correct Answer: Strengthen
     Logical Quality of the Four Incorrect Answers:
          the opposite of Strengthen = not Strengthen (could be neutral or weaken)

3.   Logical Quality of the Correct Answer: Weaken
     Logical Quality of the Four Incorrect Answers:
          the opposite of Weaken = not Weaken (could be neutral or strengthen)

Even though there is only one correct answer choice and this answer choice is unique, you still are faced with a difficult task when attempting to determine the correct answer. The test makers have the advantage of time and language on their side. Because identifying the correct answer at first glance can be quite hard, you must always read all five of the answer choices. Students who fail to read all five answer choices open themselves up to missing questions without ever having read the correct answer. There are many classic examples of Law Services placing highly attractive wrong answer choices just before the correct answer. If you are going to make the time investment of analyzing the stimulus and the question stem, you should also make the wise investment of considering each answer choice.

Primary Objective #7: Always read each of the five answer choices.

As you read through each answer choice, sort them into contenders and losers. If an answer choice appears somewhat attractive, interesting, or even confusing, keep it as a contender and move on to the next answer choice. You do not want to spend time debating the merits of an answer choice only to find

When we speak of opposites on the LSAT, we mean logical opposites. For example, what is the opposite of "wet?" Most people would say "dry." But, that is the polar opposite, not the logical opposite. The logical opposite of "wet" is "not wet." Logical opposites break the topic under discussion into two parts. In this case, everything in the spectrum of moisture would be classified as either "wet" or "not wet."

There may be times when you would not read all five answer choices, For example, if you only have two minutes left in the section and you determine that answer choice (B) is clearly correct. In that case, you would choose answer choice (B) and then move on to the next question.

that the next answer choice is superior. However, if an answer choice immediately strikes you as incorrect, classify it as a loser and move on. Once you have evaluated all five answer choices, return to the answer choices that strike you as most likely to be correct and decide which one is correct.

Primary Objective #8: Separate the answer choices into Contenders and Losers. After completing this process, review the contenders and decide which answer is the correct one.

The Contender/Loser separation process is exceedingly important, primarily because it saves time. Consider two students—1 and 2—who each approach the same question, one of whom uses the Contender/Loser approach and the other who does not. Answer choice (D) is correct:

Student 1 (using Contender/Loser)

> Answer choice A: considers this answer for 10 seconds, keeps it as a
>   Contender.
> Answer choice B: considers this answer for 5 seconds, eliminates it as
>   a Loser.
> Answer choice C: considers this answer for 10 seconds, eliminates it as
>   a Loser.
> Answer choice D: considers this answer for 15 seconds, keeps it as a
>   Contender, and mentally notes that this answer is preferable to
>   (A).
> Answer choice E: considers this answer for 10 seconds, would
>   normally keep as a contender, but determines answer choice
>   (D) is superior.

> After a quick review, Student 1 selects answer choice (D) and moves to the next question. Total time spent on the answer choices: 50 seconds (irrespective of the time spent on the stimulus).

Student 2 (considering each answer choice in its entirety)

> Answer choice A: considers this answer for 10 seconds, is not sure if
>   the answer is correct or incorrect. Returns to stimulus and
>   spends another 15 seconds proving the answer is wrong.
> Answer choice B: considers this answer for 5 seconds, eliminates it.
> Answer choice C: considers this answer for 10 seconds, eliminates it.
> Answer choice D: considers this answer for 15 seconds, notes this is
>   the best answer without further consideration.
> Answer choice E: considers this answer for 10 seconds, but determines
>   answer choice (D) is superior.

> After a quick review, Student 2 selects answer choice (D) and moves to the next question. Total time spent on the answer choices: 65 seconds.

Some companies assert that only two of the five answer choices have merit. This type of "rule" is valueless because only one answer choice can be correct; the other four answers can be eliminated for concrete and identifiable reasons.

Comparison: both students answer the problem correctly, but Student 2 takes 15 more seconds to answer the question than Student 1.

Some students, on reading this comparison, note that both students answered the problem correctly and that the time difference was small, only 15 seconds more for Student 2 to complete the problem. Doesn't sound like that big a difference, does it? But, the extra 15 seconds was for just one problem. Imagine if that same thing occurred on every single Logical Reasoning problem in the section: that extra 15 seconds per question would translate to a loss of 6 minutes and 15 seconds when multiplied across 25 questions in a section! And that lost time would mean that student 2 would get to four or five fewer questions than Student 1, just in this one section. This example underscores an essential LSAT truth: little things make a big difference, and every single second counts. If you can save even five seconds by employing a certain method, then do so!

Occasionally, students will read and eliminate all five of the answer choices. If this occurs, return to the stimulus and re-evaluate the argument. Remember— the information needed to answer the question always resides in the stimulus, either implicitly or explicitly. If none of the answers are attractive, then you must have missed something key in the stimulus.

Primary Objective #9: If all five answer choices appear to be Losers, return to the stimulus and re-evaluate the argument.

Take a moment to review the methods discussed in Chapters Two and Three. Together, these recommendations form a cohesive strategy for attacking any Logical Reasoning question. Let us start by reviewing the Primary Objectives™:

Memorize this process and make it second nature! These steps constitute the basic approach you must use to attack each question.

> Primary Objective #1: Determine whether the stimulus contains an argument or if it is only a set of factual statements.

> Primary Objective #2: If the stimulus contains an argument, identify the conclusion of the argument. If the stimulus contains a fact set, examine each fact.

> Primary Objective #3: If the stimulus contains an argument, determine if the argument is strong or weak.

> Primary Objective #4: Read closely and know precisely what the author said. Do not generalize!

> Primary Objective #5: Carefully read and identify the question stem. Do not assume that certain words are automatically associated with certain question types.

> Primary Objective #6: Prephrase: after reading the question stem, take a moment to mentally formulate your answer to the question stem.

> Primary Objective #7: Always read each of the five answer choices.

> Primary Objective #8: Separate the answer choices into Contenders and Losers. After you complete this process, review the Contenders and decide which answer is the correct one.

> Primary Objective #9: If all five answer choices appear to be Losers, return to the stimulus and re-evaluate the argument.

As you attack each problem, remember that each question stem governs the flow of information within the problem:

- The First family uses the stimulus to prove one of the answer choices must be true. No information outside the sphere of the stimulus is allowed in the correct answer choice.

- The Second Family takes the answer choices as true and uses them to help the stimulus. Information outside the sphere of the stimulus is allowed in the correct answer choice.

- The Third Family takes the answer choices as true and uses them to hurt the stimulus. Information outside the sphere of the stimulus is allowed in the correct answer choice.

- The Fourth Family uses the stimulus to prove that one of the answer choices cannot occur. No information outside the sphere of the stimulus is allowed in the answer choices.

By consistently applying the points above, you give yourself the best opportunity to succeed on each question.

Tricks of the Trade

The individuals who construct standardized tests are called *psychometricians*. Although this job title sounds ominous, breaking this word into its two parts reveals a great deal about the nature of the LSAT. Although we could make a number of jokes about the *psycho* part, this portion of the word refers to psychology; the *metrician* portion relates to metrics or measurement. Thus, the purpose of these individuals is to create a test that measures you in a precise, psychological way. As part of this process, the makers of the LSAT carefully analyze reams of data from every test administration in order to assess the tendencies of test takers. As Sherlock Holmes observed, "You can, for example, never foretell what any one man will do, but you can say with precision what an average number will be up to." By studying the actions of all past test takers, the makers of the exam can reliably predict where you will be most likely to make errors. Throughout this book we will reference those pitfalls as they relate to specific question and reasoning types. For the moment, we would like to highlight one mental trap you must avoid at all times in any LSAT section: the tendency to dwell on past problems. Many students fall prey to "answering" a problem, and then continuing to think about it as they start the next problem. Obviously, this is distracting and creates an environment where missing the next problem is more likely. When you finish a problem, you must immediately put it out of your mind and move to the next problem with 100% focus. If you are uncertain of your answer on the previous problem, simply make a note in the test booklet and then return to that problem later, if time allows. If you let your mind wander back to previous problems, you fall into a deadly trap.

Answer Transferring

Transferring your answers from the test booklet to your answer sheet is one of the most important tasks that you will perform on the LSAT. Our research indicates that approximately 10% of all test takers make some type of transcription error during a typical five section test. Since one question can mean a difference of several percentile points, we strongly advise you to follow one of the two approaches discussed below. The method you choose is entirely dependent upon your personal preferences.

1. <u>Logical Grouping</u>. This method involves transferring several answer choices at once, at logical break points throughout the test. For the Reading Comprehension and Logic Games sections, transfer answer choices after you complete the questions for each passage or game. For the Logical Reasoning section, transfer answer choices after you complete each two-page question group. This method generally allows for faster transferring of answers, but some students find they are more likely to make errors in their transcription.

2. <u>Question By Question</u>. As the name implies, this method involves filling in the answer ovals on your answer sheet after you complete each individual question. This method generally consumes more time than the Logical Grouping method, but it usually produces a higher transfer accuracy rate. If you use the Logical Grouping method and find yourself making errors, use this method instead.

Filling in the Ovals

Be sure to blacken the entire oval for the answer choice you select. Do not use checks or X's, and do not select two answers.

Although Law Services prints dire warnings against making stray marks on the answer sheet or incompletely filling in the ovals, these errors are not fatal to your LSAT score. If you believe that Law Services has incorrectly scored your test due to an answer sheet problem, you can have your answer sheet hand scored for an additional fee. Although rarely an issue, machine scoring errors can occur from stray marks, incompletely or improperly filled-in ovals, partially erased answers, or creases in your answer sheet. Remember, answers in your test booklet will not be scored, and two fully blackened answer choices to the same question will be marked incorrect and will not be reviewed by hand scoring.

Practicing with Time

In the last chapter we will discuss time management in detail. However, most students begin practicing with the ideas in this book before reaching that chapter, and we wanted to take a moment to give you advice on how to properly practice for the time element of the LSAT.

Students often ask if they should time themselves while practicing. While every student should take a timed practice LSAT at the very start of their preparation in order to gauge where they stand, not all preparation should be composed of timed exercises. When you learn a new concept or are practicing with a certain technique, you should begin by doing the first several problems untimed in order to get a feel for how the idea operates. Once you feel comfortable with the concept, begin tracking the time it takes you to complete each question. At first, do not worry about completing the question within a specified time frame, but rather examine how long it takes you to do each question when you are relaxed. After doing another 3 or 4 questions in this fashion, then begin attempting to complete each question in the time frame allowed on the test. Thus, you can "ramp up" to the appropriate time per question by following these steps:

1. Do the first 3 to 4 questions untimed; do not worry about how long you take to complete each question.
2. Do the next 3 to 4 questions without pre-setting a time per question, but track the amount of time it takes to complete each question.
3. Do the remaining questions at or near the appropriate time per question, approximately 1 minute and 25 seconds per question.

We are also often asked if every LSAT PrepTest must be done as a timed exercise. The answer is no. Although we recommend doing as many of the PrepTests as possible, you can break up individual tests and do section challenges (completing just one or two sections in the required time) or simply work through a section as a challenge exercise where you focus on answering a variety of question types without worrying about the time component.

Final Chapter Note

This concludes our general discussion of the Logical Reasoning section. In subsequent chapters we will deconstruct each question type and some of the reasoning types frequently used by the test makers. At all times we will use the principles presented in these first chapters. If, in the future, you find yourself unclear about some of these ideas, please return to these chapters and re-read them.

If you feel as if you are still hazy on some of the ideas discussed so far, do not worry. When discussing the theory that underlies all questions, the points can sometimes be a bit abstract and dry. In the future chapters we will be discussing the application of these ideas to real questions, and working with actual questions often helps a heretofore confusing idea become clear.

Average completion times for the other two sections:

Logic Games: 8 minutes and 45 seconds per game.

Reading Comprehension: 8 minutes and 45 seconds per passage.

A number of LSAT PrepTests can be purchased through our website, powerscore.com.

CHAPTER FOUR: MUST BE TRUE QUESTIONS

Must Be True Questions

Must Be True questions require you to select an answer choice that is proven by the information presented in the stimulus. The correct answer choice can be a paraphrase of part of the stimulus or it can be a logical consequence of one or more parts of the stimulus. However, when selecting an answer choice, you must find the proof that supports your answer in the stimulus. We call this the Fact Test™:

> The correct answer to a Must Be True question can always be proven by referring to the facts stated in the stimulus.

The test makers will try to entice you by creating incorrect answer choices that could possibly occur or are likely to occur, but are not certain to occur. You must avoid those answers and select the answer choice that is most clearly supported by what you read. Do not bring in information from outside the stimulus (aside from commonsense assumptions); all of the information necessary to answer the question resides in the stimulus.

Must Be True question stems appear in a variety of formats, but one or both of the features described below appear consistently:

1. The stem often indicates the information in the stimulus should be taken as true, as in:

   "If the statements above are true..."
   "The statements above, if true..."
   "If the information above is correct..."

   This type of phrase helps indicate that you are dealing with a First Family question type.

2. The stem asks you to identify a single answer choice that is proven or supported, as in:

   "...which one of the following must also be true?"
   "...which one of the following conclusions can be properly drawn on the basis of it?"
   "...most strongly support which one of the following?"
   "Which one of the following can be properly inferred..."

First Family Information Model:

Because Must Be True is the first question type under discussion, we will make test-taking comments that relate to other question types as well.

In each case, the question stem indicates that one of the answer choices is proven by the information in the stimulus.

Here are several Must Be True question stem examples from actual LSATs:

"If the statements above are true, which one of the following must also be true?"

"If the information above is correct, which one of the following conclusions can be properly drawn on the basis of it?"

"The statements above, if true, most strongly support which one of the following?"

"Which one of the following can be properly inferred from the passage?"

"Which one of the following is most strongly supported by the information above?"

Remember, "infer" means "must be true."

The majority of the questions in the Reading Comprehension section are Must Be True questions.

Although difficult questions can appear under any type, Must Be True questions are often considered one of the easier question types.

Must Be True questions are considered the foundation of the LSAT because the skill required to answer a Must Be True question is also required for every other LSAT Logical Reasoning question. Must Be True questions require you to read text and understand the facts and details that logically follow. To Weaken or Strengthen an argument, for example, you first need to be able to ascertain the facts and details. The same goes for every other type of question. Because every question type relies on the fact-finding skill used to answer Must Be True questions, your performance on Must Be True questions is often a predictor of your overall Logical Reasoning score. For this reason you must lock down the understanding required of this question category: what did you read in the stimulus and what do you know on the basis of that reading?

Prephrasing with Must Be True Questions

When you read an argument, you are forced to evaluate the validity of a conclusive statement generated by a framework designed to be persuasive (that is, after all, what argumentation is all about). When judging an argument, people tend to react with agreement or disagreement depending on the persuasiveness of the conclusion. Fact sets do not engender that same level of response because no argument is present, and, as mentioned in Chapter Two, many Must Be True stimuli are fact sets. Because prephrasing relies in part on your reaction to what you read, prephrasing Must Be True questions can often be difficult. There are exceptions (for example, when Sufficient and Necessary Conditions are present, as will be discussed in Chapter Six) but if you find yourself having difficulty prephrasing an answer to a Must Be True question, do not worry.

The following is a question from the June 1999 LSAT and will be used to further discuss prephrasing. Please take a moment to read through the problem and corresponding answer choices:

1. Flavonoids are a common component of almost all plants, but a specific variety of flavonoid in apples has been found to be an antioxidant. Antioxidants are known to be a factor in the prevention of heart disease.

   Which one of the following can be properly inferred from the passage?

   (A) A diet composed largely of fruits and vegetables will help to prevent heart disease.
   (B) Flavonoids are essential to preventing heart disease.
   (C) Eating at least one apple each day will prevent heart disease.
   (D) At least one type of flavonoid helps to prevent heart disease.
   (E) A diet deficient in antioxidants is a common cause of heart disease.

Do not worry if you have never heard of a flavonoid. The question does not depend on your knowledge, or lack thereof, of flavonoids.

Applying Primary Objective #1 we can make the determination that since there is no conclusion in the stimulus, this is a fact set and not an argument. In this case the stimulus is short, and according to Primary Objective #2 can be broken down into three components:

Remember, you can often predict the occurrence of Must Be True questions because the stimulus of most Must Be True questions does not contain a conclusion.

First Statement: Flavonoids are a common component of almost all plants,

Second Statement: a specific variety of flavonoid in apples has been found to be an antioxidant.

Third Statement: Antioxidants are known to be a factor in the prevention of heart disease.

The question stem is obviously a Must Be True, and to prephrase (Primary Objective #6), take a moment to consider what the elements in the stimulus add up to. To do so, consider the premises together, and look for the connection between the elements: the first and second premises have "flavonoid" in common, and the second and third premises have "antioxidant" in common. Take a moment to examine each connection.

Review the Primary Objectives on page 68!

The flavonoid connection between the first two premises proves to be non-informative. The first premise indicates flavonoids appear frequently in plants and the second premise cites a specific instance in apples.

The antioxidant connection in the last two premises is more revealing. The second premise indicates that a flavonoid in apples is an antioxidant, and the third premise states that antioxidants are a factor in preventing heart disease. Adding these two points together, we can deduce that the specific flavonoid in apples is a factor in preventing heart disease. Since that statement must be true based on the premises, we can attack the five answer choices with this prephrase in mind. Note that if you did not see that connection between the premises, you would simply move on and attack each answer choice with the facts at hand.

If you did not follow this exact pattern of analysis, or if you classified some answers as Contenders when we classified them as Losers, do not worry. Everyone has their own particular style and pace for attacking questions. The more questions you complete, the better you will get at understanding why answers are correct or incorrect.

Answer choice (A): This is an interesting answer choice, and most people take a moment before categorizing this as a Loser. The answer choice *could be true*, but it is too broad to be supported by the facts: nowhere are we told that a *diet* of fruits and vegetables will help prevent heart disease (and in this sense the answer fails the Fact Test). Perhaps apples are the only fruit with the antioxidant flavonoid and there is nothing beneficial about other fruits and vegetables. And, eating a diet of fruits and vegetables is no guarantee that the diet includes apples. Regardless, this answer choice can be especially attractive because it plays on the general perception that fruits and vegetables are good for you.

Answer choice (B): This answer is also a Loser. Nothing in the stimulus supports the rather strong statement that flavonoids are *essential* to preventing heart disease.

Answer choice (C): Many people hold this answer as a Contender and then move on to answer choice (D). As it will turn out, this answer is incorrect because the language is too strong: the stimulus only stated that apples contain an element that was a *factor* in preventing heart disease, not that they definitely *will* prevent heart disease.

Answer choice (D): This answer is the closest to our prephrase, and this is the correct answer. Notice how the language of this answer choice—"helps to prevent"—matches the stimulus language—"factor in the prevention."

Answer choice (E): This answer choice also could be true, but it cannot be correct because the stimulus makes no mention of the causes of heart disease. Just because an antioxidant can help prevent heart disease does not mean that a lack of antioxidants causes heart disease.

The scope of the stimulus— especially if that scope is broad— often helps eliminate one or more of the answer choices.

Notice how the scope of the stimulus plays a role in how we attack the answer choices. The language of the stimulus is relatively broad—"almost all," "factor in the prevention,"—and the author shies away from making definite statements. Because the stimulus does not contain much in the way of direct, absolute information, selecting an answer choice that contains a direct, absolute statement is difficult to justify. This reasoning helps us eliminate answer choices (B) and (C), both of which contain strong statements that are ultimately unsupportable (literally, they both fail the Fact Test because they are too strong).

Returning to the Stimulus

As you attack the answer choices, do not be afraid to return to the stimulus to re-read and confirm your perceptions. Most LSAT stimuli contain a large amount of tricky, detailed information, and it is difficult to gain a perfect understanding of many of the stimuli you encounter. There is nothing wrong with quickly looking back at the stimulus, especially when deciding between two or more answer choices.

This advice also holds true for the Reading Comprehension section.

Please note that there is a difference between returning to the stimulus and re-reading the entire stimulus. On occasion, you will find yourself with no other option but to re-read the entire passage, but this should not be your normal mode of operation.

Primary Objective #4 and Modifier Words Revisited

Primary Objective #4 states: "Read closely and know precisely what the author said. Do not generalize!" This is especially important in Must Be True questions because the details are all the test makers have to test you on. Consider the following stimulus:

In Must Be True questions you are like the detective Sherlock Holmes, looking for clues in the stimulus and then matching those clues to the answer choices.

2. The importance of the ozone layer to terrestrial animals is that it entirely filters out some wavelengths of light but lets others through. Holes in the ozone layer and the dangers associated with these holes are well documented. However, one danger that has not been given sufficient attention is that these holes could lead to severe eye damage for animals of many species.

When reading the stimulus, your eye should be drawn to the modifier and indicator words, which are underlined below:

The importance of the ozone layer to terrestrial animals is that it <u>entirely</u> filters out <u>some</u> wavelengths of light <u>but</u> lets others through. Holes in the ozone layer and the dangers associated with these holes are well documented. However, one danger that has <u>not</u> been given sufficient attention is that these holes <u>could lead to</u> severe eye damage for animals of <u>many</u> species.

The scope of the stimulus is relatively broad, and aside from the word "entirely," most of the modifiers are not absolute.

Words like "some," "could," and "many" encompass many different possibilities and are broad scope indicators. Words like "must" and "none" indicate a narrow scope.

Now, look at the rest of the problem and see how several of the answer choices attempt to prey upon those who did not read the stimulus closely. Here are the question stem and corresponding answer choices for the stimulus above:

2. The importance of the ozone layer to terrestrial animals is that it entirely filters out some wavelengths of light but lets others through. Holes in the ozone layer and the dangers associated with these holes are well documented. However, one danger that has not been given sufficient attention is that these holes could lead to severe eye damage for animals of many species.

Which one of the following is most strongly supported by the statements above, if they are true?

(A) All wavelengths of sunlight that can cause eye damage are filtered out by the ozone layer where it is intact.
(B) Few species of animals live on a part of the earth's surface that is not threatened by holes in the ozone layer.
(C) Some species of animals have eyes that will not suffer any damage when exposed to unfiltered sunlight.
(D) A single wavelength of sunlight can cause severe damage to the eyes of most species of animals.
(E) Some wavelengths of sunlight that cause eye damage are more likely to reach the earth's surface where there are holes in the ozone layer than where there are not.

With the previous discussion in mind, let us analyze the answer choices:

Answer choice (A): The very first word—"all"—should be a red flag. Nowhere in the stimulus do we have support for stating that *all* damaging wavelengths are filtered out by the ozone layer. The stimulus only states that the ozone layer filters "some" wavelengths and lets others through. Some of those that are filtered are dangerous, as indicated by the last sentence. Surprisingly, about 10% of all test takers select this answer choice.

Answer choice (B): We know that many animal species could suffer severe eye damage, and from this we can infer that some of them live in areas threatened by the ozone layer. We do *not* know that few of the species live in non-threatened areas. Do not forget the Fact Test—it will eliminate any answer choice without support.

Answer choice (C): Nothing in the passage proves this answer choice. If you selected this answer thinking that "many" implied "not all," then you made a simple, correctable mistake. As we will discuss in the chapter on Formal Logic, "many" can include "all."

Answer choice (D): Again, watch those modifiers! One reason the answer choice is incorrect is because it references "most" species when the stimulus only discusses "many" species.

Answer choice (E): This is the correct answer. We can follow the chain of connections in the stimulus to prove this answer: the ozone layer filters some wavelengths of light; holes in the ozone layer are dangerous, but one previously overlooked danger of the holes is possible eye damage for many species. From these two statements we can infer that the holes must be letting some damaging wavelengths of light through. This is essentially what answer choice (E) states.

The lesson from this question is simple: read closely and pay strict attention to the modifiers used by the author. Even though you must read quickly, the test makers expect you to know exactly what was said, and they will include answer choices specifically designed to test whether you understood the details.

Correct Answers in Must Be True Questions Reviewed

Let us take a moment to review two types of answers that will always be correct in a Must Be True question.

1. Paraphrased Answers

   Paraphrased Answers are answers that restate a portion of the stimulus in different terms. Because the language is not exactly the same as in the stimulus, Paraphrased Answers can be easy to miss. Paraphrased Answers are designed to test your ability to discern the author's exact meaning. Sometimes the answer can appear to be almost too obvious since it is drawn directly from the stimulus.

2. Answers that are the sum of two or more stimulus statements (Combination Answers)

   Any answer choice that would result from combining two or more statements in the stimulus will be correct. The correct answer to the flavonoid question earlier in this chapter is an excellent example of this idea in action.

Should you encounter either of the above as answer choices in a Must Be True question, go ahead and select the answer with confidence.

Paraphrased answers occur primarily in Must Be True and Main Point questions. Some students have said they missed paraphrased answer choices because they did not feel the test makers would simply change the language of the text. They will!

There are other classic LSAT tricks that we will discuss in this and future chapters.

There are several types of answers that appear in Must Be True questions that are incorrect. These answers appear frequently enough that we have provided a review of the major types below. Each answer category below is designed to attract you to an incorrect answer choice, and after this brief review we will examine several LSAT questions and analyze actual instances of these types of answers.

1. Could Be True or Likely to Be True Answers

   Because the criteria in the question stem requires you to find an answer choice that Must Be True, answers that only could be true or are even likely to be true are incorrect. These answers are attractive because there is nothing demonstrably wrong with them (for example, they do not contain statements that are counter to the stimulus). Regardless, like all incorrect answers these answers fail the Fact Test. Remember, you must select an answer choice that must occur based on what you have read.

   This category of incorrect answer is very broad, and some of the types mentioned below will fall under this general idea but place an emphasis on a specific aspect of the answer.

2. Exaggerated Answers

   Exaggerated Answers take information from the stimulus and then stretch that information to make a broader statement that is not supported by the stimulus. In that sense, this form of answer is a variation of a could be true answer since the exaggeration is possible, but not proven based on the information. Here is an example:

   If the stimulus states, "*Some* software vendors recently implemented more rigorous licensing procedures."

   An incorrect answer would exaggerate one or more of the elements: "*Most* software vendors recently implemented more rigorous licensing procedures." In this example, *some* is exaggerated to *most*. While it could be true that most software vendors made the change, the stimulus does not prove that it must be true. This type of answer is often paraphrased, creating a deadly combination where the language is similar enough to be attractive but different enough to be incorrect.

   Here is another example:

   If the stimulus states, "Recent advances in the field of molecular biology make it *likely* that many school textbooks will be rewritten."

The exaggerated and paraphrased version would be: "Many school textbooks about molecular biology will be re-written." In this example, *likely* has been dropped, and this omission exaggerates the certainty of the change. The paraphrase also is problematic because the stimulus referenced school textbooks whereas the paraphrased answer refers to school textbooks *about molecular biology*.

3. "New" Information Answers

Because correct Must Be True answers must be based on information in the stimulus or the direct result of combining statements in the stimulus, be wary of answers that present so-called new information—that is, information not mentioned explicitly in the stimulus. Although these answers can be correct when they fall under the umbrella of a statement made in the stimulus, they are often incorrect. For example, if a stimulus discusses the economic policies of Japan, be careful with an answer that mentions U.S. economic policy. Look closely at the stimulus—does the information about Japanese economic policy apply to the U.S., or are the test makers trying to get you to fall for an answer that sounds logical but is not directly supported? To avoid incorrectly eliminating a New Information answer, take the following two steps:

1. Examine the scope of the argument to make sure the "new" information does not fall within the sphere of a term or concept in the stimulus.

2. Examine the answer to make sure it is not the consequence of combining stimulus elements.

4. The Shell Game

The LSAT makers have a variety of psychological tricks they use to entice test takers to select an answer choice. One of their favorites is one we call the Shell Game: an idea or concept is raised in the stimulus, and then a very similar idea appears in the answer choice, but the idea is changed just enough to be incorrect but still attractive. This trick is called the Shell Game because it abstractly resembles those street corner gambling games where a person hides a small object underneath one of three shells, and then scrambles them on a flat surface while a bettor tries to guess which shell the object is under (similar to three-card Monte). The object of a Shell Game is to trick the bettor into guessing incorrectly by mixing up the shells so quickly and deceptively that the bettor mistakenly selects the wrong shell. The intent of the LSAT makers is the same.

Shell Game answers occur in all LSAT question types, not just Must Be True.

As we will see in later chapters, the Shell Game can also be played with elements in a stimulus.

5. The Opposite Answer

As the name suggests, the Opposite Answer provides an answer that is completely opposite of the stated facts of the stimulus. Opposite Answers are very attractive to students who are reading too quickly or carelessly. Because Opposite Answers appear quite frequently in Strengthen and Weaken questions, we will discuss them in more detail when we cover those question types.

6. The Reverse Answer

Here is a simplified example of how a Reverse Answer works, using italics to indicate the reversed parts:

The stimulus might state, "*Many* people have *some* type of security system in their home."

An incorrect answer then reverses the elements: "*Some* people have *many* types of security systems in their home."

The Reverse Answer is attractive because it contains familiar elements from the stimulus, but the reversed statement is incorrect because it rearranges those elements to create a new, unsupported statement.

Reverse Answers can occur in any type of question.

Idea Application: An Analysis of Correct and Incorrect Answers

In this section we will analyze three Logical Reasoning questions drawn from real LSATs. We will use the examples to discuss the various answer types you learned in the previous section.

Please take a moment to complete the following problem:

3. In an experiment, two-year-old boys and their fathers made pie dough together using rolling pins and other utensils. Each father-son pair used a rolling pin that was distinctively different from those used by the other father-son pairs, and each father repeated the phrase "rolling pin" each time his son used it. But when the children were asked to identify all of the rolling pins among a group of kitchen utensils that included several rolling pins, each child picked only the one that he had used.

    Which one of the following inferences is most supported by the information above?

    (A) The children did not grasp the function of a rolling pin.
    (B) No two children understood the name "rolling pin" to apply to the same object.
    (C) The children understood that all rolling pins have the same general shape.
    (D) Each child was able to identify correctly only the utensils that he had used.
    (E) The children were not able to distinguish the rolling pins they used from other rolling pins.

The "rolling pin" problem above is a famous question from the 1990s that lured many people to incorrectly select answer choice (D), a Shell Game answer. Answer choice (D) looks perfect at first glance, but the author never indicated that the children could identify only the *utensils* that they used. Rolling pins, yes; utensils, no. The correct answer choice is (B), which many test takers quickly pass over. Let's examine each answer:

Answer choice (A): From the text, it seems possible that the children did understand the function of a rolling pin; certainly, they were able to identify the rolling pin they used.

Answer choice (B): This is the correct answer choice. The answer must be true because we know that despite being asked to identify all the rolling pins, each child selected *only* the rolling pin he had used. No two children picked the same rolling pin and therefore no two children understood the name "rolling pin" to apply to the same object.

Shell Game answers are exceedingly dangerous because, when selected, not only do you miss the question but you walk away thinking you got it right. This misperception makes it difficult to accurately assess your performance after the test.

Answer choice (C): Apparently not, otherwise logic would say the children would pick other rolling pins aside from the one they used.

Answer choice (D): Do not be concerned if you fell into this trap, but consider it a lesson for the future. The test makers smoothly slip "utensils" into the answer choice, and most students make the mistake of equating utensils with rolling pins. Yes, a rolling pin is a utensil, but there are other utensils as well, and the stimulus does not give us information about whether the children could identify those utensils. This is the essence of the Shell Game: you expect one thing and the test makers slip something quite similar but essentially different into its place.

Answer choice (E): This is an Opposite Answer. As indicated by the final sentence of the stimulus, the children were able to distinguish the rolling pin they used from the other rolling pins. This circumstance is exactly opposite of that stated in answer choice (E), which declares, "The children were *not* able to distinguish..." In this case, if you miss the "not," this answer choice is very attractive.

Let's continue looking at the way answers are constructed. Please take a moment to complete the following problem:

4. The increasing complexity of scientific inquiry has led to a proliferation of multiauthored technical articles. Reports of clinical trials involving patients from several hospitals are usually coauthored by physicians from each participating hospital. Likewise, physics papers reporting results from experiments using subsystems developed at various laboratories generally have authors from each laboratory.

    If all of the statements above are true, which one of the following must be true?

    (A) Clinical trials involving patients from several hospitals are never conducted solely by physicians from just one hospital.
    (B) Most reports of clinical trials involving patients from several hospitals have multiple authors.
    (C) When a technical article has multiple authors, they are usually from different institutions.
    (D) Physics papers authored by researchers from multiple laboratories usually report results from experiments using subsystems developed at each laboratory.
    (E) Most technical articles are authored solely by the researchers who conducted the experiments these articles report.

Answer choice (A): The stimulus never discusses who *conducts* the studies, only who authors the reports. Thus, there is no proof for this answer choice and it fails the Fact Test. Even if you mistook "conducted" for "reported," the answer choice is still incorrect because the stimulus indicates that reports involving patients from several hospitals are *usually* coauthored physicians from each hospital. Although "usually" could mean "always," it does not have to, and hence it is possible that a clinical trial could be reported by physicians from just one hospital.

Answer choice (B): This answer choice is a direct paraphrase of the second sentence. The second sentence states, "Reports of clinical trials involving patients from several hospitals are usually coauthored by physicians from each participating hospital." Answer choice (B) translates "usually" into "most," and "coauthored by physicians from each participating hospital" into "multiple authors." Thus, the answer choice passes the Fact Test and is correct.

Answer choice (C): This is a Shell Game answer choice. Although the stimulus says there has been a proliferation of multiauthored technical articles, no comment is made about the frequency of multiauthored technical articles. In the next sentence, a frequency—"usually"—is given, but only for multiauthored clinical trial reports. The test makers give you hard data about the clinical trial reports, and then try to entice you into picking a broader answer involving technical reports.

Answer choice (C) shows how the Shell Game can occur in the stimulus as well as in the answer choices. The stimulus of this problem switches from "technical articles" to "reports of clinical trials." Answer choice (C) plays on that substitution.

Answer choice (D): This is a Reverse answer that contains a complex pair of reversed elements when matched against the stimulus. Let us compare the stimulus and the answer choice, using italics to indicate the reversed parts:

The stimulus states, "physics papers reporting results from experiments using *subsystems developed at various laboratories* generally have *authors from each laboratory*."

Answer choice (D) states, "Physics papers authored by *researchers from multiple laboratories* usually report results from experiments using *subsystems developed at each laboratory*."

The reversed pair has two notable features:

1. The numbers are reversed—authors from *each* laboratory have become researchers (authors) from *multiple* laboratories, and subsystems from *various* laboratories have become subsystems from *each* laboratory. In a nutshell, the "various" and "each" elements have been reversed in the sentences.

2. The pair also reverses logical position within the argument, as the stimulus states that the experiments generally have authors from each

laboratory and the answer choice states that the researchers usually report experiments from each laboratory.

Answer choice (E): As with answer choice (C), we do not know enough about technical articles to support this answer choice.

Stimulus Opinions versus Assertions

Please take a moment to complete the following problem:

5. Some environmentalists question the prudence of exploiting features of the environment, arguing that there are no economic benefits to be gained from forests, mountains, or wetlands that no longer exist. Many environmentalists claim that because nature has intrinsic value it would be wrong to destroy such features of the environment, even if the economic costs of doing so were outweighed by the economic costs of not doing so.

    Which one of the following can be logically inferred from the passage?

    (A) It is economically imprudent to exploit features of the environment.
    (B) Some environmentalists appeal to a noneconomic justification in questioning the defensibility of exploiting features of the environment.
    (C) Most environmentalists appeal to economic reasons in questioning the defensibility of exploiting features of the environment.
    (D) Many environmentalists provide only a noneconomic justification in questioning the defensibility of exploiting features of the environment.
    (E) Even if there is no economic reason for protecting the environment, there is a sound noneconomic justification for doing so.

The "Some environmentalists question..." construction at the start of the stimulus does not lead to the usual counter-conclusion because the stimulus does not contain an argument.

This is a very interesting stimulus because the author repeats the opinions of others and never makes an assertion of his or her own. When a stimulus contains only the opinions of others, then in a Must Be True question you can eliminate any answer choice that makes a flat assertion without reference to those opinions. For example, answer choice (A) makes a factual assertion ("It is...") that cannot be backed up by the author's survey of opinions in the stimulus—the opinions do not let us know the actual facts of the situation. Answer choice (E) can be eliminated for the very same reason.

Answer choices (B), (C), and (D) each address the environmentalists, and thus each is initially a Contender.

THE POWERSCORE LSAT LOGICAL REASONING BIBLE

Answer choice (B): This is the correct answer. The second sentence references the views of many environmentalists, who claim that "nature has intrinsic value" (for example, beauty). This view is the noneconomic justification cited by the answer choice.

This answer can be a bit tricky because of the convoluted language the test makers use. "Questioning the defensibility of exploiting features of the environment" is a needlessly complex phrase. A more direct manner of writing that phrase would be "attacking the exploitation of the environment."

To increase the difficulty of this problem, this language was then repeated in answer choices (C) and (D).

Answer choice (C): We only know the opinions of "some" and "many" environmentalists, and these numbers do not provide enough information to discern the views of "most" environmentalists, which is the term used in the answer choice ("many" is not the same as "most").

Answer choice (D): This answer choice cannot be proven. While we know that many environmentalists claim an noneconomic justification, we do not know that that is the *only* justification they provide.

With the analysis of these three LSAT questions, examples of each of the incorrect answer categories have been presented.

When you are reading a stimulus, keep a careful watch on the statements the author offers as fact, and those that the author offers as the opinion of others. In a Must Be True question, the difference between the two can sometimes be used to eliminate answer choices.

Final Note

This chapter is only the start of our question analysis. The ideas discussed so far represent a fraction of what you will learn from this book. Future chapters will build on the ideas discussed herein, and present new concepts that will help you attack all types of questions.

On the following page is a review of some of the key points from this chapter. After the review, there is a short problem set to help you test your knowledge of some of the ideas. An answer key follows with explanations. Good luck!

Must Be True Question Type Review

Must Be True questions require you to select an answer choice that is proven by the information presented in the stimulus. The question format can be reduced to, "What did you read in the stimulus, and what do you know on the basis of that reading?"

You cannot bring in information from outside the stimulus to answer the questions; all of the information necessary to answer the question resides in the stimulus.

All Must Be True answer choices must pass the Fact Test™:

> The correct answer to a Must Be True question can always be proven by referring to the facts stated in the stimulus.

If you find yourself having difficulty prephrasing an answer to a Must Be True question, do not be concerned.

The scope of the stimulus—especially if that scope is broad—often helps eliminate one or more of the answer choices.

You can often predict the occurrence of Must Be True questions because the stimulus of most Must Be True questions does not contain a conclusion.

Correct Answer Types:

> Paraphrased answers are answers that restate a portion of the stimulus in different terms. When these answers mirror the stimulus, they are correct.

> Combination answers result from combining two or more statements in the stimulus.

Incorrect Answer Types:

> Could Be True answers are attractive because they can possibly occur, but they are incorrect because they do not have to be true.

> Exaggerated answers take information from the stimulus and then stretch that information to make a broader statement that is not supported by the stimulus.

> New Information answers include information not explicitly mentioned in the stimulus. Be careful with these answers: first examine the scope of the stimulus to make sure the "new" information does not fall under the

umbrella of a term or concept in the stimulus. Second, examine the answer to make sure it is not the consequence of combining stimulus elements.

The Shell Game occurs when an idea or concept is raised in the stimulus, and then a very similar idea appears in the answer choice, but the idea is changed just enough to be incorrect but still attractive.

The Opposite answer is completely opposite of the facts of the stimulus.

The Reverse answer is attractive because it contains familiar elements from the stimulus, but the reversed statement is incorrect because it rearranges those elements to create a new, unsupported statement.

Must Be True Question Problem Set

The following questions are drawn from actual LSATs. Please complete the problem set and review the answer key and explanations. *Answers on Page 93*

1. Some argue that laws are instituted at least in part to help establish a particular moral fabric in society. But the primary function of law is surely to help order society so that its institutions, organizations, and citizenry can work together harmoniously, regardless of any further moral aims of the law. Indeed, the highest courts have on occasion treated moral beliefs based on conscience or religious faith as grounds for making exceptions in the application of laws.

    The statements above, if true, most strongly support which one of the following?

    (A) The manner in which laws are applied sometimes takes into account the beliefs of the people governed by those laws.
    (B) The law has as one of its functions the ordering of society but is devoid of moral aims.
    (C) Actions based on religious belief or on moral conviction tend to receive the protection of the highest courts.
    (D) The way a society is ordered by law should not reflect any moral convictions about the way society ought to be ordered.
    (E) The best way to promote cooperation among a society's institutions, organizations, and citizenry is to institute order in that society by means of law.

2. Newtonian physics dominated science for over two centuries. It found consistently successful application, becoming one of the most highly substantiated and accepted theories in the history of science. Nevertheless, Einstein's theories came to show the fundamental limits of Newtonian physics and to surpass the Newtonian view in the early 1900s, giving rise once again to a physics that has so far enjoyed wide success.

    Which one of the following logically follows from the statements above?

    (A) The history of physics is characterized by a pattern of one successful theory subsequently surpassed by another.
    (B) Long-standing success or substantiation of a theory of physics is no guarantee that the theory will continue to be dominant indefinitely.
    (C) Every theory of physics, no matter how successful, is eventually surpassed by one that is more successful.
    (D) Once a theory of physics is accepted, it will remain dominant for centuries.
    (E) If a long-accepted theory of physics is surpassed, it must be surpassed by a theory that is equally successful.

3. The solidity of bridge piers built on pilings depends largely on how deep the pilings are driven. Prior to 1700, pilings were driven to "refusal," that is, to the point at which they refused to go any deeper. In a 1588 inquiry into the solidity of piers for Venice's Rialto Bridge, it was determined that the bridge's builder, Antonio Da Ponte, had met the contemporary standard for refusal: he had caused the pilings to be driven until additional penetration into the ground was no greater than two inches after twenty-four hammer blows.

   Which one of the following can properly be inferred from the passage?

   (A) The Rialto Bridge was built on unsafe pilings.
   (B) The standard of refusal was not sufficient to ensure the safety of a bridge.
   (C) Da Ponte's standard of refusal was less strict than that of other bridge builders of his day.
   (D) After 1588, no bridges were built on pilings that were driven to the point of refusal.
   (E) It is possible that the pilings of the Rialto Bridge could have been driven deeper even after the standard of refusal had been met.

4. Every moral theory developed in the Western tradition purports to tell us what a good life is. However, most people would judge someone who perfectly embodied the ideals of any one of these theories not to be living a good life—the kind of life they would want for themselves and their children.

   The statements above, if true, most strongly support which one of the following?

   (A) Most people desire a life for themselves and their children that is better than a merely good life.
   (B) A person who fits the ideals of one moral theory in the Western tradition would not necessarily fit the ideals of another.
   (C) Most people have a conception of a good life that does not match that of any moral theory in the Western tradition.
   (D) A good life as described by moral theories in the Western tradition cannot be realized.
   (E) It is impossible to develop a theory that accurately describes what a good life is.

5. Mystery stories often feature a brilliant detective and the detective's dull companion. Clues are presented in the story, and the companion wrongly infers an inaccurate solution to the mystery using the same clues that the detective uses to deduce the correct solution. Thus, the author's strategy of including the dull companion gives readers a chance to solve the mystery while also diverting them from the correct solution.

   Which one of the following is most strongly supported by the information above?

   (A) Most mystery stories feature a brilliant detective who solves the mystery presented in the story.
   (B) Mystery readers often solve the mystery in a story simply by spotting the mistakes in the reasoning of the detective's dull companion in that story.
   (C) Some mystery stories give readers enough clues to infer the correct solution to the mystery.
   (D) The actions of the brilliant detective in a mystery story rarely divert readers from the actions of the detective's dull companion.
   (E) The detective's dull companion in a mystery story generally uncovers the misleading clues that divert readers from the mystery's correct solution.

6. Cézanne's art inspired the next generation of artists, twentieth-century modernist creators of abstract art. While most experts rank Cézanne as an early modernist, a small few reject this idea. Françoise Cachin, for example, bluntly states that such an ascription is "overplayed," and says that Cézanne's work is "too often observed from a modern point of view."

   Which one of the following statements is most strongly supported by the information above?

   (A) Cézanne's work is highly controversial.
   (B) Cézanne was an early creator of abstract art.
   (C) Cézanne's work helped to develop modernism.
   (D) Modern art owes less to Cézanne than many experts believe.
   (E) Cézanne's work tends to be misinterpreted as modernist.

7. Light is registered in the retina when photons hit molecules of the pigment rhodopsin and change the molecules' shape. Even when they have not been struck by photons of light, rhodopsin molecules sometimes change shape because of normal molecular motion, thereby introducing error into the visual system. The amount of this molecular motion is directly proportional to the temperature of the retina.

Which one of the following conclusions is most strongly supported by the information above?

(A) The temperature of an animal's retina depends on the amount of light the retina is absorbing.
(B) The visual systems of animals whose body temperature matches that of their surroundings are more error-prone in hot surroundings than in cold ones.
(C) As the temperature of the retina rises, rhodopsin molecules react more slowly to being struck by photons.
(D) Rhodopsin molecules are more sensitive to photons in animals whose retinas have large surface areas than in animals whose retinas have small surface areas.
(E) Molecules of rhodopsin are the only pigment molecules that occur naturally in the retina.

8. One of the most vexing problems in historiography is dating an event when the usual sources offer conflicting chronologies of the event. Historians should attempt to minimize the number of competing sources, perhaps by eliminating the less credible ones. Once this is achieved and several sources are left, as often happens, historians may try, though on occasion unsuccessfully, to determine independently of the usual sources which date is more likely to be right.

Which one of the following inferences is most strongly supported by the information above?

(A) We have no plausible chronology of most of the events for which attempts have been made by historians to determine the right date.
(B) Some of the events for which there are conflicting chronologies and for which attempts have been made by historians to determine the right date cannot be dated reliably by historians.
(C) Attaching a reliable date to any event requires determining which of several conflicting chronologies is most likely to be true.
(D) Determining independently of the usual sources which of several conflicting chronologies is more likely to be right is an ineffective way of dating events.
(E) The soundest approach to dating an event for which the usual sources give conflicting chronologies is to undermine the credibility of as many of these sources as possible.

92

Must Be True Problem Set Answer Key

All answer keys in this book indicate the source of the question by giving the month and year the LSAT was originally administered, the Logical Reasoning section number, and the question number within that section. Each LSAT has two Logical Reasoning sections, and so the Section 1 and Section 2 designators will refer to the first or second Logical Reasoning section in the test, not the physical section number of the booklet.

Question #1. Must. October 2003 LSAT, Section 2, #6. The correct answer choice is (A)

Unlike many Must Be True question stimuli, this stimulus contains an argument. The conclusion is in the second sentence: "the primary function of law is surely to help order society so that its institutions, organizations, and citizenry can work together harmoniously, regardless of any further moral aims of the law." The stimulus also begins with the "Some argue that..." construction, and as usual, is followed by a conclusion that argues against the position established in the first sentence (see "A Commonly Used Construction" in Chapter Two if this sounds unfamiliar). The last sentence is a premise that proves to be key for choosing the correct answer.

Answer choice (A): This correct answer is largely a paraphrase of the last sentence.

Answer choice (B): While the author certainly agrees with the first part of the sentence, in the second part the phrase "devoid of moral aims" is too strong to be supported by the information in the stimulus. The last sentence indicates that morality has some effect on the law and invalidates the "devoid" claim.

Answer choice (C): This is an Exaggerated answer. Although the last sentence indicates that religious faith has been grounds for making exceptions in the application of law, the stimulus does not indicate that actions based on religious or moral belief *tend* to receive the protection of the highest courts.

Answer choice (D): The author indicates that the "primary function" of law is to help order society; the author does not indicate that this is the one and only function of law. The answer choice overstates the case by saying that a society ordered by law should *not reflect any* moral convictions about the ordering.

Answer choice (E): No mention is made of the "best way" to promote cooperation, only that the primary function of law is to promote such cooperation.

Question #2. Must. June 2002 LSAT, Section 1, #7. The correct answer choice is (B)

The stimulus tells the story of recent physics theories: Newtonian physics was preeminent for over two centuries, and despite widespread acknowledgment and confirmation it was surpassed by Einsteinian physics in the early 1900s.

Answer choice (A): The two theories cited in the stimulus are not sufficient to form a *pattern*, which is the basis of answer choice (A).

Answer choice (B): This is the correct answer. As shown by the case of Newtonian physics, success and substantiation is no guarantee of dominance.

Answer choice (C): This is an Exaggerated answer that takes one instance and exaggerates it into a pattern. Although Newtonian physics was surpassed, this does not prove that *every* theory of physics will be eventually surpassed. The answer goes farther than the facts of the stimulus and fails the Fact Test.

Answer choice (D): Like answer choice (C), this answer goes too far. Although some theories of physics have been dominant for centuries, there is no guarantee that every theory will be dominant for that long.

Answer choice (E): Even though Einsteinian physics has enjoyed wide success in surpassing Newtonian physics, nowhere in the stimulus is there evidence to prove that each theory *must be* surpassed by an equally successful theory.

Question #3. Must. June 2002 LSAT, Section 1, #2. The correct answer choice is (E)

This interesting stimulus contains two definitions of "refusal:" an initial definition that implies refusal is a point at which pilings will go no further, and then a second, contemporary standards definition of refusal that reveals that refusal is a point at which additional penetration into the ground is no greater than two inches after twenty-four hammer blows. The stimulus is a fact set, and thus there is no conclusion present.

Answer choice (A): Although there was an inquiry into the solidity of the piers of the Rialto Bridge, the results of that inquiry are not disclosed. The only other information we are given is that the pilings of the Rialto Bridge met the contemporary standard of refusal, but this is not sufficient to indicate whether the pilings of this particular bridge were safe. Hence, this answer fails the Fact Test and is incorrect.

Answer choice (B): Similar to answer choice (A), we have insufficient information to make this judgment.

Answer choice (C): This answer is somewhat opposite of the information in the stimulus, which states that Da Ponte had met the contemporary standard of refusal.

Answer choice (D): This is another Opposite answer. The stimulus indicates that bridges built prior to 1700 were driven to the point of refusal.

Answer choice (E): This is the correct answer. As stated in the stimulus, "he had caused the pilings to be driven until additional penetration into the ground was no greater than two inches after twenty-four hammer blows." The statement indicates that additional penetration was possible with a sufficient number of hammer blows.

Must Be True Problem Set Answer Key

Question #4. Must. October 2000 LSAT, Section 2, #10. The correct answer choice is (C)

This is a fact set. Note the strength of the modifiers in this stimulus—"every," "most," and "any." We should be able to use this narrow scope to support a fairly strong statement, but be careful: the test makers know this too and they will supply several answer choices that are worded strongly. Make sure you select an answer that conforms to the facts.

Answer choice (A): The phrase "better than a merely good life" goes beyond the statements in the stimulus.

Answer choice (B): This answer is incorrect because we are not given information about how the moral theories are different, or if they are different at all. The only detail we are told is that the theories all have one thing in common—they tell us what a good life is. Since the answer choice makes a claim based on differences between theories, it cannot be correct.

Answer choice (C): This is the correct answer. At first glance, this answer choice may seem a bit strong in saying the conception would not match that of *any* moral theory. But, as discussed above, we can support this because the stimulus uses very strong language, specifically stating "*most* people would judge someone who perfectly embodied the ideals of *any* one of these theories *not* to be living a good life." (italics added).

Answer choice (D): This answer is worded strongly but it quickly fails the Fact Test. Nothing is said to indicate that the life described by one of the moral theories cannot be realized.

Answer choice (E): This answer also has strong language, but it goes too far in saying that it is *impossible* to develop a theory that accurately describes a good life.

Question #5. Must. October 2002 LSAT, Section 1, #15. The correct answer choice is (C)

The last sentence contains a conclusion, and this conclusion is the primary evidence that supports answer choice (C).

Answer choice (A): The word "often" in the first sentence is the key to this answer choice. "Often" means frequently, but frequently is not the same as "most." Had the stimulus said "more often than not," that would mean "most" and this answer choice would be correct.

Answer choice (B): We cannot determine if readers of mystery stories solve the mystery simply by spotting the errors of the dull companion.

Answer choice (C): This is the correct answer. The second sentence indicates that "clues are presented in the story...the detective uses to deduce the correct solution." Combined with the last sentence, which states "the author's strategy...gives readers a chance to solve the mystery," this answer choice is proven by facts.

Must Be True Problem Set Answer Key

Answer choice (D): Look for the facts in the stimulus—do they support this answer? Although the dull companion diverts readers from the correct solution, we do not know if actions of the brilliant detective rarely divert readers from the actions of the dull companion.

Answer choice (E): This is a tricky answer choice if you do not read closely. The stimulus states that the dull companion infers a wrong solution from clues that the brilliant detective ultimately uses to solve the mystery. Answer choice (E) states that the dull companion uncovers misleading clues. This is incorrect; the interpretation of the clues is misleading, not the clues themselves.

Question #6. Must. December 2002 LSAT, Section 2, #16. The correct answer choice is (C)

The final three problems in this section are harder than the previous five. This problem is answered correctly by about 45% of test takers and is classified as difficult (the hardest LSAT questions have success rates under 20%. Fortunately, questions this difficult appear infrequently). Students can miss questions for a variety of reasons:

1. The stimulus is difficult to understand.
2. The question stem is difficult to classify (very rare) or confusing.
3. The correct answer is deceptive, causing students to avoid it.
4. One (or more) of the incorrect answers is attractive, drawing students to it.

Given that the stimulus is a simple fact set and that none of the incorrect answers attracted more than 15% of test takers, the difficulty in this problem apparently lies in the correct answer.

Answer choice (A): The controversy in the stimulus is about the categorization of Cézanne as an artist, not about Cézanne's work. Further, even if the answer did correctly reference the categorization controversy, the answer would still be suspect because of the word "highly." The stimulus indicates that only a small few reject the categorization of Cézanne as an early modernist and most experts accept it.

Answer choice (B): The stimulus asserts that Cézanne *inspired* the creators of abstract art, not that Cézanne himself created abstract art.

Answer choice (C): This correct answer is a paraphrase of the first sentence. The deceptiveness of this answer lies in two areas:

1. The substitution of "develop" for "inspire." Some students feel the word "develop" is too strong, but if Cézanne inspired the creators of the next generation of art then he helped develop it.

2. The use of the word "modernism." Some students are thrown off by "modernism" because they expect to see "abstract" instead. The stimulus is careful about saying "twentieth-century modernist creators of abstract art." Notice how the test makers use answer choice (B)—which mentions "abstract"—to subtly prepare you to make this error.

Answer choice (D): The first sentence indicates that Cézanne inspired the modernist creators. The rest of the stimulus discusses a disagreement about the categorization of Cézanne that is not resolved in favor of either group. Hence, there is no way for us to determine if modern art owes less to Cézanne than many experts believe.

Answer choice (E): The word "tends" is the problem in this answer choice. Logically, "tends" means "most." So, according to answer choice (E), Cézanne's work is usually misinterpreted as modernist. The stimulus disagrees with this view: only a "small few" reject the categorization of Cézanne as a modernist whereas the majority accepts it. Further, the disagreement in the stimulus involves art experts, and from their view we would dispute answer choice (E). Answer choice (E) can also be understood as involving all interpretation of Cézanne's work—whether by art expert or not—and from this perspective the answer is still unsupported since the views of others are not discussed in the stimulus.

Question #7. Must. June 2001 LSAT, Section 2, #19. The correct answer choice is (B)

The stimulus is a fact set. Part of the difficulty with this problem is the scientific subject matter. Many people are intimidated by the mention of rhodopsin, with which they are unfamiliar. As with the flavonoids in problem #1 of the chapter text, you do not need to know what rhodopsin is to complete the problem. The stimulus can be broken into several easily digestible parts:

> Premise: Light is registered in the retina when photons hit rhodopsin molecules and the molecules change shape.

> Premise: Due to normal molecular motion, rhodopsin molecules sometimes change shape without having been hit by light. This change causes errors in the visual system.

> Premise: The amount of molecular motion is directly proportional to the temperature of the retina.

Answer choice (A): The stimulus does not indicate that the temperature of the retina *depends on* the amount of light. It could easily be affected by other factors, such as body temperature. About 15% of test takers fell prey to this answer.

Answer choice (B): This is the correct answer and just over 40% of test takers correctly choose this answer. To prove this answer you must link together several pieces of information. First, the last sentence of the stimulus shows that the amount of rhodopsin molecular motion is directly proportional to the temperature of the retina, and the second sentence of the stimulus shows that this motion causes visual errors, so the higher the retinal temperature, the more errors in the visual system. The answer choice ties body temperature (remember, the retina is a body part) to the temperature of the surroundings and then rightly notes that hot surroundings would cause more visual errors than cold surroundings if body temperature matched those surroundings.

Answer choice (C): This was the most popular incorrect answer, and just under a quarter of test takers fell for this answer. The answer is wrong because we do not know that temperature causes the rhodopsin to *react more slowly*. Higher retinal temperature causes the rhodopsin molecules to change shape, but no mention is made of reaction time. This answer falls under the "New information" category.

Must Be True Problem Set Answer Key

Answer choice (D): Another New Information answer choice. Similar to answer choice (C), this answer fails the Fact Test because no information is given about the surface area of the retina. Answer choices (C) and (D) are great examples of how an answer can contain information unmentioned by the stimulus. These answers are somewhat attractive because there is nothing actively wrong about them and thus they could be true. To avoid them, always keep in mind that your goal is to find the answer that must occur based on the information in the stimulus.

Answer choice (E): While the stimulus focuses on rhodopsin, no indication is given that rhodopsin is the only naturally occurring pigment molecule—there could be others.

Question #8. Must. June 2000 LSAT, Section 1, #20. The correct answer choice is (B)

This is a very challenging problem, and only about a quarter of students answer this problem correctly. The stimulus is a fact set and offers a solution for dating an event when the usual sources offer conflicting chronologies:

1. Minimize the number of competing sources, possibly by eliminating the less credible ones.

2. Independent of the usual sources, determine which date is more likely to be right.

Notice how the test makers throw in the word "historiography" in order to be intimidating. As usual, you do not need to know the meaning of this word (or any unusual word) in order to continue with the problem. The remainder of the sentence makes clear that dating an event is the point of discussion, and you can comfortably connect the "historio" word root to "date an event" and "historians" and confidently move on with a good idea that historiography is connected to history in some way. By definition, historiography is the writing of history.

Answer choice (A): The stimulus discusses dates where there is conflict between sources. In no way does the stimulus support answer choice (A).

Answer choice (B): This is the correct answer. As stated in the last sentence, historians are on occasion unsuccessful in determining independently the date of an event. If the usual sources offered are in conflict about the date of a particular event and an analysis independent of the usual sources fails to confirm a date, then a date cannot be reliably determined for the event.

Answer choice (C): About one-third of all test takers choose this answer. The stimulus speaks specifically of dating an event *when the usual sources offer conflicting chronologies*. The stimulus does not discuss dating an event when there is no conflict of chronologies, and most likely many dates could be set with certainty in the absence of any conflict. With this in mind, the language of the answer choice becomes problematic because "attaching a reliable date to *any* event" would not "*require* determining which of several conflicting chronologies is most likely to be true."

Answer choice (D): The language of the answer choice is too strong in saying that an independent determination is an *ineffective* way of dating events. There is simply not enough information about what constitutes a "determination independent of the usual sources" to say it is ineffective.

Answer choice (E): This is another tricky answer, and just under a quarter of test takers incorrectly select this answer. The answer claims that the soundest approach to dating an event is to *undermine the credibility* of as *many* of the competing sources as possible. First, the stimulus suggests that the historian should, perhaps, eliminate the less credible ones. No mention is made of eliminating as many as possible, and the stimulus indicates that several remaining sources are to be expected. Second, that same section discusses eliminating less credible sources, not undermining the credibility of those sources.

CHAPTER FIVE: MAIN POINT QUESTIONS

Main Point Questions

Main Point questions may be the question type most familiar to test takers. Many of the standardized tests you have already encountered, such as the SAT, contain questions that ask you to ascertain the Main Point. Even in daily conversation you will hear, "What's your point?" Main Point questions, as you might suspect from the name, ask you to summarize the author's point of view.

From a classification standpoint, Main Point questions are a subcategory of Must Be True questions and fall into the First Family type. As with all First Family questions, the answer you select must follow from the information in the stimulus. But be careful: even if an answer choice must be true according to the stimulus, if it fails to capture the main point it cannot be correct. This is the central truth of Main Point questions: like all Must Be True question variants the correct answer must pass the Fact Test, but with the additional criterion that the correct answer choice must capture the author's point.

Because every Main Point question stimulus contains an argument, if you apply the methods discussed in Chapters Two and Three you should already know the answer to a Main Point question by the time you read the question stem. Primary Objective #2 states that you should identify the conclusion of the argument, and the correct answer choice to these problems will be a rephrasing of the main conclusion of the argument. So, by simply taking the steps you would take to solve any question, you already have the answer to a Main Point question at your fingertips. Be careful, though: many Main Point problems feature a structure that places the conclusion either at the beginning or in the middle of the stimulus. Most students have an unstated expectation that the conclusion will appear in the last sentence, and the test makers are able to prey upon this expectation by creating wrong answers that paraphrase the last sentence of the stimulus. To avoid this trap, simply avoid assuming that the last sentence is the conclusion.

The Main Point question stem format is remarkably consistent, with the primary feature being a request for you to identify the conclusion or point of the argument, as in the following examples:

> "Which one of the following most accurately expresses the main conclusion of the argument?"

> "Which one of the following most accurately expresses the conclusion of the journalist's argument?"

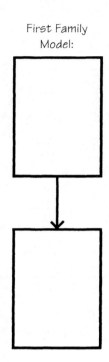

First Family Model:

There has never been a Main Point Except question, because the four wrong answers would be identical in meaning and thus easy to spot.

"Which one of the following most accurately restates the main point of the passage?"

"The main point of the argument is that"

Two Incorrect Answer Types

Two types of answers typically appear in Main Point questions. Both are incorrect:

    1. Answers that are true but do not encapsulate the author's point.

    2. Answers that repeat premises of the argument.

Each answer type is attractive because they are true based on what you have read. However, neither summarizes the author's main point and therefore both are incorrect.

Because you have already learned the skills necessary to complete these questions, we will use the following two questions for discussion purposes. Please take a moment to complete the following problem:

1.   Journalist: A free marketplace of ideas ensures that all ideas get a fair hearing. Even ideas tainted with prejudice and malice can prompt beneficial outcomes. In most countries, however, the government is responsible for over half the information released to the public through all media. For this reason, the power of governments over information needs to be curtailed. Everyone grants that governments should not suppress free expression, yet governments continue to construct near monopolies on the publication and dissemination of enormous amounts of information.

Which one of the following most accurately expresses the conclusion of the journalist's argument?

(A)   The freedom of the marketplace of ideas is in jeopardy.
(B)   Preserving a free marketplace of ideas is important.
(C)   The control that governments have over information needs to be reduced.
(D)   Ideas that have malicious content or stem from questionable sources can be valuable.
(E)   Governments have near monopolies on the dissemination of many kinds of information.

The conclusion to this argument is the fourth sentence, which begins with the conclusion indicator "For this reason..." By applying the Primary Objectives you should have identified this conclusion while reading, and then, upon classifying the question stem you should have looked for a paraphrase of this sentence. Answer choice (C) fits the bill, and is the correct answer.

Answer choice (A): The author would agree with this statement but this is not the Main Point of the argument; rather, it is closer to a premise that might support the conclusion.

Incidentally, the author's general agreement with this answer choice is signalled by the use of "however" in the third sentence. In the stimulus, the author begins by mentioning that a free marketplace of ideas, including dangerous ideas, ensures a fair hearing of ideas. In the third sentence, the author then says, "however, the government is responsible for over half the information released to the public," indicating the author feels the government is a threat to this free marketplace.

Answer choice (B): The author would also agree with this statement, but again this is not the Main Point of the argument. As discussed in the analysis of answer choice (A), the author believes that the freedom of the marketplace of ideas is at risk, and in stating that we should curtail the government's power over information, the author assumes that preserving a free marketplace of ideas is important. Thus this answer choice would be better described as an unstated premise that supports the conclusion.

Answer choice (C): This is the correct answer. Remember, any answer that is a paraphrase of the conclusion of the argument will be the correct answer to a Main Point question.

Answer choice (D): The stimulus specifically notes that malicious or prejudicial ideas can "prompt beneficial outcomes." The outcome of an idea is different from stating the ideas themselves "can be valuable."

Answer choice (E): The stimulus states that "governments continue to construct near monopolies on the publication and dissemination of enormous amounts of information." This phrasing is not the same as answer choice (E), which asserts that the government *already* has a monopoly on the dissemination of *many* kinds of information.

The lesson learned from this particular problem is that you must isolate the conclusion and then look for a paraphrase of that conclusion.

Unlike the question above, many Main Point question stimuli avoid using traditional conclusion indicators and this lack of argument indicator "guideposts" makes your task more challenging. Remember, if you are struggling to identify the conclusion in an argument, you can always use the

Always identify the conclusion of any argument you read!

Paraphrased answers are always correct in Must Be True questions. Answers that paraphrase the conclusion are correct in Main Point questions.

Conclusion Identification Methodology discussed in Chapter Two:

> Take the statements under consideration for the conclusion and place them in an arrangement that forces one to be the conclusion and the other(s) to be the premise(s). Use premise and conclusion indicators to achieve this end. Once the pieces are arranged, determine if the arrangement makes logical sense. If so, you have made the correct identification. If not, reverse the arrangement and examine the relationship again. Continue until you find an arrangement that is logical.

If you cannot identify the conclusion in a Main Point question, you must go back and apply this methodology. Otherwise, without the conclusion how can you answer the question?

Please take a moment to complete the following problem:

2. I agree that Hogan's actions resulted in grievous injury to Winters. And I do not deny that Hogan fully realized the nature of his actions and the effects that they would have. Indeed, I would not disagree if you pointed out that intentionally causing such effects is reprehensible, other things being equal. But in asking you to concur with me that Hogan's actions not be wholly condemned I emphasize again that Hogan mistakenly believed Winters to be the robber who had been terrorizing west-side apartment buildings for the past several months.

    Which one of the following most accurately expresses the conclusion of the argument?

    (A) Hogan should not be considered responsible for the injuries sustained by Winters.
    (B) The robber who had been terrorizing west-side apartment buildings should be considered to be as responsible for Winters's injuries as Hogan.
    (C) The actions of Hogan that seriously injured Winters are not completely blameworthy.
    (D) Hogan thought that Winters was the person who had been terrorizing west-side apartment buildings for the last few months.
    (E) The actions of Hogan that seriously injured Winters were reprehensible, other things being equal.

The conclusion of this argument is difficult to identify because the author does not use a traditional conclusion indicator. The first three sentences are admissions by the author regarding the nature of Hogan's actions. The fourth sentence contains the conclusion and a premise, and the conclusion is that "Hogan's actions should not be wholly condemned."

If you struggled to identify the conclusion, consider how you might have applied the Conclusion Identification Methodology to the pieces of the argument. For example, consider the two parts of the last sentence. If you thought one of them might be the conclusion, place one as the conclusion and the other as a premise, as follows:

> "Because I ask that Hogan's actions not be wholly condemned, therefore I emphasize again that Hogan mistakenly believed Winters to be the robber who had been terrorizing west-side apartment buildings for the past several months."

Does that configuration sound right? No. Try again by reversing the premise and conclusion pieces:

> "Because Hogan mistakenly believed Winters to be the robber who had been terrorizing west-side apartment buildings for the past several months, therefore I ask you to concur with me that Hogan's actions not be wholly condemned."

The relationship now sounds much more logical.

Answer choice (A): The author admits that Hogan fully realized his actions and the author asks that "Hogan's actions not be wholly condemned." Both of these statements are counter to the idea that Hogan should not be considered responsible for Winter's injuries.

Answer choice (B): The only reference to the robber is that Hogan mistakenly believed that Winters was the robber. Thus, there is no evidence in the stimulus to support this answer.

Answer choice (C): This correct answer is a paraphrase of the conclusion of the argument.

Answer choice (D): According to the information in the stimulus, this answer must be true. Regardless, the answer is still incorrect because it fails to summarize the author's main point. This type of answer—one that is true but misses the main point—is frequently featured as an incorrect answer in Main Point questions.

Answer choice (E): Like answer choice (D), this statement is true according to the stimulus. But, it is incorrect because it does not capture the main point.

Remember: Main Point questions are Must Be True questions with an additional criterion—you must also identify the author's point.

Main Point—Fill in the Blank Questions

In recent years there has been a rise in the number of questions that contain a stimulus that ends with a blank space. The question stem asks you to fill in the blank with an appropriate answer. While not one of the most common question types, a Fill in the Blank question can throw off test takers who are surprised by the unusual stimulus formation. No need to worry; these are almost always Main Point questions in disguise (and when they are not Main Point questions they are Must Be True questions).

The June 2002 LSAT had three Fill in the Blank questions, the most on a recent single test.

The placement of the blank in the stimulus is not random—the blank is always at the very end of the stimulus. There is a conclusion indicator at the start of the sentence to help you recognize that you are being asked to fill in the conclusion of the argument. In every case, you should fill the blank with the answer choice that best represents the main point of the argument. In order to achieve this goal, you must read the stimulus for clues revealing the direction of the argument and the author's intent.

First, here are some sample final sentences drawn from real LSAT questions to give you an example of how the sentence with the blank appears:

"Therefore, _____."

"Hence, in the new century, the stability of a nation's cultural identity will likely _____."

"Thus, in many cases, by criminals' characterization of their situations, _____."

As you can see, each sentence above begins with a conclusion indicator that modifies the blank. This is the signal that you must supply the conclusion.

Now, take a look at a complete question from the June 2002 LSAT in order to get a better sense of how to analyze the stimulus for contextual clues.

Please take a moment to complete the following problem:

3. Psychologist: Although studies of young children
        have revealed important facts about the
        influence of the environment on language
        acquisition, it is clear that one cannot attribute
        such acquisition solely to environmental
        influences: innate mechanisms also play a role.
        So, the most reasonable question that ought to
        be studied is whether _____.

    Which one of the following most logically completes
    the passage?

    (A)   language acquisition can ever be fully
            explained
    (B)   innate mechanisms are a contributing factor in
            language learning
    (C)   language acquisition is solely the product of
            innate mechanisms
    (D)   parents and peers are the most important
            influence on a child's learning of a language
    (E)   innate mechanisms play a more important role
            in language acquisition than a child's
            immediate environment

Fill in the Blank questions should be approached in the same manner as any First Family question, but the emphasis is on using contextual clues provided in the stimulus to find the answer choice that best fits the blank.

The single sentence prior to the last sentence is lengthy and contains the information required to fill in the blank at the end of the question. The argument topic is language acquisition; the author indicates that "one cannot attribute such acquisition solely to environmental influences" and then immediately follows that phrase by saying "innate mechanisms also play a role." Hence, the author feels that both environment and innate mechanisms play a role. The last sentence then prefaces the blank by saying, "the most reasonable question that ought to be studied is whether _____." The most logical answer would be one that addresses the relative roles played by environment and innate mechanisms in language acquisition. Let's examine the answer choices:

Answer choice (A): The argument is not about whether language acquisition can ever be explained, but about what influences exist on language acquisition and to what degree.

Answer choice (B): The psychologist asserts this statement at the end of the first sentence and if this were a Must Be True question, this would be the correct answer. But, this is more than a Must Be True question and the correct answer must meet the Main Point criterion. So, although this answer choice is true according to the psychologist, it does not capture the point of the argument as indicated by the last sentence and is therefore incorrect.

Answer choice (C): The argument does not attempt to establish that language acquisition is *solely* the product of innate mechanisms, but that innate mechanisms have some influence, as does environment. This answer choice tries to confuse test takers by going in the opposite direction of the psychologist's statement that "one cannot contribute such acquisition solely to environmental influences." This does not mean that we can therefore attribute such acquisition solely to innate mechanisms.

Answer choice (D): "Parents and peers" would qualify as environmental influences and the argument is not about determining if the environmental influence is the most important factor, but about the relative roles played by environment and innate mechanisms in language acquisition.

Answer choice (E): This is the correct answer, and this is the only answer that addresses the relative roles of environment and innate mechanisms. Note that the language of the answer choice could have indicated that either plays a greater role because what ought to be studied is a question that determines which is a greater influence.

Final Chapter Note

There are three elements remaining in this chapter: a review of Main Point questions; a brief Must Be True and Main Point Question Stem Mini-Drill; and two more Main Point questions with complete explanations. Please complete each element in the order presented and read the explanations carefully.

Main Point Question Type Review

From a classification standpoint, Main Point questions are a subcategory of Must Be True questions and thus fall into the First Family type.

The Main Point is the same as the conclusion of the argument. By applying the Primary Objectives you should already have the answer to a Main Point question by the time you read the question stem.

The correct answer choice must not only be true according to the stimulus, it must also summarize the author's point. Avoid answers that are true but miss the point of the author's argument.

Fill in the Blank questions are simply Main Point questions in disguise. They are approached in the same manner as any First Family question, but the emphasis is on using the contextual clues provided in the stimulus to find the choice that best fits the blank.

Must Be True and Main Point Question Stem Mini-Drill

Each of the following items contains a question stem from a recent LSAT question. In the space provided, categorize each stem as either a Must Be True or Main Point question, and notate any Except (X) identifier you see. *Answers on Page 110*

1. Question Stem: "Which one of the following statements is most strongly supported by the information above?"

   Question Type: _____

2. Question Stem: "The information above provides the LEAST support for which one of the following?"

   Question Type: _____

3. Question Stem: "Which one of the following most logically completes the argument?"

   Question Type: _____

4. Question Stem: "The educators' reasoning provides grounds for accepting which one of the following statements?"

   Question Type: _____

5. Question Stem: "Which one of the following most accurately expresses the argument's conclusion?"

   Question Type: _____

6. Question Stem: "Which one of the following can be inferred from the passage above?"

   Question Type: _____

1. Question Type: Must Be True
Stem drawn from the October 2002 LSAT. In this case, the "most strongly supported" is used with the intent of proving one of the answers correct. Hence, this is a Must Be True question.

2. Question Type: Must Be True X
Stem drawn from the September 1998 LSAT. The presence of "LEAST" makes this an Except question and the presence of the phrase "support for which one of the following" adds the Must Be True element. The four incorrect answer choices Must Be True; the correct answer choice is not necessarily true.

3. Question Type: Main Point-FITB
Stem drawn from the October 2002 LSAT. This is the question stem for a Fill in the Blank (FITB) question , which asks you to identify the Main Point of the argument.

4. Question Type: Must Be True
Stem drawn from the October 2002 LSAT. "Accepting which one of the following statements" is identical to asking you to find the answer that is proven by the information in the stimulus. Hence, this is a Must Be True question.

5. Question Type: Main Point
Stem drawn from the June 2003 LSAT. In asking for the argument's conclusion, the stem asks you to identify the Main Point of the argument.

6. Question Type: Must Be True
Stem drawn from the June 2000 LSAT. The word "inferred" means must be true. Hence, this is a Must Be True question.

Main Point Question Problem Set

The following questions are drawn from actual LSATs. Please complete the problem set and review the answer key and explanations. *Answers on Page 112*

1. Last month OCF, Inc., announced what it described as a unique new product: an adjustable computer workstation. Three days later ErgoTech unveiled an almost identical product. The two companies claim that the similarities are coincidental and occurred because the designers independently reached the same solution to the same problem. The similarities are too fundamental to be mere coincidence, however. The two products not only look alike, but they also work alike. Both are oddly shaped with identically placed control panels with the same types of controls. Both allow the same types of adjustments and the same types of optional enhancements.

    The main point of the argument is that

    (A) the two products have many characteristics in common
    (B) ErgoTech must have copied the design of its new product from OCF's design
    (C) the similarities between the two products are not coincidental
    (D) product designers sometimes reach the same solution to a given problem without consulting each other
    (E) new products that at first appear to be unique are sometimes simply variations of other products

2. Prediction, the hallmark of natural sciences, appears to have been possible by reducing phenomena to mathematical expressions. Some social scientists also want the power to predict accurately and assume they ought to perform the same reduction. But this would be a mistake; it would neglect data that are not easily mathematized and thereby would only distort the social phenomena.

    Which one of the following most accurately expresses the main conclusion of the argument?

    (A) The social sciences do not have as much predictive power as the natural sciences.
    (B) Mathematics plays a more important role in the natural sciences than it does in the social sciences.
    (C) There is a need in the social sciences to improve the ability to predict.
    (D) Phenomena in the social sciences should not be reduced to mathematical formulas.
    (E) Prediction is responsible for the success of the natural sciences.

Main Point Problem Set Answer Key

All answer keys in this book indicate the source of the question by giving the month and year the LSAT was originally administered, the Logical Reasoning section number, and the question number within that section. Each LSAT has two Logical Reasoning sections, so the Section 1 and Section 2 designators will refer to the first or second Logical Reasoning section in the test, not the physical section number of the booklet.

Question #1. MP. October 2002 LSAT, Section 1, #2. The correct answer choice is (C)

Like the majority of Main Point question stimuli, the argument does not contain a traditional conclusion indicator. Thus, you must look at the pieces of the argument in order to determine the point the author is making. In this case, the conclusion is "The similarities are too fundamental to be mere coincidence." Use the Conclusion Identification Methodology to help establish that point if you are unsure. The argument uses the fact that the two workstations are similar and were released in the same timespan to assume that the similarity is not caused by coincidence.

Answer choice (A): This is a repeat of a premise of the argument, not the main point. As mentioned in the discussion, in Main Point questions you should expect to see incorrect answers that repeat premises from the argument.

Answer choice (B): The statement does not pass the Fact Test. The scenario could be reversed: OCF could have copied Ergotech. Regardless, this is not the main point.

Answer choice (C): This correct answer is a paraphrase of the conclusion.

Answer choice (D): This would undermine the argument and thus it cannot be the main point.

Answer choice (E): Although the author would likely agree with this statement, this does not capture the main point, which addresses the two named products.

Question #2. MP. December 2003 LSAT, Section 2, #10. The correct answer choice is (D)

Like the previous problem, the conclusion is in the middle of the argument and is not prefaced by a conclusion indicator. Get used to seeing this format on Main Point questions! The author states that prediction has been made possible by reducing phenomena to mathematical expressions and that some social scientists want to have this same power. The author argues that it would be a mistake to allow social scientists to have this ability. The conclusion, therefore, is "But this would be a mistake."

Answer choice (A): The author says, "some social scientists also want the power to predict accurately," so the author would likely agree with this statement. Regardless, this is not the main point of the argument. Again, be careful with answers that are true according to the author—do they also address the main point?

Answer choice (B): The author might very well agree with this statement, although there is not enough information to assert that this statement is true based on the stimulus (the words "more important" are a bit strong). Regardless, this answer choice does not address the main point of the argument and is therefore wrong.

Answer choice (C): While the social scientists may believe this is true, the author's point is a different one—that social scientists ought not perform a mathematical reduction. And, because the author believes that prediction is apparently made possible by reducing phenomena to mathematical expressions, the author would likely disagree with this statement.

Answer choice (D): This is the correct answer. The conclusion states that it would be a mistake for social scientists to have the ability to reduce phenomena to mathematical expressions. Answer choice (D) is a paraphrase of that idea.

Answer choice (E): This point is not addressed in the stimulus.

CHAPTER SIX: CONDITIONAL REASONING

Sufficient and Necessary Conditions

Conditional reasoning is a fundamental component of both the Logical Reasoning and Logic Games sections of the LSAT. If you have already read the PowerScore LSAT Logic Games Bible, then you have encountered basic conditional reasoning. In this chapter we will further explore the concept.

Conditional reasoning is one of the pillars of the LSAT, and appears in a large number of problems.

Conditional reasoning is the broad name given to logical relationships composed of sufficient and necessary conditions. Any conditional statement consists of at least one sufficient condition and one necessary condition. Let us begin by defining each condition:

> A sufficient condition can be defined as an event or circumstance whose occurrence indicates that a necessary condition must also occur.

> A necessary condition can be defined as an event or circumstance whose occurrence is required in order for a sufficient condition to occur.

Now, let's try that in English! In other words, if a sufficient condition occurs, you automatically know that the necessary condition also occurs. If a necessary condition occurs, then it is possible but not certain that the sufficient condition will occur.

In everyday use, conditional statements are often brought up using the "if...then" construction. Consider the following statement, which we will use for the majority of our discussion:

> If someone gets an A+ on a test, then they must have studied for the test.

If the above statement is true, then anyone who receives an A+ on a test must have studied for the test. Anyone who studied might have received an A+, but it is not guaranteed. Since getting an A+ automatically indicates that studying must have occurred, the sufficient condition is "get an A+" and it follows that "must have studied" is the necessary condition.

Conditional reasoning can occur in any question type.

In the real world, we know that a statement such as the above is usually true, but not always. There could be a variety of other ways to get an A+ without studying, including cheating on the test, bribing the teacher for a higher grade, or even breaking into the school computer system and changing the grade. However, in the LSAT world, when an author makes a conditional statement, he or she believes that statement to be true *without exception*. So, if the statement above is made in the LSAT world, then according to the author anyone who gets an A+ must have studied.

To efficiently manage the information in conditional statements, we use arrow diagrams. For a basic conditional relationship, the arrow diagram has three parts: a representation of the sufficient condition, a representation of the necessary condition, and an arrow pointing from the sufficient condition to the necessary condition. Most often, this arrow points from left to right (exceptions will be discussed in the chapter on Formal Logic).

The diagram for the previously discussed statement would be as follows:

<u>Sufficient</u>   <u>Necessary</u>

A+ $\longrightarrow$ Study

To Diagram or Not to Diagram

As we begin using diagrams to represent conditional relationships, students often ask how much diagramming they should do on the test. The answer depends on the individual. In Logical Reasoning, some students diagram much more than others and the level of your diagramming depends on your comfort and ability to juggle the ideas mentally. A diagram is exceptionally helpful because it represents a complex relationship in picture form (think of the old saying that a picture is a worth a thousand words). Some test takers (including many high scorers) feel that making the diagram is less work because you do not need to "remember" the statement, and there is no loss of time because good diagrammers can diagram almost as fast as they read. Others feel comfortable enough with the statements to simply juggle them mentally. Regardless of your preference, at first you must learn how to diagram because there will likely be problems that you have to diagram during the test (some LSAT problems contain relationships with eight or more elements and juggling these elements mentally is challenging to say the least). Once you establish that you can accurately diagram any statement, then you can confidently make decisions during the test about whether to diagram a given problem.

Three Logical Features of Conditional Reasoning

Conditional Reasoning statements have several unique features that you must know. When considering the diagram above, remember the following:

1. The sufficient condition does not *make* the necessary condition occur. That is, the sufficient condition does not actively cause the necessary condition to happen. That form of reasoning is known as Causal

Reasoning, which will be discussed in Chapter Eight. Instead, in a conditional statement the occurrence of the sufficient condition is a sign or indicator that the necessary condition will occur, is occurring, or has already occurred. In our discussion example, the occurrence of someone receiving an A+ is a sign that indicates that studying must also have occurred. The A+ does not *make* the studying occur.

2. Temporally speaking, either condition can occur first, or the two conditions can occur at the same time. In our discussion example, the necessary condition (studying) would most logically occur first. Depending on the example, the sufficient condition could occur first.

3. The conditional relationship stated by the author does not have to reflect reality. This point may help some students who thought that our diagram might be backwards. Some people read the statement and think, "studying would logically lead to an A+, so studying is the sufficient condition." As reasonable as that may sound, that way of thinking is incorrect because it does not reflect what the author said, but rather what you think of what the author said. *Your job is not to figure out what sounds reasonable, but rather to perfectly capture the meaning of the author's sentence.*

Valid and Invalid Statements

Although the discussion example may seem relatively easy, the makers of the LSAT often use conditional reasoning to ensnare unwary test takers, especially in the Logical Reasoning section. When analyzing a basic conditional statement, there are certain observations that can be inferred from the statement and there are observations that may appear true but are not certain.

Taking our discussion example *as undeniably true*, consider the following four statements:

1. John received an A+ on the test, so he must have studied for the test.

2. John studied for the test, so he must have received an A+ on the test.

3. John did not receive an A+ on the test, so he must not have studied on the test.

4. John did not study for the test, so he must not have received an A+ on the test.

Two of the four statements above are valid, and two of the four statements are invalid. Can you identify which two are valid? The answers are on the next page.

Conditional reasoning occurs when a statement containing sufficient and necessary conditions is used to draw a conclusion based on the statement.

<u>Statement 1 is valid</u>. According to the original statement, because John received an A+, he must have studied for the test. We call this type of inference the Repeat form because the statement basically repeats the parts of the original statement and applies them to the individual in question, John.

We would use the following diagram for statement 1:

<u>Sufficient</u>   <u>Necessary</u>

$A+_J \longrightarrow Study_J$

Note how the A+ and Study elements are in the same position as our original statement, hence the "Repeat" form moniker. The "J" subscript represents "John." John is not a separate diagramming element because John is simply someone experiencing the conditions in the statement.

<u>Statement 2 is invalid</u>. Just because John studied for the test does not mean he actually received an A+. He may have only received a B, or perhaps he even failed. To take statement 2 as true is to make an error known as a Mistaken Reversal™. We use this name because the attempted inference looks like the reverse of the original statement:

<u>Sufficient</u>   <u>Necessary</u>

$Study_J \longrightarrow A+_J$

The form here reverses the Study and A+ elements, and although this statement *might* be true, it is not definitely true. Just because the necessary condition has been fulfilled does not mean that the sufficient condition must occur.

<u>Statement 3 is also invalid</u>. Just because John did not receive an A+ does not mean he did not study. He may have studied but did not happen to receive an A+. Perhaps he received a B instead. To take this statement as true is to make an error known as a Mistaken Negation™.

<u>Sufficient</u>   <u>Necessary</u>

$\cancel{A+}_J \longrightarrow \cancel{Study}_J$

The form here negates the A+ and Study elements (this is represented by the slash through each term), and although this statement *might* be true, it is not definitely true. Just because the sufficient condition has not been fulfilled does not mean that the necessary condition cannot occur.

Statement 4 is valid. If studying is the necessary condition for getting an A+, and John did not study, then according to the original statement there is no way John could have received an A+. This inference is known as the contrapositive, and you can see that when the necessary condition fails to occur, then the sufficient condition cannot occur.

<u>Sufficient</u>   <u>Necessary</u>

$$\cancel{Study}_J \longrightarrow \cancel{A+}_J$$

The form here reverses *and* negates the Study and A+ elements. When you are looking to find the contrapositive, do not think about the elements and what they represent. Instead, simply reverse and negate the two terms.

There is a contrapositive for every conditional statement, and if the initial statement is true, then the contrapositive is also true. The contrapositive is simply a different way of expressing the initial statement. To analogize, it is like examining a penny: both sides look different but intrinsically the value is the same.

These four valid and invalid inferences are used by the test makers to test your knowledge of what follows from a given statement. Sometimes you will need to recognize that the contrapositive is present in order to identify a correct answer, other times you made need to recognize a Mistaken Reversal in order to avoid a wrong answer, or that an argument is using a Mistaken Negation, and so forth. When you analyze a conditional statement, you simply need to be aware that these types of statements exist. At first that will require you to actively think about the possibilities and this will slow you down, but as time goes by this recognition will become second nature and you will begin to solve certain questions extraordinarily fast.

One word of warning: many people read the analysis of valid and invalid statements and ignore the discussion of the form of the relationships (reversal of the terms, negation of the terms, etc.). This is very dangerous because it forces them to rely on their knowledge of the grading system to understand why each statement is valid or invalid, and if their perception differs from that of the author, they make mistakes. At first, it is difficult to avoid doing this, but as time goes on, focus more on the form of the relationship and less on the content. If you simply try to think through the content of the relationship, you will likely be at a loss when faced with a conditional relationship involving, for example, the hemolymph of arthropods.

Because the contrapositive both reverses and negates, it is a combination of a Mistaken Reversal and Mistaken Negation. Since the contrapositive is valid, it is as if two wrongs do make a right.

A contrapositive denies the necessary condition, thereby making it impossible for the sufficient condition to occur. Contrapositives can often yield important insights into a game.

Symbolic Representation and Diagramming Negatives

As you diagram each conditional statement, you will face a decision about how to represent each element of the relationship. Because writing out the entire condition would be onerous, the best approach is to use a symbol to represent each condition. For example, we have already used "A+" to represent the idea of "If someone gets an A+ on a test." The choice of symbol is yours, and different students will choose different representations. For example, to represent "they must have studied for the test," you could choose "Study" or the more efficient "S." Whatever you decide to choose, the symbolization must make sense to you and it must be clear. For example, if faced with diagramming a sentence such as, "If you study, then you will be successful," you would not want to choose "S" to represent each term as that would be confusing. A better choice would be "St" for "Study" and "Su" for "Successful." Regardless of how you choose to diagram an element, once you use a certain representation within a problem, stick with that representation throughout the duration of the question.

As briefly discussed above, negatives can be diagrammed as slashes. Thus, when faced with a negative term such as "John did not receive an A+," we diagram the term as:

A̸+

Some students ask if they can simply put an "N" in front of the A+ to represent the "not" or negative idea (as in NA+). We do not recommend this approach because if that term is later negated by some other part of the stimulus, you will have a diagram that contains two negatives:

Because the two negatives translate into a positive (A+), a better approach is to diagram any negative with a slash, because when the slash is removed the term returns to "clear" or "positive" status. For those of you also using the Logic Games Bible, this approach integrates seamlessly with the PowerScore games diagramming method.

In considering the form of the statements, the position of the slashes is irrelevant when determining if you are looking at a Repeat, Contrapositive, Mistaken Reversal, or Mistaken Negation. Consider the following two pairs of statements, both of which contain contrapositives:

Negating statements largely consists of adding a "not" if a negative is not present in the sentence, or removing a "not" if a negative is present. In the disucussion of Assumptions in Chapter Nine we will discuss statement negation in more detail.

First Pair:

	Sufficient		Necessary
Original statement:	A	$\longrightarrow$	B
Contrapositive:	B̸	$\longrightarrow$	A̸

Second Pair:

	Sufficient		Necessary
Original statement:	C	$\longrightarrow$	D̸
Contrapositive:	D	$\longrightarrow$	C̸

In each pair, the second statement is a contrapositive, and in each contrapositive the terms are both reversed and negated. Thus, even though the slashes may be in different places (or nonexistent) in each of the original statements, both can yield a contrapositive. The *form* determines the result.

Valid and Invalid Statement Recognition Mini-Drill

Each of the following problems presents a pair of arrow diagrams which feature a statement and then an attempted inference. The attempted inference is either a valid Repeat form or Contrapositive, or an invalid Mistaken Reversal or Mistaken Negation. Identify the form of the attempted inference in each problem. *Answer on Page 123*

1. Original statement: $A \longrightarrow \overline{B}$

   Attempted Inference: $\overline{B} \longrightarrow A$

2. Original statement: $C \longrightarrow \overline{D}$

   Attempted Inference: $D \longrightarrow \overline{C}$

3. Original statement: $\overline{E} \longrightarrow F$

   Attempted Inference: $E \longrightarrow \overline{F}$

4. Original statement: $\overline{G} \longrightarrow H$

   Attempted Inference: $\overline{H} \longrightarrow G$

5. Original statement: $I \longrightarrow J$

   Attempted Inference: $I \longrightarrow J$

6. Original statement: $\overline{K} \longrightarrow \overline{L}$

   Attempted Inference: $\overline{L} \longrightarrow \overline{K}$

7. Original statement: $M \longrightarrow N$

   Attempted Inference: $\overline{M} \longrightarrow \overline{N}$

8. Original statement: $\overline{O} \longrightarrow \overline{P}$

   Attempted Inference: $P \longrightarrow O$

Valid and Invalid Statement Recognition Mini-Drill Answer Key

1. Mistaken Reversal

    Invalid. The A and B terms are reversed, but not negated. This is the classic Mistaken Reversal form.

2. Contrapositive

    Valid. The C and D terms are both reversed *and* negated, which is the mark of the contrapositive.

3. Mistaken Negation

    Invalid. The E and F terms are negated, but not reversed. This is the classic Mistaken Negation form.

4. Contrapositive

    Valid. The G and H terms are both reversed and negated. Compare this problem to #2. Although the "slashes" are in different places, each is a contrapositive because the terms are reversed and negated.

5. Repeat

    Valid. The terms are simply repeated.

6. Mistaken Reversal

    Invalid. Despite all the slashes, the only thing that occurs in this problem is that the K and L terms are reversed.

7. Mistaken Negation

    Invalid. The M and N terms are negated, but not reversed.

8. Contrapositive

    Valid. Although this may look "upside down," both terms are reversed and negated. Compare this with the example at the top of page 121. They are basically the same problem.

The Multiplicity of Indicator Words

So far we have discussed the nature of conditional relationships and what inferences can be made from a conditional statement. Now we turn to recognizing conditionality when it is present. One of the factors that makes identifying conditional statements difficult is that so many different words and phrases can be used to introduce a sufficient or necessary condition. The test makers have the advantage of variety in this regard, and so you must learn to recognize conditional reasoning when it is present in a stimulus. Take a moment to examine each of the following statements. Are they similar or different?

1. To get an A+ you must study.

2. Studying is necessary to get an A+.

3. When someone gets an A+, it shows they must have studied.

4. Only someone who studies can get an A+.

5. You will get an A+ only if you study.

You may be surprised to discover that each statement is diagrammed exactly the same way:

<u>Sufficient</u>   <u>Necessary</u>

A+ $\longrightarrow$ Study

In Logical Reasoning problems it is essential that you be able to recognize the many terms that identify and precede sufficient and necessary terms. The test makers frequently use the following words or phrases to introduce conditional reasoning:

Yes, you must memorize these two lists! They are incredibly helpful when you are trying to identify the presence of conditional reasoning.

To introduce a sufficient condition:	To introduce a necessary condition:
If	Then
When	Only
Whenever	Only if
Every	Must
All	Required
Any	Unless
People who	Except
In order to	Until
	Without

These lists are by no means comprehensive. Due to the vagaries of the English language many different terms can be used to introduce conditional statements. Since these lists can assist you in recognizing the types of situations where conditional statements arise, your first step should be to memorize the indicator words on each list. After you are comfortable with each word, focus on understanding the meaning of each conditional statement you encounter. Ultimately, your understanding of the relationship between sufficient and necessary conditions will allow you to easily manipulate any problem.

How to Recognize Conditionality

Using the words from the indicator lists, let's re-examine each of the five statements in the previous page. In each sentence, the conditional indicator is in italics:

Any synonym of the terms in the lists will also suffice.

1. To get an A+ you *must* study.

2. Studying is *necessary* to get an A+.

3. *When* someone gets an A+, it shows they *must* have studied.

4. *Only* someone who studies can get an A+.

5. You will get an A+ *only if* you study.

Comparing these five sentences reveals two critical rules about how conditional reasoning appears in a given sentence:

1. Either condition can appear first in the sentence.

   The order of presentation of the sufficient and necessary conditions is irrelevant. In statements 1, 3, and 5 the sufficient condition appears first in the sentence; in statements 2 and 4 the necessary condition appears first. Thus, when you are reading, you cannot rely on encountering the sufficient condition first and instead you must keep an eye out for conditional indicators.

2. A sentence can have one or two indicators.

Looking for conditionality is like being an air traffic controller: you must recognize and track the elements when they appear in a problem. If no conditional elements appear in a problem, then you do not have to worry about it.

   Sentences do not need both a sufficient condition indicator and a necessary condition indicator in order to have conditional reasoning present. As shown by statements 1, 2, 4, and 5, a single indicator is enough. Note that once you have established that one of the conditions is present, you can examine the remainder of the sentence to determine the nature of the other condition. For example, in statement 5, once the "only if" appears and you establish that "study" is the necessary condition, return to the first part of the sentence and establish that "A+" is the sufficient condition.

The Unless Equation™

In the case of "unless," "except," "until," and "without," a special two-step process called the Unless Equation is applied to the diagram:

1. Whatever term is modified by "unless," "except," "until," or "without" becomes the necessary condition.

2. The remaining term is negated and becomes the sufficient condition.

For example, consider the following:

Unless a person studies, he or she will not receive an A+.

Since "unless" modifies "a person studies," "Study" becomes the necessary condition. The remainder, "he or she will not receive an A+," is negated by dropping the "not" and becomes "he or she will receive an A+." Thus, the sufficient condition is "A+," and the diagram is as follows:

Sufficient	Necessary
A+ $\longrightarrow$	Study

Here is another example:

There can be no peace without justice.

Apply the Unless Equation"

1. Since "without" modifies "justice," "justice" becomes the necessary condition and we represent this with a "J."

2. The remainder, "There can be no peace ," is negated by dropping the "no," and becomes the sufficient condition "P."

The diagram is as follows:

Sufficient	Necessary
P $\longrightarrow$	J

Thus, if peace occurs, there must be justice.

To diagram a statement that contains "unless," convert the variable modified by "unless" into the necessary condition. Take the remainder, negate it, and convert it into the sufficient condition. The same technique applies to statements that contain "until," "except," and "without."

Conditional Reasoning Diagramming Drill

Each of the following statements contains a sufficient condition and a necessary condition and therefore each statement can be described as a "conditional statement." In the spaces provided write the proper arrow diagram for each of the following conditional statements. Then write the proper arrow diagram for the contrapositive of each of the following conditional statements. *Answers on Page 129*

Example: If that vehicle is a bus, then it is yellow.   B = Bus Y = Yellow

original diagram: ___B___ ⟶ ___Y___

contrapositive: ___Y̸___ ⟶ ___B̸___ (the contrapositive)

1. Every law student must take a class in ethics.

_____ ⟶ _____

_____ ⟶ _____

2. People who exercise have an increased life span.

_____ ⟶ _____

_____ ⟶ _____

3. No robot can think.

_____ ⟶ _____

_____ ⟶ _____

4. If the law does not pass, then wildlife will be endangered.

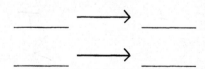

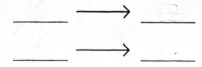

5. The meeting cannot begin unless at least six people are present.

_____ ⟶ _____

_____ ⟶ _____

6. The strike will end only if management concedes a pay raise.

$$S \longrightarrow P$$
$$\longrightarrow$$

7. The park closes when the sun goes down.

$$\longrightarrow$$
$$\longrightarrow$$

8. A computer cannot operate without an operating system.

$$\longrightarrow$$
$$\longrightarrow$$

9. The only way to achieve success is to work hard.

$$\longrightarrow$$
$$\longrightarrow$$

10. Only a professional consultant can solve the organization's problems.

$$\longrightarrow$$
$$\longrightarrow$$

11. Any decryption program can break this code.

$$\longrightarrow$$
$$\longrightarrow$$

12. No citizen can be denied the right to vote.

$$\longrightarrow$$
$$\longrightarrow$$

Conditional Reasoning Diagramming Drill Answer Key

The answer key for each problem contains a duplicate of the problem with the conditional indicators in italics, a legend for the symbols used to represent each condition, a diagrammatic representation of the statement and its contrapositive, a translation of each representation in "if...then" format, and occasional notes for each problem.

Note: Because a conditional statement and its contrapositive are identical in meaning, the order in which the two arrow diagrams appear is not important.

1. *Every* law student *must* take a class in ethics.

LS = law student   TCE = take a class in ethics

LS $\longrightarrow$ TCE
(If a person is a law student, then they must take a class in ethics.)

T̸C̸E $\longrightarrow$ L̸S̸
(If a person does not take a class in ethics, then they are not a law student.)

2. *People who* exercise have an increased life span.

E = people who exercise   ILS = increased life span

E $\longrightarrow$ ILS
(If a person exercises, then they have an increased life span.)

I̸L̸S̸ $\longrightarrow$ E̸
(If a person does not have an increased life span, then they do not exercise.)

3. *No* robot can think.

R = robot   T = think

R $\longrightarrow$ T̸
(If an entity is a robot, then it cannot think.)

T $\longrightarrow$ R̸
(If an entity can think, then it is not a robot.)

This is a tough question because the word "no" does not appear on the indicator lists in this chapter. The "No" at the beginning of the sentence (as distinguished from the "not" in #4) actually modifies the necessary condition. If you say "No robot can think," you mean that every single robot does not have the characteristic of being able to think. Thus, if an entity is a robot, then it cannot think. "None" at the beginning of the sentence would operate in the exactly the same way.

4. *If* the law does not pass, *then* wildlife will be endangered.

      LP = law passes   WE = wildlife will be endangered

        L̶P̶   ⟶   WE
        (If the law does not pass, then wildlife will be endangered.)

        W̶E̶   ⟶   LP
        (If wildlife is not endangered, then the law passed.)

The "not" directly modifies the sufficient condition and the first clause in this sentence refers to the law not passing.

5. The meeting cannot begin *unless* at least six people are present.

      MB = meeting begins   6 = at least six people are present

        MB   ⟶   6
        (If the meeting begins, then at least six people are present.)

        6̶   ⟶   M̶B̶
        (If at least 6 people are not present, then the meeting cannot being.)

Apply the Unless Equation to easily solve this problem.

6. The strike will end *only if* management concedes a pay raise.

      SE = strike will end   MCPR = management concedes a pay raise

        SE   ⟶ MCPR
        (If the strike ends, then management conceded a pay raise.)

        M̶C̶PR   ⟶   S̶E̶
        (If management does not concede a pay raise, then the strike will not end.)

The presence of the "only" overpowers the "if" in this sentence, and thus "only if" is a necessary condition indicator.

7. The park closes *when* the sun goes down.

PC = park closes   SGD = the sun goes down

SGD ⟶ PC
(If the sun goes down, then the park closes.)

P̸C̸ ⟶ S̸G̸D̸
(If the park does not close, then the sun does not go down.)

This may be the most missed problem in this set. The term "when" typically introduces a sufficient condition, and so "sun goes down" is the sufficient condition. However, many test takers reverse the statement because they take a moment to actually think about the relationship in the their head. Reasoning that a park closing cannot be a necessary condition for the sun going down (sounds crazy, doesn't it?), they make PC the sufficient condition. Again, when diagramming your task is to assess *what the author said*, and in this case the author has stated that the sun going down is the necessary condition. The fastest approach is a mechanistic one: observe the form of the problem by identifying the indicators (like "when"), then diagram the problem using those as your guides. Only resort to weighing the merits of each condition if no indicators are present to assist you. In this way you can avoid over-thinking a problem and introducing errors into the system.

Also, the form of this problem—where a word such as "if" or "when" appears in the second half of a sentence and introduces the sufficient condition—often occurs on the LSAT. When you encounter this form, you must realize that the first part of the stimulus is normally the necessary condition.

8. A computer cannot operate *without* an operating system.

CO = computer operates   OS = operating system

CO ⟶ OS
(If a computer operates, then it must have an operating system.)

O̸S̸ ⟶ C̸O̸
(If there is no operating system, then a computer cannot operate.)

As with problem #5, apply the Unless Equation.

Conditional Reasoning Diagramming Drill Answer Key

9. The *only* way to achieve success is to work hard.

   AC = achieve success   WH = work hard

   AC $\longrightarrow$ WH
   (If success is achieved, then hard word was done.)

   W̶H̶ $\longrightarrow$ A̶C̶
   (If hard work is not done, then success cannot be achieved.)

This is another tricky problem. As usual, "only" introduces the necessary condition, but the test makers use a deceptive device: in this sentence "only" modifies "way," and the "only way" refers to working hard. Thus, "work hard" is in fact the necessary condition. This type of construction appears on the LSAT with enough frequency that you should be familiar with it.

10. *Only* a professional consultant can solve the organization's problems.

   PC = professional consultant COP = solve the organization's problems.

   COP $\longrightarrow$ PC
   (If the organization's problems can be solved, then a professional consultant must solve them.)

   P̶C̶ $\longrightarrow$ C̶O̶P̶
   (If a professional consultant cannot solve the problems, then the organization's problems cannot be solved.)

11. *Any* decryption program can break this code.

   DP = decryption program   BC = break this code

   DP $\longrightarrow$ BC
   (If the entity is a decryption program, then it can break this code.)

   B̶C̶ $\longrightarrow$ D̶P̶
   (If the entity cannot break the code, then it is not a decryption program.)

12. *No* citizen can be denied the right to vote.

    C = citizen   DRV = denied the right to vote

        C   ⟶   D̶R̶V̶
        (If this person is a citizen, then they cannot be denied the right to vote.)

        DRV   ⟶   C̶
        (If this person has been denied the right to vote, then they are not a citizen.)

This problem is similar to #3. Again, "no" begins the sentence, but do not make the mistake of thinking that because "no" is next to "citizen" that it must modify "citizen." Instead, the "no" actually modifies the "denied the right to vote." Compare this problem and #9 to better understand how the LSAT can separate indicator words from the terms they modify.

Conditional Reasoning and Must Be True Problems

Now that we have reviewed conditional statements and how to identify them, let us examine two Must Be True questions that feature conditional statements in the stimulus. Please take a moment to complete the following problem:

1. People with serious financial problems are so worried about money that they cannot be happy. Their misery makes everyone close to them—family, friends, colleagues—unhappy as well. Only if their financial problems are solved can they and those around them be happy.

    Which one of the following statements can be properly inferred from the passage?

    (A) Only serious problems make people unhappy.
    (B) People who solve their serious financial problems will be happy.
    (C) People who do not have serious financial problems will be happy.
    (D) If people are unhappy, they have serious financial problems.
    (E) If people are happy, they do not have serious financial problems.

This problem is a classic example of how the LSAT attempts to disguise conditional reasoning. The stimulus can be diagrammed as follows:

SF = serious financial problems   H = happy

Sentence 1: SF ⟶ H̶

Sentence 3: H ⟶ S̶F̶   (solving SF = S̶F̶)

The sufficient condition in the first sentence is introduced by the phrase "people with." The necessary condition in the third sentence is introduced by the phrase, "only if." Note that the third sentence provides the contrapositive of the first sentence. The second sentence is not conditional and contains only general statements about the effects of their misery.

The question stem uses the word "inferred" and can be classified as a Must Be True. When you encounter a stimulus that contains conditional reasoning and a Must Be True question stem, immediately look for a contrapositive or a repeat form in the answer choices. In problems with this same combination, avoid Mistaken Reversals and Mistaken Negations as they are attractive but wrong answer traps.

Answer choice (A): One reason answer choice (A) is incorrect is because it only refers to serious problems, not serious *financial* problems as in the stimulus. Even if the answer correctly referred to serious financial problems, it would still be incorrect because it would be a Mistaken Reversal of the first sentence and a Mistaken Negation of the third sentence.

Answer choice (B): The answer choice can be diagrammed S̶F̶ ⟶ H. This answer is incorrect because it is the Mistaken Negation of the first sentence. However, it is also the Mistaken Reversal of the third sentence, which you should recognize as the contrapositive of the first statement. This leads to the interesting point that the Mistaken Negation of a statement and the Mistaken Reversal of the same statement are contrapositives of each other. This fact reveals how important it is to diagram conditional statements correctly; otherwise, the makers of the test can lure you with answer choices which contain contrapositives of Mistaken Negations or Reversals.

Answer choice (C): This answer choice would be diagrammed the same way as answer choice (B), and it is incorrect for the same reasons.

Answer choice (D): The answer choice can be diagrammed as H̶ ⟶ SF. As such, it is the Mistaken Reversal of the first sentence and also the Mistaken Negation of the third sentence.

Answer choice (E): This is the correct answer. Answer choice (E) is the contrapositive of the first sentence and a repeat of the third sentence.

Classic Combination:

When a stimulus that contains Conditional Reasoning is combined with a Must Be True question stem, immediately look for the repeat or contrapositive in the answer choices. Avoid mistaken Reversal and Mistaken Negations.

A Mistaken Reversal of a given statement and a Mistaken Negation of the same given statement are contrapositives of each other.

Please take a moment to complete the following problem:

2. Some types of organisms originated through endosymbiosis, the engulfing of one organism by another so that a part of the former becomes a functioning part of the latter. An unusual nucleomorph, a structure that contains DNA and resembles a cell nucleus, has been discovered within a plant known as a chlorarachniophyte. Two versions of a particular gene have been found in the DNA of this nucleomorph, and one would expect to find only a single version of this gene if the nucleomorph were not the remains of an engulfed organism's nucleus.

Which one of the following is most strongly supported by the information above?

(A) Only organisms of types that originated through endosymbiosis contain nucleomorphs.

(B) A nucleomorph within the chlorarachniophyte holds all of the genetic material of some other organism.

(C) Nucleomorphs originated when an organism endosymbiotically engulfed a chlorarachniophyte.

(D) Two organisms will not undergo endosymbiosis unless at least one of them contains a nucleomorph.

(E) Chlorarachniophytes emerged as the result of two organisms having undergone endosymbiosis.

This challenging problem is from the June 2000 LSAT. The stimulus can be intimidating because it contains several formidable scientific terms, but as usual these terms are explained as the stimulus progresses. Let us take a moment to recap the information in this problem. The stimulus begins by defining endosymbiosis, which is when one organism engulfs another such that the "conquered" organism still functions. Next, we are told that a nucleomorph—a DNA-containing, nucleus-like structure—has been discovered in a plant known as a chlorarachniophyte. As the last sentence begins we are told that this nucleomorph contains two versions of a particular gene. The remainder of the final sentence is the key to the problem and it illustrates how the test makers force students to maintain an awareness of conditional indicators. The conditional relationship in the final sentence is contained in the following section of text:

> "one would expect to find only a single version of this gene
> if the nucleomorph were not the remains of an engulfed
> organism's nucleus"

In the middle of this section of text the word "if" appears, and produces the following conditional relationship:

R = nucleomorph is the remains of an engulfed organism's nucleus
1 = find only a single version of this gene

However, as we know from our discussion of the last sentence, there was not a single version of the gene but two versions. This is equivalent to the necessary condition not occurring:

Combining the two above diagrams, if the necessary condition does not occur, then the contrapositive is enacted and we can conclude that the sufficient condition does not occur:

R

We can see the contrapositive in action more clearly if we link the two conditions in an arrow diagram: $\cancel{1} \longrightarrow$ R. In LSAT problems, the contrapositive is often introduced in this fashion, where a premise is given that contains both a sufficient and necessary condition, and then the necessary condition is denied. Adding those two pieces together produces a conclusion via the contrapositive that the sufficient condition cannot occur, as the following summary reveals:

Premise 1: $\cancel{R} \longrightarrow$ 1

Premise 2: $\cancel{1}$

Conclusion: R

Premise 2 and the conclusion link together in the traditional contrapositive relationship we have seen previously: $\cancel{1} \longrightarrow$ R.

Thus, the contrapositive produces the inference that the nucleomorph is the remains of an engulfed organism's nucleus. With this information in hand, we can combine some of the other elements in the stimulus. Given that the nucleomorph is part of the chlorarachniophyte and is the remains of an engulfed organism's nucleus, we have strong evidence that the chlorarachniophyte came about as the result of endosymbiosis (the engulfing of one organism by another). This is most clearly stated in answer choice (E), the correct answer.

Answer choice (A): This is an Exaggerated answer: the word "only" at the beginning of the answer choice is too strong, and there is no evidence in the stimulus to suggest that a conditional relationship exists between endosymbiosis and nucleomorphs.

Answer choice (B): This is also an Exaggerated answer: the word "all" in the middle of the answer choice is too strong.

Answer choice (C): The stimulus discusses one unusual nucleomorph whereas the answer choice attempts to make a general statement about *all* nucleomorphs. As such, the answer choice exaggerates the situation and is incorrect. Note that the first three answer choices in this problem all exaggerate some aspect of the stimulus. This is not surprising: in a stimulus with complex terminology, the test makers wisely attempt to prey upon that difficulty by presenting answers that have a degree of truth but go just a bit too far. These answer choices are attractive to a test taker who fails to lock down the facts of the stimulus.

Answer choice (D): This answer choice is similar to answer choice (A), and is incorrect for similar reasons: no conditional relationship is established where nucleomorphs are necessary for endosymbiosis.

Answer choice (E): As explained previously, this is the correct answer choice.

Conditional Linkage

In an effort to create complexity, the test makers often link two or more conditional statements. If an identical condition is sufficient in one statement and necessary in another, the two can be linked to create a chain, as follows:

Statement 1:   A ⟶ B

Statement 2:   B ⟶ C

Chain: A ⟶ B ⟶ C

Inference: A ⟶ C

The "B" condition is common to both Statement 1 and 2, and serves as the linking point. In this instance, because all A's are B's, and all B's are C's, we can make the inference that all A's are C's: A ⟶ C. Of course, the contrapositive, $\cancel{C} \longrightarrow \cancel{A}$ would follow from this inference.

Not all linkage is the same. The above example is one of the most frequently used constructions, but the test makers can also link two sufficient conditions, or two necessary conditions. These linkages yield different inferences (or none at all), and they will be discussed in more detail in Chapter Eleven.

The next two LSAT problems each feature conditional linkage. Please take a moment to complete the following problem:

3. If you have no keyboarding skills at all, you will not be able to use a computer. And if you are not able to use a computer, you will not be able to write your essays using a word processing program.

    If the statements above are true, which one of the following must be true?

    (A) If you have some keyboarding skills, you will be able to write your essays using a word processing program.
    (B) If you are not able to write your essays using a word processing program, you have no keyboarding skills.
    (C) If you are able to write your essays using a word processing program, you have at least some keyboarding skills.
    (D) If you are able to use a computer, you will probably be able to write your essays using a word processing program.
    (E) If you are not able to write your essays using a word processing program, you are not able to use a computer.

When you begin reading this stimulus, your first action should be to notice the sufficient condition indicator "if" at the beginning of the first sentence. There is another "if" near the beginning of the second sentence, and the two sentences produce the following conditional relationships, which can be linked together:

KS = keyboarding skills
AUC = able to use a computer
WEWP = able to write your essays using a word processing program

Sentence 1:   K̷S ————→ A̷U̷C

Sentence 2:   A̷U̷C ————→ WE̷W̷P

Chain: K̷S ————→ A̷U̷C ————→ WE̷W̷P

Perhaps the most problematic element of the stimulus is that each term is negated, but as you continue to work with the arrow statements and get more comfortable symbolizing the elements, working with the negated statements will become second nature.

Now that we have controlled the elements of the stimulus, we can attack this Must Be True question by looking for the two most likely answers: the chain inference that K̷S ————→ WE̷W̷P, or the contrapositive of that inference, WEWP ————→ KS. Of these two, the contrapositive is the more likely correct answer because it requires more steps and thus more work.

As we approach the answers, remember to avoid Mistaken Reversals and Mistaken Negations of the individual statements and of the chain inference.

Answer choice (A): This is a Mistaken Negation of the chain inference and is therefore incorrect. The diagram for this answer choice would be:

KS ————→ WEWP

Answer choice (B): This is a Mistaken Reversal of the chain inference and is therefore incorrect. The diagram for this answer choice would be:

WEWP ————→ KS

Answer choice (C): This is the correct answer, and this answer is the contrapositive of the chain inference.

Answer choice (D): This answer is a Mistaken Negation of the second sentence and is therefore incorrect. The diagram for this answer choice is:

$$\text{AUC} \longrightarrow \text{WEWP}$$

Answer choice (E): This answer is a Mistaken Reversal of the second sentence and is therefore incorrect. The diagram for this answer choice is:

$$\text{W}\cancel{\text{E}}\text{WP} \longrightarrow \text{A}\cancel{\text{U}}\text{C}$$

If a test taker is trained to recognize conditional statements, each of the incorrect answers as well as the correct answer is predictable and easy to handle. Recognizing and attacking problems of this nature is how you build extra time while taking the LSAT: by dominating this problem and finishing it in less than the allotted time, you build extra seconds to attack other, more difficult problems.

The following problem features more complex language. Please take a moment to complete the following problem:

4. The axis of Earth's daily rotation is tilted with respect to the plane of its orbit at an angle of roughly 23 degrees. That angle can be kept fairly stable only by the gravitational influence of Earth's large, nearby Moon. Without such a stable and moderate axis tilt, a planet's climate is too extreme and unstable to support life. Mars, for example, has only very small moons, tilts at wildly fluctuating angles, and cannot support life.

   If the statements above are true, which one of the following must also be true on the basis of them?

   (A) If Mars had a sufficiently large nearby moon, Mars would be able to support life.
   (B) If Earth's Moon were to leave Earth's orbit Earth's climate would be unable to support life.
   (C) Any planet with a stable, moderate axis tilt can support life.
   (D) Gravitational influences other than moons have little or no effect on the magnitude of the tilt angle of either Earth's or Mars's axis.
   (E) No planet that has more than one moon can support life.

To attack this problem effectively, you must recognize the conditional indicators in each sentence: "only" in the second sentence and "without" in the third sentence. Do not be intimidated by the science topic! As we will see, if you can understand the conditional form of the stimulus, the topic is of little concern.

The two sentences produce the following conditional relationships, which can be linked:

AS = angle stable
GI = gravitational influence of Earth's large, nearby Moon
PCE = planet's climate too extreme and unstable to support life

Sentence 2:   AS $\longrightarrow$ GI

Sentence 3:   P̸CE $\longrightarrow$ AS

Chain: P̸CE $\longrightarrow$ AS $\longrightarrow$ GI

Again, consider the answers that are most likely to appear in a problem like this: either the chain inference P̸CE $\longrightarrow$ GI, or the contrapositive of that chain inference, G̸I $\longrightarrow$ PCE.

Answer choice (A): This incorrect answer is the Mistaken Reversal of the chain inference. The diagram for this answer choice would be as follows, with the sub-M indicating Mars:

$GI_M \longrightarrow P̸CE_M$

Answer choice (B): This is the correct answer. As expected, this is the contrapositive of the chain inference.

Answer choice (C): This incorrect answer is the Mistaken Reversal of the third sentence, and is diagrammed as follows:

AS $\longrightarrow$ P̸CE

Answer choice (D): This answer discusses issues that were not raised in the stimulus, and is thus incorrect.

Answer choice (E): The stimulus indicates that Earth's large Moon has been necessary for the stable angle of Earth's tilt, and this stable angle has been necessary for a climate that can support life. Mars, with many small moons, tilts at fluctuating angles and cannot support life. The key difference is that Earth's Moon is large, and that creates a greater gravitational influence. It is possible therefore, that a planet with more than one moon could have a stable angle as long as at least one of the moons was of sufficient size (in Mars' case, the stimulus indicates each moon is small). Thus, it is possible that a planet can have more than one moon and support life. This scenario is contrary to the answer choice, and thus this answer is incorrect.

Diagramming Either/Or Statements

The appearance of the "either/or" sentence construction often presents difficulty for LSAT students. In its everyday use outside of the LSAT, "either/or" has come to mean "one or the other, but not both," but this usage is incorrect on the LSAT. For the purposes of the test, the definition of "either/or" is *"at least one of the two."* Note that this definition implicitly allows for the possibility that both elements occur, and the existence of this possibility makes diagramming sentences containing the "either/or" term confusing. A careful examination of the definition of "either/or" reveals that a conditional relationship is at the heart of the construction: since at least one of the terms must occur, if one fails to occur then the other *must* occur. Consider the following statement:

The LSAT definition of "either/or" is "at least one of the two, possibly both."

Either John or Jack will attend the party.

The proper diagram for this statement is:

> 1:   J~~oh~~n ⟶ Jack
> or
> 2:   J~~ac~~k ⟶ John

Note that the second diagram is the contrapositive of the first diagram and thus is functionally identical. The two diagrams indicate that if John fails to attend the party, then Jack must attend, and if Jack fails to attend the party, then John must attend. The diagrams reflect the fact that if one of the two fails to attend, then the other must attend in order to satisfy the "at least one of the two" condition imposed by the "either/or" term. Note that neither of these two diagrams preclude both John and Jack from attending the party. For example, let us assume that John is in fact attending the party. This information automatically satisfies the "either/or" condition above (again, "at least one of the two"). But the information that John is attending the party does not affect Jack in the least. He is now free to attend or not attend the party as he chooses.

To further complicate the issue, occasionally our "outside" (but public domain) knowledge of the elements involved in the "either/or" construct allows us to make additional inferences. Consider the following statement:

You are either in Los Angeles or San Francisco

According to the "either/or" term, the statement is diagrammed as follows:

Los Angeles $\longrightarrow$ San Francisco

San Francisco $\longrightarrow$ Los Angeles

These diagrams correctly indicate that if you are not in one of the cities, then you must be in the other city. But we also know that if you are in one of the cities, then you are not in the other. However, this knowledge does not come to us from the "either/or" term above, but from our public domain knowledge of geography. Thus, the original statement has another set of diagrams which also apply, as follows:

Los Angeles $\longrightarrow$ San Francisco

San Francisco $\longrightarrow$ Los Angeles

These two sets of diagrams, both correct and applicable in this case, indicate that you are always in one of the two cities and in one city only. Hence, if you are in one city, you are not in the other city, and if you are not in one city, then you must be in the other city. Note that the makers of the LSAT could create a statement about two fictional or little-known cities, such as "You are either in Monroe or Tipiwanee." Without being provided further information about these cities, we could only diagram for the "either/or" term. A diagram that attempts to reflect geographic knowledge such as:

Monroe $\longrightarrow$ Tipiwanee

would not apply since we cannot be sure that Monroe and Tipiwanee do not overlap geographically. The use of "outside" knowledge with "either/or" terms also appears in other forms. Consider the following statement:

You are either short or tall.

This "either/or" statement would be diagrammed as follows:

Short $\longrightarrow$ Tall

Tall $\longrightarrow$ Short

But again, analogous to the Los Angeles/San Francisco example, our "outside" knowledge of the English language indicates that no person can be both short and tall at the same time. Thus, the following set of diagrams also applies:

Short $\longrightarrow$ Tall

Tall $\longrightarrow$ Short

Thus, it is true that if you are not short, you must be tall, and if you are short, you are not tall; it is also true that if you are not tall, you must be short, and if you are tall, you are not short. Please note that using our "outside" knowledge in the Los Angeles/San Francisco example or the short/tall example does not constitute a violation of the LSAT dictate to "not make assumptions that are by commonsense standards implausible, superfluous, or incompatible with the passage." The general geographic location of major cities and the definition of English terms falls into the category of information Law Services expects you to know as an educated test taker.

There are ways for the test makers to indicate that the items in the two conditions cannot both occur. Consider the following statement:

Either Cindy or Clarice will attend the party, but not both.

This statement will prove to have similar diagrams to the Los Angeles/San Francisco statement and the short/tall statement, but for a different reason. In this case, as always, the "either/or" construct gives us the following diagram:

C~~i~~ndy $\longrightarrow$ Clarice

Cl~~a~~rice $\longrightarrow$ Cindy

But since the original statement also includes the phrase, "but not both," this precludes the possibility of both attending the party, and the statement is also diagrammed as follows:

Cindy $\longrightarrow$ Cl~~a~~rice

Clarice $\longrightarrow$ C~~i~~ndy

Thus, it is true that one and only one of the two will attend the party. If Cindy attends, Clarice will not attend, and if Cindy does not attend, Clarice must attend. Also, if Clarice attends the party, Cindy will not attend, and if Clarice does not attend the party, Cindy must attend.

Multiple Sufficient and Necessary Conditions

So far, all of the conditional statements we have examined have contained only one sufficient condition and one necessary condition. However, there are many statements on the LSAT that contain either multiple sufficient conditions or multiple necessary conditions. Consider the following statement:

> To graduate from Throckmorton College you must be both smart and resourceful.

In this statement there are two necessary conditions that must be satisfied if you are to graduate from Throckmorton: 1. you must be smart and 2. you must be resourceful. Thus, the proper diagram for this statement is:

$$\text{Graduate}_T \longrightarrow \begin{array}{c} \text{Smart} \\ \text{and} \\ \text{Resourceful} \end{array}$$

Whenever you take a contrapositive of a statement with multiple terms in the sufficient or necessary condition, "and" turns into "or," and "or" turns into "and."

The difficulty in handling multiple necessary conditions is with the contrapositive. In this case, if *either one* of the two necessary conditions is not met, then you cannot graduate from Throckmorton. It is *not* required that both necessary conditions *fail* to be met in order to prevent the sufficient condition from occurring. Thus, the proper diagram of the contrapositive of the statement is:

$$\begin{array}{c} \cancel{\text{Smart}} \\ \text{or} \\ \cancel{\text{Resourceful}} \end{array} \longrightarrow \cancel{\text{Graduate}}_T$$

Note that in taking the contrapositive, the "and" in the necessary condition is changed to "or." The reverse would be true if the necessary conditions had originally been linked by the term "or." Consider the following statement:

> To graduate from Throckmorton College you must be smart or resourceful.

The proper diagram for this statement is:

$$\text{Graduate}_T \longrightarrow \begin{array}{c} \text{Smart} \\ \text{or} \\ \text{Resourceful} \end{array}$$

In this case, to graduate from Throckmorton you only need to satisfy one of the two necessary conditions. This does not preclude the possibility of satisfying both conditions, but it is not necessary to do so. Now let's take the contrapositive of this statement:

Smart
and ⟶ Gra̶d̶uate_T
Resou̶rceful

This diagram indicates that if you are not smart *and* not resourceful, then you cannot graduate from Throckmorton College. Again, note that as the contrapositive occurred the "or" joining the original necessary conditions changed to "and."

Now let us examine a statement with two sufficient conditions. Consider the following statement:

If you are rich and famous, then you are happy.

The proper diagram for this statement is:

Rich
and ⟶ Happy
Famous

Note that you must be *both* rich and famous to meet the sufficient condition, and if you were both rich and famous then you would also be happy. Now let us take the contrapositive:

Ha̶ppy ⟶ Ri̶ch
or
Fam̶ous

The contrapositive indicates that if you are not happy, then you are either not rich or not famous. Thus, if you are not happy, then you are not rich, not famous, or not both. Note that once again the "and" has become "or."

Consider the following statement:

If you are rich or famous, then you are happy.

The proper diagram for this statement is:

Rich
or ⟶ Happy
Famous

Note that you can either be rich or famous, or both, to meet the sufficient condition. Now let us take the contrapositive:

$$\text{Happy} \longrightarrow \begin{array}{c} \cancel{\text{Rich}} \\ \text{and} \\ \cancel{\text{Famous}} \end{array}$$

The contrapositive indicates that if you are not happy, then you are neither rich nor famous. Thus, if you are not happy, then you are not rich and not famous. Also note that once again the "or" has become "and."

The Double Arrow

The double arrow indicates that the two terms *must* always occur together.

The majority of conditional statements in the LSAT Logical Reasoning feature arrows that point in only one direction. But, there are some statements that produce arrows that point in both directions. These arrows, also known as biconditionals, indicate that each term is both sufficient and necessary for the other. As such, they create a very limited set of possibilities. Consider the following example:

Ann will attend if and only if Basil attends.

As you can see, this sentence contains the conditional indicators "if" and "only if" connected by the term "and." This effectively creates two separate conditional statements:

Be careful with statement 1: do not forget that "if" introduces a sufficient condition!

1. "A   if   B"

and

2. "A   only if   B"

The "A if B" portion creates the following diagram: B $\longrightarrow$ A
The "A only if B" portion creates the following diagram: A $\longrightarrow$ B

Combined, the two statements create the double arrow: A $\longleftrightarrow$ B

Terms in a double arrow relationship either occur together or both do not occur.

Only two scenarios are possible under this double arrow:

1. A and B both attend   (A and B)
2. Neither A nor B attend   ($\cancel{A}$ and $\cancel{B}$)

Any scenario where one of the two attends occurs but the other does not is impossible.

148

The double arrow is typically introduced in any of the following three ways:

1. Use of the phrase "if and only if" (as in the example above).
2. Use of the phrase "vice versa" (as in "If A attends then B attends, and vice versa").
3. By repeating and reversing the terms (as in "If A attends then B attends, and if B attends then A attends").

If you encounter a double-arrow statement in a Logical Reasoning question, immediately assume that you will be tested on your knowledge of the double arrow and attack the answer choices accordingly. The test makers purposefully use the double-arrow statement knowing that most students will miss the subtlety of the relationship. By reacting to the double arrow, you can accelerate through the problem and complete the question with confidence.

The Double Not-Arrow

Just as the double arrow indicates that two terms must occur together, the double not-arrow indicates that two terms cannot occur together. Consider the following statement:

The double not-arrow is also used frequently in the Logic Games section of the LSAT.

If Gomez runs for president, then Hong will not run for president.

According to our conditional diagramming, we should diagram this statement as follows:

$$G \longrightarrow \cancel{H}$$

Let us further analyze this relationship. If G runs for president, then H will not run for president. Via the contrapositive, we can also infer that if H runs for president, then G will not run for president. Thus, if G or H runs for president, then the other will *not* run for president, and we can infer that the two can never run for president together. To represent this relationship accurately, we use the double not arrow:

$$G \longleftarrow\!\!+\!\!\longrightarrow H$$

In the symbolization above, the two terms at the ends of the sign cannot be selected together. In this sense the double not-arrow is a "super symbol," one that captures all meanings of the negative relationship.

The double not-arrow is similar to the "not equal" sign of logic; the two terms at the end of the sign cannot be selected at the same time.

If you diagram statements with the single arrow and slash in the first diagram, you will *not* be making a mistake. We raise the issue of the double not-arrow because later when we discuss Formal Logic, you will need to know the meaning of the sign. The double not-arrow is a conditional symbol, and in Formal Logic there will be times when you must know the meaning and use of the symbol in order to efficiently solve a problem.

The double not-arrow only prohibits one scenario—that where the two terms occur together. Using our Gomez/Hong example, several possible scenarios can occur:

1. G runs for president, H does not.   (G and H̸)
2. H runs for president, G does not.   (G̸ and H)
3. Neither G nor H runs for president.   (G̸ and H̸)

Either/Or, Multiple Condition, and Double Arrow Diagramming Drill

Each of the following statements contains at least one sufficient condition and at least one necessary condition; therefore, each of the following statements can be described as a "conditional statement." In the spaces provided write the proper arrow diagram for each of the following conditional statements. Then write the proper arrow diagram for the contrapositive of each of the following conditional statements. In some cases you may have to modify the given arrow to indicate that a double arrow is present. *Answers on Page 153*

1. The budget will be approved only if the amendment is withdrawn and there is a compromise on education spending.

   _____ ⟶ _____

   _____ ⟶ _____

2. Either Jones or Kim will win the election.

   _____ ⟶ _____

   _____ ⟶ _____

3. If the weather is good and we get approval from the city, we will hold the race on Saturday.

   _____ ⟶ _____

   _____ ⟶ _____

4. Taxes will be raised if and only if there is a government deficit.

   _____ ⟶ _____

   _____ ⟶ _____

5. If the economy has a downturn or if the food is not good, the restaurant will not survive.

   _____ ⟶ _____

   _____ ⟶ _____

6. It is either feast or famine.

$$\underline{} \longrightarrow \underline{}$$

$$\underline{} \longrightarrow \underline{}$$

7. The flight will be cancelled if it snows in Buffalo or the plane has mechanical problems.

$$\underline{} \longrightarrow \underline{}$$

$$\underline{} \longrightarrow \underline{}$$

8. Admission will be granted if and only if an application is completed.

$$\underline{} \longrightarrow \underline{}$$

$$\underline{} \longrightarrow \underline{}$$

9. Unless they find an eyewitness and put the defendant on the stand, they will lose the case.

$$\underline{} \longrightarrow \underline{}$$

$$\underline{} \longrightarrow \underline{}$$

10. When the package arrives and the meeting is arranged, call the president.

$$\underline{} \longrightarrow \underline{}$$

$$\underline{} \longrightarrow \underline{}$$

Either/Or, Multiple Condition, and Double Arrow Diagramming Drill Answer Key

The answer key for each problem contains a duplicate of the problem with the conditional indicators in italics, a legend for the symbols used to represent each condition, a diagrammatic representation of the statement and its contrapositive, and occasional notes for each problem.

Note: Because a conditional statement and its contrapositive are identical in meaning, the order in which the two arrow diagrams appear is not important.

1. The budget will be approved *only if* the amendment is withdrawn and there is a compromise on education spending.

BA = budget approved
AW = amendment withdrawn
CES = compromise on education spending

$$BA \longrightarrow \begin{matrix} AW \\ and \\ CES \end{matrix}$$

$$\begin{matrix} \cancel{AW} \\ or \\ \cancel{CES} \end{matrix} \longrightarrow \cancel{BA}$$

2. *Either* Jones or Kim will win the election.

JW = Jones wins the election   KW = Kim wins the election

$$\cancel{JW} \longrightarrow KW$$

$$\cancel{KW} \longrightarrow JW$$

The diagram above only reflects the implications of the "either/or" construction. Depending on the type of election, there may or may not be only one "winner" of the election. For example, a school board election can have multiple candidates who each win a seat on the board. On the other hand, a U.S. Presidential election can only have a single winner. If there was only one winner, a second set of diagrams would apply, indicating that if either Jones or Kim won the election, the other would *not* win the election.

Either/Or, Multiple Condition, and Double Arrow Diagramming Drill Answer Key

3. *If* the weather is good and we get approval from the city, we will hold the race on Saturday.

WG = weather good
AFC = approval from city
RS = hold race on Saturday

WG
and $\longrightarrow$ RS
AFC

R̸S̸ $\longrightarrow$ W̸G
or
A̸F̸C̸

4. Taxes will be raised *if and only if* there is a government deficit.

TR = taxes raised   GD = government deficit

TR $\longleftrightarrow$ GD

G̸D̸ $\longleftrightarrow$ T̸R̸

The contrapositive of the double arrow simply indicates the other half of the relationship: that if one of the terms fails to occur, then the other cannot occur.

5. *If* the economy has a downturn or if the food is not good, the restaurant will not survive.

ED = economic downturn
FG = food good
RS = restaurant survive

ED
or $\longrightarrow$ R̸S̸
F̸G̸

RS $\longrightarrow$ E̸D̸
and
FG

6. It is *either* feast or famine.

Fe = feast   Fa = famine

$$\cancel{Fe} \longrightarrow Fa$$

$$\cancel{Fa} \longrightarrow Fe$$

Additionally, because feast and famine are polar opposites, a second set of diagrams also applies indicating that if one occurs the other does not. Thus, one and only one of feast or famine can occur.

7. The flight will be cancelled *if* it snows in Buffalo or the plane has mechanical problems.

SB = snows in buffalo
PM = plane has mechanical problems
FC = flight cancelled

$$\begin{array}{c} SB \\ or \\ PM \end{array} \longrightarrow FC$$

$$\cancel{FC} \longrightarrow \begin{array}{c} \cancel{SB} \\ and \\ \cancel{PM} \end{array}$$

8. Admission will be granted *if and only if* an application is completed.

AG = admission granted   AC = application completed

$$AG \longleftrightarrow AC$$

$$\cancel{AC} \longleftrightarrow \cancel{AG}$$

Either/Or, Multiple Condition, and Double Arrow Diagramming Drill Answer Key

9. *Unless* they find an eyewitness and put the defendant on the stand, they will lose the case.

LC = lose the case
FE = find eyewitness
DS = put the defendant on the stand

$$\cancel{LC} \longrightarrow \begin{matrix} FE \\ and \\ DS \end{matrix}$$

$$\begin{matrix} \cancel{FE} \\ or \\ \cancel{DS} \end{matrix} \longrightarrow LC$$

10. *When* the package arrives and the meeting is arranged, call the president.

PA = package arrives
MA = meeting arranged
CP = call the president

$$\begin{matrix} PA \\ and \\ MA \end{matrix} \longrightarrow CP$$

$$\cancel{CP} \longrightarrow \begin{matrix} \cancel{PA} \\ or \\ \cancel{MA} \end{matrix}$$

Conditional Reasoning Review

A sufficient condition can be defined as an event or circumstance whose occurrence indicates that a necessary condition must also occur.

A necessary condition can be defined as an event or circumstance whose occurrence is required in order for a sufficient condition to occur.

Conditional Reasoning statements have several unique features that you must know:

1. The sufficient condition does not *make* the necessary condition occur. Rather, it is a sign or indicator that the necessary condition will occur.

2. Temporally speaking, either condition can occur first, or the two conditions can occur at the same time.

3. The conditional relationship stated by the author does not have to reflect reality. Your job is not to figure out what sounds reasonable, but rather to perfectly capture the meaning of the author's statement.

Conditional reasoning occurs when a statement containing sufficient and necessary conditions is used to draw a conclusion based on the statement.

Valid and Invalid Inferences

The Repeat form simply restates the elements in the original order they appeared. This creates a valid inference.

Because the contrapositive both reverses and negates, it is a combination of a Mistaken Reversal and Mistaken Negation. Since the contrapositive is valid, it is as if two wrongs do make a right.

A Mistaken Reversal switches the elements in the sufficient and necessary conditions, creating a statement that does not have to be true.

A Mistaken Negation negates both conditions, creating a statement that does not have to be true.

A Mistaken Reversal of a given statement and a Mistaken Negation of that same given statement are contrapositives of each other.

Conditional Reasoning Review Continued

Two critical rules govern how conditional reasoning appears in a given sentence:

1. Either condition can appear first in the sentence.

2. A sentence can have one or two indicators.

To introduce a sufficient condition: To introduce a necessary condition:

If	Then
When	Only
Whenever	Only if
Every	Must
All	Required
Any	Unless
People who	Except
In order to	Until
	Without

In the case of "unless," "except," "until," and "without," a special two-step process called the Unless Equation is applied to the diagram:

1. Whatever term is modified by "unless," "except," "until," or "without" becomes the necessary condition.

2. The remaining term is negated and becomes the sufficient condition.

Classic Combination:

When a stimulus that contains Conditional Reasoning is combined with a Must Be True question stem, immediately look for the Repeat or Contrapositive in the answer choices. Avoid Mistaken Reversal and Mistaken Negations.

In an effort to create complexity, the test makers often link together two or more conditional statements. Look for chain inferences or the contrapositive of a chain inference.

Either/Or Review

Statement #1: *Either* A or B must occur.

Diagram: A̸ ⟶ B

the contrapositive: B̸ ⟶ A

Statement #2: *Either* A or B, *but not both* occur.

Diagram: A̸ ⟹ B (from the "either/or")
the contrapositive: B̸ ⟹ A

and: A ⟹ B̸ (from the "but not both")
or the contrapositive: B ⟹ A̸

Multiple Conditions Review

Remember, when taking the contrapositive, "and" becomes "or" and vice versa.

Statement #1: If A, then B and C.

Diagram: A ⟶ B
and
C

Contrapositive: B̸
or ⟶ A̸
C̸

Statement #2: If A, then B or C.

Diagram: A ⟶ B
or
C

Contrapositive: B̸
and ⟶ A̸
C̸

Multiple Conditions Review

Statement #3: If A or B, then C.

Diagram:

$$\begin{matrix} A \\ \text{or} \\ B \end{matrix} \longrightarrow C$$

Contrapositive:

$$\cancel{C} \longrightarrow \begin{matrix} \cancel{A} \\ \text{and} \\ \cancel{B} \end{matrix}$$

Statement #4: If A and B, then C.

Diagram:

$$\begin{matrix} A \\ \text{and} \\ B \end{matrix} \longrightarrow C$$

Contrapositive:

$$\cancel{C} \longrightarrow \begin{matrix} \cancel{A} \\ \text{or} \\ \cancel{B} \end{matrix}$$

Unusual Arrows Review

A double arrow indicates that the two terms *must* always occur together. If you encounter a double-arrow statement in a Logical Reasoning question, immediately assume that you will be tested on your knowledge of the double arrow and attack the answer choices accordingly.

The double arrow is typically introduced in any of the following three ways:

1. Use of the phrase "if and only if" (as in the above example).

2. Use of the phrase "vice versa" (as in "If A attends then B attends, and vice versa").

3. By repeating and reversing the terms (as in "If A attends then B attends, and if B attends then A attends").

The double not-arrow indicates that two terms cannot occur together. In the symbolization, the two terms at the ends of the sign cannot be selected together.

Final Note

Conditional reasoning occurs in many different question types, and the discussion in this chapter is designed to acquaint you with recognizing conditional statements, diagramming, and some of the ways that conditionality appears in LSAT problems. If you are still struggling with nailing down the basics of conditional reasoning, do not worry. We will revisit the concepts as we discuss other question types.

As you examine LSAT questions, remember that conditional reasoning may or may not be present in the stimulus. Your job is to recognize conditionality when it appears and react accordingly. If conditionality is not present, you do not need to worry about it.

Following is a short problem set to help you work with some of the ideas. The problem set is followed by an answer key with explanations. Good luck!

Sufficient and Necessary Question Problem Set

The following questions are drawn from actual LSATs. Please complete the problem set and review the answer key and explanations. *Answers on Page 164*

1. It is a principle of economics that a nation can experience economic growth only when consumer confidence is balanced with a small amount of consumer skepticism.

    Which one of the following is an application of the economic principle above?

    (A) Any nation in which consumer confidence is balanced with a small amount of consumer skepticism will experience economic growth.
    (B) Any nation in which the prevailing attitude of consumers is not skepticism will experience economic growth.
    (C) Any nation in which the prevailing attitude of consumers is either exclusively confidence or exclusively skepticism will experience economic growth.
    (D) Any nation in which the prevailing attitude of consumers is exclusively confidence will not experience economic growth.
    (E) Any nation in which consumer skepticism is balanced with a small amount of consumer confidence will experience economic growth.

2. Editorialist: Drivers with a large number of demerit points who additionally have been convicted of a serious driving-related offense should either be sentenced to jail or be forced to receive driver reeducation, since to do otherwise would be to allow a crime to go unpunished. Only if such drivers are likely to be made more responsible drivers should driver re-education be recommended for them. Unfortunately, it is always almost impossible to make drivers with a large number of demerit points more responsible drivers.

    If the editorialist's statements are true, they provide the most support for which one of the following?

    (A) Drivers with a large number of demerit points who have been convicted of a serious driving-related offense should be sent to jail.
    (B) Driver re-education offers the best chance of making drivers with a large number of demerit points responsible drivers.
    (C) Driver re-education is not a harsh enough punishment for anyone convicted of a serious driving-related offense who has also accumulated a large number of demerit points.
    (D) Driver re-education should not be recommended for those who have committed no serious driving-related offenses.
    (E) Drivers with a large number of demerit points but no conviction for a serious driving-related offense should receive driver re-education rather than jail.

162

THE POWERSCORE LSAT LOGICAL REASONING

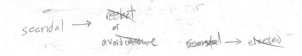

3. Muscular strength is a limited resource, and athletic techniques help to use this resource efficiently. Since top athletes do not differ greatly from each other in muscular strength, it follows that a requirement for an athlete to become a champion is a superior mastery of athletic techniques.

Which one of the following most accurately expresses the conclusion of the argument?

(A) Only champion athletes have a superior mastery of athletic techniques.
(B) Superior muscular strength is a requirement for an athlete to become a champion.
(C) No athlete can become a champion without a superior mastery of athletic techniques.
(D) The differences in muscular strength between top athletes are not great.
(E) Athletic techniques help athletes use limited resources efficiently.

→ techniq

champion → technique

technique → champion

4. If there are any inspired musical performances in the concert, the audience will be treated to a good show. But there will not be a good show unless there are sophisticated listeners in the audience, and to be a sophisticated listener one must understand one's musical roots.

inspired → good show

If all of the statements above are true, which one of the following must also be true?

good show → sophisticated
soph → understand roots

(A) If there are no sophisticated listeners in the audience, then there will be no inspired musical performances in the concert.
(B) No people who understand their musical roots will be in the audience if the audience will not be treated to a good show.
(C) If there will be people in the audience who understand their musical roots, then at least one musical performance in the concert will be inspired.
(D) The audience will be treated to a good show unless there are people in the audience who do not understand their musical roots.
(E) If there are sophisticated listeners in the audience, then there will be inspired musical performances in the concert.

inspi → good → soph → roots

insp → roots

5. A politician can neither be reelected nor avoid censure by his or her colleagues if that politician is known to be involved in any serious scandals. Several prominent politicians have just now been shown to be involved in a conspiracy that turned into a serious scandal. These politicians will therefore not be reelected.

If the statements above are all true, which one of the following statements must also be true?

(A) The prominent politicians cannot escape censure by their colleagues.
(B) If there had been no scandal, the prominent politicians would be reelected.
(C) No politician is censured unless he or she is known to be involved in a serious scandal.
(D) The prominent politicians initially benefited from the conspiracy that caused the scandal.
(E) Some politicians who are involved in scandalous conspiracies avoid detection and censure.

escape → cop exceed

Cap exceeded → escape

cap exceeded → escape

6. Leachate is a solution, frequently highly contaminated, that develops when water permeates a landfill site. If and only if the landfill's capacity to hold liquids is exceeded does the leachate escape into the environment, generally in unpredictable quantities. A method must be found for disposing of leachate. Most landfill leachate is sent directly to sewage treatment plants, but not all sewage plants are capable of handling the highly contaminated water.

Which one of the following can be inferred from the passage?

(A) The ability to predict the volume of escaping landfill leachate would help solve the disposal problem.
(B) If any water permeates a landfill, leachate will escape into the environment.
(C) No sewage treatment plants are capable of handling leachate.
(D) Some landfill leachate is sent to sewage treatment plants that are incapable of handling it.
(E) If leachate does not escape from a landfill into the environment, then the landfill's capacity to hold liquids has not been exceeded.

Insp → soph

Soph → insp

Sufficient and Necessary Question Problem Set Answer Key

All answer keys in this book indicate the source of the question by giving the month and year the LSAT was originally administered, the Logical Reasoning section number, and the question number within that section. Each LSAT has two Logical Reasoning sections, and so the Section 1 and Section 2 designators will refer to the first or second Logical Reasoning section in the test, not the physical section number of the booklet. The "SN" designation that appears after the question type indicates that the stimulus uses statements containing sufficient and necessary conditions.

Question #1. Must-SN. June 1999 LSAT, Section 1, #10. The correct answer choice is (D)

The conditionality in this short stimulus is introduced by the phrase "only when." This sets up the following conditional relationship, which is the economic principle referred to in the question stem:

EEG = a nation can experience economic growth
CCB = consumer confidence balanced with a small amount of consumer skepticism

$$EEG \longrightarrow CCB$$

The question stem, although worded a bit differently than the usual Must Be True question, requires you to select an answer that would follow from the economic principle. As discussed earlier in the chapter, when you are given a conditional statement in the stimulus and a Must Be True question stem, immediately search for an answer that is either the contrapositive of the conditional statement or the repeat form, and avoid Mistaken Reversals or Negations. Answer choice (D) is the contrapositive of the economic principle and is the correct answer.

Answer choice (A): This is a classic Mistaken Reversal incorrect answer. The answer choice simply reverses the two terms of the economic principle. Again, just because the necessary condition occurs does not mean that the sufficient condition must occur.

Answer choice (B): This answer is a version of a Mistaken Reversal: the answer reverses the terms of the economic principle and at the same time confuses the reader by attempting to equate "prevailing attitude is not skepticism" with "consumer confidence balanced with a small amount of consumer skepticism." The Reversal is sufficient to eliminate this answer, and of course the two phrases do not equate.

Answer choice (C): This is an Opposite Answer. According to the contrapositive of the economic principle, if a nation does not have a balanced consumer confidence, then that nation will *not* experience economic growth. This is the opposite of the answer choice, which stealthily drops the "not" that should appear before "experience economic growth."

Answer choice (D): This is the correct answer. The answer choice manipulates the terms a bit, forcing you to recognize that the negation of "consumer confidence balanced with a small amount of skepticism" is phrased as the "prevailing attitude of consumers is *exclusively* confidence" (italics added). This creates the contrapositive:

$$\cancel{CCB} \longrightarrow \cancel{EEG}$$

Sufficient and Necessary Question Problem Set Answer Key

Answer choice (E): This answer is another version of a Mistaken Reversal. The only difference between this answer choice and answer choice (A) is that this answer plays a Shell Game and reverses the confidence and skepticism elements from the stimulus.

Question #2. Must-SN. October 1999 LSAT, Section 2, #12. The correct answer choice is (A)

This is a fact set. The stimulus begins with the author indicating that drivers with a large number of demerit points who have also been convicted of a serious driving-related offense should either be sentenced to jail or be forced to receive driver re-education. This either/or relationship sets up the following diagram:

J = sent to jail
DE = receive driver re-education
sub-D = drivers with a large number of demerit points who have also been convicted of a serious driving-related offense

$$\cancel{J}_D \longrightarrow DE_D$$
$$\cancel{DE}_D \longrightarrow J_D$$

The next sentence begins with the conditional indicator "only if," and introduces the following conditional relationship:

R = likely to be made more responsible drivers

$$DE \longrightarrow R_D$$

The final sentence denies that drivers with a large number of demerit points who have also been convicted of a serious driving-related offense can be made into more responsible drivers. This can be represented as follows:

$$\cancel{R}_D$$

At this point the stimulus ends, but you should continue your analysis by linking the pieces of the stimulus together. The denial of the "R" condition in the final sentence enacts a contrapositive:

$$\cancel{R}_D \longrightarrow \cancel{DE}$$

Linking this contrapositive to the either/or diagram in the first sentence yields the following chain:

$$\cancel{R}_D \longrightarrow \cancel{DE} \longrightarrow J_D$$

Hence, the pieces of the argument allow us to conclude that drivers with a large number of demerit points who have also been convicted of a serious driving-related offense should go to jail. This is restated almost exactly in answer choice (A).

Sufficient and Necessary Question Problem Set Answer Key

Answer choice (A): As explained above, this is the correct answer.

Answer choice (B): Like all four of the incorrect answers, this answer contains new information, which in a Must Be True question is cause for suspicion. The stimulus does not discuss the "best chance" for making drivers more responsible.

Answer choice (C): Similar to the reasoning behind eliminating answer choice (B), the stimulus does not discuss whether driver re-education is a "harsh enough punishment" and thus we can eliminate this answer choice.

Answer choice (D): The stimulus does not address drivers who have not committed a serious driving offense, only those convicted of such an offense. Further, this answer does not indicate that the drivers under discussion have a large number of demerit points, and thus we cannot be certain the recommendations made in the stimulus apply to the drivers mentioned in this answer choice.

Answer choice (E): This is an Opposite Answer. According to the last two sentences of the stimulus, drivers with a large number of demerit points should *not* receive driver re-education.

Question #3. MP-SN. December 2001 LSAT, Section 2, #3. The correct answer choice is (C)

Unlike the first two questions in this set, this is a Main Point question. As with all Main Point questions, if you follow the Primary Objectives, the question should be easy and you should have a solid answer in mind before attacking the answer choices.

The first sentence of the argument is a premise. The second sentence is divided into a premise and a conclusion: the premise is introduced by the indicator "since," and the conclusion of the argument is introduced by the indicator "it follows that." As stated in the argument, the conclusion is "a requirement for an athlete to become a champion is a superior mastery of athletic techniques." Because the conditional indicator "requirement" is used, we can draw a conditional diagram of the conclusion:

C = champion
SM = superior mastery of athletic techniques

$$C \longrightarrow SM$$

Note that "requirement" is a necessary condition indicator, and the "requirement" referred to is "superior mastery of athletic techniques."

Answer choice (A): This is a Mistaken Reversal of the conclusion. Note how right away the test makers are trying to test you to see if you will fall for an answer that uses the elements of the conclusion but in the wrong relationship. You must be on guard at all times!

Sufficient and Necessary Question Problem Set Answer Key

Answer choice (B): Although this answer is likely to be true in the real world, this is not stated in the argument. The only comment made on muscle strength is that top athletes do not differ greatly from each other in muscular strength.

Answer choice (C): This correct answer is a paraphrase of the conclusion, and the diagram for this answer choice is the same as the diagram of the conclusion.

Answer choice (D): This is a classic incorrect Main Point question answer choice. Although the author would agree with this statement, this is not the main point of the argument.

Answer choice (E): This answer is similar to answer choice (D). Again, the answer choice repeats part of the argument, but this answer does not capture the main point of the argument.

Question #4. Must-SN. December 1999 LSAT, Section 1, #18. The correct answer choice is (A)

The stimulus is a fact set containing three conditional statements. The statements can be linked together to create one long chain:

    IMP = inspired musical performances
    GS = audience treated to a good show
    SL = sophisticated listeners in the audience
    UMR = understand one's musical roots

    1. First sentence: IMP ——⟶ GS

    2. Second sentence, first part: GS ——⟶ SL

    3. Second sentence, second part: SL ——⟶ UMR

    Chain of all statements: IMP ——⟶ GS ——⟶ SL ——⟶ UMR

With a long conditional chain and a Must Be True question, the correct answer will likely be a contrapositive of the entire chain or of a portion of the chain. Wrong answers will likely be Mistaken Reversals or Negations of the entire chain or of a portion of the chain. Keep this in mind and attack the problem!

Answer choice (A): This correct answer is a contrapositive of the chain created by the first two statements above. The diagram for this answer choice is:

    S̶L̶ ——⟶ I̶M̶P̶

Sufficient and Necessary Question Problem Set Answer Key

Answer choice (B): This answer choice is a Mistaken Negation of the chain created by the second and third statements above. The diagram for this answer choice is:

$$\cancel{GS} \longrightarrow U\cancel{M}R$$

Make sure you do not miss the "if" in the middle of the answer choice.

Answer choice (C): This answer choice is a Mistaken Reversal of the chain of all statements. The diagram for this answer choice is:

$$UMR \longrightarrow IMP$$

Answer choice (D): This answer choice is a Mistaken Negation of the chain created by the second and third statements above. This answer choice is identical to answer choice (B), and the diagram for this answer choice is:

$$\cancel{GS} \longrightarrow U\cancel{M}R$$

Answer choice (E): This answer choice is a Mistaken Reversal of the chain created by the first two statements above. The diagram for this answer choice is:

$$SL \longrightarrow IMP$$

Question #5. Must-SN. December 2002 LSAT, Section 2, #6. The correct answer choice is (A)

The argument begins with a statement that contains two necessary conditions:

> SS = involved in any serious scandal
> sub-P = politician
> R = reelected
> AC = avoid censure

$$SS_P \longrightarrow \begin{array}{c} \cancel{R} \\ \text{and} \\ \cancel{AC} \end{array}$$

This conditional relationship is introduced by the "if" in the middle of the sentence, but the statement also features a "neither/nor" construction. In this case, the neither/nor indicates that the two named events both cannot occur if a politician is involved in a serious scandal, hence the "and" in the necessary condition.

The argument continues by stating that several prominent politicians have been involved in a serious scandal. This assertion begins a Repeat form argument by indicating that the sufficient condition has occurred:

$$SS_p$$

Given this occurrence, the author now concludes that one of the two necessary conditions—"not reelected"—will happen. Because this is true based on the premises, this is a valid conclusion. Some readers object that because the author does not mention censure, the conclusion is incomplete and therefore incorrect. This point has no merit. Any LSAT author can choose what he or she wishes to address, and in this case the author has made a conclusion that follows from the premises. No false or incorrect statement has been made. The author is not compelled to address every single consequence of a given set of premises. However, as soon as the Must Be True questions stem appears, you should immediately search for an answer that addresses the censure issue. Based on the premises, we know that the prominent politicians will also be censured and answer choice (A) indicates that fact.

Answer choice (A): This correct answer is a result of the Repeat argument form enacted in the stimulus.

Answer choice (B): This answer is a Mistaken Negation of part of the conditional statement in the first sentence.

Answer choice (C): This answer is a Mistaken Reversal of part of the conditional statement in the first sentence.

Answer choice (D): This issue is not addressed in the stimulus.

Answer choice (E): While this answer is possibly true because the stimulus limits the discussion to "politicians *known* to be involved in any serious scandals," there is no evidence to prove that some politicians avoid detection and censure. Thus, this answer is incorrect.

Question #6. Must-SN. February 1992 LSAT, Section 1, #12. The correct answer choice is (E)

The key to this problem is the "if and only if" construction in the second sentence. As mentioned earlier in the chapter, when you encounter that construction, you must respond under the assumption that you will be tested on your knowledge of the relationship produced by that phrase. In this case, the following scenario is produced:

CE = the landfill's capacity to hold liquids is exceeded
LE = leachate escape into the environment

$$CE \longleftrightarrow LE$$

Sufficient and Necessary Question Problem Set Answer Key

According to your knowledge of the double-arrow relationship, only two possible scenarios can result:

1. CE and LE

or

2. C̶E̶ and L̶E̶

You should immediately glance at the question stem and determine what question you are being asked, and then attack the answer choices with the knowledge above. Answer choice (E) reflects scenario 2 above, and is therefore correct.

Answer choice (A): Although leachate escapes in "generally unpredictable" quantities, there is no evidence in the stimulus to suggest that the ability to predict the volume of escaping leachate would help solve the problem. This is a good example of an answer that sounds reasonable or likely to be true, but is incorrect.

Answer choice (B): No. Leachate escapes into the environment if the landfill's capacity is exceeded, not just if any water permeates a landfill. If the water permeating the landfill caused the capacity to be exceeded then this answer would be correct, but the answer does not indicate that the capacity is exceeded.

Answer choice (C): This is an Exaggerated answer. The stimulus indicates that "not all" sewage plants are capable of handling leachate. The answer choice exaggerates "not all" into none.

Answer choice (D): This is a tricky reworking of the final sentence. The last sentence contains two separate statements, one indicating most landfill leachate is sent to sewage plants and the other revealing that not all sewage plants can handle leachate. But, that does not mean that any leachate is sent to those plants incapable of handling leachate. Thus, answer choice (D) is incorrect.

Answer choice (E): This is the correct answer, and this is the answer you should have been seeking after identifying the presence of "if and only if" in combination with the Must Be True question. Incidentally, when looking for a correct answer in this situation, scenario 2 at the top of the page is more likely to appear than scenario 1 for the simple reason that scenario 2 represents a manipulation of the original statement.

CHAPTER SEVEN: WEAKEN QUESTIONS

Weaken Questions

Weaken questions require you to select the answer choice that undermines the author's argument as decisively as possible.

Because Weaken questions are in the Third Family, these questions require a different approach than the Must Be True and Main Point questions we have covered so far. In addition to the Primary Objectives, keep the following rules in mind when approaching Weaken questions:

1. The stimulus will contain an argument. Because you are asked to weaken the author's reasoning, and reasoning requires a conclusion, an argument will always be present. In order to maximize your chances of success you must identify, isolate, and assess the premises and the conclusion of the argument. Only by understanding the structure of the argument can you gain the perspective necessary to attack the author's position.

2. Focus on the conclusion. Almost all correct Weaken answer choices impact the conclusion. The more you know about the specifics of the conclusion, the better armed you will be to differentiate between correct and incorrect answers.

3. The information in the stimulus is suspect. There are often reasoning errors present, and you must read the argument very carefully.

4. Weaken questions often yield strong prephrases. Be sure to actively consider the range of possible answers before proceeding to the answer choices.

5. The answer choices are accepted as given, even if they include "new" information. Unlike Must Be True questions, Weaken answer choices can bring into consideration information outside of or tangential to the stimulus. Just because a fact or idea is not mentioned in the stimulus is *not* grounds for dismissing an answer choice. Your task is to determine which answer choice best attacks the argument in the stimulus.

By following the Primary Objectives and focusing on the points above, you will maximize your chances of success on Weaken questions.

Third Family Information Model:

Remember, most Weaken question stems tell you to accept the answer choices as true.

Weaken question stems typically contain the following two features:

We discuss the Third Family before the Second Family because some of the skills required to complete Third Family questions are essential for Second Family questions.

1. The stem uses the word "weaken" or a synonym. Following are some examples of words or phrases used to indicate that your task is to weaken the argument:

   weaken
   attack
   undermine
   refute
   argue against
   call into question
   cast doubt
   challenge
   damage
   counter

2. The stem indicates that you should accept the answer choices as true, usually with the following phrase:

   "Which one of the following, if true, ..."

Here are several Weaken question stem examples from actual LSATs:

"Which one of the following, if true, most seriously weakens the argument?"

"Which one of the following, if true, most undermines the researcher's argument?"

"Which one of the following, if shown to be a realistic possibility, would undermine the argument?"

"Which one of the following, if true, would most call into question the analysts' explanation of the price increase?"

"Which one of the following, if true, could be used by Cora to counter Bernard's rejection of her explanation?"

"Which one of the following, if true, is the strongest logical counter parent P can make to parent Q's objection?"

"Which one of the following, if true, most calls into question the claim above?"

How to Weaken an Argument

The key to weakening an LSAT argument is to attack the conclusion. But, keep in mind that to attack is not the same as to destroy. Although an answer that destroys the conclusion would be correct, this rarely occurs because of the minimal space allotted to answer choices. Instead, you are more likely to encounter an answer that hurts the argument but does not ultimately destroy the author's position. When evaluating an answer, ask yourself, "Would this answer choice make the author reconsider his or her position or force the author to respond?" If so, you have the correct answer.

Because arguments are made up of premises and conclusions, you can safely assume that these are the parts you must attack in order to weaken an argument. Let us discuss each part, and the likelihood that each would be attacked by an answer choice.

1. The Premises

    One of the classic ways to attack an argument is to attack the premises on which the conclusion rests. Regrettably, this form of attack is rarely used on the LSAT because when a premise is attacked, the answer choice is easy to spot. Literally, the answer will contradict one of the premises, and most students are capable of reading an argument and then identifying an answer that simply negates a premise.

    In practice, almost all correct LSAT Weaken question answers leave the premises untouched.

2. The Conclusion

    The conclusion is the part of the argument that is most likely to be attacked, but the correct answer choice will not simply contradict the conclusion. Instead, the correct answer will undermine the conclusion by showing that the conclusion fails to account for some element or possibility. In this sense, the correct answer often shows that the conclusion does not necessarily follow from the premises even if the premises are true. Consider the following example:

    > All my neighbors own blue cars. Therefore I own a blue car.

    Even though the statement that the neighbors have blue cars is entirely reasonable, the weakness in the argument is that this fact has no impact on the color of the car I own. In this overly simplified problem, the correct weakening answer would be something along the lines of, "The cars of one's neighbors have no determinative effect on the car any individual owns." Would that conclusively

You do not need to find an answer that destroys the author's position. Instead, simply find an answer that hurts the argument.

The one time you might see an answer choice attack a premise is when that "premise" is a sub-conclusion. That is, when a conclusion of one premise is used as a premise to support another conclusion.

disprove that I own a blue car? No. Does it show that perhaps I do not own a blue car? Yes. Does it disprove that my neighbors own blue cars? No.

Assumptions will be discussed in more detail in Chapter Nine.

Answers that weaken the argument's conclusion will attack assumptions made by the author. In the example above, the author assumes that the neighbors' ownership of blue cars has an impact on the color of the car that he owns. If this assumption was shown to be questionable, the argument would be undermined.

The stimuli for weaken questions contain errors of assumption. This makes sense, because the easiest argument to weaken is one that already has a flaw. Typically, the author will fail to consider other possibilities or leave out a key piece of information. In this sense the author assumes that these elements do not exist when he or she makes the conclusion, and if you see a gap or hole in the argument immediately consider that the correct answer might attack this hole.

As you consider possible answers, always look for the one that attacks the way the author arrived at the conclusion. Do not worry about the premises and instead focus on the effect the answer has on the conclusion.

Personalizing helps you see the argument from a very involved perspective, and that helps you assess the strength of each answer.

So, we know that we must first focus on the conclusion and how the author arrived at the conclusion. The second key to weakening arguments is to personalize the argument. Most students perform considerably better when they see the argument from their perspective as opposed to trying to understand the issues abstractly. When analyzing the author's argument, imagine how you would respond if you were talking directly to the author. Would you use answer choice (A) or would you prefer answer choice (B)? Students who personalize the argument often properly dismiss answer choices that they would have otherwise wasted time considering.

Common Weakening Scenarios

Although there are many classical logical fallacies, the most common of which we will discuss in the Flaw in the Reasoning section, several scenarios that occur in LSAT Weaken question stimuli are easy to recognize and attack:

1. Incomplete Information. The author fails to consider all of the possibilities, or relies upon evidence that is incomplete. This flaw can be attacked by bringing up new possibilities or information.

2. Improper Comparison. The author attempts to compare two or more items that are essentially different.

3. Qualified Conclusion. The author qualifies or limits the conclusion in such a way as to leave the argument open to attack.

While these three scenarios are not the only ways an argument can be weak, they encompass a number of the errors that appear in LSAT stimuli.

Three Incorrect Answer Traps

There are certain incorrect answer choices that appear frequently in Weaken questions:

1. Opposite Answers. As discussed in the Must Be True question chapter, these answers do the exact opposite of what is needed. In this case, they strengthen the argument as opposed to weakening it. Although you might think answers of this type are easy to avoid, they can be very tricky. To analogize, have you ever gotten on a freeway thinking you were going south when in fact you later discovered you were going north? It is easy to make a mistake when you head in the exact opposite direction. In the same way, Opposite answers lure the test taker by presenting information that relates perfectly to the argument, but just in the wrong manner.

2. Shell Game Answers. Like Opposite answers, the Shell Game is the same as in the Must Be True discussion. Remember, a Shell Game occurs when an idea or concept is raised in the stimulus and then a very similar idea appears in the answer choice, but the idea is changed just enough to be incorrect but still attractive. In Weaken questions, the Shell Game is usually used to attack a conclusion that is similar to, but slightly different from, the one presented in the stimulus. Later in this chapter you will see some excellent examples of this answer type.

3. Out of Scope Answers. These answers simply miss the point of the argument and raise issues that are either not related to the argument or tangential to the argument.

While these three answer types are not the only ways an answer choice can be attractively incorrect, they appear frequently enough that you should be familiar with each form.

Some of the wrong answer types from the Must Be True chapter do not apply to Weaken questions. For example, the New Information answer is usually wrong in a Must Be True question, but not in a Weaken question because new information is acceptable in the answer choices.

Weaken Questions Analyzed

In the following questions we will discuss the form of the stimulus and answer choices against the background of our discussion so far. Please take a moment to complete the following problem:

1. Carl is clearly an incompetent detective. He has solved a smaller percentage of the cases assigned to him in the last 3 years—only 1 out of 25—than any other detective on the police force.

   Which one of the following, if true, most seriously weakens the argument above?

   (A) Because the police chief regards Carl as the most capable detective, she assigns him only the most difficult cases, ones that others have failed to solve.

   (B) Before he became a detective, Carl was a neighborhood police officer and was highly respected by the residents of the neighborhood he patrolled.

   (C) Detectives on the police force on which Carl serves are provided with extensive resources, including the use of a large computer database, to help them solve crimes.

   (D) Carl was previously a detective in a police department in another city, and in the 4 years he spent there, he solved only 1 out of 30 crimes.

   (E) Many of the officers in the police department in which Carl serves were hired or promoted within the last 5 years.

This was the first question on one of the Logical Reasoning sections of the December 2003 LSAT, and provided a nice way to start the section. Law Services classifies this as an easy question, but as a starting point for our discussion that is helpful. The structure of the argument is simple, and it is easy to see why the premise does not undeniably prove the conclusion. The answers contain several predictable forms, and this is the type of question you should quickly destroy. You do not need to spend a great deal of time trying to find a specific prephrased answer because there are so many possibilities, and the answers can be eliminated without a great deal of time spent considering which are Losers and which are Contenders.

The stimulus uses a premise about success rate to form a conclusion about Carl's competency as a detective. Ask yourself—does the premise prove the conclusion? No, because there are many factors that could have affected Carl's performance. In this sense, the stimulus has incomplete information, and we should try to discover a relevant piece of information in one of the answer choices that will shed more light on why Carl's success rate is so low. Use this knowledge to make a general prephrase that indicates you are looking for a piece of information that shows Carl's success rate is not as low as it seems or that other factors limited Carl's performance.

The form of this problem—that a low success rate must indicate a bad performance—has appeared on several different LSATs.

Prephrasing is often easier with Weaken questions than with some other question types. Simply put, many people are good at attacking a position and prephrasing puts that skill to use.

Answer choice (A): This is the correct answer. We discover that Carl receives the hardest cases, and one would expect that the hardest cases would yield a lower success rate. Notice that this answer does not attack the premises. Even though they are still true, the conclusion is undermined by the new evidence. This is typical of most Weaken questions answers—the premises are not addressed and the focus is on the conclusion.

Answer choice (B): This answer is irrelevant. It tries to use the opinion of others about Carl's performance in one capacity to refute facts about his performance in another capacity. Personalize the answer—is this the answer you would offer to weaken the argument against Carl if he was your friend?

Answer choice (C): This is an Opposite answer that strengthens the claim that Carl is incompetent by showing that Carl was not deprived of certain resources for solving cases.

Answer choice (D): This is another Opposite answer that strengthens the claim that Carl is incompetent. This time, the answer shows that Carl has a previous record of poor performance.

Answer choice (E): This answer goes beyond the scope of the argument by discussing the promotions of other officers. These promotions do not impact Carl's job and no information is given about Carl's promotions. If you are thinking that perhaps Carl's poor performance is a result of dissatisfaction over the promotions of others, then you are assuming too much.

Now we will move to a somewhat harder question. Please take a moment to complete the following problem:

2. Beverage company representative: The plastic rings that hold six-packs of beverage cans together pose a threat to wild animals, which often become entangled in the discarded rings and suffocate as a result. Following our lead, all beverage companies will soon use only those rings consisting of a new plastic that disintegrates after only three days' exposure to sunlight. Once we all complete the switchover from the old to the new plastic rings, therefore, the threat of suffocation that plastic rings pose to wild animals will be eliminated.

Which one of the following, if true, most seriously weakens the representative's argument?

(A) The switchover to the new plastic rings will take at least two more years to complete.

(B) After the beverage companies have switched over to the new plastic rings, a substantial number of the old plastic rings will persist in most aquatic and woodland environments.

(C) The new plastic rings are slightly less expensive than the old rings.

(D) The new plastic rings rarely disintegrate during shipping of beverage six-packs because most trucks that transport canned beverages protect their cargo from sunlight.

(E) The new plastic rings disintegrate into substances that are harmful to aquatic animals when ingested in substantial quantities by them.

In two-speaker stimuli where you are asked to weaken the argument of one of the speakers, the test makers often use misdirection and place an answer choice that weakens the argument of the other speaker.

The conclusion of this argument is the final sentence, which contains the conclusion indicator "therefore," and the conclusion contains a qualification that the threat of suffocation will be eliminated *after* the switchover is complete. The premises supporting this conclusion are that the new plastic rings will be used by all companies and that the rings disintegrate after three days' exposure to sunlight. Personalize this argument and ask yourself—are there any holes in this argument? Yes, there are several. The most obvious is, "What if an animal becomes entangled in the new rings before they can disintegrate?" In this question, however, that avenue of attack is not used (this was a two-question stimuli and that idea was used in the other question) but there is no way to know this prior to attempting the question.

Answer choice (A): This answer does not hurt the argument because the author qualified the conclusion to account for the date of the switchover, thereby inoculating against this avenue of attack. From a personalizing standpoint, imagine what would happen if you raised this issue to the beverage company representative—he or she would simply say, "Yes, that may be the case, but I noted in my conclusion that the program would be effective *once the switchover is complete*." This is an attractive answer because it raises a point that would be a difficult public relations issue to address. Regardless, this does not hurt the argument given by the beverage company representative, and that is the task at hand.

Answer choice (B): This is the correct answer. Most people select answer choice (E), but as you will see, (E) is incorrect. This answer undermines the representative's conclusion by showing that even after the switchover is complete, the threat to animals from plastic rings will persist. Note the carefully worded nature of the conclusion—the representative does not say the threat from *new* plastic rings will be eliminated, but rather the threat from plastic rings, which includes both old and new rings.

Answer choice (C): This out-of-scope answer addresses an issue that is irrelevant to the representative's argument.

Answer choice (D): While this is nice information from a customer service standpoint (you do not want your six-pack of beer falling apart as you walk out of the store), this answer does not affect the conclusion because it does not address the threat of suffocation to animals.

Answer choice (E): This is the most commonly chosen answer, and it is a perfect example of a Shell Game. In this case, the answer preys upon test takers who fail to heed Primary Objective #4: "Read closely and know precisely what the author said. Do not generalize!" Many test takers read the conclusion and think, "So when they start using these new rings, it will make things better for the animals." When these test takers get to answer choice (E), the answer looks extremely attractive because it indicates that the implementation of the new rings will also have a harmful effect. With this thinking in mind, many test takers select answer choice (E) thinking it undermines the conclusion and they are certain they have nailed the question. However, the conclusion is specifically about suffocation, and answer choice (E) does not address suffocation. Instead, answer choice (E) is a shell game that attacks a conclusion that is similar to but different from the actual conclusion. Remember, one of the rules for weakening arguments is to focus on the conclusion, and knowing the details of the conclusion is part of that focus.

Answer choice (E) is only attractive if you make a mistakenly broad interpretation of the conclusion.

Finally, the placement of answer choice (E) is no accident. Most students do not immediately identify answer choice (B) as the correct answer, and even those that keep it as a Contender often feel it could be stronger. Then, just when things are starting to look bleak, answer choice (E) pops up sounding fairly reasonable. Most people breathe a sigh of relief and select the answer without carefully examining the contents. Never choose answer choice (E) just because the first four answers are not overly attractive! Always make a thorough analysis of every answer choice and remember that the test makers know that people get nervous if none of the first four answer choices jump out at them. Do not let the test makers draw you into a trap!

Please take a moment to complete the following problem:

3. There is relatively little room for growth in the overall carpet market, which is tied to the size of the population. Most who purchase carpet do so only once or twice, first in their twenties or thirties, and then perhaps again in their fifties or sixties. Thus as the population ages, companies producing carpet will be able to gain market share in the carpet market only through purchasing competitors, and not through more aggressive marketing.

Which one of the following, if true, casts the most doubt on the conclusion above?

(A) Most of the major carpet producers market other floor coverings as well.

(B) Most established carpet producers market several different brand names and varieties, and there is no remaining niche in the market for new brands to fill.

(C) Two of the three mergers in the industry's last ten years led to a decline in profits and revenues for the newly merged companies.

(D) Price reductions, achieved by cost-cutting in production, by some of the dominant firms in the carpet market are causing other producers to leave the market altogether.

(E) The carpet market is unlike most markets in that consumers are becoming increasingly resistant to new patterns and styles.

This is another difficult problem but very typical of the LSAT. As always, the key to success is to isolate the conclusion, which appears in the last sentence: "companies producing carpet will be able to gain market share in the carpet market only through purchasing competitors." As you should have noted while reading, the conclusion contains a conditional indicator and is thereby conditional in nature. The conclusion can be diagrammed as:

GMS = gain market share in the carpet market
PC = purchasing competitors

$$GMS \longrightarrow PC$$

According to the author, to gain market share in the carpet market a company must purchase a competitor. Answer choice (C) is often selected by students, but it does not attack this idea. To attack a conditional statement you must show that the necessary condition is not actually necessary for the sufficient condition to occur. Answer choice (C) simply suggests that when companies purchase their competitors the endeavor is often financially unsuccessful. Essentially, answer choice (C) fails to prove that purchasing competitors is unnecessary to gain market share. Answer choice (D), on the other hand, does suggest a way for companies to gain market share without purchasing competitors, thereby attacking the conditional statement given in the stimulus. Thus, answer choice (D) is correct.

Answer choice (A): This answer goes beyond the scope of the argument, which is limited to the carpet market (and not other floor coverings).

Answer choice (B): This is an Opposite answer that strengthens the argument. If there are no remaining niches to fill, then there is no way to expand other than to purchase a competitor.

Answer choice (C): This attractive answer is wrong for two very strong reasons:

1. A Shell Game is played with the details of the conclusion. The conclusion is about market share. Answer choice (C) is about a decline in profits and revenues. The two are not the same, and so the information in the answer choice does not weaken the conclusion.

2. Even if you assume that market share is the same thing as profits and revenues, a second Shell Game is played because the answer then attacks a conclusion that is similar but different from the given conclusion.

If the conclusion were as follows:

This question is from the February 1994 LSAT, and is known as the Carpet Market question. Although it is a few years old, this question is a great teaching tool and shows how any modern LSAT question can be useful, regardless of the date it appeared. Remember—we are discussing Logical Reasoning and logic has not changed for thousands of years. Do not fall prey to the misconception that only LSATs from the last several years are useful. Any LSAT from June 1991 to the present can teach you something about the way the test is constructed.

$$PC \longrightarrow GMS$$

then answer choice (C) would be correct (again, assuming market share is the same thing as profits and revenues). But, the above is a Mistaken Reversal of the conclusion, and so the attack is made on a statement that uses the same terms as the conclusion but puts them in a different relationship. This is a great example of the cleverness displayed by the test makers. Fortunately you can avoid this answer if you know what to look for when attacking conditional reasoning. More on this topic in the next section.

One point worth noting is that it is no accident that the most tempting wrong answer choice appears just before the correct answer. This is a classic LSAT trick, and one that is very effective because most test takers relax once they find an answer they feel is attractive. This makes them less likely to closely examine the answers that follow. Never relax during the LSAT!

Answer choice (D): This is the correct answer. If price reductions drive out some of the carpet producers, then other producers can take the market share left behind. This scenario shows that a company can gain market share without purchasing a competitor, thus attacking the necessary condition in the conclusion.

Answer choice (E): This Opposite answer strengthens the argument. If the consumers are resistant to new styles, then one fewer possibility exists if a company is trying to increase market share. By eliminating this option, the conclusion is strengthened (if you eliminate an idea that would hurt the argument, that strengthens the argument because it has fewer "competitors." More on this later).

Weakening Conditional Reasoning

As proven by the discussion of the previous problem, there is a simple rule for weakening a conditional conclusion:

> To weaken a conditional conclusion, attack the necessary condition by showing that the necessary condition does not need to occur in order for the sufficient condition to occur.

This can be achieved by presenting a counterexample or by presenting information that shows that the sufficient condition can occur without the necessary condition.

This leads to another Classic Combination:

> When you have conditional reasoning in the stimulus and a Weaken

question, immediately look for an answer that attacks the necessary condition.

Please take a moment to complete the following problem:

4. Speaker: Contemporary business firms need to recognize that avoiding social responsibility leads to the gradual erosion of power. This is Davis and Blomstrom's Iron Law of Responsibility: "In the long run, those who do not use power in a manner which society considers responsible will tend to lose it." The law's application to human institutions certainly stands confirmed by history. Though the "long run" may require decades or even centuries in some instances, society ultimately acts to reduce power when society thinks it is not being used responsibly. Therefore, a business that wishes to retain its power as long as it can must act responsibly.

Which one of the following statements, if true, most weakens the speaker's argument?

(A) Government institutions are as subject to the Iron Law of Responsibility as business institutions.
(B) Public relations programs can cause society to consider an institution socially responsible even when it is not.
(C) The power of some institutions erodes more slowly than the power of others, whether they are socially responsible or not.
(D) Since no institution is eternal, every business will eventually fail.
(E) Some businesses that have used power in socially responsible ways have lost it.

This problem is similar in form to the carpet market problem. The conclusion appears at the end and is conditional in nature: "a business that wishes to retain its power as long as it can must act responsibly."

This relationship can be diagrammed as:

WRP = business wish(es) to retain power as long as possible
AR = act responsibly

$$WRP \longrightarrow AR$$

Hopefully, you identified this conclusion as conditional when you read the stimulus. As you read the question stem, you should have immediately prephrased an answer that would allow the sufficient condition to occur without the necessary condition, namely that a business that wishes to retain power does not necessarily have to act responsibly. Let us examine the answer choices with this idea in mind:

Answer choice (A): Because this answer addresses government institutions, this cannot hurt the conclusion, which is about businesses. If anything, this may slightly support the argument. In the middle of the stimulus, the Speaker mentions that "The law's application to human institutions certainly stands confirmed by history." This answer affirms that statement by adding governments to the named list of human institutions.

Answer choice (B): This is the correct answer. If a public relations program can cause society to think an institution is socially responsible even when it is not, then an institution that wishes to retain power could act irresponsibly and then get a public relations firm to cover up the activities. In this way, the institution could wish to retain power but not act responsibly. Since this scenario allows the sufficient condition to occur without the necessary, this weakens the argument.

Answer choice (C): Many students hold this answer choice as a Contender. The answer is incorrect because the stimulus contemplates varying rates of power retention, especially between socially responsible and non-socially responsible institutions. If you read this answer thinking that the stimulus indicated socially responsible institutions do not lose power if socially responsible, then you made a quasi-Mistaken Reversal of the stimulus. There is never a presumption in the argument that power can be held indefinitely. If there were, this answer would be much more attractive.

Answer choice (D): The conclusion is clear in saying, "a business that wishes to retain power *as long as it can*..." The italicized phrase allows for the idea that businesses will eventually lose power and ultimately fail. Thus, this answer does not hurt the argument.

Answer choice (E): This is another attractive answer, and one that lured in many test takers. The answer states that even though some businesses acted responsibly (AR), they did not retain power (RP). If this difference between retaining power and wishing to retain power (WRP) is ignored, then this answer can be seen as attacking the Mistaken Reversal of the conclusion. As you learned from the discussion of answer choice (C) of the carpet market question, attacking the Mistaken Reversal of the conclusion does not hurt the conclusion. However, this answer is attractive because not only does it address elements of the conclusion, it also appears as the final answer choice. A test taker who did not like any of the earlier answers would find this answer quite attractive.

In the previous two problems, the only conditionality has been the conditional statement in the conclusion. However, Weaken questions can contain conditional statements throughout the stimulus. Consider the following problem:

5. Politician: All nations that place a high tax on income produce thereby a negative incentive for technological innovation, and all nations in which technological innovation is hampered inevitably fall behind in the international arms race. Those nations that, through historical accident or the foolishness of their political leadership, wind up in a strategically disadvantageous position are destined to lose their voice in world affairs. So if a nation wants to maintain its value system and way of life, it must not allow its highest tax bracket to exceed 30 percent of income.

Each of the following, if true, weakens the politician's argument EXCEPT:

(A) The top level of taxation must reach 45 percent before taxation begins to deter inventors and industrialists from introducing new technologies and industries.

(B) Making a great deal of money is an insignificant factor in driving technological innovation.

(C) Falling behind in the international arms race does not necessarily lead to a strategically less advantageous position.

(D) Those nations that lose influence in the world community do not necessarily suffer from a threat to their value system or way of life.

(E) Allowing one's country to lose its technological edge, especially as concerns weaponry, would be foolish rather than merely a historical accident.

This problem is a complete conditional argument containing conditional premises and a conditional conclusion. Here is a breakdown of the argument:

HT = nations that place a high tax on income
NI = negative incentive for technological innovation
FB = fall behind in the international arms race; also, wind up in a strategically disadvantageous position
LV = lose voice in world affairs

The first sentence contains two sufficient condition indicators (the word "all") and can be diagrammed as a chain:

$$HT \longrightarrow NI \longrightarrow FB$$

The next sentence paraphrases "fall behind in the international arms race" as "wind up in a strategically disadvantageous position" and can be diagrammed as:

$$FB \longrightarrow LV$$

Because the two statements have FB in common, a single long chain can be created:

$$HT \longrightarrow NI \longrightarrow FB \longrightarrow LV$$

From our discussion of conditional reasoning we know that a chain of this length contains many inferences. The conclusion, when paraphrased, tries to make a contrapositive:

> The phrase "nation wants to maintain its value system and way of life" is a very rough equivalent of "not wind up in a strategically disadvantageous position" and "not lose a voice in world affairs." The paraphrase is not a perfect equivalent because the conclusion discusses values, and the premises do not. For our purposes, we will symbolize this condition as:
>
> $\cancel{FB}$
> and
> $\cancel{LV}$

The phrase "must not allow its highest tax bracket to exceed 30 percent of income" is the equivalent of $\cancel{HT}$. Thus, the diagram for the conclusion is:

$\cancel{FB}$
and $\longrightarrow \cancel{HT}_{30}$
$\cancel{LV}$

Thus, based on the chain of reasoning provided, we have a reasonable conclusion, but not a perfect one because the paraphrase was not exact. The question stem is a WeakenX, which means that four of the answers will weaken the argument and the one correct answer will either have no effect on the argument or will strengthen the argument.

Answer choice (A): This answer attacks the necessary condition of the conclusion by showing that taxes could exceed 30% before problems occurred.

Answer choice (B): This answer attacks the first half of the first sentence, which states that high taxes necessarily produce a negative incentive for technological innovation. Because taxes lower an individual's income, the higher the tax, the greater the relative restriction on making money. Answer choice (B) shows that higher taxes would not necessarily produce low innovation because innovators do not care about the amount they earn.

Answer choice (C): This answer attacks the part of the argument that equates "fall behind in the international arms race" as "wind up in a strategically disadvantageous position." If the two are not equated, then the chain of premises breaks down.

Answer choice (D): Like (C), this attacks a portion of the argument where the author equates terms. In this case, the paraphrase in the conclusion was not exact, and this answer exploits that gap.

Answer choice (E): This is the correct answer. The answer does not hurt the argument because the stimulus specifically states that "Those nations that, through historical accident or the foolishness of their political leadership, wind up in a strategically disadvantageous position..." So, the actual reason the nation ends up in a disadvantageous position is not critical. It could be either foolishness or historical accident. So, an answer that asserts that it is foolishness and not historical accident has no effect on the argument.

Final Note

We will continue our discussion of Weaken questions in the next chapter, which addresses Cause and Effect Reasoning. We will also continue to discuss argumentation in more detail as we progress through the Second Family of questions and into Method of Reasoning and Parallel Reasoning.

The following page is a review of key points from this chapter. After the review, there is a short problem set to help test your knowledge of these ideas. The problem set is followed by an answer key with explanations. Good luck!

Weaken Question Type Review

Weaken questions require you to select an answer choice that undermines the author's argument as decisively as possible. Keep these fundamental rules in mind when you approach Weaken questions:

1. The stimulus will contain an argument.

2. Focus on the conclusion.

3. The information in the stimulus is suspect. There are often reasoning errors present, and you must read the argument very carefully.

4. Weaken questions often yield strong prephrases.

5. The answer choices are accepted as given, even if they include "new" information.

The conclusion is the part of the argument that is most likely to be attacked, but the correct answer choice will not simply contradict the conclusion. Instead, the correct answer will undermine the conclusion by showing that the conclusion fails to account for some element or possibility. In this sense, the correct answer often shows that the conclusion does not necessarily follow from the premises even if the premises are true.

Several scenarios that can occur in LSAT Weaken question stimuli are easy to recognize and attack:

1. Incomplete Information.

2. Improper Comparison.

3. Qualified Conclusion.

There are certain incorrect answer choices that appear frequently in Weaken questions:

1. Opposite Answers.

2. Shell Game Answers.

3. Out of Scope Answers.

There is a simple rule for weakening a conditional conclusion:

> To weaken a conditional conclusion, attack the necessary condition by showing that the necessary condition does not need to occur in order for the sufficient condition to occur.

Weaken Question Problem Set

The following questions are drawn from actual LSATs. Please complete the problem set and review the answer key and explanations. *Answers on Page 193*

1. Human beings have cognitive faculties that are superior to those of other animals, and once humans become aware of these, they cannot be made happy by anything that does not involve gratification of these faculties.

   Which one of the following statements, if true, most calls into question the view above?

   (A) Certain animals—dolphins and chimpanzees, for example—appear to be capable of rational communication. ×

   (B) Many people familiar both with intellectual stimulation and with physical pleasures enjoy the latter more. ×

   (C) Someone who never experienced classical music as a child will usually prefer popular music as an adult. ×

   (D) Many people who are serious athletes consider themselves to be happy.

   (E) Many people who are serious athletes love gourmet food. ×

2. Loggerhead turtles live and breed in distinct groups, of which some are in the Pacific Ocean and some are in the Atlantic. New evidence suggests that juvenile Pacific loggerheads that feed near the Baja peninsula hatch in Japanese waters 10,000 kilometers away. Ninety-five percent of the DNA samples taken from the Baja turtles match those taken from turtles at the Japanese nesting sites.

   Which one of the following, if true, most seriously weakens the reasoning above?

   (A) Nesting sites of loggerhead turtles have been found off the Pacific coast of North America several thousand kilometers north of the Baja peninsula.

   (B) The distance between nesting sites and feeding sites of Atlantic loggerhead turtles is less than 5,000 kilometers.

   (C) Loggerhead hatchlings in Japanese waters have been declining in number for the last decade while the number of nesting sites near the Baja peninsula has remained constant.

   (D) Ninety-five percent of the DNA samples taken from the Baja turtles match those taken from Atlantic loggerhead turtles.

   (E) Commercial aquariums have been successfully breeding Atlantic loggerheads with Pacific loggerheads for the last five years.

Weaken Question Problem Set

3. People who have specialized knowledge about a scientific or technical issue are systematically excluded from juries for trials where the issue is relevant. Thus, trial by jury is not a fair means of settling disputes involving such issues.

Which one of the following, if true, most seriously weakens the argument?

(A) The more complicated the issue being litigated, the less likely it is that a juror without specialized knowledge of the field involved will be able to comprehend the testimony being given.

(B) The more a juror knows about a particular scientific or technical issue involved in a trial, the more likely it is that the juror will be prejudiced in favor of one of the litigating parties before the trial begins.

(C) Appointing an impartial arbitrator is not a fair means of settling disputes involving scientific or technical issues, because arbitrators tend to favor settlements in which both parties compromise on the issues.

(D) Experts who give testimony on scientific or technical issues tend to hedge their conclusions by discussing the possibility of error.

(E) Expert witnesses in specialized fields often command fees that are so high that many people involved in litigation cannot afford their services.

4. The five senses have traditionally been viewed as distinct yet complementary. Each sense is thought to have its own range of stimuli that are incapable of stimulating the other senses. However, recent research has discovered that some people taste a banana and claim that they are tasting blue, or see a color and say that it has a specific smell. This shows that such people, called synesthesiacs, have senses that do not respect the usual boundaries between the five recognized senses.

Which one of the following statements, if true, most seriously weakens the argument?

(A) Synesthesiacs demonstrate a general, systematic impairment in their ability to use and understand words.

(B) Recent evidence strongly suggests that there are other senses besides sight, touch, smell, hearing, and taste.

(C) The particular ways in which sensory experiences overlap in synesthesiacs follow a definite pattern.

(D) The synesthetic phenomenon has been described in the legends of various cultures.

(E) Synesthesiacs can be temporarily rid of their synesthetic experiences by the use of drugs.

5. Archaeologist: A skeleton of a North American mastodon that became extinct at the peak of the Ice Age was recently discovered. It contains a human-made projectile dissimilar to any found in that part of Eurasia closest to North America. Thus, since Eurasians did not settle in North America until shortly before the peak of the Ice Age, the first Eurasian settlers in North America probably came from a more distant part of Eurasia.

Which one of the following, if true, most seriously weakens the archaeologist's argument?

(A) The projectile found in the mastodon does not resemble any that were used in Eurasia before or during the Ice Age.

(B) The people who occupied the Eurasian area closest to North America remained nomadic throughout the Ice Age.

(C) The skeleton of a bear from the same place and time as the mastodon skeleton contains a similar projectile.

(D) Other North American artifacts from the peak of the Ice Age are similar to ones from the same time found in more distant parts of Eurasia.

(E) Climatic conditions in North America just before the Ice Age were more conducive to human habitation than were those in the part of Eurasia closest to North America at that time.

6. Lobsters and other crustaceans eaten by humans are more likely to contract gill diseases when sewage contaminates their water. Under a recent proposal, millions of gallons of local sewage each day would be rerouted many kilometers offshore. Although this would substantially reduce the amount of sewage in the harbor where lobsters are caught, the proposal is pointless, because hardly any lobsters live long enough to be harmed by those diseases.

Which one of the following, if true, most seriously weakens the argument?

(A) Contaminants in the harbor other than sewage are equally harmful to lobsters.

(B) Lobsters, like other crustaceans, live longer in the open ocean than in industrial harbors.

(C) Lobsters breed as readily in sewage-contaminated water as in unpolluted water.

(D) Gill diseases cannot be detected by examining the surface of the lobster.

(E) Humans often become ill as a result of eating lobsters with gill diseases.

Weaken Question Problem Set Answer Key

All answer keys in this book indicate the source of the question by giving the month and year the LSAT was originally administered, the Logical Reasoning section number, and the question number within that section. Each LSAT has two Logical Reasoning sections, and so the Section 1 and Section 2 designators will refer to the first or second Logical Reasoning section in the test, not the physical section number of the booklet.

Question #1. Weaken. June 1999 LSAT, Section 2, #15. The correct answer choice is (B)

This is a nice straightforward question to start the problem set. The conclusion of the argument appears at the end of the stimulus: human beings "cannot be made happy by anything that does not involve gratification of these [cognitive] faculties." To weaken the argument we must show that individuals can be made happy without gratification of the cognitive faculties. If you do not know the meaning of "cognitive," the problem can be challenging. Cognitive means "relating to the mental process of knowing, including reasoning and judgment." In other words, cognitive faculties are thinking and analyzing, etc.

Answer choice (A): This answer attempts to attack the first premise, but fails. Although it is fantastic news that dolphins and chimps can rationally communicate, this fact has no impact on the argument at hand. Even though they have this communication ability, human cognitive faculties can still be superior.

Answer choice (B): This is the correct answer, and a somewhat risqué one at that. By showing that many people enjoy the physical more than the cognitive, the answer shows that people can be made happy by gratification of something other than cognitive faculties. Cognitive faculties, being mental in nature, are of course distinct from physical pleasures.

Additionally, this answer has the benefit of addressing the phrase in the stimulus regarding awareness of cognitive faculties: "once humans become aware of these..." In this answer, unlike others, the individuals are known to be familiar with cognitive faculties. While we believe that recognition of cognitive faculties is inherent in adults (or some of the named types in other answers, such as *serious athletes*, who by definition would have to be teens or adults), this answer is stronger because it explicitly addresses the issue.

Answer choice (C): A preference for a certain type of music is likely a cognition-driven preference, and this preference is expressed by an adult who would certainly be aware of cognitive faculties. And, since no suggestion is made that individuals can be made happy without gratification of the cognitive faculties, this answer is incorrect.

Answer choice (D): This can be an attractive answer at first, but it depends on the assumption that the serious athletes are happy due to their athletic endeavors. However, that connection is not explicitly stated, and it could be that the serious athletes are happy because of some gratification of their cognitive faculties, in their respective sport or otherwise.

Answer choice (E): This answer is similar to answer choice (D). A gourmet is a connoisseur of food and drink, and a connoisseur is a person with deep or special knowledge of a subject. In this sense, there would be a cognitive element to the enjoyment of gourmet food. As such, this answer may serve to slightly strengthen the argument because it shows that an individual with experience with the non-cognitive still retains a love of the cognitive.

Question #2. October 2002 LSAT, Section 2, #15. The correct answer choice is (D)

The argument uses the premise that Baja turtles and Japanese turtles share ninety-five percent of their DNA to conclude that Baja turtles hatch in Japanese waters 10,000 kilometers away. This sounds like convincing statistical evidence unless you realize that many organisms share DNA. For example, humans and chimpanzees share about 98% of their DNA (we share about 75% of our DNA with dogs, for that matter). Since Baja and Japanese turtles come from the same species, it is not surprising that they would share a high percentage of their DNA. Regardless of whether or not you saw this connection, you should have been skeptical of the reference to *juvenile* turtles travelling *10,000* kilometers. Such a lengthy trip by a juvenile animal is unlikely, and calls into question the soundness of the argument.

Answer choice (A): This answer does not impact the argument because no details—DNA or otherwise—are given about the turtles at these nesting sites off the Pacific coast of North America.

Answer choice (B): The fact that Atlantic turtles have nesting and feeding sites no more than 5,000 kilometers apart does not attack the argument because the argument is about *Baja* turtles.

Answer choice (C): This answer attempts to weaken the argument by inducing you to conclude that if the Japanese hatchlings are declining but Baja sites are constant, then the Baja sites cannot be supplied by the Japanese hatchlings. But, the answer choice moves from the number of *hatchlings* to the number of *sites*. Even with a declining number of hatchlings, the number of sites could remain constant, albeit with fewer turtles at each. Because of this possibility, the answer does not undermine the argument.

Answer choice (D): This is the correct answer. The answer shows that all turtles in the argument have the same ninety-five percent DNA, meaning that the Baja turtles did not have to take the 10,000 kilometer trip.

Answer choice (E): The breeding between species was not an issue in the stimulus.

Question #3. December 2003 LSAT, Section 1, #20. The correct answer choice is (B)

The first sentence is a premise, and the second sentence is the conclusion of this argument. To attack this conclusion, look for an answer choice that shows that the exclusion of knowledgeable individuals from scientific or technical issue trials is a fair way of proceeding in these trials.

Answer choice (A): This is an Opposite answer that strengthens the conclusion. If specialized knowledge of these issues makes it more likely that the juror can comprehend the testimony being given, then these individuals should not be excluded from juries, and their exclusion makes trial by jury an unfair means of resolving a dispute.

Answer choice (B): This is the correct answer. If the specialized knowledge is likely to produce a prejudice in a juror, then by all means they should be excluded from the jury. Thus, instead of trial by jury being an unfair means, it is made more fair by the exclusion of these individuals. The answer is a tricky one because most people initially think the answer agrees with the argument. It agrees with the principle of the premise, but not with the conclusion drawn from that premise.

Answer choice (C): This answer simply notes that arbitrators are not a fair means of settling scientific or technical issue debates. This has no impact on the fairness of jury trials involving these same issues.

Answer choice (D): This answer is about the *experts* testifying at scientific or technical issue trials. This information does not attack the claim that jury trials are unfair because of the exclusion of *jurors* with knowledge of these issues.

Answer choice (E): This answer can be eliminated by reasoning similar to that used to eliminate answer choice (D).

Question #4. June 2001 LSAT, Section 1, #12. The correct answer choice is (A)

The conclusion is in the last sentence, that some people "have senses that do not respect the usual boundaries between the five recognized senses." Instead of keeping their senses distinct, these individuals have an overlap.

Incidentally, the condition discussed in the stimulus is not made up: synesthesiacs (or synesthetes) have a real condition known as synesthesia. Regardless of that fact, you must find an answer choice that undermines the conclusion of the argument, something that would suggest their senses do respect the usual boundaries.

Answer choice (A): This is the correct answer. If the synesthesiacs have a systematic impairment in their use of language it may not be that their senses overlap but rather that they lack the ability to properly express themselves. Thus, their claim to taste a banana and see blue might not be a reflection of that actually occurring but rather a reflection of the words they use to describe taste. If so, this would undermine the conclusion that the senses of synesthesiacs do overlap. This is a difficult answer to identify as correct, and less than 50% of test takers are able to do so.

Answer choice (B): The appeal of this answer—and many students keep this as a Contender—is that it suggests that perhaps other senses are operating, and some test takers make the judgment that these additional senses account for the sensory overlap in synesthesiacs. Unfortunately, that judgment is not supported by the answer choice. Not enough information is provided by the answer choice to say what role, if any, is played by these other senses.

Answer choice (C): This is the most popular wrong answer choice. Do not forget to personalize the argument and consider how the author would react if faced with this answer. Would he or she surrender and admit the answer overpowers the argument? Doubtful. The author would probably react to this answer by saying something along these lines, "Exactly. Since all the individuals are synesthesiacs and suffer from the same condition, it is not surprising that there would be patterns in the way the senses overlap. Just as everyone afflicted with emphysema has difficulty breathing, the sensory patterns exhibited by synesthesiacs are just a product of the condition. The fact that their senses do not follow the usual boundaries and do so in certain ways is to be expected." So, instead of surrendering to the answer, the author would indicate that the answer agrees with the conclusion.

Answer choice (D): This answer is out of the scope of the argument. The "legendary" status of synesthesiacs does not shed any light on the operation of their five senses.

Answer choice (E): If anything, this may strengthen the argument by indicating that the synesthesiacs are experiencing some type of phenomenon. Beyond that point, however, no information is given to suggest that their senses do not respect the usual boundaries.

Question #5. October 2001 LSAT, Section 2, #20. The correct answer choice is (A)

The stimulus sets up an interesting argument that appears fairly reasonable. A mastodon skeleton has been found containing a human-made projectile dissimilar to those of the part of Eurasia *closest* to North America and because Eurasians did not settle in North America until shortly before the peak of the Ice Age, the first Eurasian settlers of North America probably came from a *more distant* part of Eurasia than the area nearest North America. To make a very rough analogy using dialects, it is like a resident of Washington, D.C. saying, "The visitors we just met did not sound like they were from Virginia, so they must be from a much more distant part of the U.S." Reading that rough analogy, you can see that the speaker has assumed that the visitors are from the U.S. Of course, that does not have to be the case—they could be from England or France or elsewhere. The same form of assumption has occurred in the argument, and the author has assumed that the *projectile* is of Eurasian origin.

Answer choice (A): This is the correct answer. This answer hurts the argument by indicating that the projectile is apparently not Eurasian, suggesting that the first Eurasian settlers could have come from any part of Eurasia, including the area closest to North America.

Answer choice (B): This is the most attractive wrong answer, but regardless, this answer does not hurt the argument. Some students attempt to conclude that since the people were nomadic, they could have moved to areas farther away and found projectiles like the one in the mastodon. However, even though these individuals remained nomadic, they were apparently nomadic within the area of Eurasia closest to North America because the answer clearly states, "The people who *occupied* the Eurasia area closest to North America..." Hence, they did not necessarily occupy other areas and this answer does not hurt the argument.

Answer choice (C): This Opposite answer supports the argument by showing that the projectile in the mastodon was not a one-time, anomalous occurrence. If other, similar projectiles come to light, then the author's position would be strengthened.

Answer choice (D): This Opposite answer supports the argument by connecting other artifacts of the same age as the projectile to parts of Eurasia more distant than the area of Eurasia closest to North America. This adds further evidence to the idea that the first Eurasian settlers of North America probably came from a more distant part of Eurasia than the area nearest North America.

Answer choice (E): This Opposite answer supports the argument by indicating that the part of Eurasia closest to North America may not have been inhabited just before the Ice Age. If this area was uninhabitable, then it is more likely that settlers coming to North America came from more distant regions.

Weaken Problem Set Answer Key

Question #6. October 2001 LSAT, Section 1, #8. The correct answer choice is (E)

This is a great separator question, and approximately one in three students answers this question correctly. However, some students are able to annihilate this question because they see a reference in the first line that raises an important issue that goes unanswered. That reference is to lobsters "eaten by humans." The argument asserts that diverting the sewage in the harbor is a moot point because hardly any lobsters live long enough to be harmed by the diseases caused by the sewage. This may be, but what about the humans who eat the lobsters that live in the sewage-contaminated environment? The author fails to address this point.

The conclusion of the argument is near the end: "the proposal is pointless," and this is based on the premise that "hardly any lobsters live long enough to be harmed by those diseases."

Answer choice (A): The argument is based on the sewage contamination of the harbor. Although other contaminants may be present, they are not addressed by the argument, and thus this answer does not undermine the author's position.

Answer choice (B): This answer has no impact because the argument is about lobsters that are caught *in the harbor*. So, while lobsters in the open ocean may live longer, the author's point about lobsters in the harbor not living long enough to contract a gill disease is untouched.

Answer choice (C): The issue is not breeding frequency but longevity. So, while we are pleased to hear that lobsters in sewage-contaminated waters breed frequently, this fact does not impact an argument based on the age and disease contraction.

Answer choice (D): Although whether the lobsters contract a gill disease is a critical issue in the argument, the method of determining whether a lobster has a disease is not a critical issue. Again, keep in mind the heart of the argument:

> Premise: "hardly any lobsters live long enough to be harmed by those diseases."
> Conclusion: "the proposal [to reroute harbor sewage] is pointless."

Nothing in that argument concerns the detection of the gill diseases.

Answer choice (E): This is the correct answer. As discussed above, the author fails to address the effect of the contaminated lobsters on humans who consume them, and this answer attacks that hole. If humans become ill as a result of eating lobsters with gill diseases, and gill diseases are more likely to arise when the lobsters live in the sewage-contaminated waters, then the conclusion that the proposal is pointless is incorrect.

CHAPTER EIGHT: CAUSE AND EFFECT REASONING

What is Causality?

When examining events, people naturally seek to explain why things happened. This search often results in cause and effect reasoning, which asserts or denies that one thing causes another, or that one thing is caused by another. On the LSAT, cause and effect reasoning appears in many Logical Reasoning problems, often in the conclusion where the author mistakenly claims that one event causes another. For example:

> Last week IBM announced a quarterly deficit and the stock market dropped 10 points. Thus, IBM's announcement must have caused the drop.

Like the above conclusion, most causal conclusions are flawed because there can be alternate explanations for the stated relationship: another cause could account for the effect; a third event could have caused both the stated cause and effect; the situation may in fact be reversed; the events may be related but not causally; or the entire occurrence could be the result of chance.

In short, causality occurs when one event is said to make another occur. The *cause* is the event that makes the other occur; the *effect* is the event that follows from the cause. By definition, the cause must occur before the effect, and the cause is the "activator" or "ignitor" in the relationship. The effect always happens at some point in time after the cause.

How to Recognize Causality

A cause and effect relationship has a signature characteristic—the cause *makes* the effect happen. Thus, there is an identifiable type of expression used to indicate that a causal relationship is present. The list on the following page contains a number of the phrases used by the makers of the LSAT to introduce causality, and you should be on the lookout for those when reading Logical Reasoning stimuli.

As mentioned before, this is a book about LSAT logic, not general philosophy. Therefore, we will not go into an analysis of David Hume's *Inquiry* or Mill's Methods (both of which address causality) because although those discussions are interesting, they do not apply to the LSAT.

The following terms often introduce a cause and effect relationship:

caused by
because of
responsible for
reason for
leads to
induced by
promoted by
determined by
produced by
product of
played a role in
was a factor in
is an effect of

Be sure to memorize this list!

Because of the variety of the English language, there are many alternate phrases that can introduce causality. However, those phrases would all have the similar characteristic of suggesting that one event *made* another occur.

The Difference Between Causality and Conditionality

Many people confuse causal reasoning with conditional reasoning, but the two are entirely separate! Here are several key differences:

Knowing the difference between conditionality and causality can help you determine which one is present when none of the usual indicator words appear.

1. The chronology of the two events can differ.

    In cause and effect statements there is an implied temporal relationship: the cause must happen first and the effect must happen at some point in time after the cause.

    In sufficient and necessary statements there is no implied temporal relationship: the sufficient condition can happen before, at the same time, or after the necessary condition.

2. The connection between the events is different.

    In cause and effect statements the events are related in a direct way: "She swerved to avoid hitting the dog and that caused her to hit the tree." The cause physically *makes* the effect happen.

    In conditional statements the sufficient and necessary conditions are often related directly, but they do not have to be: "Before the war can end, I must eat this ice cream cone." The sufficient condition does not make the necessary condition happen, it just *indicates* that it must occur.

3. The language used to introduce the statements is different.

Because of item 2, the words that introduce each type of relationship are very different. Causal indicators are active, almost powerful words, whereas most conditional indicators do not possess those traits.

Causality in the Conclusion versus Causality in the Premises

Causal statements can be found in the premise or conclusion of an argument. If the causal statement is the conclusion, then the reasoning is flawed. If the causal statement is the premise, then the argument may be flawed, but not because of the causal statement. Because of this difference, one of the critical issues in determining whether flawed causal reasoning is present is identifying where in the argument the causal assertion is made. The classic mistaken cause and effect reasoning we will refer to throughout this book occurs when a causal assertion is made in the *conclusion*, or the conclusion presumes a causal relationship. Let us examine the difference between an argument with a causal premise and one with a causal conclusion.

This is an argument with a causal conclusion:

Premise: In North America, people drink a lot of milk.

Premise: There is a high frequency of cancer in North America.

Conclusion: Therefore, drinking milk causes cancer.

In this case, the author takes two events that occur together and concludes that one causes the other. This conclusion is in error for the reasons discussed on the first page of this chapter.

If a causal claim is made in the premises, however, then no *causal* reasoning error exists in the argument (of course, the argument may be flawed in other ways). As mentioned previously, the makers of the LSAT tend to allow premises to go unchallenged (they are more concerned with the reasoning that follows from a premise) and it is considered acceptable for an author to begin his argument by stating a causal relationship and then continuing from there:

Premise: Drinking milk causes cancer.

Premise: The residents of North America drink a lot of milk.

Conclusion: Therefore, in North America there is a high frequency of cancer among the residents.

The second example is considered valid reasoning because the author takes a causal principle and follows it to its logical conclusion. Generally, causal reasoning occurs in a format similar to the first example, but there are LSAT problems similar to the second example.

In the LSAT world, when a cause and effect statement appears as the conclusion, the conclusion is flawed. In the real world that may not be the case because a preponderance of evidence can be gathered or visual evidence can be used to prove a relationship.

Situations That Can Lead to Errors of Causality

There are two scenarios that tend to lead to causal conclusions in Logical Reasoning questions:

1. One event occurs before another

    When one event occurs before another event, many people fall into the trap of assuming that the first event caused the second event. This does not have to be the case, as shown by the following famous example:

    > Every morning the rooster crows before the sun rises. Hence, the rooster must cause the sun to rise.

    The example contains a ludicrous conclusion, and shows why it is dangerous to simply assume that the first event must have caused the second event.

2. Two (or more) events occur at the same time

    When two events occur simultaneously, many people assume that one event caused the other. While one event could have caused the other, the two events could be the result of a third event, or the two events could simply be correlated without one causing the other.

    The following example shows how a third event can cause both events:

    > The consumption of ice cream has been found to correlate with the murder rate. Therefore, consuming ice cream must cause one to be more likely to commit murder.

    As you might imagine, the conclusion of the example does not have to be true (yes, go ahead and eat that Ben and Jerry's!), and the two events can be explained as the effects of a single cause: hot weather. When the weather is warmer, ice cream consumption and the murder rate tend to rise (this example is actually true, especially for large cities).

If you have taken a logic course, you will recognize the first scenario produces the *Post Hoc, Ergo Propter Hoc* fallacy.

In this example, the two events could simply be correlated. A positive correlation is a relationship where the two values move together. A negative correlation is one where the two values move in opposite directions, such as with age and eyesight (the older you get, the worse your eyesight gets).

The Central Assumption of Causal Conclusions

Understanding the assumption that is at the heart of a causal conclusion is essential to knowing why certain answers will be correct or incorrect. Most students assume that the LSAT makes basic assumptions that are similar to the real world; this is untrue and is a dangerous mistake to make.

When we discuss causality in the real world, there is an inherent understanding that a given cause is just one possible cause of the effect, and that there are other causes that could also produce the same effect. This is reasonable because we have the ability to observe a variety of cause and effect scenarios, and experience shows us that different actions can have the same result. The makers of the LSAT do *not* think this way. When an LSAT speaker concludes that one occurrence caused another, that speaker also assumes that the stated cause is the *only* possible cause of the effect and that consequently the stated cause will *always* produce the effect. This assumption is incredibly extreme and far-reaching, and often leads to surprising answer choices that would appear incorrect unless you understand this assumption. Consider the following example:

Understanding this assumption is absolutely critical to your LSAT success. The makers of the test will closely examine your knowledge of this idea, especially in Strengthen and Weaken questions.

Premise:	Average temperatures are higher at the equator than in any other area.
Premise:	Individuals living at or near the equator tend to have lower per-capita incomes than individuals living elsewhere.
Conclusion:	Therefore, higher average temperatures cause lower per-capita incomes.

This argument is a classic flawed causal argument wherein two premises with a basic connection (living at the equator) are used as the basis of a conclusion that states that the connection is such that one of the elements actually makes the other occur. The conclusion is flawed because it is not necessary that the one element caused the other to occur: the two could simply be correlated in some way or the connection could be random.

In the real world, we would tend to look at an argument like the one above and think that while the conclusion is possible, there are also other things that could cause the lower per-capita income of individuals residing at or near the equator, such as a lack of natural resources. *This is not how speakers on the LSAT view the relationship.* When an LSAT speaker makes an argument like the one above, he or she believes that the *only* cause is the one stated in the conclusion and that there are *no other* causes that can create that particular effect. Why is this the case? Because for an LSAT speaker to come to that conclusion, he or she must have weighed and considered every possible alternative and then rejected each one. Otherwise, why would the speaker draw the given conclusion? In the final analysis, to say that higher average temperatures cause lower per-capita incomes the speaker must also believe that nothing else could be the cause of lower per-capita incomes.

Thus, in every argument with a causal conclusion that appears on the LSAT, the speaker believes that the stated cause is in fact the only cause and all other theoretically possible causes are not, in fact, actual causes. This is an incredibly powerful assumption, and the results of this assumption are most evident in Weaken, Strengthen, and Assumption questions. We will discuss this effect on Strengthen and Assumption questions in a later chapter. Following is brief analysis of the effect of this assumption on Weaken questions.

How to Attack a Causal Conclusion

Whenever you identify a causal relationship in the conclusion of an LSAT problem, immediately prepare to either weaken or strengthen the argument. Attacking a cause and effect relationship in Weaken questions almost always consists of performing one of the following tasks:

A. Find an alternate cause for the stated effect

   Because the author believes there is only one cause, identifying another cause weakens the conclusion.

B. Show that even when the cause occurs, the effect does not occur

   This type of answer often appears in the form of a counterexample. Because the author believes that the cause always produces the effect, any scenario where the cause occurs and the effect does not weakens the conclusion.

C. Show that although the effect occurs, the cause did not occur

   This type of answer often appears in the form of a counterexample. Because the author believes that the effect is always produced by the same cause, any scenario where the effect occurs and the cause does not weakens the conclusion.

D. Show that the stated relationship is reversed

   Because the author believes that the cause and effect relationship is correctly stated, showing that the relationship is backwards (the claimed effect is actually the cause of the claimed cause) undermines the conclusion.

Answer choices that otherwise appear irrelevant will suddenly be obviously correct when you understand the central causal assumption.

Stimuli containing causal arguments are often followed by Weaken, Strengthen, Assumption, or Flaw questions.

E. Show that a statistical problem exists with the data used to make the causal statement

If the data used to make a causal statement is in error, then the validity of the causal claim is in question.

Diagramming Causality

Like conditional statements, causal statements can be quickly and easily represented by an arrow diagram. However, because causal and conditional diagrams represent entirely different relationships, we use designators ("C" for cause and "E" for effect) above the terms when diagramming (and, in corresponding fashion, we use "S" for sufficient and "N" for necessary above the terms when diagramming conditional statements). We use these designators in the book to make the meaning of the diagram clear. During the LSAT, students should not use the designators (they just use the arrow diagram) because they want to go as fast as possible and they can remember if they have a conditional or causal argument while completing the problem.

Here is an example of a causal diagram:

Statement: "Smoking causes cancer."

S = smoking
C = cancer

$$\underline{C} \qquad \underline{E}$$

$$S \longrightarrow C$$

Although the diagram looks the same as a conditional diagram, the two are different for the reasons described in "The Difference Between Causality and Conditionality" section earlier in this chapter.

During the LSAT, the choice to create an arrow diagram for a causal statement is yours.

Two Cause and Effect Problems Analyzed

Please take a moment to complete the following problem:

1. People with high blood pressure are generally more nervous and anxious than people who do not have high blood pressure. This fact shows that this particular combination of personality traits—the so-called hypertensive personality—is likely to cause a person with these traits to develop high blood pressure.

    nervous and anxious → high BP

    The reasoning in the argument is most vulnerable to criticism on the grounds that the argument

    (A) fails to define the term "hypertensive personality"
    (B) presupposes that people have permanent personality traits
    (C) simply restates the claim that there is a "hypertensive personality" without providing evidence to support that claim
    (D) takes a correlation between personality traits and high blood pressure as proof that the traits cause high blood pressure
    (E) focuses on nervousness and anxiety only, ignoring other personality traits that people with high blood pressure might have

Flaw in the Reasoning questions will be covered in Chapter Thirteen.

This is a Flaw in the Reasoning question and although we have not yet discussed this question type, based on your knowledge of causal reasoning we can proceed without a detailed understanding of the question form. You should have identified the following argument structure in the question above:

Premise: People with high blood pressure are generally more nervous and anxious than people who do not have high blood pressure.

Premise: This particular combination of personality traits is called the hypertensive personality.

Conclusion: The hypertensive personality is likely to cause a person to develop high blood pressure.

The premises indicate that certain individuals have both high blood pressure and the hypertensive personality. From this information we cannot draw any conclusions, but the author makes the classic LSAT error of concluding that one of the conditions causes the other. Your job is to find the answer that describes this error of reasoning.

From the "Situations That Can Lead to Errors of Causality" discussion, the scenario in this stimulus falls under item 2—"Two (or more) events occur at the same time." As described in that section, "While one event could have caused the other, the two events could be the result of a third event, or the two events could simply be correlated without one causing the other." Thus, you should search either for an answer that states that the author forgot that a third event could have caused the two events or that the author mistook correlation for causation. Answer choice (D) describes the latter.

Answer choice (A): This is an Opposite answer because the stimulus defines the hypertensive personality as one with the traits of nervousness and anxiety.

Answer choice (B): The permanence of the traits is not an issue in the stimulus.

Answer choice (C): Although the argument does act as described in this answer choice, this is not an error. On the LSAT, authors have the right to make premises that contain certain claims. Remember, the focus is not on the premises but where the author goes with the argument once a premise is created.

Answer choice (D): This is the correct answer. The conclusion can be diagrammed as:

HP = hypertensive personality
HBP = high blood pressure

$$\underline{C} \qquad\qquad \underline{E}$$
$$HP \longrightarrow HBP$$

This answer choice describes a classic error of causality: two events occurring simultaneously are mistakenly interpreted to be in a causal relationship. There are many other possibilities for the arrangement: the two events could be caused by a third event (for example, genetics could cause both a hypertensive personality and high blood pressure), the events could be reversed (the high blood pressure could actually cause the hypertensive personality), or there may be situations where the two do not occur together.

Answer choice (E): Although the argument does act as described in this answer choice, this is not an error. The author is allowed to focus on nervousness and anxiety to the exclusion of other traits. To analogize, imagine a speaker says, "The Kansas City Royals have bad pitching and this makes them a bad team." The Kansas City Royals might also wear blue, but the speaker is not obligated to mention that trait when discussing why the Royals are a bad baseball team. In much the same way, the author of this stimulus is not obligated to mention other traits people with high blood pressure may have.

Please take a moment to complete the following problem:

2. High school students who feel that they are not succeeding in high school often drop out before graduating and go to work. Last year, however, the city's high school dropout rate was significantly lower than the previous year's rate. This is encouraging evidence that the program instituted two years ago to improve the morale of high school students has begun to take effect to reduce dropouts.

Which one of the following, if true about the last year, most seriously weakens the argument?

(A) There was a recession that caused a high level of unemployment in the city.

(B) The morale of students who dropped out of high school had been low even before they reached high school.

(C) As in the preceding year, more high school students remained in school than dropped out.

(D) High schools in the city established placement offices to assist their graduates in obtaining employment.

(E) The antidropout program was primarily aimed at improving students' morale in those high schools with the highest dropout rates.

The argument concludes that a program instituted two years ago to increase morale has ultimately caused the recent decrease in high school dropouts. You must always recognize a causal conclusion when one is presented to you! Whenever you encounter a causal conclusion, ask yourself if the relationship must be as stated by the author or if another explanation can be found.

A good portion of the LSAT is about recognition of existing patterns. Recognizing these patterns in a stimulus will help you increase your speed and accuracy.

In simplified form, the conclusion appears as follows:

P = program to raise high school morale
RD = reduction in dropouts

$$\underline{C} \qquad \underline{E}$$

$$P \longrightarrow RD$$

Regardless of the question asked, this assessment is helpful. The question stem asks you to weaken the argument, and according to the "How to Attack a Causal Conclusion" section there are five main avenues of attack you should be prepared to encounter. The correct answer, (A), falls into one of the most frequently occurring of those categories—the alternate cause.

Answer choice (A): This is the correct answer. The answer attacks the conclusion by introducing an alternate cause: it was not the morale program that led to a decrease in high dropouts, but rather the fact that fewer jobs were available for individuals contemplating dropping out of high school. The job availability factor is important because the first sentence of the stimulus indicates that high school students who drop out go to work. Thus, if a recession led to a high level of unemployment, this could cause high school students to rethink dropping out and stay in school.

Answer choice (B): At best, the answer choice is irrelevant. At worst, this answer confirms that some of the high school students had low morale, and in that sense, the answer strengthens the argument.

Answer choice (C): The argument indicates that the dropout rate is *lower* relative to the preceding year; there is no claim that the dropout rate ever exceeded the retention rate. Thus, to suggest that more students stayed in school than dropped out has no effect on the argument.

Answer choice (D): This is a Shell Game answer. The stimulus refers to high school dropouts. This answer choice refers to high school *graduates*.

Answer choice (E): The argument uses information about the city's *overall* dropout rate. Therefore, the target high schools of the antidropout program are irrelevant.

Causal Reasoning Review

Causality occurs when one event is said to make another occur. The *cause* is the event that makes the other occur; the *effect* is the event that follows from the cause.

Most causal conclusions are flawed because there can be alternate explanations for the stated relationship: some other cause could account for the effect; some third event could have caused both the stated cause and effect; the situation may in fact be reversed; the events may be related but not causally; or the entire occurrence could be the result of chance.

Many people confuse causal reasoning with conditional reasoning. Although they can appear similar, the two are entirely separate. Here are several key differences:

As with conditional statements, causal statements can be linked together, although causal chains rarely exceed three terms.

1. The chronology of the two events can differ.

   In cause and effect statements there is an implied temporal relationship: the cause must happen first and the effect must happen at some time after the cause. In sufficient and necessary statements there is no implied temporal relationship: the sufficient condition can happen before, at the same time, or after the necessary condition.

2. The connection between the events is different.

   In cause and effect statements the events are related in a direct way: "She swerved to avoid hitting the dog and that caused her to hit the tree." The cause physically *makes* the effect happen. In conditional statements the sufficient and necessary conditions are often related directly, but they do not have to be: "Before the war can end, I must eat this ice cream cone." The sufficient condition does not make the necessary condition happen, it just *indicates* that it must occur.

3. The language used to introduce the statements is different.

   Because of item number 2, the words that introduce each type of relationship are very different. Causal indicators are active, almost powerful words, whereas most conditional indicators do not possess those traits.

Causal statements can be used in the premise or conclusion of an argument. If the causal statement is the conclusion, then the reasoning is flawed. If the causal statement is a premise, then the argument may be flawed, but not because of the causal statement.

There are two scenarios that tend to lead to causal conclusions in Logical Reasoning questions:

1. One event occurs before another
2. Two (or more) events occur at the same time

When an LSAT speaker concludes that one occurrence caused another, that speaker also assumes that the stated cause is the *only* possible cause of the effect and that consequently the stated cause will *always* produce the effect.

In Weaken questions, attacking a cause and effect relationship almost always consists of performing one of the following tasks:

A. Find an alternate cause for the stated effect
B. Show that even when the cause occurs, the effect does not occur
C. Show that although the effect occurs, the cause did not occur
D. Show that the stated relationship is in fact reversed
E. Show a statistical problem exists with the data used to make the causal statement

Final Note

Causal reasoning occurs in many different question types, and the discussion in this chapter is designed to acquaint you with situations that produce causal statements, how to identify a causal statement, and some of the ways that causality appears in LSAT problems. We will revisit these concepts as we discuss other question types.

As you examine LSAT questions, remember that causal reasoning may or may not be present in the stimulus. Your job is to recognize causality when it appears and react accordingly. If causality is not present, you do not need to worry about it.

On the following page is a short problem set to help you work with some of the ideas. The problem set is followed by an answer key with explanations. Good luck!

Causal Reasoning Problem Set

The following questions are drawn from actual LSATs. Please complete the problem set and review the answer key and explanations. *Answers on Page 214*

1. The number of airplanes equipped with a new anticollision device has increased steadily during the past two years. During the same period, it has become increasingly common for key information about an airplane's altitude and speed to disappear suddenly from air traffic controllers' screens. The new anticollision device, which operates at the same frequency as air traffic radar, is therefore responsible for the sudden disappearance of key information.

   Which one of the following, if true, most seriously weakens the argument?

   (A) The new anticollision device has already prevented a considerable number of mid-air collisions.
   (B) It was not until the new anticollision device was introduced that key information first began disappearing suddenly from controllers' screens.
   (C) The new anticollision device is scheduled to be moved to a different frequency within the next two to three months.
   (D) Key information began disappearing from controllers' screens three months before the new anticollision device was first tested.
   (E) The sudden disappearance of key information from controllers' screens has occurred only at relatively large airports.

2. Most antidepressant drugs cause weight gain. While dieting can help reduce the amount of weight gained while taking such antidepressants, some weight gain is unlikely to be preventable.

   The information above most strongly supports which one of the following?

   (A) A physician should not prescribe any antidepressant drug for a patient if that patient is overweight.
   (B) People who are trying to lose weight should not ask their doctors for an antidepressant drug.
   (C) At least some patients taking antidepressant drugs gain weight as a result of taking them.
   (D) The weight gain experienced by patients taking antidepressant drugs should be attributed to lack of dieting.
   (E) All patients taking antidepressant drugs should diet to maintain their weight.

3. Violent crime in this town is becoming a serious problem. Compared to last year, local law enforcement agencies have responded to 17 percent more calls involving violent crimes, showing that the average citizen of this town is more likely than ever to become a victim of a violent crime.

   Which one of the following, if true, most seriously weakens the argument?

   (A) The town's overall crime rate appears to have risen slightly this year compared to the same period last year.
   (B) In general, persons under the age of 65 are less likely to be victims of violent crimes than persons over the age of 65.
   (C) As a result of the town's community outreach programs, more people than ever are willing to report violent crimes to the proper authorities.
   (D) In response to worries about violent crime, the town has recently opened a community center providing supervised activities for teenagers.
   (E) Community officials have shown that a relatively small number of repeat offenders commit the majority of violent crimes in the town.

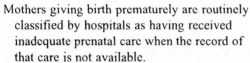

4. Medical researcher: As expected, records covering the last four years of ten major hospitals indicate that babies born prematurely were more likely to have low birth weights and to suffer from health problems than were babies not born prematurely. These records also indicate that mothers who had received adequate prenatal care were less likely to have low birth weight babies than were mothers who had received inadequate prenatal care. Adequate prenatal care, therefore, significantly decreases the risk of low birth weight babies.

Which one of the following, if true, most weakens the medical researcher's argument?

(A) The hospital records indicate that many babies that are born with normal birth weights are born to mothers who had inadequate prenatal care.

(B) Mothers giving birth prematurely are routinely classified by hospitals as having received inadequate prenatal care when the record of that care is not available.

(C) The hospital records indicate that low birth weight babies were routinely classified as having been born prematurely.

(D) Some babies not born prematurely, whose mothers received adequate prenatal care, have low birth weights.

(E) Women who receive adequate prenatal care are less likely to give birth prematurely than are women who do not receive adequate prenatal care.

5. Researcher: People with certain personality disorders have more theta brain waves than those without such disorders. But my data show that the amount of one's theta brain waves increases while watching TV. So watching too much TV increases one's risk of developing personality disorders.

A questionable aspect of the reasoning above is that it

(A) uses the phrase "personality disorders" ambiguously

(B) fails to define the phrase "theta brain waves"

(C) takes a correlation to imply a causal connection

(D) draws a conclusion from an unrepresentative sample of data

(E) infers that watching TV is a consequence of a personality disorder

6. Unlike newspapers in the old days, today's newspapers and televised news programs are full of stories about murders and assaults in our city. One can only conclude from this change that violent crime is now out of control, and, to be safe from personal attack, one should not leave one's home except for absolute necessities.

Which one of the following, if true, would cast the most serious doubt on the conclusion?

(A) Newspapers and televised news programs have more comprehensive coverage of violent crime than newspapers did in the old days.

(B) National data show that violent crime is out of control everywhere, not just in the author's city.

(C) Police records show that people experience more violent crimes in their own neighborhoods than they do outside their neighborhoods.

(D) Murder comprised a larger proportion of violent crimes in the old days than it does today.

(E) News magazines play a more important role today in informing the public about crime than they did in the old days.

Causal Reasoning Problem Set Answer Key

All answer keys in this book indicate the source of the question by giving the month and year the LSAT was originally administered, the Logical Reasoning section number, and the question number within that section. Each LSAT has two Logical Reasoning sections, and so the Section 1 and Section 2 designators will refer to the first or second Logical Reasoning section in the test, not the physical section number of the booklet.

Question #1. Weaken-CE. December 2000 LSAT, Section 1, #25. The correct answer choice is (D)

The stimulus commits the classic error of assuming that because two events occur simultaneously that one must cause the other. The phrase used to indicate causality is "responsible for."

> D = anticollision device
> SD = sudden disappearance of key information

$$\underline{C} \qquad\qquad \underline{E}$$
$$D \longrightarrow SD$$

The question stem asks you to weaken the argument, and according to the "How to Attack a Causal Conclusion" section you should be on the lookout for one of several primary methods of attacking the argument.

Answer choice (A): This answer presents *another effect* of the cause, but this additional effect does not weaken the argument. To analogize this answer to a different argument, imagine a scenario where a speaker concludes that playing football makes a person more prone to sustaining a leg injury. Would suggesting that playing football makes a person more prone to a head injury (another effect) undermine the first statement? No.

Answer choice (B): This is an Opposite answer that supports the conclusion. By showing that the key information did not disappear prior to the appearance of the anticollision device, the argument is strengthened because the likelihood that the device is at fault is increased.

Answer choice (C): This information has no effect on determining if the device causes the information to disappear from the screen because it references an event that has yet to occur.

Answer choice (D): This is the correct answer, and this answer falls into the third category for weakening a causal argument: "Show that although the effect exists, the cause did not occur." In this instance, the effect of information disappearing from the screen occurred prior to the creation of the supposed causal agent, the anticollision device.

Answer choice (E): This answer choice has no impact on the argument. We cannot make a judgment based on the size of the airport because the argument did not mention airport size or anything directly related to airport size.

Question #2. Must-CE. December 2001 LSAT, Section 1, #4. The correct answer choice is (C)

The causal relationship in this problem appears in the premise, and the argument is structured as follows:

Premise: Most antidepressant drugs cause weight gain.

Premise: Dieting can help reduce the amount of weight gained while taking such antidepressants

Conclusion: Some weight gain is unlikely to be preventable.

Note that the causal premise specifically states that "most" antidepressants cause weight gain, not necessarily all antidepressants. Also, the second premise specifically refers to antidepressants causing weight gain (the use of "such" indicates this). The second premise also indicates that the *amount gained* can be reduced, not that dieting can stop weight gain. Perhaps the antidepressants cause a twenty pound weight gain, but dieting can reduce that to a ten pound total gain.

The question stem is a Must Be True, and thus you must accept the stimulus information and find an answer that is proven by that information.

Answer choice (A): This is an Exaggerated answer. The stimulus indicates that *most* antidepressants cause weight gain, leaving open the possibility that some do not. This answer choice references *any* antidepressant drug. Further, the stimulus does not address the role of a physician or the advisability of prescribing certain drugs under certain conditions. The benefits of prescribing an antidepressant that causes weight gain to an overweight patient may well outweigh the negatives (pun intended).

Answer choice (B): This is also an Exaggerated answer. The stimulus allows for antidepressants that do not cause weight gain.

Answer choice (C): This is the correct answer. Some individuals taking antidepressants that cause weight gain will gain weight even though dieting can reduce the amount of the gain.

Answer choice (D): This is an Opposite answer. The stimulus and correct answer both indicate that people taking the weight gain-causing antidepressants will gain weight regardless of whether they diet. Thus, the weight gain cannot be attributed to a lack of dieting.

Answer choice (E): This answer is too strong. Not all patients necessarily take antidepressants that cause weight gain, so those that do not might not need to diet to maintain their weight. Also, some patients who do take weight gain-causing antidepressants might be too thin for their own good and could benefit from a weight gain-causing antidepressant.

Question #3. Weaken-CE. December 2003 LSAT, Section 2, #6. The correct answer choice is (C)

The premise contains information concerning a rise in the number of calls involving violent crimes compared to last year. This is where smart LSAT reading comes into play: does the argument say there is more crime, or does it say there are more *calls* reporting crime? Recognizing the difference is critical for successfully solving this problem. The conclusion about citizens being more likely to be victimized by a violent crime indicates the author believes the following causal relationship:

> GNC = greater number of violent crimes
> MC = more calls involving violent crimes

C   E

GNC $\longrightarrow$ MC

Literally, the author believes that there are more violent crimes and therefore the police are responding to more violent crime calls.

The question stem asks you to weaken the argument, and the correct answer falls into one of the five basic methods for weakening a causal argument.

Answer choice (A): This is an Opposite answer that strengthens the argument.

Answer choice (B): Because the argument is about "the average citizen of this town," information about victims of a certain age is not relevant.

Answer choice (C): This is the correct answer. By showing that people are more willing to report crimes (and thus call them in for response), an alternate cause for the rise in the number of calls is given.

Answer choice (D): This answer only addresses an effect of the concern over crime, and does not address the causal relationship that underlies the argument.

Answer choice (E): This answer does not address a possible rise in crime or the reasons for the rise in responses to calls involving violent crime.

Question #4. Weaken-CE. October 1999 LSAT, Section 2, #24. The correct answer choice is (B)

The premises contain correlations, and the conclusion makes a causal claim:

PC = adequate prenatal care
DR = decrease risk of low birth weight babies

$$\underline{C} \qquad\qquad \underline{E}$$

$$PC \longrightarrow DR$$

The question stem asks you to weaken the argument, and the correct answer falls into one of the five basic methods for weakening a causal argument.

Answer choice (A): The conclusion specifically states that mothers who had received adequate prenatal care were *less likely* to have low birth weight babies than mothers who had received inadequate prenatal care. Thus, although mothers who received inadequate prenatal care have a higher likelihood of having low birth weight babies, this likelihood still allows for many babies to be born of normal weight. In a later chapter we will explore the ways the LSAT uses numbers and statistics to confuse test takers, but for now, consider this analogy: The Detroit Tigers are more likely to lose a baseball game than any other team, but even so, they can still win a number of games. In the same way, the aforementioned mothers may be more likely to have low birth weight babies, but they can still give birth to babies of normal weight. Hence, answer choice (A) does not attack the argument.

Answer choice (B): This is the correct answer. The answer choice falls into the category of "Showing a statistical problem exists with the data used to make the causal statement." By indicating that all mothers without prenatal care records are automatically classified as mothers receiving inadequate prenatal care, the answer undermines the relationship in the argument because the data used to make the conclusion is unreliable.

Answer choice (C): The conclusion is about low birth weight babies, not premature babies. Even if low birth weight babies were routinely classified as premature, that would not affect the conclusion.

Answer choice (D): Similar to answer choice (A), the likelihoods discussed in the stimulus allow for this possibility. Hence, this answer cannot hurt the argument.

Answer choice (E): If anything, this answer strengthens the argument since it shows that adequate prenatal care has a powerful positive effect.

Causal Reasoning Problem Set Answer Key

Question #5. Flaw-CE. October 2003 LSAT, Section 2, #13. The correct answer choice is (C)

This Flaw in the Reasoning problem is very similar to the Flaw problem discussed in the chapter (problem #1). A correlation involving theta waves, TV watching, and personality disorders is presented in the premises, and then the author concludes that watching too much TV causes a rise in the risk of developing a personality disorder to rise.

Answer choice (A): Although "personality disorders" are left largely undefined (which is acceptable), the term is not used ambiguously.

Answer choice (B): This is not an error because the author is not obligated to define theta brain waves in order to make the argument understandable.

Answer choice (C): This is the correct answer.

Answer choice (D): There is no information to prove that the sample of data used was unrepresentative. Although the researcher says, "my data show..." it is possible the researcher's data are extensive and representative.

Answer choice (E): This is a Shell Game answer because the researcher infers that the reverse is true.

Question #6. Weaken-CE. December 2000 LSAT, Section 2, #7. The correct answer choice is (A)

The heart of the argument is a causal claim that the reason today's newspapers are full of stories about violent crime is that violent crime has now risen to a point where it is out of control.

> MVC = more violent crimes
> NFS = more news stories about violent crimes

$$\underline{C} \longrightarrow \underline{E}$$
$$\text{MVC} \qquad \text{NFS}$$

On the basis of this relationship, the author adds for good measure that one should not leave one's home!

From a form standpoint, this problem is very similar to #3 in this problem set. This is one of the keys to the LSAT—you must recognize the patterns that exist within the test and then capitalize on them when they appear. All the problems in the set include causality. From this point on, you must recognize causality when it appears and then properly respond to it. Your ability to recognize these forms will give you an advantage in both speed and confidence, and ultimately raise your score.

Answer choice (A): This is the correct answer. This answer presents an alternate cause to the scenario presented above, namely that more comprehensive coverage leads to more news stories, not more violent crime.

Causal Reasoning Problem Set Answer Key

Answer choice (B): This Opposite answer strengthens the argument.

Answer choice (C): This answer strengthens the argument, if anything.

Answer choice (D): This is an answer that many people select. The answer is incorrect because it fails to account for other violent crimes beside murder. Indicating that murder comprised a higher percentage of violent crimes in the old days than today does not address the total number of crimes being committed. Since the argument concludes that "*violent crime* is now *out of control*," this answer is incorrect. Consider the following example:

	Old Days	Today
Total number of murders	3	1,000
Total number of violent crimes	4	50,000
Percentage of violent crimes that are murders	75%	2%

In this example, although murder was a higher proportion of the violent crimes in the old days, today there are many more violent crimes. This shows that the scenario in the answer choice does not have to undermine the argument. In the chapter on Numbers and Percentages we will revisit the concept of proportion versus total numbers and discuss how the test makers use numerical ideas to attack test takers.

Answer choice (E): The role played by magazines in informing the public does not address why there are so many stories about violent crime or if violent crime is now out of control.

220

CHAPTER NINE: STRENGTHEN, JUSTIFY THE CONCLUSION, AND ASSUMPTION QUESTIONS

The Second Family

Second Family Information Model:

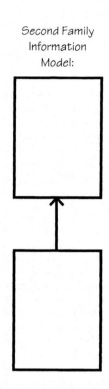

With this chapter, we begin our exposition of the Second Family of questions. Three of the question types within this family—Strengthen, Justify, and Assumption—are considered to be among the hardest Logical Reasoning question types. These three question types are closely related and will be examined consecutively in this chapter. The remaining Second Family question type—Resolve the Paradox—will be examined in the next chapter.

Although all Second Family question types are related by their shared information model, there are distinct differences between each question type that ultimately determine the exact nature of the correct answer. Your performance on these questions will depend on your ability to distinguish each question type and understand the task you must fulfill.

Some students compare the Second Family information model diagram to the Third Family (Weaken) model and assume the two groups are exact opposites. While Strengthen and Weaken questions require you to perform opposite tasks, there are many similarities between the two types in terms of how information is used in each question. Assumption and Justify questions are variations on the Strengthen theme.

In addition to the Primary Objectives, keep these fundamental rules in mind when approaching Strengthen, Justify the Conclusion, and Assumption questions:

1. The stimulus will contain an argument. Because you are being asked about the author's reasoning, and reasoning requires a conclusion, an argument will always be present. In order to maximize your chances of success you must identify, isolate, and assess the premises and the conclusion of the argument. Only by understanding the structure of the argument can you gain the perspective necessary to understand the author's position.

2. Focus on the conclusion. Almost all correct answer choices impact the conclusion. The more you know about the specifics of the conclusion, the better armed you will be to differentiate between correct and incorrect answers.

3. The information in the stimulus is suspect. There are often reasoning

errors present, and you must read the argument very carefully in order to know how to shore up the argument.

4. These questions often yield strong prephrases. Make sure you actively consider the range of possible answers before proceeding to the answer choices.

5. The answer choices are accepted as given, even if they include "new" information. Like Weaken questions, the answer choices to the problems in this chapter can bring into consideration information outside of or tangential to the stimulus. Just because a fact or idea is not mentioned in the stimulus is *not* grounds for dismissing an answer choice.

By following the Primary Objectives and focusing on the points above, you will maximize your chances for success on these questions.

The Difference Between Strengthen, Justify the Conclusion, and Assumption Questions

Chapter Three contained a basic definition of each question type. Now we will expand those definitions and compare and contrast each type:

Strengthen questions ask you to support the argument in any way possible. This type of answer has great range, as the additional support provided by the answer choice could be relatively minor or major. Speaking in numerical terms, any answer choice that strengthens the argument, whether by 1% or by 100%, is correct.

Justify the Conclusion questions ask you to strengthen the argument so powerfully that the conclusion is made logical. Compared to a Strengthen question, the answer to a Justify question must strengthen the conclusion so it is 100% proven; anything less and the answer choice is incorrect. Logically speaking, the correct answer to a Justify the Conclusion question is *sufficient* to prove the conclusion when added to the premises.

An assumption is simply an unstated premise of the argument.

Assumption questions ask you to identify a statement that the argument assumes or supposes. An assumption is simply an unstated premise— what must be true in order for the argument to be true. An assumption can therefore be defined as what is *necessary* for the argument to be true.

Because the three question types are confusingly similar, let's use a simple example to clarify the difference among the correct answer choices that appear with each question type:

THE POWERSCORE LSAT LOGICAL REASONING BIBLE

An argument concludes that a teenager is an outstanding golfer.

In an Assumption question, the correct answer could be: "The teenager always hits the ball" or "The teenager never swings and misses the ball." Either statement is an assumption of the argument; otherwise how could the teenager be an outstanding golfer?

In a Justify the Conclusion question, the correct answer could be: "The teenager recently won the Masters golf tournament" (The Masters is perhaps the most prestigious golf tournament in the world). This answer choice proves the conclusion beyond a doubt but is not an assumption of the conclusion—the teenager did not have to win the Masters to prove greatness; other professional tournaments would suffice.

In a Strengthen question, the correct answer could be: "The teenager won a local club tournament." This answer choice supports the idea that the teenager is an outstanding golfer, but does not undeniably prove the teenager to be outstanding (what if the tournament was composed primarily of pre-teen players?) nor is the answer an assumption of the conclusion.

Admittedly, this is a simple example, but take a moment to examine the different types of answers to each question. The differences are subtle and can be confusing at first, especially with Assumption and Justify the Conclusion questions.

Strengthen Questions

Strengthen questions ask you to identify the answer choice that best supports the argument. The correct answer choice does not necessarily justify the argument, nor is the correct answer choice necessarily an assumption of the argument. The correct answer choice simply helps the argument in some way.

Most Strengthen question stems typically contain the following two features:

1. The stem uses the word "strengthen" or a synonym. Following are some examples of words or phrases used to indicate that your task is to strengthen the argument:

> strengthen
> support
> helps
> *most* justifies

Whether you are finding an assumption of the argument or strengthening the conclusion, you are doing something positive for the stimulus.

2. The stem indicates that you should accept the answer choices as true, usually with the following phrase:

"Which one of the following, if true, ..."

Following are several Strengthen question stem examples from actual LSATs:

"Which one of the following, if true, most strengthens the argument?"

"Which one of the following, if true, most strongly supports the statement above?"

"Which one of the following, if true, does most to justify the conclusion above?"

"Each of the following, if true, supports the claim above EXCEPT:"

How to Strengthen an Argument

Use the following points to effectively strengthen arguments:

1. Identify the conclusion—this is what you are trying to strengthen!

    Because Strengthen questions are the polar opposite of Weaken questions, the correct approach to supporting an LSAT argument is to help the author's conclusion. When evaluating an answer, ask yourself, "Would this answer choice assist the author in some way?" If so, you have the correct answer.

2. Personalize the argument.

    Personalizing allows you to see the argument from a very involved perspective and helps you assess the strength of each answer.

3. Look for weaknesses in the argument.

    This may seem like a strange recommendation since your task is to strengthen the argument, but a weak spot in an argument is tailor-made for an answer that eliminates that weakness. If you see a weakness or flaw in the argument, look for an answer that eliminates the weakness. In other words, close any gap or hole in the argument.

    Many Strengthen questions require students to find the missing link between a premise and the conclusion. These missing links are assumptions made by the author, and bringing an assumption to light strengthens the argument because it validates part of the author's thinking. This idea will be discussed further in the Assumption section of this chapter.

4. Arguments that contain analogies or use surveys rely upon the validity of those analogies and surveys. Answer choices that strengthen the analogy or survey, or establish their soundness, are usually correct.

5. Remember that the correct answer can strengthen the argument just a little or a lot. This variation is what makes these questions difficult.

Three Incorrect Answer Traps

The same type of wrong answer traps appear in Strengthen as in Weaken questions:

1. Opposite Answers. These answers do the exact opposite of what is needed—they weaken the argument. Because of their direct relation to the conclusion they are tempting, despite the fact that they result in consequences opposite of those intended.

2. Shell Game Answers. Remember, a Shell Game occurs when an idea or concept is raised in the stimulus and then a very similar idea appears in the answer choice, but the idea is changed just enough to be incorrect but still attractive. In Strengthen questions, the Shell Game is usually used to support a conclusion that is similar to, but slightly different from, the one presented in the stimulus.

3. Out of Scope Answers. These answers simply miss the point of the argument and support issues that are either unrelated to the argument or tangential to the argument.

These three answer types are not the only ways an answer choice can be attractively incorrect, but they appear frequently enough that you should be familiar with each form.

The stimuli for Strengthen and Weaken questions tend to be similar: both often contain faulty reasoning.

Strengthen Questions Analyzed

Please take a moment to complete the following problem:

1. Advertisement: At most jewelry stores, the person assessing the diamond is the person selling it so you can see why an assessor might say that a diamond is of higher quality than it really is. But because all diamonds sold at Gem World are certified in writing, you're assured of a fair price when purchasing a diamond from Gem World.

The reasoning in the advertisement would be most strengthened if which one of the following were true?

(A) Many jewelry stores other than Gem World also provide written certification of the quality of their diamonds.

(B) The certifications of diamonds at Gem World are written by people with years of experience in appraising gems.

(C) The diamonds sold at Gem World are generally of higher quality than those sold at other jewelry stores.

(D) The diamond market is so volatile that prices of the most expensive diamonds can change by hundreds of dollars from one day to the next.

(E) The written certifications of diamonds at Gem World are provided by an independent company of gem specialists.

The stimulus is prefaced by the word "advertisement." One quirk of the LSAT is that every stimulus in LSAT history that has been preceded by this word has contained faulty or deceptive logic. Thus, whenever you see this word prefacing a stimulus, be on the lookout for misleading or flawed reasoning.

The argument is constructed as follows:

Premise: At most jewelry stores, the person assessing the diamond is the person selling it.

Premise/Sub-conclusion:
                        So you can see why an assessor might say that a diamond is of higher quality than it really is.

Premise: All diamonds sold at Gem World are certified in writing,

Conclusion: You're assured of a fair price when purchasing a diamond from Gem World.

Remember, a conclusion that is then used as a premise to support another conclusion is called a Sub-conclusion.

The first sentence contains a premise and conclusion that relies on the assumption that financial motivation might cause a person to lie about the quality of the item. According to the advertisement, at Gem World there is no such worry because the diamonds are certified in writing. Think for a moment—does that reasoning sound bulletproof? If you were standing there in the store and you were told that Gem World has written certification, wouldn't you ask *who* does the certification? This is the essence of personalizing the argument—place yourself inside the situation and think how you would react. As soon as you do that in this question, the weakness in the argument becomes apparent. Then, since this is a Strengthen question, you can look for an answer choice that eliminates this weakness. Answer choice (E) addresses the hole in the argument by indicating that the individuals who provide the written certification are not the same people who are selling the diamonds at Gem World.

There are other errors in the stimulus, such as assuming that a written certification equals a fair price. The certification may have no impact on the actual price of the diamond, or perhaps it could even be used to raise the price unjustly. These problems are ignored by the answer choices, and the test makers have that right.

Answer choice (A): The conclusion addresses the fair price of diamonds *at Gem World*, not other stores. Hence, the fact that other stores have written certification does not help the Gem World advertisement.

Answer choice (B): This is an answer many people keep as a Contender. The answer is incorrect because it fails to address the point raised in the first sentence, namely that the person assessing the diamond has a personal stake in the outcome. This "accountability" issue is the central point of the argument, and without knowing the source of the certifications, this answer does not strengthen the argument.

Answer choice (C): The argument asserts that a fair price is assured when purchasing *a* diamond at Gem World. No claim to comparative quality is made in the advertisement, and thus this answer does not strengthen the argument.

Answer choice (D): If anything, this answer may hurt the argument since it indicates that a fair price may not be obtainable at Gem World due to price volatility. If prices change daily, then Gem World may be selling diamonds at a price that does not reflect current market value. However, the answer choice specifically mentions "the most expensive diamonds" and there is no guarantee that Gem World carries diamonds in this price range. So, at best, the answer choice has no effect on the argument and is therefore incorrect.

Answer choice (E): This is the correct answer. As mentioned above, this answer addresses the separation of the certification writer from the seller and thereby strengthens the reasoning.

One thing that makes the LSAT difficult is that the test makers have so many options for testing you. In this question they could have chosen to strengthen a different part of the argument.

Please take a moment to complete the following problem:

2. Statistician: A financial magazine claimed that its
    survey of its subscribers showed that North
    Americans are more concerned about their
    personal finances than about politics. One
    question was: "Which do you think about
    more: politics or the joy of earning money?"
    This question is clearly biased. Also, the readers
    of the magazine are a self-selecting sample.
    Thus, there is reason to be skeptical about the
    conclusion drawn in the magazine's survey.

    Each of the following, if true, would strengthen the
    statistician's argument EXCEPT:

    (A) The credibility of the magazine has been called
         into question on a number of occasions.
    (B) The conclusions drawn in most magazine
         surveys have eventually been disproved.
    (C) Other surveys suggest that North Americans are
         just as concerned about politics as they are
         about finances.
    (D) There is reason to be skeptical about the results
         of surveys that are biased and
         unrepresentative.
    (E) Other surveys suggest that North Americans are
         concerned not only with politics and
         finances, but also with social issues.

This problem is more difficult than the previous problem, in part because this is
an Except question. As you recall, in a Strengthen Except question the four
incorrect answers strengthen the argument and the correct answer either has no
effect on the argument or weakens the argument.

The statistician's statement begins with a variation of the classic LSAT
construction "Some people claim..." As discussed in Chapter Two, when this
construction is used, the author almost always argues against the claim made by
the people. Here, a financial magazine has claimed that a survey proves that
North Americans are more concerned about personal finances than politics. The
statistician attacks two elements of the survey—there was a biased question and
the sampling was faulty—and concludes the magazine's claim is questionable.
Let us take a closer look at the statistician's two premises:

1. One question was biased.

    The key to understanding this claim is the phrasing of the question in the
    magazine: "the *joy* of earning money." By describing politics neutrally
    but describing earning money as a fun activity, the question
    inappropriately suggests to the magazine reader that one activity is more

228

interesting than the other. This bias undermines the integrity of the survey.

2. The sample was self-selecting.

A self-selecting sample is one in which individuals decide whether to participate. As you might expect, only those interested in the topic tend to participate and this creates a bias in the results. Because the survey was of subscribers to a financial magazine and not of the general North American population, those participating in sample are not necessarily representative of North Americans and thus the magazine cannot reliably draw a conclusion about North Americans.

Hence, the statistician's position appears reasonably strong. Nonetheless, you are asked to eliminate four answers that will strengthen it further.

Earlier in this chapter we mentioned that the test makers believe in the validity of surveys, polls, etc. This question does not affect that position; in this situation the survey itself is the topic of discussion. Normally, that is not the case, and unless a survey or poll is shown to be questionable, you can typically accept the results knowing that the test makers believe survey results are valid.

Answer choice (A): This answer asserts that the magazine has credibility issues and thereby supports the conclusion that there should be skepticism regarding the magazine's activities.

Answer choice (B): This answer attacks the integrity of magazine surveys, and therefore supports the idea that there is reason to be skeptical of this magazine survey. Frankly, this is a weak answer because the validity of surveys in other magazines do not necessarily reflect on the validity of this magazine's survey. Nonetheless, only about five percent of test takers select this answer, as most people are able to recognize the intent of the test makers.

Answer choice (C): This answer supports the argument because other surveys suggest that North Americans are not more concerned about finances than politics. Because this counters the claim of the magazine, the answer supports the statistician's conclusion that there is reason to be skeptical of the magazine's survey.

Answer choice (D): Because the statistician has shown the survey to be biased and unrepresentative, this answer choice supports the statistician's conclusion.

Answer choice (E): This is the correct answer. The answer has no impact on the statistician's argument because a third topic—social issues—was not part of the magazines' survey, nor does this answer suggest anything about the preference of North Americas for finance or politics. Because the answer has no impact, it is correct in a StrengthenX question.

> As mentioned previously, surveys that are conducted properly are considered reliable by the makers of the LSAT.

Causality and Strengthen Questions

Because Strengthen and Weaken questions require you to perform opposite tasks, to strengthen a causal conclusion you take the exact opposite approach that you would in a Weaken question.

In Strengthen questions, supporting a cause and effect relationship almost always consists of performing one of the following tasks:

A. Eliminate any alternate causes for the stated effect

Because the author believes there is only one cause (the stated cause in the argument), eliminating other possible causes strengthens the conclusion.

B. Show that when the cause occurs, the effect occurs

Because the author believes that the cause always produces the effect, any scenario where the cause occurs and the effect follows lends credibility to the conclusion. This type of answer can appear in the form of a example.

Remember, to strengthen a causal argument you must perform tasks that are opposite of those that weaken a causal argument.

C. Show that when the cause does not occur, the effect does not occur

Using the reasoning in the previous point, any scenario where the cause does not occur and the effect does not occur supports the conclusion. This type of answer also can appear in the form of a example.

D. Eliminate the possibility that the stated relationship is reversed

Because the author believes that the cause and effect relationship is correctly stated, eliminating the possibility that the relationship is backwards (the claimed effect is actually the cause of the claimed cause) strengthens the conclusion.

E. Show that the data used to make the causal statement is accurate, or eliminate possible problems with the data

If the data used to make a causal statement is in error, then the validity of the causal claim is in question. Any information that eliminates error or reduces the possibility of error will support the argument.

Take a moment to consider each of these items as they will reappear in the discussion of causality and Assumption questions—the approach will be identical for that combination.

THE POWERSCORE LSAT LOGICAL REASONING BIBLE

Please take a moment to complete the following problem:

3. Modern navigation systems, which are found in most of today's commercial aircraft, are made with low-power circuitry, which is more susceptible to interference than the vacuum-tube circuitry found in older planes. During landing, navigation systems receive radio signals from the airport to guide the plane to the runway. Recently, one plane with low-power circuitry veered off course during landing, its dials dimming, when a passenger turned on a laptop computer. Clearly, modern aircraft navigation systems are being put at risk by the electronic devices that passengers carry on board, such as cassette players and laptop computers.

    Which one of the following, if true, LEAST strengthens the argument above?

    (A) After the laptop computer was turned off, the plane regained course and its navigation instruments and dials returned to normal.
    (B) When in use all electronic devices emit electromagnetic radiation, which is known to interfere with circuitry.
    (C) No problems with navigational equipment or instrument dials have been reported on flights with no passenger-owned electronic devices on board.
    (D) Significant electromagnetic radiation from portable electronic devices can travel up to eight meters, and some passenger seats on modern aircraft are located within four meters of the navigation systems.
    (E) Planes were first equipped with low-power circuitry at about the same time portable electronic devices became popular.

The conclusion of the argument is based on the causal assumption that electronic devices cause a disturbance in low-power circuitry, creating an obvious danger:

$$ED = \text{electronic devices}$$
$$I = \text{interference with low-power circuitry}$$

$$\underline{C} \qquad\qquad \underline{E}$$

$$ED \longrightarrow I$$

The "Least equals Except" principle applies only when the terms appear in the question stem.

The question stem is a StrengthenX (remember, *Least* works like *Except* in question stems) and thus the four incorrect answers will each strengthen the argument. As you attack the answer choices, look for the five causal strengthening answer types discussed earlier.

Answer choice (A): This answer choice strengthens the argument by showing that when the cause is absent, the effect does not occur (Type C). Once the laptop was turned off, the cause disappeared, and according to the author's beliefs, the effect should then disappear as well.

Answer choice (B): This answer strengthens the argument by showing that the data used to make the conclusion is accurate (Type E). By stating that *all* electronic devices emit radiation, the answer choice closes a hole in the argument.

Answer choice (C): This answer choice strengthens the argument by showing that when the cause is absent, the effect does not occur (Type C).

Answer choice (D): This answer strengthens the argument by showing that the data used to make the conclusion is accurate (Type E). By showing that radiation can travel far enough to reach the cockpit, the cause is confirmed as possible.

This is the third Strengthen question in a row with (E) as the correct answer choice. This is not a pattern, just an incidental and meaningless result of the questions selected for this section.

Answer choice (E): This is the correct answer. The fact that the circuitry and electronic devices became popular at the same time does not offer any supporting evidence to the contention that the electronic devices cause the interference with the low power circuitry. This answer has no effect on the argument and is therefore correct.

Please take a moment to complete the following problem:

4. Amphibian populations are declining in numbers worldwide. Not coincidentally, the earth's ozone layer has been continuously depleted throughout the last 50 years. Atmospheric ozone blocks UV-B, a type of ultraviolet radiation that is continuously produced by the sun, and which can damage genes. Because amphibians lack hair, hide, or feathers to shield them, they are particularly vulnerable to UV-B radiation. In addition, their gelatinous eggs lack the protection of leathery or hard shells. Thus, the primary cause of the declining amphibian population is the depletion of the ozone layer.

Each of the following, if true, would strengthen the argument EXCEPT:

(A) Of the various types of radiation blocked by atmospheric ozone, UV-B is the only type that can damage genes.
(B) Amphibian populations are declining far more rapidly than are the populations of nonamphibian species whose tissues and eggs have more natural protection from UV-B.
(C) Atmospheric ozone has been significantly depleted above all the areas of the world in which amphibian populations are declining.
(D) The natural habitat of amphibians has not become smaller over the past century.
(E) Amphibian populations have declined continuously for the last 50 years.

This question is much more difficult than the previous question, in part because one of the wrong answer choices is very attractive.

The conclusion of the argument is a causal statement that the depletion of the ozone layer is the primary cause of the declining amphibian population:

$$DO = depletion\ of\ the\ ozone\ layer$$
$$DA = decline\ of\ amphibian\ population$$

$$\underset{DO}{\overset{C}{}} \longrightarrow \underset{DA}{\overset{E}{}}$$

This conclusion is based on the fact that the ozone layer blocks harmful UV-B radiation, which amphibians are vulnerable to in both adult and egg form.

Although the argument mentions UV-B radiation, which may sound impressive, the structure of the reasoning is easy to follow and no knowledge of the radiation is needed. The conclusion is clearly stated and easy to spot due to the indicator "thus." The question stem is a StrengthenX and therefore the four incorrect answers will each strengthen the argument. As with the previous question, look for answers that fit the five causal strengthening answer types discussed earlier.

Answer choice (A): This is the correct answer. The answer fails to shed any light—positive or negative—on the connection between the ozone depletion and the amphibian population decline. Because the argument is concerned with the damage done by UV-B radiation, the fact that UV-B is the only damaging type of radiation blocked by ozone is irrelevant.

Answer choice (B): This answer choice strengthens the argument by showing that when the cause is absent in nonamphibian populations, the effect does not occur (Type C).

Answer choice (C): This answer strengthens the argument by showing that the areas of ozone depletion and amphibian decline match each other, thereby affirming the data used to make the conclusion (Type E).

Answer choice (D): This was the answer most frequently chosen by test takers. This answer choice strengthens the argument by eliminating an alternate cause for the effect (Type A). Had the natural habitat become smaller over the years (from say, human encroachment or climatic change) then that shrinkage would have offered an alternate explanation for the decline in the amphibian population. By eliminating the possibility of habitat shrinkage, the stated cause in the argument is strengthened.

Answer choice (E): This answer strengthens the argument by showing that the decline of the amphibians has mirrored the decline of the ozone layer, thereby affirming the data used to make the conclusion (Type E).

Strengthen Question Type Review

Strengthen questions ask you to identify the answer choice that best supports the argument.

Use the following points to effectively strengthen arguments:

1. Identify the conclusion—this is what you are trying to strengthen!

2. Personalize the argument.

3. Look for weaknesses or holes in the argument.

The same type of wrong answer traps appear in Strengthen as in Weaken questions:

1. Opposite Answers.

2. Shell Game Answers.

3. Out of Scope Answers.

In Strengthen questions, supporting a cause and effect relationship almost always consists of performing one of the following tasks:

A. Eliminate any alternate causes for the stated effect

B. Show that when the cause occurs, the effect occurs

C. Show that when the cause does not occur, the effect does not occur

D. Eliminate the possibility that the stated relationship is reversed

E. Show that the data used to make the causal statement is accurate, or eliminate possible problems with the data

Although you do not need to memorize the types of wrong answer choices that appear in Strengthen questions, you must memorize the ways to strengthen a causal argument.

Strengthen Question Problem Set

The following questions are drawn from actual LSATs. Please complete the problem set and review the answer key and explanations. *Answers on Page 238*

1. According to the theory of continental drift, in prehistoric times, many of today's separate continents were part of a single huge landmass. As the plates on which this landmass rested began to move, the mass broke apart, and ocean water filled the newly created chasms. It is hypothesized, for example, that South America was once joined on its east coast with what is now the west coast of Africa.

   Which one of the following discoveries, if it were made, would most support the above hypothesis about South America and Africa?

   (A) A large band of ancient rock of a rare type along the east coast of South America is of the same type as a band on the west coast of Africa.
   (B) Many people today living in Brazil are genetically quite similar to many western Africans.
   (C) The climates of western Africa and of the east coast of South America resemble each other.
   (D) Some of the oldest tribes of people living in eastern South America speak languages linguistically similar to various languages spoken by certain western African peoples.
   (E) Several species of plants found in western Africa closely resemble plants growing in South America.

2. Medical doctor: Sleep deprivation is the cause of many social ills, ranging from irritability to potentially dangerous instances of impaired decision making. Most people today suffer from sleep deprivation to some degree. Therefore we should restructure the workday to allow people flexibility in scheduling their work hours.

   Which one of the following, if true, would most strengthen the medical doctor's argument?

   (A) The primary cause of sleep deprivation is overwork.
   (B) Employees would get more sleep if they had greater latitude in scheduling their work hours.
   (C) Individuals vary widely in the amount of sleep they require.
   (D) More people would suffer from sleep deprivation today than did in the past if the average number of hours worked per week had not decreased.
   (E) The extent of one's sleep deprivation is proportional to the length of one's workday.

3. Toxicologist: A survey of oil-refinery workers who work with MBTE, an ingredient currently used in some smog-reducing gasolines, found an alarming incidence of complaints about headaches, fatigue, and shortness of breath. Since gasoline containing MBTE will soon be widely used, we can expect an increased incidence of headaches, fatigue, and shortness of breath.

Each of the following, if true, strengthens the toxicologist's argument EXCEPT:

(A) Most oil-refinery workers who do not work with MBTE do not have serious health problems involving headaches, fatigue, and shortness of breath.

(B) Headaches, fatigue, and shortness of breath are among the symptoms of several medical conditions that are potentially serious threats to public health.

(C) Since the time when gasoline containing MBTE was first introduced in a few metropolitan areas, those areas reported an increase in the number of complaints about headaches, fatigue, and shortness of breath.

(D) Regions in which only gasoline containing MBTE is used have a much greater incidence of headaches, fatigue, and shortness of breath than do similar regions in which only MBTE-free gasoline is used.

(E) The oil-refinery workers surveyed were carefully selected to be representative of the broader population in their medical histories prior to exposure to MBTE, as well as in other relevant respects.

4. Galanin is a protein found in the brain. In an experiment, rats that consistently chose to eat fatty foods when offered a choice between lean and fatty foods were found to have significantly higher concentrations of galanin in their brains than did rats that consistently chose lean over fatty foods. These facts strongly support the conclusion that galanin causes rats to crave fatty foods.

Which one of the following, if true, most supports the argument?

(A) The craving for fatty foods does not invariably result in a rat's choosing those foods over lean foods.

(B) The brains of the rats that consistently chose to eat fatty foods did not contain significantly more fat than did the brains of rats that consistently chose lean foods.

(C) The chemical components of galanin are present in both fatty foods and lean foods.

(D) The rats that preferred fatty foods had the higher concentrations of galanin in their brains before they were offered fatty foods.

(E) Rats that metabolize fat less efficiently than do other rats develop high concentrations of galanin in their brains.

All answer keys in this book indicate the source of the question by giving the month and year the LSAT was originally administered, the Logical Reasoning section number, and the question number within that section. Each LSAT has two Logical Reasoning sections, and so the Section 1 and Section 2 designators will refer to the first or second Logical Reasoning section in the test, not the physical section number of the booklet.

Question #1. Strengthen. June 2003 LSAT, Section 1, #11. The correct answer choice is (A)

The theory discussed in the stimulus is a real scientific hypothesis, often called the "Pangaea Theory." Alfred Wegener, who has been the subject of other LSAT questions, theorized in 1915 that Pangaea was a "supercontinent" composed of all landmasses. The theory is attractive because when the shape of today's continents is examined, the continents roughly fit together.

The question stem specifically asks you to strengthen the hypothesis that South America and Africa were once joined. To do so, you must identify evidence about the landmasses, as this is the evidence that the hypothesis in the stimulus relies upon.

Answer choice (A): This is the correct answer, and this is the only answer that addresses the land. By tying the rock strata of each continent together, the answer supports the idea that there was once a physical connection between the two continents. A high percentage of test takers correctly identify this answer.

Answer choice (B): This answer addresses people, not land. As with the earlier turtle question, the genetic similarity could be the result of humans from different areas sharing a large amount of DNA.

Answer choice (C): The similarity of climates does not help establish that the landmasses were once connected. For example, the similarity could be the result of both continents largely straddling the equator.

Answer choice (D): The language of the people does not mean the continents were connected. Australians and Americans share the same language, but this is because both areas were populated in modern times by English-speaking people from Britain.

Answer choice (E): The resemblance of plants in both areas does not suggest or strengthen the idea that the continents were joined. Plant similarities could be the result of climate, or perhaps of man-made propagation efforts.

Strengthen Problem Set Answer Key

Question #2. Strengthen. December 2001 LSAT, Section 2, #7. The correct answer choice is (B)

Following is the structure of the medical doctor's argument:

Premise: Sleep deprivation is the cause of many social ills, ranging from irritability to potentially dangerous instances of impaired decision making.

Premise: Most people today suffer from sleep deprivation to some degree.

Conclusion: Therefore we should restructure the workday to allow people flexibility in scheduling their work hours.

The first premise contains a causal assertion (not a causal conclusion), and the second premise indicates that most people suffer from the stated cause. This combination would lead to the conclusion that most people have a social ill (which could be irritability or impaired decision making, or something in between). However, the conclusion in the argument leaps over this idea to conclude that the workday should be restructured. The missing link—or assumption—in the argument is that restructuring the workday would alleviate the sleep deprivation. As always, whenever you see a gap in the argument, you can strengthen the argument by eliminating that gap. By relating sleep to work, answer choice (B) closes the gap in the argument.

Answer choice (A): This is a tricky answer, and the key word is "overwork." While the author clearly believes that work schedules affect sleep, this does not mean that employees are being overworked. For example, a person may be sleep deprived because they have to come into work at 8 A.M. Perhaps they have children so they must get up very early to take care of their family. The person might then work a normal eight hour day and be sleep deprived not because of overwork but because of rising early.

Answer choice (B): This is the correct answer. By indicating that employees would avoid sleep deprivation with a revised workday, this answer affirms that the leap (or gap) made in the argument is not an unreasonable one.

Answer choice (C): This answer may hurt the argument by suggesting that some individuals cannot be helped by the restructuring of the workday. At best, this answer has no impact on the argument because we already know that most people suffer from sleep deprivation to some degree.

Answer choice (D): This answer addresses the fact that the hours worked per week has decreased. But the argument is not about the average number of hours worked, but rather the way that those hours affect sleep. Thus, this answer does not help the conclusion that people should be allowed flexibility in scheduling.

Answer choice (E): The argument does not suggest that the workday will be shortened, only that the day will be structured so that people have more flexibility in scheduling their hours. Thus, knowing that the extent of sleep deprivation is proportional to the length of one's workday does not strengthen the argument.

Strengthen Problem Set Answer Key

Question #3. StrengthenX-CE. October 2002 LSAT, Section 2, #5. The correct answer choice is (B)

The conclusion of the argument reflects a causal relationship:

> MBTE = MBTE used
> II = increased incidence of headaches, fatigue, and shortness of breath

$$\underline{\text{C}} \qquad\qquad \underline{\text{E}}$$

$$\text{MBTE} \quad\longrightarrow\quad \text{II}$$

The question stem is a StrengthenX, and therefore the four wrong answers will support the argument. With a stimulus containing causal reasoning and a StrengthenX question, expect to see wrong answers that come from the five different "Causality and Strengthen Questions" categories to help the argument.

Answer choice (A): This answer shows that when the cause is not present, then the effect is not present. Thus, the answer strengthens the argument and is incorrect.

Answer choice (B): This is the correct answer. By indicating that the symptoms discussed in the stimulus can be the effects of several potentially serious public health threats, the author offers up possible alternate causes for the symptoms. These alternate causes would weaken the argument, and therefore this is the correct answer.

Answer choice (C): This answer affirms that when the cause occurs, then the effect occurs. The answer therefore strengthens the argument.

Answer choice (D): Like answer choice (C), this answer shows that when the cause is present, then the effect is present, and makes the case stronger by comparing that scenario to regions where the cause is absent.

Answer choice (E): This answer choice strengthens the argument by showing that the data used to make the argument is accurate.

Question #4. Strengthen-CE. December 2000 LSAT, Section 2, #20. The correct answer choice is (D)

This stimulus also contains causal reasoning—the conclusion takes a correlation and turns it into a causal relationship:

G = higher concentration of galanin in the brain
CFF = crave fatty foods

<u>C</u>   <u>E</u>

G $\longrightarrow$ CFF

As with all causal arguments, once you identify the causality, you must immediately look to the question stem and then attack. In this instance, the author simply assumes that galanin is the cause. Why can't the fatty foods lead to higher concentrations of galanin?

Answer choice (A): If anything, this answer choice may hurt the argument by showing that the cravings do not always lead to choosing fatty foods. But, since the author uses the phrase "consistently chose" to describe the choices of the rats, an answer stating that rats did not "invariably" choose fatty foods has no effect on the argument.

Answer choice (B): This is a Shell Game answer because the test makers try to get you to fall for an answer that addresses the wrong issue. The argument discusses the concentration of galanin in the brains of rats; no mention is made of the fat content of the brains of rats. This answer, which focuses on the fat content in the brains of rats, therefore offers no support to the argument. Even though the brain might not contain more fat, a rat could still consistently choose and eat foods with a higher fat content.

Answer choice (C): The argument is that galanin *in the brain* causes rats to crave fatty foods. The fact that galanin is in the food does not help that assertion and may actually hurt the argument.

Answer choice (D): This is the correct answer. The answer strengthens the argument by eliminating the possibility that the stated causal relationship is reversed: if the rats had higher concentrations of galanin prior to eating the fatty foods, then the fatty foods cannot be the cause of the higher concentration of galanin. As discussed earlier in the chapter, this approach strengthens the argument by making it more likely that the author had the original relationship correct.

Answer choice (E): This answer choice hurts the argument by suggesting that the causal relationship in the conclusion is reversed. Remember that in Strengthen questions you can expect to see Opposite answers, and this is one.

Justify the Conclusion questions require you to select an answer choice that logically proves the conclusion of the argument. The correct answer proves the conclusion by adding a piece of information to the premises that makes the reasoning structure valid. In this sense, Justify questions are perfect strengthening questions: the correct answer will strengthen the argument so well that the conclusion must follow from the combination of the premises and the correct answer choice.

To solve this type of question, apply the Justify Formula™:

$$\text{Premises} + \text{Answer choice} = \text{Conclusion}$$

If the answer choice is correct, the application of the Justify Formula will produce the given conclusion. If the answer choice is incorrect, the application of the Justify Formula will fail to produce the given conclusion.

Consider the following example:

> Premise: John has exactly 2 apples.
>
> Conclusion: John has exactly 5 apples.

What statement can be added to the argument above to conclude that it must be true that John has exactly 5 apples? Apply the Justify Formula:

Premises	+	Answer choice	=	Conclusion
2 apples	+	?	=	5 apples

The correct answer would of course be 3 apples. Admittedly, this is a simple example, but all Justify questions work along this same model.

Why are Justify Questions Described in Terms of Sufficiency?

Earlier in this chapter we noted that the correct answer to a Justify the Conclusion question is *sufficient* to prove the conclusion. This is because Justify questions all conform to the following relationship:

$$\text{Answer choice}_{\text{Correct}} \longrightarrow \text{Conclusion}_{\text{Valid}}$$

As we will see when looking at Justify question stems, the language used by the stem will convey that the answer choice is sufficient to prove the conclusion, as in the following stem:

The Justify Formula is a useful tool for understanding how these questions work. When approaching a question, first separate the answers into Contenders and Losers. Then apply the Justify Formula to the remaining Contenders.

The correct answer to this problem could just as easily be, "3 apples and 2 oranges." Although the oranges are superfluous, the 3 apples alone would justify the conclusion. This separates Justify answers from Assumption answers, which would never contain extraneous information.

"The conclusion above follows logically if which one of the following is assumed?"

Using the conditional indicators in the stem, we can rearrange the stem as follows:

"*If* which one of the following is taken as true (assumed), then the conclusion above follows logically?"

From a conditional standpoint, this shows that the correct answer is sufficient to make the conclusion follow logically. This does not mean that the answer choice must contain a sufficient condition indicator or that the argument must be conditional in nature (although many are)! The sufficiency model is a way of showing that the correct answer choice will add enough to the argument to make the conclusion follow.

Identifying Justify the Conclusion Question Stems

Justify the Conclusion questions can be difficult to identify because they often appear to be Assumption questions to the uninformed test taker. Many Justify question stems use the word "assumed" or "assumption," and this leads to confusion.

Most Justify the Conclusion question stems contain some of the following three features:

1. The stem uses the word "if" or another sufficient condition indicator.

   Because a Justify question stem introduces an answer that is sufficient to prove the conclusion, a sufficient condition indicator will often be present.

2. The stem uses the phrase "allows the conclusion to be properly drawn" or "enables the conclusion to be properly drawn."

   These phrases are a way for Law Services to convey that the correct answer is sufficient. In the majority of cases, the presence of either phrase indicates a Justify question.

3. The stem does not lessen the degree of justification.

   Justifying a conclusion is an exacting task with strict requirements. Any question stem that permits a lessened degree of justification, for example by using the phrase "most justifies" or "does the most to justify," allows for an answer that does not justify the conclusion 100%. This violates the principle behind Justify questions. Thus, questions with the "most justify" construction are properly classified

The sufficiency model explained here reveals the abstract nature of the correct answer choice in a Justify question.

A large number of test preparation companies continue to erroneously classify Justify questions as Assumption questions.

A Justify the Conclusion question requires you to prove the conclusion; you are not asked to "kind of" or "somewhat" prove the conclusion. Because of this certainty, most students find these questions easier than Assumption questions.

Part of the difficulty in identifying Justify questions is that the first two indicators above are not consistently present (the third is always present). You must look at each question stem carefully and discern precisely what the test makers intend. Sometimes one of the indicators will be present, sometimes none, occasionally both.

Question stem examples:

"The conclusion above follows logically if which one of the following is assumed?"

"Which one of the following, if assumed, would allow the conclusion to be properly drawn?"

"Which one of the following, if true, enables the conclusion to be properly drawn?"

"Which one of the following, if assumed, enables the argument's conclusion to be properly inferred?"

Do not expect to see JustifyX questions—the task of proving the conclusion is too difficult for multiple answers that justify the conclusion.

"Which one of the following is an assumption that would serve to justify the conclusion above?"

"The environmentalist's conclusion would be properly drawn if it were true that the"

"The conclusion above is properly drawn if which one of the following is assumed?"

Justify the Conclusion Stimuli

Because logically proving an argument is a difficult task that requires 100% certainty, only certain types of argumentation tend to appear in Justify stimuli. In fact, most Justify stimuli either use Conditional Reasoning or contain numbers and percentages. Why? Because both forms of reasoning allow for certainty when drawing a conclusion. Consider the following example, which contains conditional reasoning:

Because justifying a conclusion is such a specific task, the logic behind the question must allow for airtight provability.

Premise: A

Premise: A $\longrightarrow$ B

Conclusion: B

This example can quickly be turned into a Justify the Conclusion question by removing either premise. For example:

Premise: A occurs.

Conclusion: B occurs.

Question: What statement can be added to the argument above to conclude that B must follow?

Answer: A $\longrightarrow$ B

Or, the other premise could be removed:

Premise: A $\longrightarrow$ B

Conclusion: B occurs.

Question: What statement can be added to the argument above to conclude that B must follow?

Answer: A occurs.

Stimuli that contain numbers or percentages in the stimulus also allow for the exactitude these questions require.

When examined abstractly, many Justify the Conclusion questions work in just this way. Please take a moment to consider the following question:

1. Maria won this year's local sailboat race by beating
   Sue, the winner in each of the four previous years. We
   can conclude from this that Maria trained hard.

   The conclusion follows logically if which one of the
   following is assumed?

   (A) Sue did not train as hard as Maria trained. ✗
   (B) If Maria trained hard, she would win the
        sailboat race.
   (C) Maria could beat a four-time winner only if she
        trained hard.
   (D) If Sue trained hard, she would win the sailboat
        race.
   (E) Sue is usually a faster sailboat racer than Maria.

win → train

The structure of the argument is:

Premise: Maria won this year's local sailboat race by beating Sue, the
                winner in each of the four previous years.

Conclusion: We can conclude from this that Maria trained hard.

A quick glance at the argument reveals a gap between the premise and
conclusion—winning does not necessarily guarantee that Maria trained hard.
This is the connection we will need to focus on when considering the answer
choices. To further abstract this relationship, we can portray the argument as
follows:

Premise: Maria won (which we could also call "A")

Conclusion: Maria trained hard (which we could also call "B")

The answer that will justify this relationship is:

$$A \longrightarrow B$$

Which is the same as:

Maria won $\longrightarrow$ Maria trained hard

A quick glance at the answer choices reveals that answer choice (C) matches
this relationship (remember, "only if" introduces a necessary condition). Thus,
the structure in this problem matches the first of the two examples discussed on
the previous page. A large number of Justify questions follow this same model,
and you should be prepared to encounter this form.

Strengthen
questions with
the phrase "most
justifies" in the
question stem
can largely be
treated like
Justify questions,
but you must
understand there
is a window that
allows for an
answer that does
not perfectly
justify the
conclusion.

Answer choice (A): This answer does not justify the conclusion that Maria trained *hard*. The answer does justify the conclusion that Maria *trained*, but because this is not the same as the conclusion of the argument, this answer is incorrect.

Another way of attacking this answer is to use the Justify Formula. Consider the combination of the following two elements:

Premise: Maria won this year's local sailboat race by beating Sue, the winner in each of the four previous years.

Answer choice (A):   Sue did not train as hard as Maria trained.

Does the combination of the two elements lead to the conclusion that Maria trained hard? No, and therefore the answer is wrong.

Answer choice (B): This is a Mistaken Reversal of what is needed (and therefore the Mistaken Reversal of answer choice (C)). Adding this answer to the premise does not result in the conclusion. In Justify questions featuring conditionality, always be ready to identify and avoid Mistaken Reversals and Mistaken Negations of the relationship needed to justify the conclusion.

Answer choice (C): This is the correct answer. Adding this answer to the premise automatically yields the conclusion.

Answer choice (D): Because we do not know anything about Sue except that she lost, this answer does not help prove the conclusion.

If you are having difficulty understanding why this answer is incorrect, use the Justify Formula. Consider the combination of the following two elements:

Premise: Maria won this year's local sailboat race by beating Sue, the winner in each of the four previous years.

Answer choice (C):   *If* Sue trained hard, she would win the sailboat race.

The combination of the two creates the contrapositive conclusion that Sue did not train hard. But, the fact that Sue did not train hard does not tell us anything about whether Maria trained hard.

Answer choice (E): Because this answer addresses only the relative speed of the two racers, it fails to help prove that Maria trained hard.

Solving Justify Questions Mechanistically

Remember, techniques that require a number of steps seem daunting at first (think about your first time driving a car). But as you practice with each technique, you will get faster and eventually your application of the technique will be transparent and effortless. To reach that level takes practice, but the rewards are great.

Although many justify the conclusion questions can be solved quickly and easily through the normal methods of breaking the argument down and analyzing the answer choices, sometimes you will find yourself unable to answer a question. Because Justify the Conclusion questions can be characterized in formulaic terms, you can often solve these questions using a mechanistic approach. This approach requires you to reduce the stimulus to its component parts (a process that occurs naturally as you identify premises and conclusions), and then identify which elements appear in the conclusion but not in the premises. The following rules apply:

1. Any "new" element in the conclusion will appear in the correct answer.

    "New" or "rogue" elements are those that did not appear in any of the premises. By definition, any new element in the conclusion must be proven to occur, and so if the new element is not in the premises then it must be introduced in the correct answer choice.

2. Elements that are common to the conclusion and at least one premise normally do not appear in the correct answer.

    If an element occurs in both the conclusion and premises, then there is a bridge already established that justifies the presence of the element in the conclusion. Hence, the correct answer need not contain this element.

3. Elements that appear in the premises but not the conclusion usually appear in the correct answer.

    Although these premise elements do not have to appear in the correct answer, they often do because they represent a convenient linking point.

In a nutshell, the rules condense to the following: link new elements in the premises and conclusion and ignore elements common to both. Consider the following example:

Premise: Every person who lives in Manhattan hates the subway.

Conclusion: Joan hates the subway.

Now we will analyze this answer from a mechanistic standpoint:

You should note that this example has a conditional structure like those discussed in the previous section.

1. "Joan" is a new element in the conclusion. The correct answer must contain "Joan." Any answer that does not contain Joan will be incorrect. Otherwise, how can we justify that *Joan* hates the subway?

2. "Hates the subway" is common to both the premise and conclusion.

Elements that are common to both the premise and conclusion in a justify question do not normally appear in the correct answer choice, hence we would not expect to see this element in the correct answer.

3. "Every person who lives in Manhattan" is an element that appears in the premise but not the conclusion. Chances are high that this element will appear in the correct answer.

As you might imagine, the correct answer to this problem will be along the lines of "Joan lives in Manhattan." This answer connects the new elements in the premise and conclusion and ignores the elements common to both. Let us try the mechanistic approach on an actual LSAT question. Please take a moment to consider the following question:

2. If something would have been justifiably regretted if it had occurred, then it is something that one should not have desired in the first place. It follows that many forgone pleasures should not have been desired in the first place.

The conclusion above follows logically if which one of the following is assumed?

(A) One should never regret one's pleasures.
(B) Forgone pleasures that were not desired would not have been justifiably regretted.
(C) Everything that one desires and then regrets not having is a forgone pleasure.
(D) Many forgone pleasures would have been justifiably regretted.
(E) Nothing that one should not have desired in the first place fails to be a pleasure.

For those of you thinking that this method is similar to the technique we will use for Assumption questions, it is. Justify answers are often assumptions of the argument, but not always. A Justify answer can contain components that, if they appeared in an Assumption question, would make the answer incorrect. Using the example to the left, an answer that would be correct for a Justify problem but incorrect for an Assumption problem would be, "Joan lives in a red house in Manhattan." When we discuss Assumption question in the next section this distinction will be clear.

This is an intimidating problem at first glance. The terminology is complex and the problem appears to be based on difficult philosophical principles. First, analyze the structure of the argument:

Premise: If something would have been justifiably regretted if it had occurred, then it is something that one should not have desired in the first place.

Conclusion: Many forgone pleasures should not have been desired in the first place.

Second, use the three steps for mechanistically solving Justify questions as described in this section.

1. Any "new" or "rogue" element in the conclusion will appear in the correct answer.

    "Many forgone pleasures" is a new element that appears only in the conclusion. Only answer choices (B), (C), and (D) contain "forgone pleasures," and only answer choice (D) contains "many." Thus, if forced to make a quick decision, answer choice (D) would be the best selection at this point in our analysis. And, fortunately, the technique is so powerful that this analysis does indeed yield the correct answer. Regardless, let's continue.

2. Elements that are common to the conclusion and at least one premise, or to two premises, normally do not appear in the correct answer.

    "Should not have (been) desired in the first place" appears in both the premise and the conclusion. This element is not likely to appear in the correct answer choice.

3. Elements that appear in the premises but not the conclusion normally appear in the correct answer.

    "Justifiably regretted" appears in the premise but not the conclusion. Only answer choices (B) and (D) contain "justifiably regretted."

Once you become used to examining the elements of the argument, the analysis above can be made very quickly. The method also correctly reveals answer choice (D) as correct with a minimum of effort.

This problem also contains conditional reasoning, and as such the argument can be diagrammed:

Premise: Justifiably Regretted $\longrightarrow$ D~~e~~sire

Conclusion: many D~~e~~sire$_{Forgone}$

This relationship is similar to the following:

Premise: A $\longrightarrow$ B

Conclusion: B occurs.

Question: What statement can be added to the argument above to conclude that B must follow?

Answer: A occurs.

In this case, a few additional elements have been added to B in the conclusion, but we can add these elements to A and make the problem work. The term that would justify the conclusion in this problem is:

many Justifiably Regretted$_{Forgone}$

A comparison of this term and answer choice (D) reveals that the two are identical. If you are still uncertain, use the Justify Formula to eliminate each of the remaining answer choices.

In reviewing Justify the Conclusion questions, you must recognize that each of the strategies described in this section are complementary. The approaches work because they all revolve around the undeniable truth of these questions: your answer, when combined with the premises, must justify the conclusion. Whether you see the conditional or numerical basis for the question or use the mechanistic approach is unimportant. The important part is that you quickly determine which answer has the components sufficient to prove the conclusion.

We will examine a numerically-based Justify question in the Numbers and Percentages Chapter.

Justify the Conclusion Question Type Review

Justify the Conclusion questions require you to select an answer choice that logically proves the conclusion of the argument.

To solve this type of question, apply the Justify Formula™:

Premises + Answer choice = Conclusion

Justify questions all conform to the following relationship:

$$\text{Answer choice}_{\text{Correct}} \longrightarrow \text{Conclusion}_{\text{Valid}}$$

Most Justify the Conclusion question stems typically contain some of the following three features:

1. The stem uses the word "if" or another sufficient condition indicator.

2. The stem uses the phrase "allows the conclusion to be properly drawn" or "enables the conclusion to be properly drawn."

3. The stem does not lessen the degree of justification.

Most Justify stimuli either use Conditional Reasoning or contain numbers and percentages.

Because Justify the Conclusion questions can be characterized in formulaic terms, you can often solve these questions using a mechanistic approach. This approach requires you to reduce the stimulus to its component parts (a process that occurs naturally as you identify premises and conclusions), and then identify which elements appear in the conclusion but not the premises. The following rules apply:

1. Any "new" element in the conclusion will appear in the correct answer.

2. Elements that are common to the conclusion and at least one premise, or to two premises, normally do not appear in the correct answer.

3. Elements that appear in the premises but not the conclusion normally appear in the correct answer.

Justify the Conclusion Question Problem Set

The following questions are drawn from actual LSATs. Please complete the problem set and review the answer key and explanations. *Answers on Page 254*

1. Psychiatrist: Take any visceral emotion you care to consider. There are always situations in which it is healthy to try to express that emotion. So, there are always situations in which it is healthy to try to express one's anger.

   The conclusion of the argument follows logically if which one of the following is assumed?

   (A) Anger is always expressible.
   (B) Anger is a visceral emotion.
   (C) Some kinds of emotions are unhealthy to express.
   (D) All emotions that are healthy to express are visceral.
   (E) An emotion is visceral only if it is healthy to express.

2. Marian Anderson, the famous contralto, did not take success for granted. We know this because Anderson had to struggle early in life, and anyone who has to struggle early in life is able to keep a good perspective on the world.

   The conclusion of the argument follows logically if which one of the following is assumed?

   (A) Anyone who succeeds takes success for granted.
   (B) Anyone who is able to keep a good perspective on the world does not take success for granted.
   (C) Anyone who is able to keep a good perspective on the world has to struggle early in life.
   (D) Anyone who does not take success for granted has to struggle early in life.
   (E) Anyone who does not take success for granted is able to keep a good perspective on the world.

3. Columnist: Almost anyone can be an expert, for there are no official guidelines determining what an expert must know. Anybody who manages to convince some people of his or her qualifications in an area—whatever those may be—is an expert.

   The columnist's conclusion follows logically if which one of the following is assumed?

   (A) Almost anyone can convince some people of his or her qualifications in some area.
   (B) Some experts convince everyone of their qualifications in almost every area.
   (C) Convincing certain people that one is qualified in an area requires that one actually be qualified in that area.
   (D) Every expert has convinced some people of his or her qualifications in some area.
   (E) Some people manage to convince almost everyone of their qualifications in one or more areas.

4. Vague laws set vague limits on people's freedom, which makes it impossible for them to know for certain whether their actions are legal. Thus, under vague laws people cannot feel secure.

   The conclusion follows logically if which one of the following is assumed?

   (A) People can feel secure only if they know for certain whether their actions are legal.
   (B) If people do not know for certain whether their actions are legal, then they might not feel secure.
   (C) If people know for certain whether their actions are legal, they can feel secure.
   (D) People can feel secure if they are governed by laws that are not vague.
   (E) Only people who feel secure can know for certain whether their actions are legal.

Justify the Conclusion Problem Set Answer Key

All answer keys in this book indicate the source of the question by giving the month and year the LSAT was originally administered, the Logical Reasoning section number, and the question number within that section. Each LSAT has two Logical Reasoning sections, and so the Section 1 and Section 2 designators will refer to the first or second Logical Reasoning section in the test, not the physical section number of the booklet.

Question #1. Justify. October 2000 LSAT, Section 2, #4. The correct answer choice is (B)

The first step in solving a Justify question is to analyze the structure of the argument:

Premise: There are always situations in which it is healthy to try to express that [visceral] emotion.

Conclusion: There are always situations in which it is healthy to try to express one's anger.

A quick mechanistic analysis reveals that the correct answer should contain "anger" and "visceral emotion." Only answer choice (B) contains these two elements, and as it turns out, (B) is correct. Answer choice (B) must also solve the Justify Formula:

Premise: There are always situations in which it is healthy to try to express that [visceral] emotion.

Answer choice (B): Anger is a visceral emotion.

Does the combination of these two elements lead to the conclusion? Yes, and so the answer must be correct. The Justify Formula can also be used to eliminate each of the other answer choices.

Question #2. Justify. October 2001 LSAT, Section 2, #14. The correct answer choice is (B)

The structure of the argument is:

Premise: Anyone who has to struggle early in life is able to keep a good perspective on the world.

Premise: Anderson had to struggle early in life.

Conclusion: Marian Anderson, the famous contralto, did not take success for granted.

A mechanistic analysis reveals that "Anderson" is common to the conclusion and a premise, and "struggle early in life" is common to the two premises. Thus, we would not expect to see either in the correct answer. New elements that should be in the correct answer are "able to keep a good perspective on the world" and "did not take success for granted." Only answer choices (B) and (E) contain both elements. Since (B) and (E) are Reversals of each other, let us look at the conditional relationship present in the stimulus:

Justify the Conclusion Problem Set Answer Key

Premise: Struggle early in life ——————→ able to keep a good perspective on the world

Premise: Struggle early in life _{Anderson}

Conclusion: Did not take success for granted _{Anderson}

Clearly, we need a connection that moves from "able to keep a good perspective on the world" to "did not take success for granted," such as the following:

able to keep a good perspective on the world ——————→ did not take success for granted

This relationship, which is the same as that presented in answer choice (B), ultimately creates a chain that can be used to prove the conclusion:

struggle ——————→ keep a good perspective ——————→ did not take success for granted

The addition of the premise "Anderson struggled early in life" to the chain above yields the conclusion "Anderson did not take success for granted." Hence, answer choice (B) is correct. Answer choice (E) is a Mistaken Reversal of the correct answer.

Question #3. Justify. October 2001 LSAT, Section 1, #20. The correct answer choice is (A)

The argument can be analyzed as follows:

Premise: Anybody who manages to convince some people of his or her qualifications in an area—whatever those may be—is an expert.

Conclusion: Almost anyone can be an expert.

The argument contains a classic conditional form: In abstract form:

Premise: Convince some people ————→ Expert   (A ————→ B)

Conclusion: Expert _{Almost anyone}   (B)

The element that must be added to justify the conclusion is:

Convince some people _{Almost anyone}   (A)

Answer choice (A) contains this element and is the correct answer. Use the Justify Formula to confirm the answer if it is still unclear.

Many students mistakenly select answer choice (D). Answer choice (D) is the Mistaken Reversal of the premise. Use the Justify Formula to reveal why this answer fails:

Premise: Convince some people $\longrightarrow$ Expert

Answer choice (D):   Expert $\longrightarrow$ Convince some people

Does the combination of these two statements prove that almost anyone can be an expert? No, and therefore the answer choice is incorrect.

Answer choice (E) is incorrect because it only justifies the conclusion that *some people* are experts.

Question #4. Justify. December 2001 LSAT, Section 2, #12. The correct answer choice is (A)

The argument can be analyzed as follows:

Premise: Vague laws set vague limits on people's freedom.

Premise: Vague limits on people's freedom makes it impossible for them to know for certain whether their actions are legal.

Conclusion: Under vague laws people cannot feel secure.

There is a new element in the conclusion—"cannot feel secure"—that must be justified. There is also an unconnected element in the premise—"know for certain whether their actions are legal"—that will likely appear in the answer choice. Unfortunately, four of the answer choices contain those two elements. Only answer choice (D) does not contain both, and as (D) also contains the "vague law" element that appears in both a premise and the conclusion, we can eliminate (D) for the moment.

Given the plethora of answers that remain in contention, first examine the conditional structure that is extant in the stimulus:

Premises: Vague laws $\longrightarrow$ Vague limits $\longrightarrow$ Know act̶i̶o̶n̶s̶ are legal

Conclusion: Vague laws $\longrightarrow$ Se̶c̶u̶re

Abstractly, this relationship is similar to:

Premises: A $\longrightarrow$ B $\longrightarrow$ C̶

Conclusion: A $\longrightarrow$ D̶

The relationship that must be added to the premise to prove the conclusion is:

C̶ $\longrightarrow$ D̶

Justify the Conclusion Problem Set Answer Key

Translating the diagram back to the terms used in our premise and conclusion, we need a statement like the following:

Know ac~~ti~~ons are legal $\longrightarrow$ Se~~cu~~re

Of course, the contrapositive of this statement would also be acceptable. Answer choice (A) is the contrapositive and thus (A) is correct.

Answer choice (B): This answer is incorrect because it has a different level of certainty than the conclusion: this answer uses the phrase "might not" when the conclusion uses "cannot." If this flaw were corrected, the answer would be correct.

Answer choice (C): This answer is the Mistaken Reversal of the correct answer.

Answer choice (D): This answer was eliminated previously.

Answer choice (E): This answer is also the Mistaken Reversal of the correct answer.

If you found yourself in trouble on this question, understanding that answers such as (C) and (E) are identical would allow you to eliminate them under the Uniqueness Rule of Answer Choices (that the correct answer must have unique properties).

An argument can be analogized to a house: the premises are like walls, the conclusion is like the roof, and the assumptions are like the foundation.

As with a house foundation, an assumption is a hidden part of the structure, but critical to the integrity of the structure—all the other elements rest upon it.

For many students, Assumption questions are the most difficult type of Logical Reasoning problem. An assumption is simply an unstated premise of the argument; that is, an integral component of the argument that the author takes for granted and leaves unsaid. In our daily lives we make thousands of assumptions, but they make sense because they have context and we have experience with the way the world works. Think for a moment about the many assumptions required during the simple act of ordering a meal at a restaurant. You assume that: the prices on the menu are correct; the items on the menu are available; the description of the food is reasonably accurate; the waiter will understand what you say when you order; the food will not sicken or kill you; the restaurant will accept your payment, etcetera. In an LSAT question, you are faced with the difficult task of figuring out the author's mindset and determining what assumption he or she made when formulating the argument. This task is unlike any other on the LSAT.

Just as we were able to describe Justify the Conclusion questions in terms of conditional reasoning, we can do the same for Assumption questions. Because an assumption is an integral component of the author's argument, a piece that must be true in order for the conclusion to be true, assumptions are *necessary* for the conclusion. Accordingly, the relationship between the conclusion and the assumption can be described as:

$$\text{Conclusion}_{\text{Valid}} \longrightarrow \text{Assumption}_{\text{True}}$$

Hence, the answer you select as correct must contain a statement that the author relies upon and is fully committed to in the argument. Think of an assumption as the foundation of the argument, a statement that the premises and conclusion rest upon. If an answer choice contains a statement that the author might only think *could* be true, or if the statement contains additional information that the author is not committed to, then the answer is incorrect. In many respects, an assumption can be considered a minimalist answer. Because the statement must be something the author believed when forming the argument, assumption answer choices cannot contain extraneous information. For example, let us say that an argument requires the assumption "all dogs are intelligent." The correct answer could be that statement, or even a subset statement such as "all black dogs are intelligent" or "all large dogs are intelligent" (black dogs and large dogs being subsets of the overall group of dogs, of course). But, additional information would rule out the answer, as in the following case: "All dogs and cats are intelligent." The additional information about cats is not part of the author's assumption, and would make the answer choice incorrect.

The correct answer to an Assumption question is a statement the author must believe in order for the conclusion to make sense.

Because assumptions are described as what must be true in order for the conclusion to be true, some students ask about the difference between Must Be True question answers and Assumption question answers. The difference is one that can be described as *before* versus *after*: Assumption answers contain statements that were *used to make* the conclusion; Must Be True answers contain statements that *follow from* the argument made in the stimulus. In both cases, however, there is a stringent requirement that must be met: Must Be True answers must be proven by the information in the stimulus; Assumption answers contain statements the author must believe in order for the conclusion to be valid.

As mentioned in the previous section, separating Justify the Conclusion questions from Assumption questions can be difficult. Assumption question stems typically contain the following features:

1. The stem uses the word "assumption," "presupposition," or some variation.

   "Presupposition" is another word for "assumes." These words are a direct reflection of the task at hand.

2. The stem *never* uses the word "if" or any other sufficient condition indicator.

   Because an assumption is a necessary part of the argument, no sufficient condition indicators can appear in the question stem. The appearance of sufficient condition indicator means that the question is either a Justify or Strengthen question. The stem of an Assumption question will likely contain a necessary condition indicator such as *required* or *unless*.

Question stem examples:

"Which one of the following is an assumption required by the argument above?"

"Which one of the following is an assumption upon which the argument depends?"

"The argument assumes which one of the following?"

"The conclusion in the passage above relies on which one of the following assumptions?"

"The position taken above presupposes which one of the following?"

"The conclusion cited does not follow unless"

The Supporter/Defender Assumption Model™

Most LSAT publications and courses present a limited description of assumptions. An assumption is described solely as a linking statement, one that links two premises or links a premise to the conclusion. If no other description of assumptions is given, this limited presentation cheats students of the possibility of fully understanding the way assumptions work within arguments and the way they are tested by the makers of the exam.

On the LSAT, assumptions play one of two roles—the Supporter or the Defender. The Supporter role is the traditional linking role, where an assumption connects the pieces of the argument. Consider the following example:

> All male citizens of Athens had the right to vote. Therefore, Socrates had the right to vote in Athens.

The linking assumption is that Socrates was a male citizen of Athens. This connects the premise element of male citizens having the right to vote and the conclusion element that Socrates had the right to vote (affiliated assumptions are "Socrates was male" and "Socrates was a citizen of Athens").

We typically use the term "new" or "rogue" to refer to an element that appears only in the conclusion or only in a premise.

Because Supporters often connect "new" or "rogue" pieces of information in the argument, the Supporter role generally appears similar to the Justify the Conclusion answers discussed in the previous section. In fact, a number of correct Justify the Conclusion answers are assumptions of the argument, especially when the argument contains a conditional structure. This is actually a benefit because if you mis-identify a Justify question as an Assumption question there is still a reasonable possibility that you can answer the question correctly.

If you see a weakness in the argument, look for an answer that eliminates the weakness or assumes that it does not exist. In other words, close the gaps in the argument.

Supporter assumptions on the LSAT are often relatively easy for students to identify because they can see the gap in the argument. The Supporter assumption, by definition, closes the hole by linking the elements together. Should you ever see a gap or a new element in the conclusion, a Supporter assumption answer will almost certainly close the gap or link the new element back to the premises.

The Defender role is entirely different, and Defender assumptions protect the argument by eliminating ideas that could weaken the argument. Consider our discussion from Chapter Two:

> "When you read an LSAT argument from the perspective of the author, keep in mind that he or she believes that their argument is sound. In other words, they do not knowingly make errors of reasoning. This is a fascinating point because it means that LSAT authors, as part of the LSAT world, function as if the points they raise and the conclusions they make have been well-considered and are airtight."

This fundamental truth of the LSAT has a dramatic impact when you consider the range of assumptions that must be made by an LSAT author. In order to believe the argument is "well-considered and airtight," an author must assume that every possible objection has been considered and rejected. Consider the following causal argument:

People who read a lot are more intelligent than other people. Thus, reading must cause a person to be intelligent.

Although the conclusion is questionable (for example, the situation may be reversed: intelligence might be the cause of reading a lot), in the author's mind *all* other alternative explanations are assumed not to exist. Literally, the author assumes that any idea that would weaken the argument is impossible and cannot occur. Consider some of the statements that would attack the conclusion above:

Sleeping more than eight hours causes a person to be intelligent.

Regular exercise causes a person to be intelligent.

A high-protein diet causes a person to be intelligent.

Genetics cause a person to be intelligent.

Each of these ideas would undermine the conclusion, but they are assumed by the author *not* to be possible, and the author therefore makes the following assumptions in the original argument:

Sleeping more than eight hours does not cause a person to be intelligent.

Regular exercise does not cause a person to be intelligent.

A high-protein diet does not cause a person to be intelligent.

Genetics do not cause a person to be intelligent.

Supporter answer choices lend themselves well to prephrasing. Defender answers do not because there are too many possibilities to choose from.

These assumptions protect the argument against statements that would undermine the conclusion. In this sense, they "defend" the argument by showing that a possible avenue of attack has been eliminated (assumed not to exist). As you can see, this list could go on and on because the author assumes *every* alternate cause does not exist. This means that although the argument only discussed reading and intelligence, we suddenly find ourselves with assumptions addressing a wide variety of topics that were never discussed in the stimulus. In a typical argument, there are an infinite number of assumptions possible, with most of those coming on the Defender side. Books and courses that focus solely on the Supporter role miss these assumptions, and students who do not understand how Defenders work will often summarily dismiss answer choices that later prove to be correct.

By assuming that any threat to the argument does not exist, the author can present the argument and claim it is valid. If the author knew of imperfections and still presented the argument without a caveat, then the author would be hard-pressed to claim that this conclusion—especially an absolute one—was reasonable.

If there is no obvious weakness in the argument and you are faced with an Assumption question, expect to see a Defender answer choice.

Let's review the two roles played by assumptions:

Supporter Assumption: These assumptions link together new or rogue elements in the stimulus or fill logical gaps in the argument.

Defender Assumption: These assumptions contain statements that eliminate ideas or assertions that would undermine the conclusion. In this sense, they "defend" the argument by showing that a possible source of attack has been eliminated.

Let us examine examples of each type. Please take a moment to complete the following question:

1. Art historian: Great works of art have often elicited outrage when first presented; in Europe, Stravinsky's *Rite of Spring* prompted a riot, and Manet's *Déjeuner sur l'herbe* elicited outrage and derision. So, since it is clear that art is often shocking, we should not hesitate to use public funds to support works of art that many people find shocking.

    Which one of the following is an assumption that the art historian's argument requires in order for its conclusion to be properly drawn?

    (A) Most art is shocking.
    (B) Stravinsky and Manet received public funding for their art.
    (C) Art used to be more shocking than it currently is.
    (D) Public funds should support art.
    (E) Anything that shocks is art.

Once you understand the way Supporters work, they can often be predicted after you read an argument.

This is a very challenging Supporter assumption, and only about half of the test takers identify the correct answer. Take a close look at the conclusion: "we should not hesitate to use public funds to support works of art that many people find shocking." Did "public funds" appear anywhere else in the argument? No. Given our discussion about linking new elements that appear in the conclusion, you should have recognized that a new element was present and responded accordingly. Given that Supporters connect new elements, one would suspect that the correct answer would include this element and that either answer choice (B) or (D) was correct. Take a look at the argument structure:

Premise:	Great works of art have often elicited outrage when first presented; in Europe, Stravinsky's *Rite of Spring* prompted a riot, and Manet's *Déjeuner sur l'herbe* elicited outrage and derision.
Premise:	Art is often shocking.
Conclusion:	We should not hesitate to use public funds to support works of art that many people find shocking.

As is often the case with LSAT stimuli, the argument is based on real events. During the notorious 1913 premiere of the ballet *Rite of Spring*, the rioting crowd inside and outside the theater was so loud the pit orchestra director had difficulty conducting.

However, because the structure of the last sentence in the stimulus ("So, since...") suggests that the author uses the second premise to prove the conclusion, you should focus on the relationship between those two pieces. For the author to say that art is shocking and therefore art should be publicly funded, the author must assume that art is worthy of public support. This assumption is reflected in answer choice (D), the correct answer.

Answer choice (A): The author states that "art is often shocking" but does not assume that *most* art is shocking.

Answer choice (B): This is the most popular wrong answer choice. In the argument, is the author committed to believing that Stravinsky and Manet received public funding? Does the author need this statement in order for the rest of the argument to work? No. The author uses Stravinsky and Manet as examples of artists whose work caused shock, but the author never assumes that those individuals received public funding. Think for a moment—does the conclusion rest on the fact that Stravinsky and Manet received public funding?

Answer choice (C): The author makes no statement regarding the "shock level" of today's art, and thus there is no way to determine if an assumption has been made comparing the shock level of past and present art.

Answer choice (D): This is the correct answer. The answer acts as a Supporter and connects the elements in the final sentence.

Answer choice (E): The author states that "art is often shocking," but there is no indication that a conditional assumption has been made stating that anything that shocks is art.

Now let us look at a Defender assumption. Please take a moment to complete the following question:

2. In Western economies, more energy is used to operate buildings than to operate transportation. Much of the decline in energy consumption since the oil crisis of 1973 is due to more efficient use of energy in homes and offices. New building technologies, which make lighting, heating, and ventilation systems more efficient, have cut billions of dollars from energy bills in the West. Since energy savings from these efficiencies save several billion dollars per year today, we can conclude that 50 to 100 years from now they will save more than $200 billion per year (calculated in current dollars).

    On which one of the following assumptions does the argument rely?

    (A) Technology used to make buildings energy efficient will not become prohibitively expensive over the next century.
    (B) Another oil crisis will occur in the next 50 to 100 years.
    (C) Buildings will gradually become a less important consumer of energy than transportation.
    (D) Energy bills in the West will be $200 billion lower in the next 50 to 100 years.
    (E) Energy-efficient technologies based on new scientific principles will be introduced in the next 50 to 100 years.

Unlike Supporter assumptions, Defender assumptions are extremely hard to prephrase because there are so many possibilities for the test makers to choose from. The correct answer in this problem is a Defender, but it is unlikely that anyone could have predicted the answer. Compare this to the previous problem, where many students were able to prephrase the correct Supporter answer.

Now, focus on the final sentence of the argument, which contains a premise and conclusion:

Premise: Energy savings from these efficiencies [new building technologies] save several billion dollars per year today.

Conclusion: 50 to 100 years from now they will save more than $200 billion per year (calculated in current dollars).

So, according to the author, the new building technologies—which are already saving billions—will continue to do the same in the future and the savings will be even greater, relatively.

Answer choice (A): This is the correct answer, and a classic Defender. If the money-saving and energy-saving technology becomes too expensive to use in the next 100 years, the savings expected will not materialize. Because this idea would clearly weaken the argument, the author assumes that it does not exist, and answer choice (A) denies that the technology will become prohibitively expensive over the next century.

Answer choice (B): Although there has been an energy usage decline since the 1973 oil crisis, the author does not assume that there will be another crisis in the next 50 to 100 years. Look at the conclusion—does there seem to be a reliance on the idea in this answer? No.

Answer choice (C): Although this answer plays with the idea mentioned in the first sentence of the stimulus—that more energy is used to operate buildings than to operate transportation—no assumption is made that buildings will become a less important consumer of energy. True, buildings have saved billions in operating in costs, but the conclusion is about future savings and not about comparing buildings to transportation.

Answer choice (D): The argument is specific about technologies *saving* more than $200 billion per year; the author does not assume that the *total* bill in the next 50 to 100 years will be lower by $200 billion.

Answer choice (E): The argument is about current technologies saving money in the future. The author does not make an assumption regarding new technologies being introduced in the future.

The Assumption Negation Technique™

Do not use the Assumption Negation Technique on all five answer choices. The process is too time-consuming and you can usually knock out a few answer choices without working too hard. Only apply the technique once you have narrowed the field.

Only a few types of LSAT questions allow you to double-check your answer. Assumption questions are one of those types, and you should use the Assumption Negation Technique to decide between Contenders or to confirm that the answer you have chosen is correct.

The purpose of this technique is to take an Assumption question, which is generally difficult for most students, and turn it into a Weaken question, which is easier for most students. *This technique can only be used on Assumption questions.* To apply the technique take the following steps:

1. Logically negate the answer choices under consideration.

   We will discuss negation later in this section, but negating a statement means to alter the sentence so the meaning is logically opposite of what was originally stated. Negation largely consists of taking a "not" out of a sentence when one is present, or putting a "not" in a sentence if one is not present. For example, "The congressman always votes for gun control" becomes "The congressman does not always vote for gun control" when properly negated.

2. The negated answer choice that attacks the argument will be the correct answer.

   When the correct answer choice is negated, the answer *must* weaken the argument. This will occur because of the conditional nature of an assumption. Take a moment to examine this diagram from the Assumption question introduction:

$$\text{Conclusion}_{\text{Valid}} \longrightarrow \text{Assumption}_{\text{True}}$$

   The diagram represents the statement "If the conclusion is valid, then the assumption must be true." The contrapositive shows that when the assumption is not true, then the conclusion is not true. Take the contrapositive of this statement:

$$\cancel{\text{Assumption}}_{\text{True}} \longrightarrow \cancel{\text{Conclusion}}_{\text{Valid}}$$

   The consequence of negating an assumption is that the validity of the conclusion is called into question. In other words, when you take away (negate) an assumption—a building block of the argument—it calls into question the integrity of the entire reasoning structure. Accordingly, negating the answer choices turns an Assumption question into a Weaken question.

Negating Statements

Negating a statement consists of creating the *logical* opposite of the statement. The logical opposite is the statement that denies the truth of the original statement, and a logical opposite is different than the *polar* opposite. For example, consider the following statement:

> I went to the beach every day last week.

The logical opposite is the statement requiring the least amount of "work" to negate the original statement:

> I did not go to the beach every day last week.

The polar opposite typically goes much further:

> I did not go to the beach *any* day last week.

For LSAT purposes, the logical opposite is the statement you should seek when negating, and in order to do this you must understand logical opposition.

Logical Opposition

The concept of logical opposition appears frequently on the LSAT in a variety of forms. A complete knowledge of the logical opposites that most often appear will provide you with a framework that eliminates uncertainties and ultimately leads to skilled LSAT performance. Consider the following question:

> What is the logical opposite of sweet?

Most people reply "sour" to the above question. While "sour" is an opposite of "sweet," it is considered the polar opposite of "sweet," not the logical opposite. A logical opposite will always completely divide the subject under consideration into two parts. Sweet and sour fail as logical opposites since tastes such as bland or bitter remain unclassified. The correct logical opposite of "sweet" is in fact "not sweet." "Sweet" and "not sweet" divide the taste spectrum into two complete parts, and tastes such as bland and bitter now clearly fall into the "not sweet" category. This same type of oppositional reasoning also applies to other everyday subjects such as color (what is the logical opposite of white?) and temperature (what is the logical opposite of hot?).

To help visualize pairs of opposites within a subject, we use an Opposition Construct. An Opposition Construct efficiently summarizes subjects within a limited spectrum of possibilities, such as quantity:

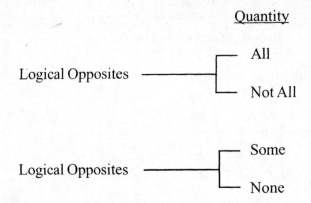

<u>Quantity</u>

Logical Opposites — All / Not All

Logical Opposites — Some / None

In this quantity construct, the range of possibilities extends from All to None. Thus, these two "ends" are polar opposites. There are also two pairs of logical opposites: All versus Not All and Some versus None. These logical opposites hold in both directions: for example, Some is the precise logical opposite of None, and None is the precise logical opposite of Some. The relationship between the four logical possibilities of quantity becomes more complex when we examine pairs such as Some and All. Imagine for a moment that we have between 0 and 100 marbles. According to the above construct, each logical possibility represents the following:

<u>Quantity</u>

All	= 100
Not All	= 0 to 99 (everything but All)
Some	= 1 to 100 (everything but None)
None	= 0

The definitions of All, Not All, Some, and None will reappear in the Formal Logic chapter.

By looking closely at the quantities each possibility represents, we can see that Some (1 to 100) actually includes All (100). This makes sense because Some, if it is to be the exact logical opposite of None, should include every other possibility besides None. The same relationship also holds true for Not All (0 to 99) and None (0).

The relationship between Some and Not All is also interesting. Some (1 to 100) and Not All (0 to 99) are largely the same, but they differ significantly at the extremes. Some actually includes All, the opposite of Not All, and Not All includes None, the opposite of Some. As a point of definition Not All is the same as Some Are Not.

The same line of reasoning applies to other subjects that often appear on the LSAT:

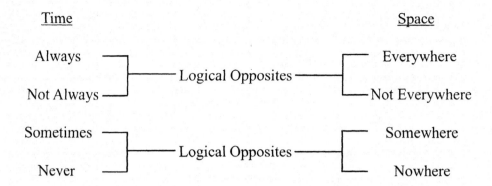

The Time and Space constructs are very similar to the Quantity construct. For example, Always is somewhat equivalent to "All of the time." Everywhere could be said to be "All of the space." Thus, learning one of these constructs makes it easy to learn the other two.

Negating Conditional Statements

To negate a conditional statement you must show that the necessary condition is not in fact necessary. For example, "To be rich, you must be smart" becomes "To be rich, you do not necessarily have to be smart." Assumption question answer choices containing conditional answer choices occur frequently on the LSAT and you must understand how to properly negate them.

To logically negate a conditional statement, negate the necessary condition.

It is also worth noting that the logical negation of a conditional statement is different than the Mistaken Negation of that statement. The Mistaken Negation is a failed inference that follows from negating both sides of the statement. A logical negation negates just the necessary condition in an attempt to produce the opposite of the statement. Example:

Original Statement: If A occurs, then B occurs.

Diagram: A $\longrightarrow$ B

Logical Negation: A $\longrightarrow$ B̸

Mistaken Negation: A̸ $\longrightarrow$ B̸

Statement Negation Drill

This drill will test your ability to use the Assumption Negation Technique™, which requires the conversion of Assumption question answer choices to Weaken answer choices. In the spaces provided write the proper logical negation of each of the following statements. *Answers on Page 271*

1. The tax increase will result in more revenue for the government.

    _____

2. The councilmember could reverse her position.

    _____

3. The voting patterns in this precinct changed significantly in the past year.

    _____

4. The pattern of behavior in adolescents is not necessarily determined by the environment they are raised in.

    _____

5. Organic farming methods promote crop resistance to pest attack.

    _____

6. All of the missions succeeded.

    _____

7. If the policy is implemented, the education budget will be cut.

    _____

8. The positive effects of the U.S. immigration policy are everywhere.

    _____

9. Unless the stock market rebounds, the economy will not recover this year.

    _____

10. Exactly one police car will reach the scene in time.

    _____

Statement Negation Drill Answer Key

The correct answer is listed below, with the negating elements italicized.

1. The tax increase *might not* result in more revenue for the government.

   The negation of "will" is "might not." In practice the polar opposite "will not" tends to be acceptable.

2. The councilmember *cannot* reverse her position.

   "Cannot" is the opposite of "could."

3. The voting patterns in this precinct *did not* change significantly in the past year.

4. The pattern of behavior in adolescents is *necessarily* determined by the environment they are raised in.

5. Organic farming methods *do not* promote crop resistance to pest attack.

6. *Not all* of the missions succeeded.

7. If the policy is implemented, the education budget will *not* be cut.

   Negate the necessary condition using "will not" or "might not."

8. The positive effects of the U.S immigration policy are *not* everywhere.

   Note that "positive" in this sentence does not become "negative." To say "The negative effects of the U.S immigration policy are everywhere" would not negate the original.

9. The economy will recover this year even if the stock market does *not* rebound.

   This is a conditional statement, and to most easily negate the statement you should turn it into an "if...then" sentence construction.

10. *Not exactly one* police car will reach the scene in time.

    Typically, there are two ways to negate a phrase containing the words "only one" or "exactly one." One possibility is to use the term "none" and the other possibility is to use the phrase "more than once." Both are logical negations since you are attempting to negate a statement where something occurred a precise number of times. In this case, any statement that differs in number from the original statement will be a negation.

Three Quirks of Assumption Question Answer Choices

Over the years, certain recurring traits have appeared in Assumption answer choices. Recognizing these quirks may help you eliminate wrong answers or more quickly identify the correct answer at crunch time.

1. Watch for answers starting with the phrase "at least one" or "at least some."

    For some reason, when an Assumption answer choice starts with either of the above constructions the chances are unusually high that the answer will be correct. However, if you spot an answer with that construction, do not simply assume the answer is correct; instead, use the proper negation ("None") and check the answer with the Assumption Negation Technique.

2. Avoid answers that claim an idea was the most important consideration for the author.

    These answers typically use constructions such as "the primary purpose," "the top priority," or "the main factor." In every Assumption question these answers have been wrong. And, unless, the author specifically discusses the prioritization of ideas in the stimulus, these answers will continue to be wrong because an author can always claim that the idea under discussion was very important but not necessarily the most important idea.

3. Watch for the use of "not" or negatives in assumption answer choices.

    Because most students are conditioned to think of assumptions as positive connecting elements, the appearance of a negative in an Assumption answer choice often causes the answer to be classified a Loser. Do not rule out a negative answer choice just because you are used to seeing assumptions as a positive part of the argument. As we have seen with Defender answer choices, one role an assumption can play is to eliminate ideas that could attack the argument. To do so, Defender answer choices frequently contain negative terms such as "no," "not," and "never." One benefit of this negative language is that Defender answer choices can usually be negated quite easily.

    Law Services is clearly aware that negative language in an Assumption answer confuses most people, and at one point in the 1980s there were numerous problems where the first answer choice contained negative language and was correct. This phenomenon has faded, but the implications are clear: the test makers expect you to routinely bypass answers with negative language. Remember, you can quickly drop the negative term and see if the negated answer attacks the argument.

Assumptions and Conditionality

Problems containing conditional reasoning tend to produce two types of assumption answer choices:

1. If conditional statements are linked together in the argument, the correct answer choice for an Assumption question will typically supply a missing link in the chain, as in the following example:

    Premises: A $\longrightarrow$ B $\longrightarrow$ C

    Conclusion: A $\longrightarrow$ D

    Assumption: C $\longrightarrow$ D   (or the contrapositive)

    Thus, if you encounter linked statements and an Assumption question, be prepared to supply the missing link or the contrapositive of that link.

2. The assumption underlying a conditional statement is that the necessary condition *must occur* in order for the sufficient condition to occur. Thus, the author always assumes that any statement that would challenge the truth of the relationship is false. If no conditional chains are present and only a conditional conclusion exists, the correct answer will usually deny scenarios where the sufficient condition occurs and the necessary does not. In other words, the assumption in these arguments always protects the necessary condition (that is, it works as a Defender). If you see a conditional conclusion and then are asked an Assumption question, immediately look for an answer that confirms that the necessary condition is truly necessary or that eliminates possible alternatives to the necessary condition.

Please take a moment to complete the following problem:

3. Emissions from automobiles that burn gasoline and automobiles that burn diesel fuel are threatening the quality of life on our planet, contaminating both urban air and global atmosphere. Therefore, the only effective way to reduce such emissions is to replace the conventional diesel fuel and gasoline used in automobiles with cleaner-burning fuels, such as methanol, that create fewer emissions.

Which one of the following is an assumption on which the argument depends?

(A) Reducing the use of automobiles would not be a more effective means to reduce automobile emissions than the use of methanol.

(B) There is no fuel other than methanol that is cleaner-burning than both diesel fuel and gasoline.

(C) If given a choice of automobile fuels, automobile owners would not select gasoline over methanol.

(D) Automobile emissions constitute the most serious threat to the global environment.

(E) At any given time there is a direct correlation between the level of urban air pollution and the level of contamination present in the global atmosphere.

The last sentence contains the conclusion of the argument, which is conditional (note the use of the necessary condition indicator "only"):

ERE = Effectively reduce emissions
Replace = Replace the conventional diesel fuel and gasoline used in automobiles with cleaner-burning fuels, such as methanol, that create fewer emissions.

$$ERE \longrightarrow Replace$$

According to the author, to effectively reduce emissions, conventional fuels *must* be replaced. Based on our discussion, since the stimulus does not present any conditional chains, you should look for an answer that protects the necessary condition. Answer choice (A) is a Defender that does just that, eliminating an idea that would undermine the relationship.

Answer choice (A): This is the correct answer. Consider the author's position that the only effective way to reduce emissions is fuel replacement. Wouldn't it be more effective to simply stop using cars altogether? Of course this is true, but this would undermine the conditional nature of the conclusion and so the author assumes that this possibility cannot occur.

If this answer is troubling you, use the Assumption Negation Technique and ask yourself if the following statement would undermine the argument:

> Reducing the use of automobiles *would be* a more effective means to reduce automobile emissions than the use of methanol.

This answer clearly shows that there are other, more effective ways of reducing emissions and therefore the answer attacks the argument. This must be the correct answer.

Answer choice (B): The author is not committed to methanol because the stimulus clearly references "fuels such as methanol." Accordingly, this answer is not an assumption of the argument.

Answer choice (C): The choices automobile owners would make are not part of the argument made by the author. The author simply states that the only effective way to achieve reduced emissions is fuel replacement. No assumption is made about whether automobile owners would follow that way. The problem with the answer can be highlighted by this example:

> An argument is made that the best way to achieve long-lasting fame is to commit suicide. Does the author assume that people will or will not choose that path? No, because the *best way* does not involve an assumption about how people will actually act.

Answer choice (D): This answer falls under the second of the three quirks discussed in the previous section. The author clearly believes that automobile emissions are a serious threat to the environment, but this does not mean that the author has assumed they are the *most* serious threat. Negate the answer and ask yourself, "What would the author say to the negation?" The author would reply that he or she never indicated that emissions were the most serious threat, so it is fine that they are not.

Answer choice (E): We know that both urban air and the global atmosphere are contaminated by cars, but the author does not indicate that there is a direct correlation between the two. This answer, when negated, has no effect on the argument (and must therefore be incorrect).

In an Assumption question, there can be only one answer that will hurt the argument when negated. If you negate the answers and think that two or more hurt the argument, you have made a mistake.

Assumptions and Causality

The central assumption of causality was stated in the last chapter:

> "When an LSAT speaker concludes that one occurrence caused another, that speaker also assumes that the stated cause is the *only* possible cause of the effect and that consequently the stated cause will *always* produce the effect."

Thus, because the author always assumes that the stated cause is the only cause, Assumption answer choices tend to work exactly like Strengthen answer choices in arguments with causal reasoning. The correct answer to an Assumption question will normally fit one of the following categories:

A. Eliminates any alternate cause for the stated effect

   Because the author believes there is only one cause (the stated cause in the argument), the author assumes no other cause exists.

B. Shows that when the cause occurs, the effect occurs

   Because the author believes that the cause always produces the effect, assumption answers will affirm this relationship.

C. Shows that when the cause does not occur, the effect does not occur

   Using the reasoning in the previous point, the author will always assume that when the cause does not occur, the effect will not occur.

D. Eliminates the possibility that the stated relationship is reversed

   Because the author believes that the cause-and-effect relationship is correctly stated, the author assumes that the relationship cannot be backwards (the claimed effect is actually the cause of the claimed cause).

E. Shows that the data used to make the causal statement are accurate, or eliminates possible problems with the data

   If the data used to make a causal statement are in error, then the validity of the causal claim is in question. The author assumes that this cannot be the case and that the data are accurate.

The above categories should be easy to identify because you should have already memorized them from the Strengthen question section. From now on, when you encounter Assumption questions containing causal reasoning, you will be amazed at how obvious the correct answer will seem. These types of patterns within questions are what makes improvement on the LSAT possible, and when you become comfortable with the ideas, your speed will also increase.

Please take a moment to complete the following problem:

4. Doctors in Britain have long suspected that patients who wear tinted eyeglasses are abnormally prone to depression and hypochondria. Psychological tests given there to hospital patients admitted for physical complaints like heart pain and digestive distress confirmed such a relationship. Perhaps people whose relationship to the world is psychologically painful choose such glasses to reduce visual stimulation, which is perceived as irritating. At any rate, it can be concluded that when such glasses are worn, it is because the wearer has a tendency to be depressed or hypochondriacal.

The argument assumes which one of the following?

(A) Depression is not caused in some cases by an organic condition of the body.
(B) Wearers do not think of the tinted glasses as a means of distancing themselves from other people.
(C) Depression can have many causes, including actual conditions about which it is reasonable for anyone to be depressed.
(D) For hypochondriacs wearing tinted glasses, the glasses serve as a visual signal to others that the wearer's health is delicate.
(E) The tinting does not dim light to the eye enough to depress the wearer's mood substantially.

The conclusion of this argument is causal in nature ("because" is the indicator):

Depression = tendency to be depressed or hypochondriacal
Glasses = glasses are worn

The answer choices are very interesting as they all relate to either the cause or effect, or both. Answer choices (A) and (C) are similar in that they both discuss what causes depression (the cause of the cause). But the author has made no assumption about what *causes* depression, only that depression causes a person to wear glasses. Therefore, both of these answers are incorrect. Similarly, answer choices (B) and (D) both discuss the effects of wearing glasses (the effects of the effect). Again, this is not a part of the author's argument. Because answer choices (A), (B), (C), and (D) discuss issues that occur either "before" or "after" the causal relationship in the conclusion, they are incorrect.

Answer choice (E): This is the correct answer. Answer choice (E) is a Defender that eliminates the possibility that the stated relationship is reversed (Type D in the Assumptions and Causality discussion). Remember, if the glasses actually cause the wearer to be depressed, this scenario would hurt the argument, so the author assumes the possibility cannot exist. Note how tricky this answer could be, especially if you had not been exposed to the way the test makers think about causality and assumptions. With the right information, the answer can be identified as part of a larger pattern on the LSAT, and this allows you to solve the problem quickly and confidently. While it may take a bit of work to memorize the different assumptions inherent in causal arguments, the payoff is more than worth the effort.

Assumption Question Type Review

An assumption is simply an unstated premise of the argument; that is, an integral component of the argument that the author takes for granted and leaves unsaid.

The relationship between the conclusion and the assumption can be described as:

$$\text{Conclusion}_{\text{Valid}} \longrightarrow \text{Assumption}_{\text{True}}$$

Hence, the answer you select as correct must contain a statement that the author relies upon and is fully committed to in the argument.

Assumption question stems typically contain the following features:

1. The stem uses the word "assumption" or "presupposition" or some variation.

2. The stem does *not* use the word "if" or another sufficient condition indicator.

On the LSAT, assumptions play one of two roles: the Supporter or the Defender:

Supporter Assumption: These assumptions link together new or rogue elements in the stimulus or fill logical gaps in the argument.

Defender Assumption: These assumptions contain statements that eliminate ideas or assertions that would undermine the conclusion. In this sense, they "defend" the argument by showing that a possible avenue of attack has been eliminated (assumed not to exist).

Use the Assumption Negation Technique to decide between Contenders or to confirm that the answer you have chosen is correct. The purpose of this technique is to take an Assumption question, which is generally more difficult, and turn it into a Weaken question. *This technique can only be used on Assumption questions.* Take the following step to apply this technique:

1. Logically negate the answer choices under consideration.

2. The negated answer choice that attacks the argument will be the correct answer.

Assumption Question Type Review

Negating a statement consists of creating the *logical* opposite of the statement. The logical opposite is the statement that denies the truth of the original statement, and a logical opposite is different than the polar opposite.

To negate a conditional statement you must show that the necessary condition is not in fact necessary.

The assumption underlying conditional reasoning is that the necessary condition *must occur* in order for the sufficient condition to occur. Thus, the author always assumes that any statement that challenges the truth of the relationship is false. If you see a conditional conclusion and then are asked an Assumption question, immediately look for an answer that confirms that the necessary condition is truly necessary or one that eliminates possible alternatives to the necessary condition.

Assumption answer choices tend to work exactly like Strengthen answer choices in arguments with causal reasoning. Because the author always assumes the stated cause is the only cause, the correct answer to an Assumption question will normally fit one of the following categories:

A. Eliminates any alternate cause for the stated effect

B. Shows that when the cause occurs, the effect occurs

C. Shows that when the cause does not occur, the effect does not occur

D. Eliminates the possibility that the stated relationship is reversed

E. Shows that the data used to make the causal statement are accurate, or eliminates possible problems with the data

Assumption Question Problem Set

The following questions are drawn from actual LSATs. Please complete the problem set and review the answer key and explanations. *Answers on Page 283*

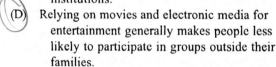

1. Columnist: A democratic society cannot exist unless its citizens have established strong bonds of mutual trust. Such bonds are formed and strengthened only by participation in civic organizations, political parties, and other groups outside the family. It is obvious then that widespread reliance on movies and electronic media for entertainment has an inherently corrosive effect on democracy.

    Which one of the following is an assumption on which the columnist's argument depends?

    (A) Anyone who relies on movies and electronic media for entertainment is unable to form a strong bond of mutual trust with a citizen.
    (B) Civic organizations cannot usefully advance their goals by using electronic media.
    (C) Newspapers and other forms of print media strengthen, rather than weaken, democratic institutions.
    (D) Relying on movies and electronic media for entertainment generally makes people less likely to participate in groups outside their families.
    (E) People who rely on movies and electronic media for entertainment are generally closer to their families than are those who do not.

2. Barnes: The two newest employees at this company have salaries that are too high for the simple tasks normally assigned to new employees and duties that are too complex for inexperienced workers. Hence, the salaries and the complexity of the duties of these two newest employees should be reduced.

    Which one of the following is an assumption on which Barnes's argument depends?

    (A) The duties of the two newest employees are not less complex than any others in the company.
    (B) It is because of the complex duties assigned that the two newest employees are being paid more than is usually paid to newly hired employees.
    (C) The two newest employees are not experienced at their occupations.
    (D) Barnes was not hired at a higher-than-average starting salary.
    (E) The salaries of the two newest employees are no higher than the salaries that other companies pay for workers with a similar level of experience.

3. The current pattern of human consumption of resources, in which we rely on nonrenewable resources, for example metal ore, must eventually change. Since there is only so much metal ore available, ultimately we must either do without or turn to renewable resources to take its place.

    Which one of the following is an assumption required by the argument?

    (A) There are renewable resource replacements for all of the nonrenewable resources currently being consumed.
    (B) We cannot indefinitely replace exhausted nonrenewable resources with other nonrenewable resources.
    (C) A renewable resource cannot be exhausted by human consumption.
    (D) Consumption of nonrenewable resources will not continue to increase in the near future.
    (E) Ultimately we cannot do without nonrenewable resources.

Assumption Question Problem Set

4. In humans, ingested protein is broken down into amino acids, all of which must compete to enter the brain. Subsequent ingestion of sugars leads to the production of insulin, a hormone that breaks down the sugars and also rids the bloodstream of residual amino acids, except for tryptophan. Tryptophan then slips into the brain uncontested and is transformed into the chemical serotonin, increasing the brain's serotonin level. Thus, sugars can play a major role in mood elevation, helping one to feel relaxed and anxiety-free.

    Which one of the following is an assumption on which the argument depends?

    (A) Elevation of mood and freedom from anxiety require increasing the level of serotonin in the brain.
    (B) Failure to consume foods rich in sugars results in anxiety and a lowering of mood.
    (C) Serotonin can be produced naturally only if tryptophan is present in the bloodstream.
    (D) Increasing the level of serotonin in the brain promotes relaxation and freedom from anxiety.
    (E) The consumption of protein-rich foods results in anxiety and a lowering of mood.

5. Publicity campaigns for endangered species are unlikely to have much impact on the most important environmental problems, for while the ease of attributing feelings to large mammals facilitates evoking sympathy for them, it is more difficult to elicit sympathy for other kinds of organisms, such as the soil microorganisms on which large ecosystems and agriculture depend.

    Which one of the following is an assumption on which the argument depends?

    (A) The most important environmental problems involve endangered species other than large mammals.
    (B) Microorganisms cannot experience pain or have other feelings.
    (C) Publicity campaigns for the environment are the most effective when they elicit sympathy for some organism.
    (D) People ignore environmental problems unless they believe the problems will affect creatures with which they sympathize.
    (E) An organism can be environmentally significant only if it affects large ecosystems or agriculture.

6. Historian: Leibniz, the seventeenth-century philosopher, published his version of calculus before Newton did. But then Newton revealed his private notebooks, which showed he had been using these ideas for at least a decade before Leibniz's publication. Newton also claimed that he had disclosed these ideas to Leibniz in a letter shortly before Leibniz's publication. Yet close examination of the letter shows that Newton's few cryptic remarks did not reveal anything important about calculus. Thus, Leibniz and Newton each independently discovered calculus.

    Which one of the following is an assumption required by the historian's argument?

    (A) Leibniz did not tell anyone about calculus prior to publishing his version of it.
    (B) No third person independently discovered calculus prior to Newton and Leibniz.
    (C) Newton believed that Leibniz was able to learn something important about calculus from his letter to him.
    (D) Neither Newton nor Leibniz knew that the other had developed a version of calculus prior to Leibniz's publication.
    (E) Neither Newton nor Leibniz learned crucial details about calculus from some third source.

    FUCK

282

THE POWERSCORE LSAT LOGICAL REASONING BIBLE

Assumption Problem Set Answer Key

All answer keys in this book indicate the source of the question by giving the month and year the LSAT was originally administered, the Logical Reasoning section number, and the question number within that section. Each LSAT has two Logical Reasoning sections, and so the Section 1 and Section 2 designators will refer to the first or second Logical Reasoning section in the test, not the physical section number of the booklet.

Question #1. Assumption-SN. June 2001 LSAT, Section 2, #5. The correct answer choice is (D)

The stimulus contains conditional reasoning, and can be diagrammed as follows:

DS = democratic society exists
SB = citizens establish strong bonds of mutual trust
PCO = participation in civic organizations, political parties, and other groups outside the family

Premises: DS $\longrightarrow$ SB $\longrightarrow$ PCO

Conclusion: Widespread reliance on movies and electronic media for entertainment has an inherently corrosive effect on democracy.

The conclusion brings in a new element—reliance on movies and electronic media—and you should expect to see that element in the correct answer choice. First, let us take a moment to closely examine the conclusion. The wording in the conclusion is interesting: "has an inherently corrosive effect on democracy." We know from the premises that a democratic society relies on both citizens and participation in groups outside the family. How then can the author suggest that democracy is being corroded? Since corrosion implies an undermining force, democracy can be undermined by attacking the conditions it relies upon. If, for example, the participation in organizations outside the family was curtailed, this would eventually enact a contrapositive that would undermine the existence of democratic society. The assumption that is needed therefore, is to show that movies and other electronic media somehow lead to a lessening of participation in civic organizations, political parties, and other groups outside the family. This is the connection made in answer choice (D), the correct answer.

Answer choice (A): This was the most commonly selected wrong answer, and this answer is incorrect because it exaggerates the situation. The author does not assume that *anyone* would be *unable* to form a strong bond of trust. The argument was clear about a *corrosive* effect on democracy. This answer, if it were an assumption, would lead to the end of democracy. That result is too strong for the author's conclusion.

Answer choice (B): The author makes no assumption regarding organizations advancing their agenda.

Answer choice (C): The argument is not about newspapers and print media.

Answer choice (D): This is the correct answer. This Supporter assumption connects the new element in the conclusion back to the conditional relationship in the premises.

Answer choice (E): The author does not assume that closeness to the family is a bad thing, but that one must also participate outside the family. This answer does not suggest otherwise, and it is not an assumption of the argument.

Question #2. Assumption. October 1999 LSAT, Section 1, #5. The correct answer choice is (C)

The stimulus to this problem contains a Shell Game, and you must read closely in order to identify it: in the first sentence the author equates "new employees" with "inexperienced workers." Of course, a new employee is not necessarily inexperienced (the employee could have transferred from another company, etc.). The assumption that new employees are inexperienced is reflected in the correct answer, (C).

Answer choice (A): The author notes that the duties of the two new employees are too complex for them, but the author does not compare or imply a comparison to the tasks of other workers.

Answer choice (B): The author makes no assumption as to why the two new employees are being paid the salary they receive, only that their salary should be reduced. For example, the reason the employees are paid more could be that they are related to the owner of the company.

Answer choice (C): This is the correct answer, a Supporter.

Answer choice (D): This answer is an immediate Loser. No discussion or assumption is made about Barnes' salary.

Answer choice (E): This answer would hurt the argument, and therefore it can never be an assumption of the argument.

Question #3. Assumption. October 2001 LSAT, Section 1, #18. The correct answer choice is (B)

The structure of the argument is as follows:

Premise:	There is only so much metal ore available.
Subconclusion/ Premise:	Ultimately we must either do without or turn to renewable resources to take its place.
Conclusion:	The current pattern of human consumption of resources, in which we rely on nonrenewable resources, for example metal ore, must eventually change.

At first glance the argument does not seem to have any holes. This would suggest a Defender answer is coming, and indeed that is the case.

Answer choice (A): The author does not need to assume this statement because the stimulus specifically indicates that "we must either *do without* or turn to renewable resources." Since doing without is an option, the author is not assuming there are renewable replacements for all nonrenewable resources currently being consumed.

Assumption Problem Set Answer Key

Answer choice (B): This is the correct answer. This answer defends the conclusion that the consumption pattern must change by indicating that it would *not* be possible to simply replace one nonrenewable resource with another nonrenewable resource. If this answer did not make sense at first glance, you should have noted the negative language and then negated the answer. Using the Assumption Negation Technique, the following would clearly attack the conclusion: "We *can* indefinitely replace exhausted nonrenewable resources with other nonrenewable resources." If the nonrenewable resources can be indefinitely replaced, why do we need to change our consumption habits?

Answer choice (C): The author's argument concerns changing current consumption habits. Although the author does suggest turning to renewable resources, this alone would represent a change. The author does not make a long-term assumption that renewable resources can never be depleted. When faced with the negation of the answer choice, the author would likely reply: "If that eventuality does occur, then perhaps we will have to do without. In the meantime, we still need to change our consumption habits." As you can see, the negation has not undermined the author's position, and so this answer is incorrect.

Answer choice (D): The author does not make statements or assumptions about actual consumption patterns in the *near future*, only statements regarding what must *eventually* occur.

Answer choice (E): This answer, when rephrased to eliminate the double negative, reads as "Ultimately we must have nonrenewable resources." Because this answer hurts the argument, the answer is incorrect.

Question #4. Assumption. October 2002 LSAT, Section 2, #22. The correct answer choice is (D)

The importance of this problem is not just in answering it correctly, but also in answering it quickly. A major portion of LSAT success is speed related, and a question like this is an opportunity to gain time. The first step is to recognize the argument structure:

Premise:	In humans, ingested protein is broken down into amino acids, all of which must compete to enter the brain.
Premise:	Subsequent ingestion of sugars leads to the production of insulin, a hormone that breaks down the sugars and also rids the bloodstream of residual amino acids, except for tryptophan.
Premise:	Tryptophan then slips into the brain uncontested and is transformed into the chemical serotonin, increasing the brain's serotonin level.
Conclusion:	Sugars can play a major role in mood elevation, helping one to feel relaxed and anxiety-free.

At this point in your preparation, you should constantly be on the lookout for new elements that appear in the conclusion. This problem contains the new conclusion element of "a major role in mood elevation, helping one to feel relaxed and anxiety-free." Because this element immediately follows the assertion that the brain's serotonin level has been increased, you should attack the answer choices by looking for an answer that fits the Supporter relationship that an increase serotonin leads to an elevated mood. Only answer choices (A) and (D) contain these two elements, and you should examine them first as you seek to accelerate through this problem:

Answer choice (A): Although the author assumes that raising the level of serotonin is sufficient to elevate mood, this answer claims that it is necessary. Hence, this answer is incorrect.

Answer choice (D): This is the correct answer. The author states that after the action of the sugars, more serotonin enters the brain. The author then concludes that this leads to a mood elevation. Thus, the author assumes that serotonin has an effect on the mood level.

Answer choice (B): The argument refers to what happens when sugars are ingested. No assumption is made about what occurs when foods rich in sugars are not ingested.

Answer choice (C): Although the argument states that tryptophan is transformed into serotonin, no assumption is made that this is the only way serotonin is produced.

Answer choice (E): The author does not assume the statement in this answer. We know from the first sentence of the stimulus that ingested protein is broken down into amino acids which compete to enter the brain. This competition could result in mood elevation even without the ingestion of sugars since some amino acids will enter the brain (some could be tryptophan, for example). Thus, since the author's argument contains a scenario that would allow for the opposite of this answer choice to occur, this answer is not an assumption of the argument.

Question #5. Assumption. October 2001 LSAT, Section 2, #16. The correct answer choice is (A)

This is a challenging problem because two of the wrong answer choices are attractive. The argument itself is not overly complex, but you must pay attention to the language. Consider the conclusion of the argument:

> "Publicity campaigns for endangered species are unlikely to have much impact on the most important environmental problems."

Ask yourself, why is it that these campaigns are unlikely to have much impact on the *most important* problems? According to the premises, the reason is that "it is more difficult to elicit sympathy for other kinds of organisms [than large mammals]." The reasoning shows that the author believes there is a connection between the important problems and organisms that are not large mammals. This Supporter connection is perfectly reflected in answer choice (A), the correct answer. Again, when faced with an Assumption question, remember to look for connections between rogue elements in the argument, and then seek that connection in the answer choices.

Answer choice (B): The argument is about eliciting sympathy, and no assumption is made about microorganisms *experiencing* pain.

Assumption Problem Set Answer Key

Answer choice (C): This is a Shell Game answer. The conclusion is specific about "publicity campaigns for endangered species" as they relate to environmental problems. This answer refers to "publicity campaigns" in general—a different concept. It may be that the most effective publicity campaign for the environment has nothing to do with organisms. Consequently, this answer is not an assumption of the argument.

Answer choice (D): This answer choice is worded too strongly and is an Exaggerated answer. "Ignore" goes further than what the author implies. The author indicates that it is "*more difficult* to elicit sympathy for other kinds of organisms," but the author does not say it is impossible to get sympathy from individuals if a non-large mammal is involved. Further, the argument is specific about the impact on the "most important" problems, and this answer goes well beyond that domain.

Answer choice (E): The microorganisms discussed at the end of the argument are an example ("such as"); therefore, the author does not assume this type of relationship must be true in order for the conclusion to be true.

Question #6. Assumption. June 2000 LSAT, Section 1, #14. The correct answer choice is (E)

The conclusion of the argument asserts that Leibniz and Newton each independently discovered calculus, and in drawing the conclusion the author addresses the possibility Newton may have influenced Leibniz, and then rejects that possibility. A review of the argument does not reveal any conspicuous flaws, and so upon encountering the question stem, you should expect to see a Defender answer. As such, do not spend time trying to prephrase an answer—just make sure you know the facts of the argument.

Answer choice (A): The argument is about the independent discovery of calculus; the author makes no assumption that Leibniz did not tell anyone else, and indeed the fact that Newton did tell Leibniz is not accepted by the author as undermining the conclusion.

Answer choice (B): Negate the answer: "A third person independently discovered calculus prior to Newton and Leibniz." Would this negated answer attack the argument? No, the author would just assert that three different parties independently discovered calculus.

Answer choice (C): The author cites Newton's letter as evidence that Newton felt he had disclosed ideas to Leibniz prior to Leibniz's publication date. No assumption is made that Newton felt that what was disclosed allowed Leibniz to learn something important. If you are uncertain of this answer, negate the choice to see if it weakens the argument.

Answer choice (D): This is clearly not an assumption of the argument because the author discusses Newton's letter to Leibniz prior to Leibniz's publication date.

Answer choice (E): This is the correct answer. The answer can be difficult because it is somewhat similar to answer choice (B), which many people already eliminated by the time they reached this answer. Answer (E) is different from answer (B) because it involves learning details from a third source. This is important because the conclusion references the *independent discovery* of calculus, and so the author must believe that neither Newton nor Leibniz learned anything substantial about calculus from other sources.

This elimination of an idea that weakens the argument is the essence of a Defender answer choice. To further confirm the answer, consider the negation of this answer choice ("neither...nor" becomes "either...or"): "*Either* Newton *or* Leibniz learned crucial details about calculus from some third source." This negated answer undermines the assertion that Leibniz and Newton each independently discovered calculus. Consequently, this is the correct answer.

Strengthen, Justify the Conclusion, and Assumption Identify The Question Stem Drill

The following items contain a question stem from a recent LSAT question. In the space provided, categorize each stem into one of the three Logical Reasoning Question Types: Strengthen, Justify the Conclusion, or Assumption. *Answers on Page 290*

1. Question Stem: "Which one of the following, if true, most strongly supports the statement above?"

   Question Type: _____

2. Question Stem: "Which one of the following is an assumption on which Patti's argument depends?"

   Question Type: _____

3. Question Stem: "The conclusion drawn by the professor follows logically if which one of the following is assumed?"

   Question Type: _____

4. Question Stem: "Which one of the following is an assumption required by the argument?"

   Question Type: _____

5. Question Stem: "Which one of the following, if assumed, would allow the conclusion to be properly drawn?"

   Question Type: _____

6. Question Stem: "Which one of the following, if true, does most to justify the apparently contradictory conclusion above?"

   Question Type: _____

1. Question Type: Strengthen
Stem drawn from the December 2003 LSAT. The presence of the phrase "most strongly supports" indicates that this question stem is a Strengthen.

2. Question Type: Assumption
Stem drawn from the October 2003 LSAT. The presence of the word "assumption" without any sufficient condition indicators classifies this question as an Assumption. Further, the phrase "depends upon" indicates the answer will have a necessary quality, a hallmark of assumption questions.

3. Question Type: Justify the Conclusion
Stem drawn from the December 2003 LSAT. The presence of the words "if" and "assumed" indicates that this question stem is a Justify.

4. Question Type: Assumption
Stem drawn from the October 2003 LSAT. The key words in this stem are "required" and "assumption," making this an Assumption question. You must be careful when you see the word "assumption" because that word can also be used in Justify the Conclusion questions.

5. Question Type: Justify the Conclusion
Stem drawn from the October 2003 LSAT. The presence of the words "if" and "assumed" indicates that this question stem is a Justify, as does the phrase "allow the conclusion to be properly drawn."

6. Question Type: Strengthen
Stem drawn from the December 2002 LSAT. The presence of the phrase "does *most* to justify" indicates that this question stem is a Strengthen. The presence of "most" opens the door to an answer that does not 100% justify the conclusion, hence the question is not a true Justify the Conclusion question.

CHAPTER TEN: RESOLVE THE PARADOX QUESTIONS

Resolve the Paradox Questions ████████████

Resolve the Paradox questions are generally easy to spot because of their distinctive stimuli: each stimulus presents a situation where two ideas or occurrences contradict each other. Because most people are very good at recognizing these paradox scenarios, they usually know after reading the stimulus that a Resolve the Paradox question is coming up.

Stimulus Peculiarities

Besides the discrepant or contradictory facts, most Resolve the Paradox stimuli contain the following features:

1. No conclusion

   One of the hallmarks of a Resolve the Paradox question is that the stimulus does not contain a conclusion. The author is not attempting to persuade you, he or she just presents two sets of contradictory facts. Thus, when you read a stimulus without a conclusion that contains a paradox, expect to see a Resolve question. If you read a fact set that does not contain a paradox, expect to see a Must Be True question or a Cannot Be True question (less likely).

2. Language of contradiction

   In order to present a paradox, the test makers use language that signals a contradiction is present, such as:

   > But
   > However
   > Yet
   > Although
   > Paradoxically
   > Surprisingly

If you can recognize the paradox present in the stimulus, you will have a head start on prephrasing the answer and completing the problem more quickly.

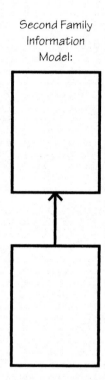

Second Family
Information
Model:

Question Stem Features

Resolve the Paradox question stem are easy to identify, and typically contain the following features:

You should attempt to prephrase an answer; many students are able to successfully predict a scenario that would explain the situation.

1. An indication that the answer choices should be accepted as true

   Because Resolve the Paradox questions fall into the Second Question Family, you must accept the answer choices as true and then see if they resolve the paradox. Typically, the question stem will contain a phrase such as, "which one of the *following*, if true, ..."

2. Key words that indicate your task is to resolve a problem

   To convey the nature of your task, Resolve the Paradox question stems usually use words from both of the lists below. The first list contains words used to describe the action you must take, the second list contains words used to describe the paradox present in the stimulus:

Action	Problem
Resolve	Paradox
Explain	Discrepancy
Reconcile	Contradiction
	Conflict
	Puzzle

A ResolveX question would present four incorrect answers that resolve or explain the situation. The one correct answer would either confuse the situation, or, more likely, have no impact on the situation.

Here are several Resolve the Paradox question stem examples from actual LSATs:

"Which one of the following, if true, would most effectively resolve the apparent paradox above?"

"Which one of the following, if true, most helps to resolve the apparent discrepancy in the passage above?"

"Which one of the following, if true, most helps to explain the puzzling fact cited above?"

"Which one of the following, if true, most helps to reconcile the discrepancy indicated above?"

"Which one of the following, if true, most helps to resolve the apparent conflict described above?"

Active Resolution

When first presented with a Resolve question, most students seek an answer choice that destroys or disproves one side of the situation. They follow the reasoning that if one side can be proven false, then the paradox will be eliminated. While this is true, the test makers know that such an answer would be obvious (it would simply contradict part of the facts given in the stimulus) and thus this type of answer does not appear in these questions. Instead, the correct answer will actively resolve the paradox, that is, it will allow both sides to be factually correct and it will either explain how the situation came into being or add a piece of information that shows how the two ideas or occurrences can coexist.

Because you are not seeking to disprove one side of the situation, you must select the answer choice that contains a *possible cause* of the situation. So, when examining answers, ask yourself if the answer choice could lead to the situation in the stimulus. If so, the answer is correct.

Please take a moment to complete the following problem:

1. Provinces and states with stringent car safety requirements, including required use of seat belts and annual safety inspections, have on average higher rates of accidents per kilometer driven than do provinces and states with less stringent requirements. Nevertheless, most highway safety experts agree that more stringent requirements do reduce accident rates.

    Which one of the following, if true, most helps to reconcile the safety experts' belief with the apparently contrary evidence described above?

    (A) Annual safety inspections ensure that car tires are replaced before they grow old.
    (B) Drivers often become overconfident after their cars have passed a thorough safety inspection.
    (C) The roads in provinces and states with stringent car safety programs are far more congested and therefore dangerous than in other provinces and states.
    (D) Psychological studies show that drivers who regularly wear seat belts often come to think of themselves as serious drivers, which for a few people discourages reckless driving.
    (E) Provinces and states with stringent car safety requirements have, on average, many more kilometers of roads then do other provinces and states.

The correct answer will positively resolve the paradox so that both sides are true and the conditions in the stimulus have been met.

If an answer supports or proves only one side of the paradox, that answer will be incorrect. The correct answer must show how both sides coexist.

If the stimulus contains a paradox where two items are similar, then an answer choice that explains a difference between the two cannot be correct.

Conversely, if the stimulus contains a paradox where two items are different, then an answer choice that explains why the two are similar cannot be correct.

In short, a similarity cannot explain a difference, and a difference cannot explain a similarity.

The paradox in the argument is that the provinces and states that have more stringent safety requirements also have higher average rates of accidents. Even so, experts agree that the more stringent requirements actually are effective. This type of "surprisingly low/high rate of success" scenario has appeared in a number of Resolve the Paradox questions, including the following:

An anti-theft device is known to reduce theft, but cars using the anti-theft device are stolen at a higher rate than cars without the device.

Explanation: The device is placed on highly desirable cars that are prone to being stolen, and the device actually lessens the rate at which they are stolen.

A surgeon has a low success rate while operating, but the director of the hospital claims the surgeon is the best on the staff.

Explanation: The surgeon operates on the most complex and challenging cases.

A bill collector has the lowest rate of success in collecting bills, but his manager claims he is the best in the field.

Explanation: The bill collector is assigned the toughest cases to handle.

These scenarios underscore the issue present in the question: other factors in the situation make it more difficult to be successful. With the car safety requirements, you should look for an answer that shows that there is a situation with the roads that affects the accident rates. A second possible explanation is that the seat belts are not actually used by a majority of drivers and the safety inspections are not made or are rubber-stamp certifications. This answer is less likely to appear because it is fairly obvious.

Answer choice (A): The stimulus specifies that annual safety inspections—regardless of what is examined—are already in place. Therefore, this answer does not explain why the average rate of accidents is higher in those states.

Answer choice (B): Assuming that overconfidence leads to accidents, the answer could support the assertion that states with more stringent requirements have higher accident rates. But, this answer would also suggest that the experts are wrong in saying that more stringent standards reduce accident rates, so this answer cannot be correct.

Answer choice (C): This is the correct answer, and the answer conforms to the discussion above. If the roads are generally more dangerous, then the stringent requirements could reduce the accident rate while at the same time the accident rate could remain relatively high. Since this scenario allows all sides of the situation to be correct and it explains how the situation could occur, this is the correct answer.

Answer choice (D): This answer supports only one side of the paradox. The answer confirms that the experts are correct, but it does not explain why these provinces have higher accident rates. Thus, as explained in the second sidebar on page 293, it does not resolve the paradox.

Answer choice (E): This answer appears attractive at first, but the number of miles of roadway in the provinces is irrelevant because the stimulus specifically references "accidents per kilometer driven." Since the accident rate is calculated as per-miles-driven, the actual number of miles of roadway is irrelevant.

Address the Facts

When attempting to resolve the paradox in the stimulus, you must address the facts of the situation. Many incorrect answers will try to lure you with reasonable solutions that do not quite meet the stated facts. These answers are incorrect. The correct answer *must* conform to the specifics of the stimulus otherwise how could it resolve or explain the situation?

Please take a moment to complete the following problem:

2. Calories consumed in excess of those with which the body needs to be provided to maintain its weight are normally stored as fat and the body gains weight. Alcoholic beverages are laden with calories. However, those people who regularly drink two or three alcoholic beverages a day and thereby exceed the caloric intake necessary to maintain their weight do not in general gain weight.

    Which one of the following, if true, most helps to resolve the apparent discrepancy?

    (A) Some people who regularly drink two or three alcoholic beverages a day avoid exceeding the caloric intake necessary to maintain their weight by decreasing caloric intake from other sources.
    (B) Excess calories consumed by people who regularly drink two or three alcoholic beverages a day tend to be dissipated as heat.
    (C) Some people who do not drink alcoholic beverages but who eat high-calorie foods do not gain weight.
    (D) Many people who regularly drink more than three alcoholic beverages a day do not gain weight.
    (E) Some people who take in fewer calories than are normally necessary to maintain their weight do not lose weight.

The paradox in this problem is that alcohol drinkers who surpass the threshold for calorie intake should gain weight, but they do not. Most people, upon reading the stimulus, prephrase an answer involving exercise or some other way to work off the expected weight gain. Unfortunately, a perfect match to this prephrase does not appear, and instead students are faced with a tricky answer that preys upon this general idea while at the same time it fails to meet the circumstances in the stimulus.

Answer choice (A): Read closely! The stimulus specifies that people who regularly drink two or three alcoholic beverages a day thereby *exceed* the necessary caloric intake. This answer, which discusses individuals who *avoid exceeding* the caloric intake necessary, therefore addresses a different group of people from that in the stimulus. Since information about a different group of people does not explain the situation, this answer is incorrect.

This answer is attractive because it uses the idea of getting rid of or avoiding calories, but it violates one of the precepts of the stimulus. Remember, you must look very closely at the circumstances in the stimulus and make sure that the answer you select matches those circumstances.

Answer choice (B): This is the correct answer. If the excess calories are dissipated as heat, then there would be no weight gain. Hence, alcohol drinkers can consume excess calories and still not gain weight.

Some students object to this answer because the situation seems unrealistic. Can heat dissipation actually work off dozens if not hundreds of calories? According to the question stem, yes. Remember, the question stem tells you that each answer choice should be taken as true. Since this answer choice clearly states that the excess calories tend to be dissipated, you must accept that as true and then analyze what effect that would have.

Answer choice (C): The stimulus discusses "people who regularly drink two or three alcoholic beverages a day and thereby exceed the caloric intake necessary." This answer choice addresses a different group of people than those discussed in the stimulus.

Answer choice (D): The first flaw in this answer is that it simply states that individuals consuming alcohol do not gain weight but it offers no *explanation* for why these people have no weight gain. The second flaw in the problem is that it addresses the wrong group of people. The stimulus discusses people who drink two or three alcoholic beverages a day; this answer addresses people who drink *more than* three alcoholic beverages a day.

Answer choice (E): Again, this answer discusses a different group of people than those in the stimulus. The stimulus discusses people who exceed the necessary caloric intake; this answer addresses people who do not meet the necessary caloric intake.

Resolve the Paradox Question Review

Each Resolve the Paradox stimulus presents a situation where two ideas or occurrences contradict each other.

Besides the discrepant or contradictory facts, most Resolve the Paradox stimuli contain the following features:

1. No conclusion
2. Language of contradiction

The correct answer will actively resolve the paradox—it will allow both sides to be factually correct and it will either explain how the situation came into being or add a piece of information that shows how the two ideas or occurrences can coexist.

Because you are not seeking to disprove one side of the situation, you must select the answer choice that contains a *possible cause* of the situation. So, when examining answers, ask yourself if the answer choice could lead to the situation in the stimulus. If so, the answer is correct. The following types of answers are incorrect:

1. Explains only one side of the paradox

   If an answer supports or proves only one side of the paradox, that answer will be incorrect. The correct answer must show how both sides coexist.

2. Similarities and differences

   If the stimulus contains a paradox where two items are similar, then an answer choice that explains a difference between the two cannot be correct.

   Conversely, if the stimulus contains a paradox where two items are different, then an answer choice that explains why the two are similar cannot be correct.

   In short, a similarity cannot explain a difference, and a difference cannot explain a similarity.

When attempting to resolve the problem in the stimulus, you must address the facts of the situation. Many answers will try to lure you with reasonable solutions that do not quite meet the stated facts. These answers are incorrect.

All Resolve the Paradox questions require you to seek a cause of the scenario in the stimulus. However, we do not classify these questions as "CE" questions because the causality does not appear in the stimulus. The CE designator is reserved solely for indicating when causality is featured as the form of reasoning in an argument.

Resolve the Paradox Question Problem Set

The following questions are drawn from actual LSATs. Please complete the problem set and review the answer key and explanations. *Answers on Page 300*

1. Industry experts expect improvements in job safety training to lead to safer work environments. A recent survey indicated, however, that for manufacturers who improved job safety training during the 1980s, the number of on-the-job accidents tended to increase in the months immediately following the changes in the training programs.

    Which one of the following, if true, most helps to resolve the apparent discrepancy in the passage above?

    (A) A similar survey found that the number of on-the-job accidents remained constant after job safety training in the transportation sector was improved.
    (B) Manufacturers tend to improve their job safety training only when they are increasing the size of their workforce.
    (C) Manufacturers tend to improve job safety training only after they have noticed that the number of on-the-job accidents has increased.
    (D) It is likely that the increase in the number of on-the-job accidents experienced by many companies was not merely a random fluctuation.
    (E) Significant safety measures, such as protective equipment and government safety inspections, were in place well before the improvements in job safety training.

2. Cigarette companies claim that manufacturing both low- and high-nicotine cigarettes allows smokers to choose how much nicotine they want. However, a recent study has shown that the levels of nicotine found in the blood of smokers who smoke one pack of cigarettes per day are identical at the end of a day's worth of smoking, whatever the level of nicotine in the cigarettes they smoke.

    Which one of the following, if true, most helps to explain the finding of the nicotine study?

    (A) Blood cannot absorb more nicotine per day than that found in the smoke from a package of the lowest-nicotine cigarettes available.
    (B) Smokers of the lowest-nicotine cigarettes available generally smoke more cigarettes per day than smokers of high-nicotine cigarettes.
    (C) Most nicotine is absorbed into the blood of a smoker even if it is delivered in smaller quantities.
    (D) The level of tar in cigarettes is higher in low-nicotine cigarettes than it is in some high-nicotine cigarettes.
    (E) When taking in nicotine by smoking cigarettes is discontinued, the level of nicotine in the blood decreases steadily.

3. Raisins are made by drying grapes in the sun. Although some of the sugar in the grapes is caramelized in the process, nothing is added. Moreover, the only thing removed from the grapes is the water that evaporates during the drying, and water contains no calories or nutrients. The fact that raisins contain more iron per calorie than grapes do is thus puzzling.

Which one of the following, if true, most helps to explain why raisins contain more iron per calorie than do grapes?

(A) Since grapes are bigger than raisins, it takes several bunches of grapes to provide the same amount of iron as a handful of raisins does.

(B) Caramelized sugar cannot be digested, so its calories do not count toward the calorie content of raisins.

(C) The body can absorb iron and other nutrients more quickly from grapes than from raisins because of the relatively high water content of grapes.

(D) Raisins, but not grapes, are available year-round, so many people get a greater share of their yearly iron intake from raisins than from grapes.

(E) Raisins are often eaten in combination with other iron-containing foods, while grapes are usually eaten by themselves.

4. Vervet monkeys use different alarm calls to warn each other of nearby predators, depending on whether the danger comes from land or from the air.

Which one of the following, if true, contributes most to an explanation of the behavior of vervet monkeys described above?

(A) By varying the pitch of its alarm call, a vervet monkey can indicate the number of predators approaching.

(B) Different land-based predators are responsible for different numbers of vervet monkey deaths.

(C) No predators that pose a danger to vervet monkeys can attack both from land and from the air.

(D) Vervet monkeys avoid land-based predators by climbing trees but avoid predation from the air by diving into foliage.

(E) Certain land-based predators feed only on vervet monkeys, whereas every predator that attacks vervet monkeys from the air feeds on many different animals.

Resolve the Paradox Problem Set Answer Key

All answer keys in this book indicate the source of the question by giving the month and year the LSAT was originally administered, the Logical Reasoning section number, and the question number within that section. Each LSAT has two Logical Reasoning sections, and so the Section 1 and Section 2 designators will refer to the first or second Logical Reasoning section in the test, not the physical section number of the booklet.

Question #1. Resolve. October 2003 LSAT, Section 1, #4. The correct answer choice is (B)

The paradox in the stimulus is: for manufacturers who improved job safety training during the 1980s there was an increase in the number of on-the-job accidents.

Answer choice (A): This answer does not provide an explanation for the paradox in the stimulus. Some students eliminate this answer because it addresses the transportation industry, but information about the transportation industry could be used to analogically explain the issue in the manufacturing industry (but, to be correct the answer would have to offer some further relevant parallel between the two industries).

Answer choice (B): This is the correct answer. If the workforce is increasing, more accidents would be expected. Thus, safety training could improve the safety of the work environment (as measured by average number of accidents per worker, for example) while at the same time the number of total accidents could increase. Because this answer allows both sides to be true and it explains the circumstance in the stimulus, this answer is correct. In Chapter Fifteen we will discuss average versus total numbers, and that will further explain the construction of this question.

Answer choice (C): This would explain an increase in accidents *before* job safety training, but the issue in the stimulus is an increase *after* the safety training.

Answer choice (D): This answer further confuses the issue. If the fluctuation *was* random, that could explain how an increase in accidents could follow safety training. By stating that the increase was *not* random, a possible cause of the scenario is eliminated.

Answer choice (E): This answer shows that the level of safety was at least minimal prior to the safety training, but this does not help explain why an increase in accidents followed the training.

Question #2. Resolve. October 2000 LSAT, Section 2, #5. The correct answer choice is (A)

In rough terms, the paradox in the stimulus is that smokers of one pack of low-nicotine cigarettes have an identical nicotine level at the end of the day as smokers of one pack of high-nicotine cigarettes. This similarity must be explained by a similarity, not a difference.

Answer choice (A): This is the correct answer. The answer choice indicates that there is a similarity in the blood such that the maximum amount of nicotine absorbed is identical for everyone. Because the maximum amount of nicotine absorbed per day is equal to the nicotine in a pack of low-nicotine cigarettes, each person absorbs the amount of nicotine equal to the low-nicotine pack regardless of the type of cigarette smoked. Additional nicotine is not absorbed into the blood of smokers of the high-nicotine brand. Since this answer explains the paradox, this is the correct answer.

Resolve the Paradox Problem Set Answer Key

Answer choice (B): Read closely! The stimulus is specifically about smokers who "smoke one pack of cigarettes per day." This answer discusses smoking different numbers of cigarettes and thus it fails to meet the circumstances in the stimulus.

Answer choice (C): This answer confuses the issue because it indicates that most nicotine is absorbed into the system. From this fact one would expect that those smoking high-nicotine cigarettes would have higher nicotine levels than low-nicotine cigarette smokers.

Answer choice (D): The stimulus does not address the level of tar in cigarettes, nor can we make any judgment about how tar affects nicotine levels.

Answer choice (E): This would apply to any smoker, and as this addresses an effect that occurs after smoking is stopped, it does not help us understand why the nicotine rose to identical levels regardless of the kind of cigarette smoked.

Question #3. Resolve. December 2001 LSAT, Section 1, #9. The correct answer choice is (B)

The paradox in the stimulus is that raisins contain more iron per calorie than grapes even though the two are almost identical in composition. But there is a difference: "some of the sugar in grapes is caramelized" as the grapes are dried in the sun. Since this is the only stated difference between the two that could affect the calorie count (water has no calories), you should focus on an answer that discusses this difference.

Answer choice (A): This answer essentially states that grapes are bigger than raisins, and you need several bunches to equal a handful of raisins. The issue is not the size of the grapes or raisins!

Answer choice (B): This is the correct answer. If the iron content in the raisins and grapes is identical, but raisins have fewer calories for counting purposes, then the iron per calorie will be higher for raisins, as highlighted by the following example:

	Raisins	Grapes
Units of Iron	100	100
Countable Calories	10	20
Iron per Calorie	10	5

Note that the paradox could have addressed any common element between raisins and grapes (such as fiber or fat), and raisins would always have the higher per calorie content since they contain fewer countable calories.

Answer choice (C): The paradox in the stimulus does not involve the rate at which the body can absorb iron or any other nutrient. This answer misses the point and is incorrect.

Answer choice (D): The availability of raisins and grapes is not an issue in the stimulus. The answer then discusses iron, but the point made about yearly intake is irrelevant.

Answer choice (E): The comparison in the stimulus is between grapes and raisins. This answer, which brings in other food items, is irrelevant.

Question #4. Resolve. October 2003 LSAT, Section 1, #8. The correct answer choice is (D)

The situation in the stimulus is that vervet monkeys use different calls depending on where predators come from. The correct answer must explain why the calls are different (again, difference versus similarity is an issue). Note that the stimulus does not contain a true paradox, just an odd situation that is presented without explanation.

Answer choice (A): This answer states that vervet monkeys vary the calls in order to indicate the number of predators, but the answer does not explain why different calls are used for land versus air predators. This answer is attractive because it shows that different calls can be used to indicate different things, but it is wrong because it does not explain the behavior of the monkeys as described in the stimulus.

Answer choice (B): This answer addresses only land-based predators and does not explain the difference described in the stimulus.

Answer choice (C): This answer states that the predators using land attacks are different from the predators using air attacks, but this information does not explain why vervet monkeys use different calls to indicate that fact.

Answer choice (D): This is the correct answer. Because vervet monkeys react to predators in different ways, they would need to know if the predator was coming by land or air. Hence, the different calls are used to tell the monkeys whether they should climb trees or dive into the foliage. Since this answer explains the behavior of vervet monkeys, this answer is correct.

Answer choice (E): The diet of selected predators of vervet monkeys is irrelevant and does not help explain why vervet monkeys use different calls depending on the direction of the attack.

CHAPTER ELEVEN: FORMAL LOGIC

The PowerScore Definitive LSAT Formal Logic Deconstruction

Many students struggle with Formal Logic when it appears on the LSAT. Although an understanding of the rules of Formal Logic indicates a strong grasp of important principles such as sufficient and necessary conditions, please do not overemphasize the importance of Formal Logic in your studies. The typical LSAT contains only one to three Formal Logic Problems, so the majority of your study time is better spent on more heavily tested elements such as Cause and Effect reasoning. Regardless, this section will cover every Formal Logic concept from the most basic to the most complex.

Formal Logic Defined

Formal Logic—also known as Symbolic Logic—is defined by Webster's as, "The study of the properties of propositions and deductive reasoning by abstraction and analysis of the form rather than the content of propositions under consideration." That definition is quite a mouthful, but the important part is in the middle: "reasoning by analysis and abstraction of *form* rather than the content." Formal Logic is simply a standard way of translating relationships into symbols and then making inferences from those symbolized relationships. And, because certain combinations always yield the same inference regardless of the underlying topic, a close study of the combinations that appear frequently on the test allows you to move quickly and confidently when attacking Formal Logic problems.

On the LSAT, the basis for Formal Logic relationships are terms such as "all," "none," "some," and "most." Here is an example of how Formal Logic works, using a few of those terms:

First we examine a statement containing Formal Logic:

"Every author works long hours, and if you work long hours you are never happy. Some authors are female."

Second, swiftly translate the statement into a set of symbols that represent the concepts and relationships:

$$F \xleftrightarrow{\;S\;} A \longrightarrow LH \xleftrightarrow{\;|\;} H$$

(where F = female; A = author; LH = long hours; and H = happy)

Third, examine the symbolic notation and make additive inferences:

> Students interested in improving their Formal Logic skills sometimes wonder if taking a university-level symbolic logic class in addition to an LSAT course is a good idea. While symbolic logic classes do help improve your understanding of certain LSAT concepts, unfortunately these logic classes also teach a wide variety of concepts that have no application on the LSAT. We feel your time is better spent studying LSAT problems than by taking a symbolic logic course. In this chapter, we will focus on presenting those areas of Formal Logic that are specifically applicable to the LSAT.

Inferences:
$$F \xleftrightarrow{\ s\ } LH$$
$$F \xleftrightarrow{\ s\ } \cancel{H}$$
$$A \xleftrightarrow{\ \ |\ \ } H$$

Although the example above may appear daunting, with practice you will be able to translate the statement into notation and then make the inferences rapidly and with certainty. Later in this section we will return to the problem above and fully explain each inference, and in the following pages we will discuss each of the general relationships above and the standardized inferences that follow from combining certain relationships. By the end of this chapter you should not only understand how to diagram any Formal Logic problem, but also how to make inferences quickly and efficiently from your diagram.

Formal Logic Terms and Diagrams Defined

Every Formal Logic relationship features at least two separate variables linked in a relationship. The variables represent groups or ideas. For instance, in the example on the previous page, "A" represented "authors" and "H" represented "happy." These variables—and LH and F—were linked in relationships that were represented by the diagrammatic elements of " $\xleftrightarrow{\ s\ }$," " $\longrightarrow$," and " $\longleftrightarrow\!\!\!\!|$." Below, the components of Formal Logic diagrams are discussed in more detail.

1. Choosing Symbols to Represent Each Variable

    Choosing symbols to represent each group or idea is easy: simply choose the letter or letters that, *to you*, best represent the element. For most people, the best symbols are the first letter of each word or words. For example, using "A" to represent "authors" makes it easy to remember "authors" when you are examining your diagram. The exact letters you choose to represent each group are *not* critical; what is important is that you use those same letters to represent the group throughout your diagram and inferences. This is especially important when terms are negated. For example, if you represent "happy" with "H" as you begin your diagram, and later you are presented with a seemingly new element, "unhappy," do *not* create a new variable, "UH." Instead, simple negate "happy" and use "$\cancel{H}$."

2. Conditional Reasoning Terms and Diagrams

    Many of the relationship indicators used within Formal Logic problems are terms you are familiar with from Conditional Reasoning. Conditional indicators such as "if" and "only" yield exactly the same diagrams that were used in Sufficient and Necessary problems. Let us briefly review those terms and their resultant diagrams:

The second section of the October 2003 LSAT contained three problems that contained Formal Logic.

Formal Logic is present when chain relationships involving "some" and "most" are used.

A. The Single Arrow (⟶)

Introduced by sufficient and necessary words such as: *if...then*, *when*, *all*, *every*, and *only*, where both elements are positive or both elements are negative.

Example Statement: All X's are Y's   (X and Y both positive)

     Diagram: X ⟶ Y

Example Statement: If you are not T, then you are not V   (T and V both negative)

     Diagram: T̸ ⟶ V̸

You can, of course take the contrapositive of this diagram and force both terms to be positive:

     V ⟶ T

B. The Double Arrow (⟷)

Introduced by "if and only if" or by situations where the author implies that the arrow goes "both ways," such as by adding "vice versa" after a conditional statement.

Example Statement: X if and only if Y

     Diagram: X ⟷ Y

Example Statement: All W's are Z's, and all Z's are W's

     Diagram: W ⟷ Z

Double-arrow statements allow for only two possible outcomes: the two variables occur together, or the neither of the two variables occur.

C. The Double-Not Arrow ($\longleftrightarrow\!\!\!|\!\!\longrightarrow$)

Introduced by conditional statements where exactly one of the terms is negative, or by statements using words such as "no" and "none" that imply the two variables cannot "go together."

Example Statement: No X's are Y's

Diagram: X $\longleftrightarrow\!\!\!|\!\!\longrightarrow$ Y

Example Statement: If you are a T, then you are not a V

Diagram: T $\longleftrightarrow\!\!\!|\!\!\longrightarrow$ V

Remember, the statement above produces a diagram,   T $\longrightarrow \cancel{V}$, which can more properly be diagrammed as T $\longleftrightarrow\!\!\!|\!\!\longrightarrow$ V.

3. New Terms and Diagrams

A. Relationships involving *Some*

The word "some" can be defined as *at least one, possibly all*. Take a close look at that definition—it is different than what most people expect because *some* includes the possibility of *all*. Thus, if a person says, "Some of my friends graduated last week," using the definition above it could be true that *all* of the person's friends graduated last week.

When you diagram statements involving *some*, simply place a double-arrow with the letter "S" between the two elements:

Some students prefer to place the "S" right on the double arrow instead of above it. That representation is equally valid.

Example Statement: Some X's are Y's

Diagram: X $\overset{s}{\longleftrightarrow}$ Y

When "some" appears as "some are not" (as in "Some X's are not Y's"), the interpretation changes due to the *not*. "Some are not" can be defined as *at least one is not, possibly all are not*. Thus, if I say, "Some of my friends are not present," then it could be true that *none* of my friends are present.

One of the most popular ways to introduce the idea that *some are not* is to use the phrase *not all*, which is functionally equivalent to *some are not*.

When diagramming statements involving *some are not*, simply place the word *some* between the two elements and negate the second element:

Example Statement: Some W's are not Z's

Diagram: W $\xleftrightarrow{\text{ S }}$ Z̸

Example Statement: Not all T's are V's

Diagram: T $\xleftrightarrow{\text{ S }}$ V̸

The LSAT introduces the concept of *some* in a variety ways, including the following relationship indicators:

some
at least some
at least one
a few
a number
several
part of
a portion
many

B. Relationships involving *Most*

The word "most" can be defined as *a majority, possibly all*. Again, take a careful look at that definition—it is different than what most people expect because *most* includes the possibility of *all*. Thus, if I say, "Most of my friends graduated last week," using the definition above it could in fact be true that *all* of my friends graduated last week.

When diagramming statements involving *most*, simply place the letter "M" between the two elements and place an arrow under the "M" pointing at the second element:

Example Statement: Most X's are Y's

Diagram: X $\xrightarrow{\text{ M }}$ Y

When "most" appears as "most are not," the interpretation changes due to the *not*. "Most are not" can be defined as *a majority are not, possibly all are not*. Thus, if I say, "Most of my friends are not present," it could be true that *none* of my friends are present.

Just as with "some," it is acceptable to place the "M" directly on the arrow.

When you diagram a statement involving *most are not*, simply place the word *most* between the two elements, place an arrow under the *most* pointing at the second element, and negate the second element:

Example Statement: Most W's are not Z's

Diagram: $W \xrightarrow{M} \not{Z}$

The LSAT introduces the concept of *most* in a variety ways, including the following relationship indicators:

> most
> a majority
> more than half
> almost all
> usually
> typically

C. Contrapositives

Some students ask if there is a contrapositive for *some* and *most* statements. The answer is *No*. Only the arrow statements like *all* have contrapositives; *some* and *most* do not because they do not necessarily encompass an entire group.

The makers of the LSAT will often try to trick unwary test takers by offering wrong answer choices that are similar to the would-be contrapositive of a "some" or "most" statement.

Formal Logic Relationship Indicators Defined Numerically

Now that we have individually reviewed each of the major relationship indicators that appear in Formal Logic statements, we will list them in relation to each other using a 0 to 100 unit scale:

All	=	100
Most	=	51 to 100 ("a majority")
Some are not	=	0 to 99 (also "Not All")
Most are not	=	0 to 49
Some	=	1 to 100 ("at least one")
None	=	0

Two of the terms—*All* and *None*—are very precise and thus one or both appear in almost every inference chain. They represent constant states with no uncertainty. The other terms cover a wide array of possibilities, and for that reason they can, at times, be more difficult to manipulate.

Some and *Most* Diagramming Drill

Each of the following statements has two elements linked in a *some* or *most* relationship. First, determine the nature of the relationship, and then make a simple diagram for each statement that uses either the *some* or *most* symbolization to link the two elements. *Answers on page 310*

Example: Some drivers are reckless.

Diagram: D $\xleftarrow{\quad s \quad}$ R

 (where D stands for *drivers* and R stands for *reckless*)

1. At least one heron has blue feathers.

 Diagram:

2. A majority of senators are wealthy.

 Diagram:

3. Not all of the Smallville roads are safe.

 Diagram:

4. A few of the schools no longer offer business degrees.

 Diagram:

5. More often than not, dinner for two is expensive.

 Diagram:

6. Most of the time playing the stock market is not profitable.

 Diagram:

Some and *Most* Diagramming Drill Answer Key

1. Diagram: H $\longleftrightarrow^{S}$ BF

    (where H stands for *heron* and BF stands for *blue feathers*)

2. Diagram: S $\xrightarrow{M}$ W

    (where S stands for *senators* and W stands for *wealthy*)

3. Diagram: SR $\longleftrightarrow^{S}$ S̸

    (where SR stands for *Smallville roads* and S stands for *safe*)

4. Diagram: S $\longleftrightarrow^{S}$ O̶B̶D̶

    (where S stands for *schools* and OBD stands for *offer business degrees*)

5. Diagram: D2 $\xrightarrow{M}$ E

    (where D2 stands for *dinner for two* and E stands for *expensive*)

6. Diagram: PSM $\xrightarrow{M}$ P̸

    (where PSM stands for *playing the stock market* and P stands for *profitable*)

The Rules of Reversibility

Certain Formal Logic relationships have a natural "reversibility." Reversibility in the context of Formal Logic means that the relationship between the two variables has exactly the same meaning regardless of which "side" of the relationship is the starting point of your analysis. Statements that are non-reversible have a single "direction," that is, the relationship between the two variables is not the same.

First, examine a relationship that is not reversible:

$$A \longrightarrow B$$

Starting from the A side, we know that every single A is a B. If we start at B, does the relationship reverse? That is, is every single B an A? No—that would be a Mistaken Reversal. From B's side, we do not know if every B is an A. Instead, we only know that some B's are A's (this inherent inference will be discussed in greater detail in the "Inherent versus Additive Inferences" section). Thus, the arrow between A and B in the diagram above has a direction: the "all" travels only from A to B and it does not additionally travel from B to A. The relationship is therefore not reversible.

Now, examine a reversible relationship. "Some" is a classic example of a reversible statement. Consider the following example:

$$A \xleftrightarrow{\;s\;} B$$

Starting from A yields, "Some A's are B's" (A some B). Starting from B yields "Some B's are A's" (B some A). Because of the nature of "some," these two statements are functionally identical (if some A's are B's, by definition some B's must also be A's; alternatively, if some A's are B's, then somewhere in the world there is an AB pair, and thus somewhere a B is with an A and we can conclude some B's are A's).

Reversible statements are easily identifiable because the relationship symbol is symmetrical and the arrow points in both directions. Non-reversible terms have arrows that point in only one direction.

<table>
<tr><td>Reversible Relationships</td><td>Non-reversible Relationships</td></tr>
<tr><td>None (⟵┼⟶)</td><td>All (⟶)</td></tr>
<tr><td>Some (⟵ˢ⟶)</td><td>Most (⟶ᴹ⟶)</td></tr>
<tr><td>Double-arrow (⟷)</td><td></td></tr>
</table>

The reversibility of any given term is immediately evident from the use of a single arrow or double arrow.

The beauty of reversible terms is that you can analyze the relationship from either "side" and still arrive at the same conclusion.

The Special Case of "Some are Not"

Because *some* is a reversible term, *some are not* statements are also reversible. However, students are warned to be careful when working with these statements (in fact, so many students make mistakes with this relationship that in teaching this method to students we start by saying that *some are not* is non-reversible as a way to simplify the introduction to this concept).

This is a typical *some are not* diagram:

$$A \longleftrightarrow^{S} \not{B}$$

Starting from the A side, we know that some A's are not B's. Most students have no difficulty making that judgment. Trouble can arise when we look at the relationship from the other side. Correctly reversed, the relationship reads, "Some things that are not B are A's." To most people this sounds strange and useless; nonetheless, that is the correct phrasing of the reversed statement. But, most students will incorrectly reverse the statement to read, "Some B's are not A's." That is not necessarily true! In effect, this incorrect reverse interpretation is the same as:

The test makers know how easy it is to mix up "some are not" statements and they create wrong answer choices to prey upon that mistake. Make sure you are comfortable handling the reversibility of this relationship!

$$B \longleftrightarrow^{S} \not{A}$$

Obviously, this diagram is different from our original diagram because the "not" slash is now on A, whereas the slash was originally on B.

Thus, you can reverse a *some are not* statement, but you must be careful when doing so in order to avoid accidentally moving the "not."

Reversibility Recognition Mini-Drill

Each of the following statements has two elements linked in a relationship. First, determine whether the relationship is reversible, and if so, identify the reversed statement. *Answers on page 314*

Example: A $\longrightarrow$ B

Analysis: Not reversible

1. A $\xleftrightarrow{\text{ } S \text{ }}$ B

    Analysis:

2. C $\xrightarrow{\text{ } M \text{ }}$ D

    Analysis:

3. E $\longleftrightarrow$ F

    Analysis:

4. G $\xleftrightarrow{\text{ } S \text{ }}$ H̸

    Analysis:

Reversibility Recognition Mini-Drill Answer Key

1. Analysis: Reversible; diagram as B $\xleftrightarrow{\text{ s }}$ A.
2. Analysis: Not reversible
3. Analysis: Reversible; diagram as F $\xleftrightarrow{\quad|\quad}$ E.
4. Analysis: Reversible; diagram as ~~H~~ $\xleftrightarrow{\text{ s }}$ G.

Inherent versus Additive Inferences

There are two types of Formal Logic inferences: inherent and additive.

Additive inferences result from combining multiple statements through a common term and then deducing a relationship that does not include the common term. Consider the following diagram:

$$A \longrightarrow B \xleftarrow{\quad|\quad} C$$

Individually, the two relationships have "B" in common. But, as we will discuss shortly, we can ultimately connect A and C in a relationship that drops B, and make the inference that $A \xleftrightarrow{\quad|\quad} C$. This is an additive inference, so-called because it comes from "adding" two statements together to make the inference. In Logical Reasoning, additive inferences are often the correct answer choice on Formal Logic problems.

Inherent inferences follow from a single statement such as $A \longrightarrow B$, and they are inferences that are known to be true simply from the relationship between the two variables. In the statement above we know that all A's are B's. Of course, if all A's are B's, then it must also be true that most A's are B's and that some A's are B's—these last two statements are inherently true because of the nature of the initial relationship. And, because we know from the last inference that some A's are B's, if we analyze the initial relationship from B's perspective (also called "coming backward" against the arrow) we can deduce that some B's are A's. This deduction can be incredibly useful when you are trying to attack complex problems and you need, in effect, to work "against" the arrow. We will discuss this process in more detail when we begin analyzing the inference-making process.

Because inherent inferences are for the most part obvious, when we speak of making inferences in the future we will almost always be referring to the process of making additive inferences. Thus, when writing out inferences, do *not* include the inherent inferences. However, sometimes the process of making an additive inference involves recognizing the inherent inferences present. Later, we will discuss this process in greater detail. First, let us analyze the presence of inherent inferences a bit more closely.

The past is prologue: the patterns that appear on past LSATs continue to appear in new LSATs, and by learning those patterns you can increase your speed on the test.

The contrapositive is an example of an inherent inference.

The Logic Ladder™

The Logic Ladder details the relationship between *all*, *most*, and *some*:

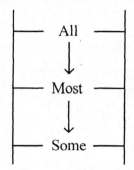

In the Ladder, each term represents a "rung," and the upper rung terms automatically imply that the lower rung terms are known to be true. Thus, if you have an *all* relationship, you automatically know that the *most* and *some* relationships for that same statement are true. So, if a statement is made that "All waiters like wine," then you immediately know that "Most waiters like wine," and "Some waiters like wine."

The same is true for *most* relationships, but to a more limited extent. If "Most waiters like wine," then you automatically know that "Some waiters like wine." But, because *most* is below *all* on the Logic Ladder, you do *not* know with certainty that "All waiters like wine" (it is possibly true, but not known for certain). This reveals a truth about the Logic Ladder: the upper rungs automatically imply the lower rungs, but the lower rungs do not automatically imply the upper rungs. In other words, as you go down the rungs the lower relationships *must* be true, but as you go up the rungs the higher relationships *might* be true but are not certain.

At the lowest rung—*some*—no inherent inferences follow. From the definition of *some* we know that *most* and *all* are possible, but we cannot know for sure that they are true.

A close analysis of the Logic Ladder explains the presence of inherent inferences in *all* and *most* statements. For example, if "All doctors are lawyers," then from the Logic Ladder we know that "Some doctors are lawyers." And, because *some* is a reversible term, we then know that "Some lawyers are doctors." The presence of inherent inferences in non-reversible terms such as *all* and *most* helps to make complex inferences easier to follow.

The Logic Ladder is an easy way to visualize the relationship between "some," "most," and "all" relationships.

Inherent Inference Recognition Drill

Each of the following statements has two elements linked in a relationship. First, diagram the relationship, and then list out each inherent inference, if any, that results from the relationship. *Answers on the next page*

Example: Most football players are male.

Diagram: FP $\xrightarrow{\text{M}}$ M
(where FP stands for *football players* and M stands for *male*)

Inherent Inferences: FP $\xleftarrow{\text{S}}\rightarrow$ M

1. All licensed attorneys must have a law degree.

Diagram:

Inherent Inference(s):

2. Some cities have subway systems.

Diagram:

Inherent Inference(s):

3. More often than not, professional athletes are wealthy.

Diagram:

Inherent Inference(s):

4. A few of these houses do not meet city architectural codes.

Diagram:

Inherent Inference(s):

5. Airlines fly a route if and only if the route is profitable.

Diagram:

Inherent Inference(s):

Inherent Inference Recognition Drill Answer Key

1. Diagram: LA ——————→ LD   (where LA stands for *licensed attorney* and LD stands for
                                                       law degree)

    Inherent Inferences: LA $\xrightarrow{\text{M}}$ LD
                                   LA $\xleftrightarrow{\text{S}}$ LD

    If you wrote out *LD* $\xleftrightarrow{\text{S}}$ *LA* as an inherent inference that would also be correct. But, because
    we already have *LA* $\xleftrightarrow{\text{S}}$ *LD* on our list, and that reverses to *LD* $\xleftrightarrow{\text{S}}$ *LA* and is therefore
    identical, we did not place *LD* $\xleftrightarrow{\text{S}}$ *LA* on the inherent inference list. Although *LD* $\xleftrightarrow{\text{S}}$ *LA*
    is correct, to write out both *LD* $\xleftrightarrow{\text{S}}$ *LA* and *LA* $\xleftrightarrow{\text{S}}$ *LD* is redundant and time-wasting.
    Simply write out one of the two and recognize that the statement reverses.

2. Diagram: C $\xleftrightarrow{\text{S}}$ S   (where C stands for *city* and S stands for *subway systems*)

    Inherent Inferences: None

3. Diagram: PA $\xrightarrow{\text{M}}$ W   (where PA stands for *professional athletes* and W stands for
                                                       wealthy)

    Inherent Inferences: PA $\xleftrightarrow{\text{S}}$ W

4. Diagram: H $\xleftrightarrow{\text{S}}$ ~~MCAC~~   (where H stands for *houses* and MCAC stands for *meet city
                                                       architectural codes)

    Inherent Inferences: None

5. Diagram: AFR $\longleftrightarrow$ RP   (where AFR stands for *airline flies route* and RP stands for
                                                       route profitable)

    Inherent Inferences: AFR $\xrightarrow{\text{M}}$ RP
                                   RP $\xrightarrow{\text{M}}$ AFR
                                   AFR $\xleftrightarrow{\text{S}}$ RP

    This is a very tricky problem. Because the arrow between AFR and RP goes in both directions, we can
    infer that the *most* relationships are inherent in both directions.

The Negative Logic Ladder™

The Positive and
Negative Logic
Ladders are
identical except
for the terms in
each.

The Logic Ladder presented in the previous section deals only with the "positive terms." There is also a Logic Ladder for negative terms, although this Ladder is less useful since the inherent inferences revealed by this Ladder rarely appear in LSAT Formal Logic problems. Nonetheless, in the interests of full disclosure we present the Logic Ladder for negative terms:

The Negative Logic Ladder

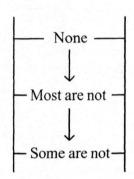

As in the first Ladder, each term represents a "rung," and the upper rung terms automatically imply that the lower rung terms are known to be true. Thus, if you have an *none* relationship, you automatically know that the *most are not* and *some are not* relationships for that same statement are true. So, if a statement is made that "None of the waiters like wine," then you immediately know that "Most waiters do not like wine," and "Some waiters do not like wine."

The same is true for *most are not* relationships, but to a more limited extent. If "Most waiters do not like wine," then you automatically know that "Some waiters do not like wine." But, because *most are not* is below *none* on the Logic Ladder, you do *not* know with certainty that "None of the waiters like wine" (it is possibly true, but not known for certain). Thus, just as in the positive Logic Ladder, in the negative Logic Ladder the upper rungs automatically imply the lower rungs, but the lower rungs do not automatically imply the upper rungs. In other words, as you go down the rungs the lower relationships *must* be true, but as you go up the rungs the higher relationships *might* be true but are not certain.

At the lowest rung—*some are not*—no inferences follow. From the definition of *some are not* we know that *most are not* and *none* are possible, but we cannot know for sure that either is true.

Two Rules of Diagram Creation

Rule #1. Always combine common terms

In order to make complete and effective Formal Logic diagrams, you must always combine like terms through linkage. For example, most students tend to write statements separately, as in the following:

$$A \xleftrightarrow{\ s\ } B$$

$$B \longrightarrow C$$

Instead, you should recognize that "B" is common to both diagrams, and combine the two diagrams into one linked diagram:

$$A \xleftrightarrow{\ s\ } B \longrightarrow C$$

In your Formal Logic diagrams, *each variable should appear only one time*; variables should not be duplicated if at all possible.

Rule #2. There is no traditional direction in logic

Because English speakers read from left to right, most people assume that inference-making patterns *always* travel from left to right. This assumption is false. For example, consider the following four diagrams:

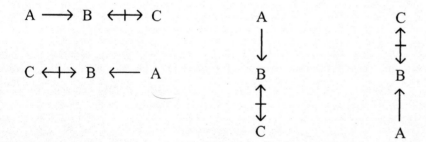

The four diagrams contain identical relationships—and produce identical inferences—but they look different because the variables are placed in different relative positions. Yet, the underlying relationships are the same in each instance: all A's are B's, and no B's are C's. Thus, you can create a diagram in any shape or direction because the physical placement of the variables is not critical as long as the relationships are properly represented.

In the next section we will discuss how to reliably make inferences regardless of the configuration and "direction" of the relationships. For the moment, the best way to consider logic is to think of logical relationships as following train tracks—you simply follow the path of the track regardless of whether it is to the left, to the right, downwards, diagonal, etcetera.

Some students ask why we do not use Venn diagrams. Despite their popularity with certain test preparation programs, Venn diagrams are inappropriate for the LSAT because they force the test taker to make certain dangerous assumptions while diagramming.

If you would like more information about the limitations of Venn diagrams, please visit the Free LSAT Help section on the powerscore.com website. The website contains a lengthy discussion of the problems with Venn diagramming.

The 11 Principles of Making Formal Logic Inferences

One of the challenges of Formal Logic is that there is no room for error in your diagramming and interpretation. The system is tightly structured and complex, and it is easy to spend hours and hours working with the ideas. Again, we emphasize that students should not spend a disproportionate amount of time learning Formal Logic.

Once you have created a diagram that connects all of the elements in a Formal Logic problem, your task is to quickly and efficiently make additive inferences. As discussed previously, you may be required to use inherent inferences to achieve this goal.

The key to analyzing Formal Logic diagrams is to know where to begin your inferential analysis. The most reliable method of making inferences is to look for known patterns and relationships within the diagram. There are different ways of memorizing these relationships, but within these pages we will teach the PowerScore inference analysis methodology, which we are certain is the easiest and most dependable method for making inferences.

Below is a list of eleven principles that you must consider when making inferences. While discussing these principles, we will occasionally refer to the following example diagram:

$$A \xleftrightarrow{\ \ s\ \ } B \longrightarrow C \xleftarrow{\ \ |\ \ }\rightarrow D$$

1. Start by looking at the ends of the chain.

Variables that are linked in only one relationship are "open"; variables that are linked in two or more relationships are "closed." Because the ends of a chain are naturally open variables and are involved in fewer relationships, they are easier to analyze. Always begin your analysis by looking at the ends of the chain.

In the example diagram above, variables A and D are open; variables B and C are closed. To make inferences, first examine variables A and D, and thereafter examine variables B and C.

2. The vast majority of additive inferences require either an *all* or *none* statement somewhere in the chain.

Because *all* and *none* statements affect the entire group under discussion (for example, in A $\longrightarrow$ B, every single A must be a B), they are very restrictive and when other variables are joined to these relationships then inferences often result. In fact, either *all* or *none* (or both) are present in almost every Formal Logic diagram that produces additive inferences. Later, we will discuss the few situations where they are not present.

3. When making inferences, do *not* start with a variable involved in a double-not arrow relationship and then try to "go across" the double-not arrow.

In the example diagram, we know that the open ends are A and D, but, because D is involved in a double-not arrow relationship, we should not start at D and attempt to make an additive inference with B or A. Instead, as you will find later, starting at A or B will make it easier to create inferences involving D.

4. The Some Train

To make an inference with a variable involved in a *some* relationship, either an *all* arrow, a *none* arrow, or double-arrow "leading away" from the *some* relationship is required. Consider the first part of the example diagram:

$$A \xleftrightarrow{\ s\ } B \xrightarrow{\quad\quad} C$$

In this case, the arrow from B to C "leads away" from the *some* relationship. From this configuration, we can deduce the presence of an additive inference: $A \xleftrightarrow{\ s\ } C$. Logically, if some A's are B's, and every single B is a C, then it must be true that some A's are C's.

In the example above, the direction of the arrow is critical. Consider the following example:

$$A \xleftrightarrow{\ s\ } B \xleftarrow{\quad\quad} C$$

At first glance, you might think that this relationship will produce the same inference as the example above. There are three variables and the same internal relationships exist—*some* and *all*. But, because the direction of the *all* arrow is different, ultimately we will not be able to make an inference from this diagram. Logically, the group of B's could be so large that even though every C is a B, and some A's are B's, the groups of A's and C's do not overlap, and thus no inference between A and C is present.

To help remember the difference between these relationships, we use a mnemonic trick called the *Some Train*. In the Some Train, each variable is considered a "station," and the relationships between each variable are "tracks." A successful "journey" (defined as a journey of at least two stops) yields an inference. An unsuccessful journey means no inference is present. Consider again the first part of the example diagram:

$$A \xleftrightarrow{\ s\ } B \xrightarrow{\quad\quad} C$$

We start at station A because A is the open variable in the *some* relationship. From A, we can ride over to station B because we get a free pass on the Some Train when we travel over *some*. Once at station B, we need a track "away"

To move from the second station, a "some" or "most" arrow will not be strong enough to make the leap. You must have an "all," "none," or double-arrow to make the trip to the third station.

from B going to another station. Since the tracks are arrows, we need either an *all* arrow, a double arrow, or a double-not arrow (*some* and *most* arrows do not count because they do not necessarily include the entire group). In this case we have the *all* arrow, and thus we can ride over to C. We now have a successful journey between A and C. Now, to make our inference, we look at two elements:

     1. The weakest link in the chain
     2. The presence of relevant negativity

In our example, looking back on the journey, the weakest link is *some*, and there are no negative terms. Thus, our inference is A $\xleftrightarrow{\text{ s }}$ C.

Consider again the second example from above:

$$A \xleftrightarrow{\text{ s }} B \xleftarrow{\hspace{1cm}} C$$

In this example, we again start at station A and ride over to station B. Once at station B, we need a track "away" from B going to another station, but there is no track away, only an incoming track. Thus, we are stopped and there is no inference that can be made in this example.

Some students fall into the trap of believing that the Some Train works only from left to right. Consider the following example:

$$A \xleftarrow{\hspace{1cm}} B \xleftrightarrow{\text{ s }} C$$

In this diagram, following the first principle of making inferences, we begin at station C and then ride over to station B (remember, going "backwards" is acceptable since there is no true direction in logic, just relationships). Once we arrive at station B, we look for a track leading away, and we find one pointing to station A. Thus, we can ride from C to A, the weakest link is *some*, and our inference is A $\xleftrightarrow{\text{ s }}$ C. The Some Train can work in any direction as long as it is following the rules discussed previously.

Now, let us examine the Some Train when used with a double-not arrow. Consider the following example:

$$A \xleftrightarrow{\text{ s }} B \xleftrightarrow{\hspace{0.3cm}|\hspace{0.3cm}} C$$

Starting at station A, we ride over to station B. Once at station B, we need a track "away" from B going to another station. In this case we have the double-not arrow, and therefore we can ride over to C. We now know we can travel from A to C, and, to make our inference, we again look at two elements:

     1. The weakest link in the chain
     2. The presence of relevant negativity

In our example, looking back on the journey, the weakest link is *some*, so we know that at least we have A some C. But, there is negativity between B and C, and that negativity transfers to C, and thus our inference is A $\xleftrightarrow{\quad S \quad}$ C̸ (we will discuss the concept of relevant negativity in principle #8).

As mentioned before, direction has no effect on the relationships. Consider the following example:

$$A \xleftrightarrow{\quad|\quad} B \xleftrightarrow{\quad S \quad} C$$

Starting at station C, we ride over to station B. Once at station B, we need a track "away" from B going to another station. In this case we have the double-not arrow, and we can ride over to A. Thus, we know we can travel from C to A, and adding the relevant negativity between B and A produces our inference: C $\xleftrightarrow{\quad S \quad}$ A̸.

In general, the Some Train is an incredibly easy tool to help you quickly and easily make inferences. Simply remember to look for the weakest link in the chain and to consider the relevant negativity.

Some Train Diagramming Mini-Drill

Each of the following problems has three elements linked in a relationship containing *some*. On the basis of the diagram, please identify each additive inference, if any. *Answers on page 325*

1. A $\xleftrightarrow{\ s\ }$ B $\longrightarrow$ C

2. D $\xleftrightarrow{\ s\ }$ E̸ $\longrightarrow$ F

3. G $\longrightarrow$ H $\xleftrightarrow{\ s\ }$ I

4. J $\longleftarrow$ K $\xleftrightarrow{\ s\ }$ L

5. M $\xleftrightarrow{\ s\ }$ N $\longleftrightarrow$ O

6. P $\xleftrightarrow{\ s\ }$ Q $\longleftrightarrow\!\!\!+\!\!\!\longrightarrow$ R

7. S $\longleftarrow\!\!\!+\!\!\!\longrightarrow$ T $\xleftrightarrow{\ s\ }$ U

8. V $\xleftrightarrow{\ s\ }$ W $\longleftarrow$ X

Some Train Diagramming Mini-Drill Answer Key

1. Inference: A $\xleftrightarrow{\;\;S\;\;}$ C
2. Inference: D $\xleftrightarrow{\;\;S\;\;}$ F
3. Inference: None
4. Inference: L $\xleftrightarrow{\;\;S\;\;}$ J
5. Inference: M $\xleftrightarrow{\;\;S\;\;}$ O
6. Inference: P $\xleftrightarrow{\;\;S\;\;}$ R̸
7. Inference: U $\xleftrightarrow{\;\;S\;\;}$ S̸
8. Inference: None

5. The Most Train

The Most Train works in a very similar fashion to the Some Train, but because *most* is one step higher than *some* on the Logic Ladder, the Most Train produces stronger inferences. Consider the following example:

$$A \xrightarrow{\;\;M\;\;} B \xrightarrow{\quad\quad} C$$

Starting at station A, we ride over to station B because we get a one-way pass on the Most Train when we travel over *most*. Once at station B, we need a track "away" from B going to another station. Since the tracks are arrows, we either need an *all* arrow, a double arrow, or a double-not arrow (when we reach the second track, *most* arrows do not count because they do not necessarily include the entire group). In this case we have the *all* arrow, and thus we can ride over to C. Thus, we know we can travel from A to C. Now, just as in the Some Train, to make our inference we look at two elements:

1. The weakest link in the chain
2. The presence of relevant negativity

Looking back at the "example journey," the weakest link is Most, and there are no negative terms. Thus, our inference is A $\xrightarrow{\;\;M\;\;}$ C.

The critical difference between the Some Train and Most Train is that because *most* has direction, you can only follow the *most*-arrow to make a *most* inference. If you go "against" the arrow, the relationship will devolve to *some*, which is the inherent inference.

Some students ask how to determine the weakest link. The weakest link is simply the least definite link, and so the major terms are in this order:

1. Some—this is the broadest term and the least definite; therefore it is the weakest.
2. Most—this is more definite than Some.
3. All and None—these two terms are the most definite, and although they are polar opposites, they are equal in power.

Most Train Mini-Diagramming Drill

Each of the following problems has three elements linked in a relationship containing *most*. On the basis of the diagram, please identify each additive inference, if any. *Answers page 327*

1. A $\xrightarrow{M}$ B $\longrightarrow$ C

2. D $\xrightarrow{M}$ E̸ $\longrightarrow$ F

3. G $\longrightarrow$ H $\xrightarrow{M}$ I

4. J $\longleftarrow$ K $\xleftarrow{M}$ L

5. M $\xrightarrow{M}$ N $\longleftrightarrow$ O

6. P $\xrightarrow{M}$ Q $\longleftrightarrow\!\!\!|$ R

7. S $\longleftrightarrow\!\!\!|$ T $\xleftarrow{M}$ U

8. V $\xrightarrow{M}$ W $\longleftarrow$ X

Most Train Diagramming Drill Answer Key

1. Inference: A $\xrightarrow{\text{M}}$ C
2. Inference: D $\xrightarrow{\text{M}}$ F
3. Inference: None
4. Inference: L $\xrightarrow{\text{M}}$ J
5. Inference: M $\xrightarrow{\text{M}}$ O
6. Inference: P $\xrightarrow{\text{M}}$ R̸
7. Inference: U $\xrightarrow{\text{M}}$ S̸
8. Inference: None

6. Arrows and double-not arrows

Because arrows and double-not arrows are so powerful, they almost always elicit additive inferences. Perhaps the most familiar inference is the following:

$$A \longrightarrow B \longleftarrow\!\!\!|\!\!\!\longrightarrow C$$

This popular combination, which often appears in Logic Games, yields the inference A $\longleftarrow\!\!\!|\!\!\!\longrightarrow$ C.

Any combination of an arrow and a double-not arrow in succession will yield an inference (although inherent inferences may be needed to make the inference). Any combination of two arrows may yield an inference depending on the configuration. A combination of two double-not arrows in succession does not yield an inference.

Two double-not arrows in a row will not yield an inference. The same is true for two "somes" in a row.

7. Use inherent inferences

So far in our discussion we have avoided using inherent inferences to make additive inferences—none of the examples provided in this section has required the use of an inherent inference. On the LSAT, however, you will at times be forced to use an inherent inference to make an additive inference. Consider the following example:

$$A \longleftarrow\!\!\!|\!\!\!\longrightarrow B \longrightarrow C$$

By using the principles we have established for making inferences, we should start at A or C. But, A is involved in a double-not arrow relationship, and thus we should not begin there. So, we should start at C. But, C is at the end of an *all* arrow—how can we go against the arrow? Remember, going "backwards" against the arrow is the inherent inference *some*, and thus we can use the Some Train. Starting at C, we can ride the Some "backwards" over to B. Once at B, we can take the arrow to A, and derive the inference C $\xleftarrow{\text{S}}$ A̸.

Some of the more challenging LSAT Formal Logic questions require the use of an inherent inference to make an additive inference.

Thus, the Some Train does not require the explicit presence of *some* in a relationship. If the *some* relationship is implicit (as in the inherent inferences present in *all* and *most*), then the Some Train can be used.

As previously discussed, inherent inferences are most useful when they appear as part of *all* or *most* relationships. Because the inherent inference in these statements is *some*, we can use the Some Train in a variety of unexpected relationships. Consider the following examples:

Example: A ⟵⟶ B ⟵⫠⟶ C

Inference: A ⟵ˢ⟶ C̸

(Start at A and use the inherent inference *some* to ride the Some Train)

Certain inferences that are useful in Logical Reasoning are largely worthless in Logic Games. Take, for example, each of the relationships to the right. Each yields a "some" inference, and in almost every Logic Game a "some" inference is useless. Not so in Logical Reasoning questions where a "some" inference can be the correct answer.

Example: A ⟵ᴹ⟶ B ⟵⫠⟶ C

Inference: A ⟵ˢ⟶ C̸

(Start at A and use the inherent inference *some* to ride the Some Train)

Example: A ⟵⫠⟶ B ⟶ C

Inference: C ⟵ˢ⟶ A̸

(Start at C and use the inherent inference *some* to ride the Some Train)

Example: A ⟵⫠⟶ B ⟶ᴹ⟶ C

Inference: C ⟵ˢ⟶ A̸

(Start at C and use the inherent inference *some* to ride the Some Train)

Example: A $\longleftarrow\cdot$ B $\longrightarrow$ C

Inference: C $\xleftrightarrow{\ S\ }$ A (or, A $\xleftrightarrow{\ S\ }$ C—the two are identical)

(Start at A or C and use the inherent inference *some* to ride the Some Train)

Example: A $\longleftarrow$ B $\xrightarrow{\ M\ }$ C

Inference: C $\xleftrightarrow{\ S\ }$ A
(Start at C and use the inherent inference *some* to ride the Some Train)

8. Watch for the relevant negativity

When making inferences—especially with the Some and Most Trains—special care must be paid to identifying relevant negativity. The presence of relevant negativity is defined as the following:

1. Either the first or last term in the inference chain is negated, as in $\cancel{A}$ $\xleftrightarrow{\ S\ }$ B $\longrightarrow$ C

or

2. There is a double-not arrow in the chain (which will always appear just before the last station)

Consider the following example:

$$\cancel{A}\ \xleftrightarrow{\ S\ }\ B\ \longrightarrow\ C$$

In this case, we start with $\cancel{A}$ as the first term and then use the Some Train to connect to C. The inference is then $\cancel{A}$ $\xleftrightarrow{\ S\ }$ C.

One point of irrelevant negativity is if the negative is on the middle station, as follows:

$$A\ \xleftrightarrow{\ S\ }\ \cancel{B}\ \longrightarrow\ C$$

The inference from the relationship above is A $\xleftrightarrow{\ S\ }$ C; the negativity on B is bypassed. This is true for all "intermediate" stations in a three-variable chain such as the one above.

Negativity on a variable will only appear in the inference if the negativity is on the first or last variable in the inference chain. "Intermediate" negativity will be bypassed.

9. Some and Most Combinations

In general, two consecutive *some's*, two consecutive *most's*, or a *some* and *most* in succession will not yield any inferences. Thus, a statement such as the following does not yield an additive inference:

$$A \xleftrightarrow{\ S\ } B \xleftrightarrow{\ S\ } C$$

Nor will the following:

$$A \xleftrightarrow{\ S\ } B \xrightarrow{\ M\ } C$$

Usually, two *most's* in sequence do not yield an inference. For example,

$$A \xrightarrow{\ M\ } B \xrightarrow{\ M\ } C$$

No inference can be made with this statement, unless you have further numerical information about the size of the groups, such that A has 7 members, B has 5 members and C has 3 members. Then we could deduce that some A's are C's. A problem with this configuration and corresponding information has never appeared on the LSAT.

A problem involving two *most's* that has appeared on the LSAT and does yield an inference is the following:

$$A \xleftarrow{\ M\ } B \xrightarrow{\ M\ } C$$

Although from all appearances no inference can be made, the fact that most B's are both A's and C's allows us to conclude that some A's are C's. For example, if there are five B's, and three of the B's are A's, and three of the B's are C's, then there must be an overlap of at least one A and C, and therefore we can conclude that some A's are C's. This inference can only occur when the two *most's* each "lead away" from the middle variable. Otherwise, there is no inference, as in the following cases:

Example: $\quad A \xrightarrow{\ M\ } B \xrightarrow{\ M\ } C$

Inference: No inference

Example: $\quad A \xrightarrow{\ M\ } B \xleftarrow{\ M\ } C$

Inference: No inference

10. Analyzing Compound Statements

Up to this point we have only analyzed statements with three variables and two connecting relationships. On the LSAT you will see even more complex relationships, but the skills we have discussed so far still apply to these more complex relationships, and, to some extent all compound relationships can be reduced to three-variable statements.

When working with compound statements (statements where there are four or more variables), keep in mind the following guidelines:

   A. Recycle your inferences to see if they can be used to create further inferences.

   B. Make sure to check the closed variables.

Now return to the original diagram on the first page of this chapter:

$$F \xleftrightarrow{\ \ S\ \ } A \xrightarrow{\hspace{2cm}} LH \xleftarrow{\ |\ } \rightarrow H$$

(where F = female, A = author, LH = long hours, and H = happy)

Let us fully analyze the chain:

The ends of the chain are F and H, but since H is at the end of a double-not arrow, we should begin our analysis at F. Starting at F, we can ride the Some Train through A to LH, yielding the additive inference $F \xleftrightarrow{\ \ S\ \ } LH$. At this point, we must apply the guidelines given above. First, we can recycle the $F \xleftrightarrow{\ \ S\ \ } LH$ inference we just made by adding $LH \xleftarrow{\ |\ } \rightarrow H$ to the end, creating the following chain:

$$F \xleftrightarrow{\ \ S\ \ } LH \xleftarrow{\ |\ } \rightarrow H$$

This diagram—which can easily be created mentally without drawing the diagram out physically—yields the additive inference $F \xleftrightarrow{\ \ S\ \ } \cancel{H}$.

We can now apply the second guideline, which is to examine the closed variables A and LH. Starting at LH does not yield an inference (see principle #11 for more details). But, starting at A, we can follow the arrow to LH and then to H, making the inference $A \xleftarrow{\ |\ } \rightarrow H$.

Thus, by methodically attacking each part of the chain, we have made three separate inferences, representing all the possible additive inferences:

$$F \xleftrightarrow{\ \ S\ \ } LH$$
$$F \xleftrightarrow{\ \ S\ \ } \cancel{H}$$
$$A \xleftarrow{\ |\ } \rightarrow H$$

In our answer keys, LSAT stimuli that contain Formal Logic will be designated with "FL," as in "Must-FL."

11. Once an inference bridge is built, it does not need to be built again

One question often asked by students is, "Does an inference have to be makeable from both sides in order to be valid?" The answer is *No*. Consider the following example:

$$A \longleftarrow B \xleftrightarrow{\ s\ } C$$

Starting at A, we can ride backwards across the arrow using the inherent inference, *some*. But, once we arrive at B, there is no *all*, *none*, or true double-arrow leading away, and thus we are stopped: no inference.

Starting at C, we can ride *some* over to B. Once we arrive at B, there is a track leading over to A, so we can ride the Some Train from C to A and make the inference C $\xleftrightarrow{\ s\ }$ A.

Reviewing the example above, some students get confused. We cannot make an inference from A to C, but we can make an inference from C to A? That sounds odd. Does this make the second inference invalid? *No*. If an inference can be made from one "side" of the relationship, that is enough to establish the inference even if the inference cannot be made from the other side. In this sense, making an inference is like building a bridge—you may start on one side, but once you build the bridge the relationship is made between both sides.

The reason we cannot get from A to C is because of the system we use to make inferences. But, our system easily allows us to get from C to A, and once we establish the inference C $\xleftrightarrow{\ s\ }$ A (which is also reversible to A $\xleftrightarrow{\ s\ }$ C), that inference is valid. The fact that we cannot first build the inference from A to C is irrelevant.

The Complete Table of Formal Logic Additive Inference Relationships™

The following table lists all the major additive inferences that can be drawn by combining two relationships. A close examination of this table should help strengthen your understanding of the combinations that produce inferences.

The table does not attempt to identify which term is first or second; instead, the table simply lists whether the two terms in combination will yield an inference, and with what frequency. For example, in the Some-Some box (second row, second box), the word "Never" appears because *some* and *some* in any combination (A $\xleftrightarrow{S}$ B $\xleftrightarrow{S}$ C, etcetera) never produce an additive inference.

Several of the boxes in the Table are identical. For example, the Most-All box (third row, fourth box) is identical to the All-Most box (fourth row, third box). Below the table there are footnotes to help clarify each relationship.

Relationship	None	Some	Most	All
None	Never	Always[1]	Always[2]	Always[3]
Some	Always[1]	Never	Never	Sometimes[4]
Most	Always[2]	Never	Sometimes[5]	Sometimes[6]
All	Always[3]	Sometimes[4]	Sometimes[6]	Always[7]

Table Footnotes:

1. The inference is always a "some are not" inference.

2. The inference can be a "some are not" or "most are not" inference depending on the direction of the Most arrow.

3. The inference can be a "some are not" or "all are not" inference depending on the direction of the All arrow.

4. Some and All can produce an additive inference depending on the direction of the arrow. For example, A $\xleftrightarrow{S}$ B $\longrightarrow$ C produces the inference A $\xleftrightarrow{S}$ C; A $\xleftrightarrow{S}$ B $\longleftarrow$ C does not produce an inference.

5. The only relationship with two Mosts that will produce an inference is A $\xleftarrow{M}$ B $\xrightarrow{M}$ C. The inference is A $\xleftrightarrow{S}$ C.

6. Most and All can produce an additive inference depending on the direction of the All arrow. For example, A $\xrightarrow{M}$ B $\longrightarrow$ C produces the inference A $\xrightarrow{M}$ C; A $\xrightarrow{M}$ B $\longleftarrow$ C does not produce an inference.

7. The inference can be a "some" or "all" inference depending on the direction of the two All arrows.

Formal Logic Additive Inference Drill

Each of the following statements has three or more elements linked in a relationship. First, diagram the relationship, and then list each additive inference, if any, that result from the relationship. Do *not* list inherent inferences; they will not appear in the answer key. *Answers on page 336*

Example: Most A's are B's.
            All B's are C's.

Diagram: A $\xrightarrow{\text{M}}$ B $\longrightarrow$ C

Inference(s): A $\xrightarrow{\text{M}}$ C

1.   Some A's are B's.
      No B's are C's.
      All C's are D's.

      Diagram:

      Inference(s):

2.   All X's are Y's.
      Some Y's are Z's.
      Most X's are W's.

      Diagram:

      Inference(s):

3.   No E's are F's.
      All F's are G's.
      All G's are H's.

      Diagram:

      Inference(s):

4.   Some T are U's.
        All U's are V's.
        All T's are S's.

        Diagram:

        Inference(s):

5.   Most I's are J's.
        All J's are K's, and all K's are J's.
        All K's are L's.

        Diagram:

        Inference(s):

6.   Some N's are O's.
        No O's are P's.
        No P's are Q's.
        All Q's are R's.

        Diagram:

        Inference(s):

1. Diagram: A ⟷^{S} B ⟵|⟶ C ⟶ D

   Inferences: A ⟷^{S} ~~C~~
                        D ⟷^{S} ~~B~~

2. Diagram: W ⟵^{M} X ⟶ Y ⟷^{S} Z

   Inference: W ⟷^{S} Y

3. Diagram: E ⟵|⟶ F ⟶ G ⟶ H

   Inferences: G ⟷^{S} ~~E~~
                        F ⟶ H
                        H ⟷^{S} ~~E~~   (made by recycling either one of the two previous inferences)

4. Diagram: S ⟵ T ⟷^{S} U ⟶ V

   Inferences: T ⟷^{S} V
                        U ⟷^{S} S
                        S ⟷^{S} V   (made by recycling either one of the two previous inferences. This form has appeared in several LSAT questions and this final inference has always been the correct answer)

5. Diagram: I ⟶^{M} J ⟷ K ⟶ L

   Inferences: The presence of the double-arrow between J and K creates more powerful inferences than usual.

                        I ⟶^{M} K
                        J ⟶ L   (this inherently includes the inference L some J)
                        I ⟶^{M} L

6. Diagram: N ⟷^{S} O ⟵|⟶ P ⟵|⟶ Q ⟶ R

   Inferences: N ⟷^{S} ~~P~~
                        R ⟷^{S} ~~P~~

Formal Logic Problem Set

The following questions are drawn from actual LSATs. Please complete the problem set and review the answer key and explanations. *Answers on Page 338*

1. Political theorist: The vast majority of countries that have a single political party have corrupt national governments, but some countries with a plurality of parties also have corrupt national governments. What all countries with corrupt national governments have in common, however, is the weakness of local governments.

   If all of the political theorist's statements are true, which one of the following must also be true?

   (A) Every country with weak local government has a single political party.
   (B) Some countries with weak local governments have a plurality of political parties.
   (C) Some countries with weak local governments do not have corrupt national governments.
   (D) The majority of countries with weak local governments have a single political party.
   (E) Fewer multi-party countries than single-party countries have weak local governments.

2. Some of the world's most beautiful cats are Persian cats. However, it must be acknowledged that all Persian cats are pompous, and pompous cats are invariably irritating.

   If the statements above are true, each of the following must also be true on the basis of them EXCEPT:

   (A) Some of the world's most beautiful cats are irritating.
   (B) Some irritating cats are among the world's most beautiful cats.
   (C) Any cat that is not irritating is not a Persian cat.
   (D) Some pompous cats are among the world's most beautiful cats.
   (E) Some irritating and beautiful cats are not Persian cats.

3. Most serious students are happy students, and most serious students go to graduate school. Furthermore, all students who go to graduate school are overworked.

   Which one of the following can be properly inferred from the statements above?

   (A) Most overworked students are happy students.
   (B) Some happy students are overworked.
   (C) All overworked students are serious students.
   (D) Some unhappy students go to graduate school.
   (E) All serious students are overworked.

4. No chordates are tracheophytes, and all members of Pteropsida are tracheophytes. So no members of Pteropsida belong to the family Hominidae.

   The conclusion above follows logically if which one of the following is assumed?

   (A) All members of the family Hominidae are tracheophytes.
   (B) All members of the family Hominidae are chordates.
   (C) All tracheophytes are members of Pteropsida.
   (D) No members of the family Hominidae are chordates.
   (E) No chordates are members of Pteropsida.

Formal Logic Problem Set Answer Key

All answer keys in this book indicate the source of the question by giving the month and year the LSAT was originally administered, the Logical Reasoning section number, and the question number within that section. Each LSAT has two Logical Reasoning sections, and so the Section 1 and Section 2 designators will refer to the first or second Logical Reasoning section in the test, not the physical section number of the booklet.

Question #1. Must-FL. October 1997 LSAT, Section 1, #12. The correct answer choice is (B)

The stimulus does not contain a conclusion and can be diagramed as follows:

> SP = counties with a single political party
> P = countries with a plurality of parties
> CG = corrupt national governments
> WLG = weakness of local governments

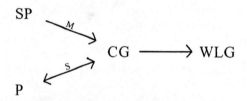

The diagram yields two inferences:

$$SP \xrightarrow{\ M\ } WLG \qquad \text{(use the Most Train to make this inference)}$$

and

$$P \xleftrightarrow{\ S\ } WLG \qquad \text{(use the Some Train to make this inference)}$$

Given that the question stem is a Must Be True, you should look for an answer choice that contains one of the two inferences. Answer choice (B) contains the second inference and is correct.

Answer choice (A): This answer contains two errors, both of which are fatal: first, it attempts to reverse the chain between the single party and weak local governments and second it tries to change a *most* statement into an *all* statement.

Answer choice (B): This is the correct answer. The answer can be a bit tricky to spot since the statement is reversible, and the wording of the answer is given from the reversed perspective. This is a common trick used by the test makers, and you should be prepared for it when solving Formal Logic problems.

Answer choice (C): Although this answer could be true, it does not have to be true. From the inherent inference of the statement contained in the last sentence of the stimulus, we can conclude that some countries with weak local governments *do* have corrupt governments, and thus it is possible that *all* countries with weak local governments have corrupt governments.

Formal Logic Problem Set Answer Key

Answer choice (D): This answer choice improperly reverses the first inference.

Answer choice (E): The stimulus does not provide information as to the total number of countries with single political parties or a plurality of parties. Thus, the statement in this answer choice cannot be proven true. Remember, the *most* and *some* statements in the stimulus relate to different entities, hence no comparative inference can be drawn. The following example shows why this answer is incorrect:

	Single Party (*most*)	Plurality of Parties (*some*)
Total number of countries that fall in this category	10	100
Total number of parties with corrupt governments and hence weak local governments	7	40

Thus, this hypothetical scenario disproves answer choice (E).

Question #2. MustX-FL. December 1994 LSAT, Section 2, #14. The correct answer choice is (E)

The stimulus does not contain a conclusion and can be diagramed as follows:

BC = world's most beautiful cats
P = Persian cats
Po = pompous
I = irritating

$$BC \xleftrightarrow{\ s\ } P \longrightarrow Po \longrightarrow I$$

The diagram yields the following inferences:

$BC \xleftrightarrow{\ s\ } Po$ (use the Some Train to make this inference)

$BC \xleftrightarrow{\ s\ } I$ (use the Some Train to make this inference)

$P \longrightarrow I$ (note: you should not write down the contrapositive of this inference because you should, by now, see the contrapositive as an immediate and obvious consequence of any conditional statement)

Formal Logic Problem Set Answer Key

Because the question stem is a MustX, you should expect to see all of the above inferences as wrong answer choices.

Answer choice (A): This is the second inference, and therefore the answer is incorrect.

Answer choice (B): This answer choice is identical to answer choice (A)—remember to expect the reversibility of statements to be used by the test makers.

Answer choice (C): This is the contrapositive of the third inference.

Answer choice (D): This is the first inference, reworded to reflect the reversibility of the statement.

Answer choice (E): This is the correct answer. Notice that the presence of *some are not* should have been a tip off that this answer was problematic because the only possible negative in the statement would be via the contrapositive of the third inference.

Question #3. Must-FL. October 2003 LSAT, Section 2, #25. The correct answer choice is (B)

This question was used in Chapter Two as an example stimulus, and in that chapter we mentioned the question would be fully explained in this chapter. Here is the diagram for the stimulus, which does not contain a conclusion:

SS = serious students
H = happy students
GS = go to graduate school
O = overworked

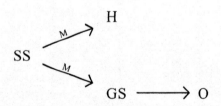

The diagram yields the following three inferences:

$$SS \xrightarrow{\ M\ } O \qquad \text{(use the Most Train to make this inference)}$$

$$H \xleftrightarrow{\ S\ } GS \qquad \text{(uses the special double-most inference)}$$

$$H \xleftrightarrow{\ S\ } O \qquad \text{(uses the special double-most inference and the Some Train)}$$

The first inference is simply an application of the Most Train from SS to O. The second and third inferences rely on the double-most inference discussed earlier in this chapter on page 330. The presence of two *most* relationships emanating from a single group (in this case, SS) allows a *some* inference to be drawn. In this case, the inference H ⟵—ˢ—⟶ GS can be made.

When an inference this tricky is present, you should expect to be tested on it. With that in mind, spend some time learning to recognize the special double-most relationship and the *some* inference that follows. The makers of the LSAT have had a recent emphasis on testing this relationship, and questions appeared on the test in 2000, 2002, and 2003 (this question) that feature the special double-most configuration presented in this problem.

Answer choice (A): Although some overworked students are happy (see the third inference), we do not know that *most* overworked students are happy.

Answer choice (B): This is the correct answer. The inference in this answer is identical to the third inference drawn from the diagram. This is a classic separation problem. Students who are properly prepared will be able to quickly diagram the problem, make inferences, and identify the correct answer. Other students will struggle to diagram the problem and have difficulty with the challenging inferences, resulting in lost time and possibly an incorrect answer choice. This is the essence of LSAT preparation: by learning the patterns used by the test makers you give yourself a tremendous advantage over unprepared students.

Answer choice (C): At best, we can infer that *some* overworked students are serious students (this is the inherent inference present in the first inference). Thus, this answer is too strong.

Answer choice (D): No inference can be made about *unhappy* students.

Answer choice (E): The stimulus allows for the inference that *most* serious students are overworked. Although it may be possible that *all* serious students are overworked, this is not certain, and therefore this answer choice is incorrect.

Question #4. Justify-FL. October 2001 LSAT, Section 1, #22. The correct answer choice is (B)

Unlike the three previous problems, this stimulus contains a conclusion. Therefore, argumentation is present and the chances of a Must Be True question appearing are diminished. Indeed, a Justify the Conclusion question is presented, and when combined with the complex relationship in the stimulus, the result is a challenging problem. The stimulus can be diagrammed as follows:

C = chordates
T = tracheophytes
P = member of Pteropsida
H = member of family Hominidae

Premise Chain: C ⟵—|—⟶ T ⟵——— P

Conclusion: P ⟵—|—⟶ H

Formal Logic Problem Set Answer Key

Given that we need to justify the conclusion, try to solve the problem mechanically:

1. The conclusion contains the new element H, and thus the correct answer should contain H. This analysis eliminates answer choices (C) and (E) from contention.

2. The element P is common to both the conclusion and the premises, and the correct answer should not contain P. Unfortunately, this has no impact on the three answer choices in contention.

3. The premises contain elements C and T that are unconnected to the conclusion. Again, answer choices (A), (B), and (D) contain one or the other.

Based on the analysis above, we should expect the correct answer to either link H and C or to link H and T. Given that C would involve a longer chain of deduction, you should suspect that the correct answer will link H and C. The question becomes what is exact relationship that will connect the premises to the conclusion? The first relationship that comes to mind is H $\longleftrightarrow$ T. But the only answer that involves H and T is answer choice (A), and the relationship there is the opposite of what is needed. Answer choice (A) would not lead to the conclusion and is therefore incorrect.

The elimination of answer choice (A) leaves two answers that involve H and C. Answer choice (B) stipulates that all H's are C's, and answer choice (D) stipulates that no H's are C's. Keep in mind that with a Justify question you can simply add the answer choice under consideration to the premise diagram and then check to see if one of the inferences that follows matches the conclusion. If so, then that answer is correct. If not, then the answer is incorrect. Let use that method with the remaining two answer choices:

The addition of answer choice (B) to the premises leads to the following diagram:

$$H \longrightarrow C \longleftrightarrow T \longleftarrow P$$

Initial inferences can be made that H $\longleftrightarrow$ T and P $\longleftrightarrow$ C. Recycling either inference leads to the super inference that H $\longleftrightarrow$ P. Because this inference matches the conclusion, answer choice (B) is correct.

The addition of answer choice (D) to the premises leads to the following diagram:

$$H \longleftrightarrow C \longleftrightarrow T \longleftarrow P$$

Because no inference can be made from H to T, the diagram above does not allow for an inference to be made between H and P. Therefore, this answer choice is incorrect.

This is an extremely challenging question because it contains a Formal Logic structure that is complex. The addition of the Justify question forces you to find the missing link, but by quickly eliminating answer choices that do not match the Justify paradigm, you can narrow the field to two contenders and then make a decision. But, as you can see, you must have complete control of the diagrams and you must be able to make inferences quickly, accurately, and confidently. This is not for the faint-hearted or lazy!

CHAPTER TWELVE: METHOD OF REASONING QUESTIONS

Method of Reasoning Questions

Method of Reasoning questions require you to select the answer choice that best describes the method used by the author to make the argument. Structurally, Method of Reasoning questions are simply abstract Must Be True questions: instead of identifying the facts of the argument, you must identify the logical organization of the argument.

As part of the First Family of Questions, Method of Reasoning questions feature the following information structure, modified slightly for the abstract nature of these questions:

1. You can use only the information in the stimulus to prove the correct answer choice.

2. Any answer choice that describes an element or a situation that does not occur in the stimulus is incorrect.

Method of Reasoning question stems use a variety of formats, but in each case the stem refers to the method, technique, strategy, or process used by the author while making the argument. Here are several question stem examples:

"The method of the argument is to"

"The argument proceeds by"

"The argument derives its conclusion by"

"Which one of the following describes the technique of reasoning used above?"

"Which one of the following is an argumentative strategy employed in the argument?"

"The argument employs which one of the following reasoning techniques?"

"Aiesha responds to Adam's argument by"

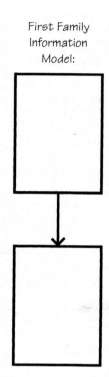

First Family Information Model:

As you attack each question, keep in mind that Method of Reasoning questions are simply abstract Must Be True questions. Use the information in the stimulus to prove or disprove each answer choice.

Prephrasing in Method of Reasoning Questions

You may not have noticed, but this book began with the most concrete questions and slowly moved towards the most abstract questions. For example, we began with Must Be True questions, which require you to identify the details of an argument. Later we discussed Weaken and Strengthen questions, which require you identify both the structure and details of an argument. Now we have arrived at Method questions, which focus much more on structure. Because abstract thinking requires more work than concrete thinking, most students find abstract questions difficult.

Method of Reasoning questions are challenging because they involve abstract thinking, which focuses on the *form* of the argument instead of the concrete facts of the argument. The answer choices will therefore describe the argument in abstract terms, and many students have difficulty because the test makers are experts at manipulating those terms to describe the argument in unexpected and deceptive ways. Often, students will have a firm grasp of the structure of the argument only to struggle when none of the answers match their prephrase. This situation occurs because the test makers can use one or two words to describe entire sections of the stimulus, and you are rigorously tested on your knowledge of the mechanics of the argument and your ability to discern the references in the answer choice.

When prephrasing in Method of Reasoning questions, you may understand the details of the stimulus but not understand the structure of the argument. Thus, each answer may sound implausible since they are related primarily to the logical organization of the argument. Therefore, you must think about the structure of the argument *before* examining the answer choices. However, do not expect to see your exact prephrase as the answer; there are simply too many variations on the way an argument can be described. Instead, make a general, abstract prephrase of what occurred in the argument and then rigorously examine each answer choice to see if the test makers have created an answer that paraphrases your prephrase. Many students are deceived by the description used by the test makers, and the only way to overcome this problem is to compare the description given in the answer choice to the stimulus.

The Fact Test in Method of Reasoning Questions

Because Method of Reasoning questions are similar to Must Be True questions, you can use the principle behind the Fact Test to destroy incorrect answers. In a Method Reasoning question, the Fact Test works as follows:

> If an answer choice describes an event that did not occur in the stimulus, then that answer is incorrect.

The test makers will try to entice you by creating incorrect answer choices that contain elements that did not occur, and you must avoid those answers and select the answer choice that describes what occurred in the stimulus. For example, if an answer choice states, "The argument accepts a claim on the basis of public opinion of the claim," *all* parts of the answer must be identifiable in the stimulus. First you must be able to identify where the author "accepts a claim," and then you must be able to identify where that is done "on the basis of public opinion of the claim." If you cannot identify part of an answer as having occurred in the stimulus, that answer is incorrect.

Watch out for answers that are partially true—that is, answers that contain a description of something that happened in the argument but that also contain additional things that did not occur. For example, an answer choice states that, "The author disagrees with the analogy used by the critic." When examining this answer, you must find both the "disagreement" and the "analogy"; if you can only find one, or neither, the answer is wrong. But let us say you know the author disagrees with the critic. That is a good start, but you will still have to find disagreement with the analogy for the answer to be correct.

Stimulus Notes

The stimulus for a Method Reasoning question will contain an argument, and the argument can contain either valid or invalid reasoning. As you read the stimulus, you should naturally make an assessment of the validity of the argument, and you can expect that many Method of Reasoning answer choices will reflect that assessment.

Because recognizing argument structure is such an important part of attacking Method questions, you must watch for the presence of the premise and conclusion indicators discussed in Chapter Two. These indicators will help you identify the structure of the argument and better help you understand the answer choices.

In the next chapter we will cover Flaw in the Reasoning questions, which are Method of Reasoning questions where the stimulus must contain flawed reasoning.

Incorrect Answers in Method of Reasoning Questions

In Chapter Four we discussed several types of incorrect answers that appear in Must Be True questions. In this section we will review selected answer types from that chapter that apply to Method of Reasoning questions and add an additional wrong answer type.

1. "New" Element Answers

   Because correct Method of Reasoning answers must be based on elements of the stimulus, an answer that describes something that did not occur or describes an element new to the argument cannot be correct. All of the wrong answer choices described below are simply very specific variations on this theme.

Some Method of Reasoning answer choices can be difficult to understand because they are written in a way that is obviously designed to be confusing. The test makers excel at using deceptive language to make wrong answers attractive and to hide the correct answer.

2. Half Right, Half Wrong Answers

   The makers of the LSAT love to present answers that start out by describing something that in fact occurred in the stimulus. Unfortunately, they often end by describing something that did *not* occur in the stimulus. The rule for these answers is that half wrong equals all wrong, and these answers are always incorrect.

As part of the
First Family,
Method of
Reasoning
questions are
grouped with
Must Be True,
Main Point, etc.
Each type of
question shares
similar
characteristics,
but the exact
execution of each
is different. For
example, one way
to compare Must
Be True questions
to Method of
Reasoning
questions is to
use an analogy
about trees in a
forest. A Must Be
True question is
like examining a
single tree and
looking at the
details: the bark,
the branches, the
leaves, etc. A
Method of
Reasoning
question requires
you to look at
that same tree,
but from a
different
perspective, one
that is farther
away and places
that tree in the
context of the
forest. You are no
longer looking at
the individual
branches and
leaves, but rather
at the general
structure of the
tree.

3. Exaggerated Answers

Exaggerated Answers take a situation from the stimulus and stretch that situation to make an extreme statement that is not supported by the stimulus. Be careful, though! Just because an answer choice contains extreme language does not mean that the answer is incorrect.

4. The Opposite Answer

As the name suggests, the Opposite Answer provides an answer that is exactly opposite of correct.

5. The Reverse Answer

The Reverse Answer is attractive because it contains familiar elements from the stimulus, but reverses them in the answer. Since the reversed statement does not describe what occurred in the stimulus, it must be incorrect.

Interestingly, the incorrect answer choices in any Method of Reasoning question can be a helpful study aid in preparing for future questions. Since the makers of the LSAT tend to reuse certain methods of reasoning, familiarizing yourself with those methods and the language used to describe them helps you prepare for when you encounter them again. You should carefully study all Method of Reasoning answers—correct and incorrect—and it would not be unreasonable to keep a list of the different types of methods you encounter. Remember, the wrong answer choice on one question could be right answer choice on another question. After you complete the problem and are reviewing each wrong answer choice, try to imagine what type of argument would be needed to fit that answer. This exercise will strengthen your ability to recognize any type of argument structure.

Idea Application: Correct and Incorrect Answers Analyzed

In this section we present and analyze two Logical Reasoning questions drawn from real LSATs. We will use the two examples to discuss the various answer types presented in the previous section and to discuss the language used by the test makers in the answer choices.

Please take a moment to complete the following problem:

1. Garbage in this neighborhood probably will not be collected until Thursday this week. Garbage is usually collected here on Wednesdays, and the garbage collectors in this city are extremely reliable. However, Monday was a public holiday, and after a public holiday that falls on a Monday, garbage throughout the city is supposed to be collected one day later than usual.

The argument proceeds by

(A) treating several pieces of irrelevant evidence as though they provide support for the conclusion

(B) indirectly establishing that one thing is likely to occur by directly ruling out all of the alternative possibilities

(C) providing information that allows application of a general rule to a specific case

(D) generalizing about all actions of a certain kind on the basis of a description of one such action

(E) treating something that is probable as though it were inevitable

As usual, we begin by analyzing the structure of the problem:

Premise: Garbage is usually collected here on Wednesdays, and the garbage collectors in this city are extremely reliable.

Premise: Monday was a public holiday.

Premise: After a public holiday that falls on a Monday, garbage throughout the city is supposed to be collected one day later than usual.

Conclusion: Garbage in this neighborhood probably will not be collected until Thursday this week.

The argument is sound and the conclusion seems reasonable. The language in the conclusion is not absolute ("probably"), and this is justified since the language used in the argument—"usually" and "supposed to be"—is also probabilistic. Knowing that the argument is valid, the question you must ask yourself is, "How would I describe the structure of this argument?"

Answer choice (A): This answer forces you to make an assessment of the premises (the "evidence") as they relate to the conclusion. Are the premises irrelevant to the conclusion? Clearly not. Therefore, this answer is incorrect.

Answer choice (B): This is a Half Right, Half Wrong answer. The argument does establish "that one thing is likely to occur." But, is this established by ruling out *all* of the alternative possibilities? No, to do that would mean presenting arguments against the garbage being collected on Friday, Saturday, Sunday, etc. Since this section of the answer choice does not occur, this answer is incorrect.

Also, because the argument does not rule out all the alternatives, the conclusion is not established "indirectly."

Answer choice (C): This is the correct answer. Consider each piece of the argument:

"providing information"—a variety of information about the garbage situation is provided.

"application of a general rule"—the general rule is that "After a public holiday that falls on a Monday, garbage throughout the city is supposed to be collected one day later than usual."

"to a specific case"—the specific case is the pickup of garbage this week in this neighborhood.

Given that all elements occurred and the answer presents an accurate

THE POWERSCORE LSAT LOGICAL REASONING BIBLE

description of the way the author made his or her argument, this answer is correct. Now, take a moment and compare this answer to the prephrase you made after reading the stimulus. How similar are the two? Given that you may not be familiar with the language used by the test makers, the two may not be very similar. As your preparation continues, you will become more comfortable with the language and your Method of Reasoning prephrasing will improve. For example, note the use in this answer of "general rule" to describe the last sentence of the stimulus. The test makers could also have used a phrase like "basic principle" to achieve the same result. Your job is to match their language to what occurred in the stimulus.

Answer choice (D): This answer is an overgeneralization—a situation where one instance is used to make a broad based conclusion. This is a Reverse Answer since the stimulus actually uses a general principle and applies it to one instance. In addition, the language in the answer is far too strong in saying "all actions of a certain kind" when the language in the stimulus was probabilistic.

Answer choice (E): This is an Exaggerated Answer. The conclusion states that "Garbage in this neighborhood *probably* will not be collected until Thursday this week" and the use of "probably" is a clear and obvious indication that the author does not think the Thursday garbage pickup is inevitable.

Now try another. Please take a moment to complete the following problem:

2. Jane: Professor Harper's ideas for modifying the design of guitars are of no value because there is no general agreement among musicians as to what a guitar should sound like and, consequently, no widely accepted basis for evaluating the merits of a guitar's sound.

    Mark: What's more, Harper's ideas have had enough time to be adopted if they really resulted in superior sound. It took only ten years for the Torres design for guitars to be almost universally adopted because of the improvement it makes in tonal quality.

    Which one of the following most accurately describes the relationship between Jane's argument and Mark's argument?

    (A) Mark's argument shows how a weakness in Jane's argument can be overcome.
    (B) Mark's argument has a premise in common with Jane's argument.
    (C) Mark and Jane use similar techniques to argue for different conclusions.
    (D) Mark's argument restates Jane's argument in other terms.
    (E) Mark's argument and Jane's argument are based on conflicting suppositions.

This is one of the greatest LSAT Method of Reasoning questions of all time. First take a close look at the statements made by Jane and Mark.

> Jane's position: Jane concludes that Professor Harper's ideas are valueless because there is no way to evaluate a guitar sound and determine what constitutes a better-sounding guitar.

> Mark's position: Mark also agrees that Professor Harper's ideas are valueless, but Mark's reasoning is that if Harper's ideas really worked, then they would have been adopted by now. In making this analysis, Mark reveals that he believes there is a way to determine that one guitar sounds better than another.

Like all LSAT questions, you must lock down the exact nature of the premises and conclusions! Mark's initial comment of "What's more" leads most people to believe he is in complete agreement with Jane. Yes, he agrees with her conclusion, but his reason for doing so is completely contrary to Jane's reason. Mark actually misinterprets Jane's claim, and this is why he says "What's more," as if he is adding an additional piece of information that supports her position. He is not; the premise that he uses contradicts Jane's premises. If you simply accept "What's more" to mean that he is in complete agreement with Jane, you will most certainly miss the question, and have no idea you have done so.

The problem becomes even more challenging because the answer choices are brilliantly constructed:

Answer choice (A): Mark does not address a weakness in Jane's argument or show how one could be overcome. Do not mistake the use of "What's more" to automatically mean that he is adding something helpful to the situation.

Answer choice (B): This is an answer chosen by many people, and it has Shell game aspects. Mark's argument does not have a *premise* in common with Jane's argument; rather, Mark's argument has the *conclusion* in common with Jane's argument.

Before you select this answer, use the Fact Test and ask yourself, "Which premise do the two arguments have in common?" You won't be able to find one, and that would instantly disprove the answer.

Answer choice (C): This is a very clever Reverse Answer choice. The answer states:

> "Mark and Jane use *similar* techniques to argue for *different* conclusions."

THE POWERSCORE LSAT LOGICAL REASONING BIBLE

In fact, the following happens in the stimulus:

> "Mark and Jane use *different* techniques to argue for *similar* conclusions."

If you had any doubt that the makers of the LSAT put the same amount of work into the wrong answers as the correct answers, this answer choice should be convince you that they do.

Answer choice (D): An argument is the sum of the premises and conclusion. Although Mark restates Jane's conclusion, he does not restate her premises. Therefore, he does not restate her argument and this answer is incorrect.

Answer choice (E): This is the correct answer. As discussed in the argument analysis, Jane believes that there is no way to evaluate the merit of a guitar's sounds. On the opposite side, Mark's response indicates he believes that there is a way to evaluate the merit of a guitar's sound ("because of the improvement it makes in tonal quality") and thus the two have conflicting positions.

This is another great example of a separator question: one that scorers in a certain range will get and scorers in a lower range will not get. This is also a dangerous question because many people think they have chosen the correct answer when in fact they have missed it. The lesson here is that you must be an active, prepared reader. Do not allow yourself to be lulled by Mark's comment of "What's more" into believing that he automatically is in agreement with Jane. The test makers use that phrase to see if you will read closely enough to discern his real argument or if you will simply gloss over his comments on the basis of how they are introduced. The LSAT always makes you pay if you gloss over any section of a stimulus.

Method of Reasoning-Argument Part Questions ▌

Argument Part (AP) questions are a subset of Method of Reasoning questions. In Method-AP questions, the question stem cites a specific portion of the stimulus and then asks you to identify the role the cited portion plays in the structure of the argument. Here are several example question stems:

> "The claim that inventors sometimes serve as their own engineers plays which one of the following roles in the argument?"

> "The statement 'thinking machines closely modeled on the brain are also likely to fail' serves which one of the following roles in Yang's argument?"

> "The assertion that a later artist tampered with Veronese's painting serves which one of the following functions in the curator's argument?"

The answer choices in each problem then describe the structural role of the citation, often using terms you are already familiar with such as "premise," "assumption," and "conclusion." At this point in the book, you are uniquely positioned to answer these questions because the Primary Objectives have directed you from the start to isolate the structure of each argument and to identify each piece of the argument. Method-AP questions reward the knowledge you naturally gain from this process.

Method-AP Stimulus Structure

The stimuli that accompany Method-AP questions tend to be more complex than the average LSAT stimulus. Some problems feature two conclusions (one is the main conclusion, the other is a subsidiary conclusion), and often the stimulus includes two different viewpoints or the use of counterpremises. Thus, the ability to identify argument parts using indicator words is important.

As you know from the discussion in Chapter Two, the order in which the conclusion and premises are presented is not relevant to the logical validity of the argument. Still, many people have difficulty becoming accustomed to arguments where the conclusion appears first, and we will discuss those arguments in a moment. Regardless, a large number of Method-AP problems feature the traditional formation with the conclusion at the end of the argument. If you do see the main conclusion at the end of a Method-AP problem, be prepared to answer a question about a part of the argument *other than* the conclusion. The test makers do this because they know students are very good at identifying the conclusion when it appears in the last sentence.

Please take a moment to complete the following problem:

3. It is well documented that people have positive responses to some words, such as "kind" and "wonderful," and negative responses to others, such as "evil" and "nausea." Recently, psychological experiments have revealed that people also have positive or negative responses to many nonsense words. This shows that people's responses to words are conditioned not only by what the words mean, but also by how they sound.

The claim that people have positive or negative responses to many nonsense words plays which one of the following roles in the argument?

(A) It is a premise offered in support of the conclusion that people have either a positive or a negative response to any word.

(B) It is a conclusion for which the only support provided is the claim that people's responses to words are conditioned both by what the words mean and by how they sound.

(C) It is a generalization partially supported by the claim that meaningful words can trigger positive or negative responses in people.

(D) It is a premise offered in support of the conclusion that people's responses to words are engendered not only by what the words mean, but also by how they sound.

(E) It is a conclusion supported by the claim that people's responses under experimental conditions are essentially different from their responses in ordinary situations.

The argument is structured as follows:

Premise: It is well documented that people have positive responses to some words, such as "kind" and "wonderful," and negative responses to others, such as "evil" and "nausea."

Premise: Recently, psychological experiments have revealed that people also have positive or negative responses to many nonsense words.

Conclusion: This shows that people's responses to words are conditioned not only by what the words mean, but also by how they sound.

Like many Method-AP arguments, the conclusion is in the final sentence and is introduced by the conclusion indicator "this shows that." As discussed earlier, you should not expect to be asked about the conclusion if it appears in the last sentence of a Method-AP question, and indeed the statement referenced in question stem is clearly a premise used to support the conclusion. With this in mind, we will examine the answers.

The first few words of each answer indicate the general role the statement is claimed to play. Answer choices (B) and (E) both name the statement as a conclusion, and both are unlikely to be correct. Answer choices (A) and (D) are early Contenders, and answer choice (C) bears further analysis.

The presence of Method-AP questions signals that the makers of the LSAT expect you to understand argument structure. At the same time, the presence of this question type indicates that many students are unable to do so. Amazingly, you can gain time and points on the LSAT simply by doing the very things you already learned in order to succeed on the test.

Answer choice (A): We know that the statement is a premise, so this is answer is possibly correct based on the first line of the answer. But, the answer claims the statement is used to support a conclusion that "people have either a positive or a negative response to any word," and that is not the conclusion of the argument. Thus, although the answer starts out correctly describing the statement, it finishes by incorrectly describing the statement. As we know, half-right, half-wrong answers are always incorrect.

Answer choice (B): This answer is immediately eliminated since the statement is not a conclusion. A further reading reveals that the answer also characterizes the conclusion of the argument as a premise, another reason to dismiss this answer.

Answer choice (C): Although the statement could probably be characterized as a generalization, it is not one supported by the first premise. This answer tries to claim the statement is a conclusion, whereas we know that the first two statements are both separate premises.

Answer choice (D): This is the correct answer. We know the statement is a premise designed to support the conclusion, and this answer choice describes that role perfectly.

Answer choice (E): We know this answer is incorrect because it claims the statement is a conclusion. The remainder of the answer choice would also cause the answer to be eliminated since it describes a claim that does not occur in the argument.

Method-AP questions often feature two conclusions—a main conclusion and subsidiary conclusion—where the main conclusion is typically placed in the first or second sentence, and the last sentence contains the subsidiary conclusion. In addition, the subsidiary conclusion is often preceded by a conclusion indicator such as "thus" or "therefore" while the main conclusion is not prefaced by an indicator. This is an intentional stimulus formation designed to trick many students into erroneously believing that the last sentence contains the main point. Let's take a look at an example.

Please take a moment to complete the following question:

4. Psychologist: The obligation to express gratitude cannot be fulfilled anonymously. However much society may have changed over the centuries, human psychology is still driven primarily by personal interaction. Thus, the important social function of positively reinforcing those behaviors that have beneficial consequences for others can be served only if the benefactor knows the source of the gratitude.

Which one of the following most accurately describes the role played in the psychologist's argument by the claim that the obligation to express gratitude cannot be fulfilled anonymously?

(A) It is an illustration of a premise that is used to support the argument's conclusion.

(B) It is used to counter a consideration that might be taken to undermine the argument's conclusion.

(C) It is used to support indirectly a claim that the argument in turn uses to support directly the conclusion.

(D) It is used to identify the social benefit with which the argument is concerned.

(E) It is the conclusion that the argument is intended to support.

If the use of premise/ conclusion identifier words fails to identify the main conclusion, then use the Conclusion Identification Method described in Chapter Two: use one statement as a conclusion and the other as a premise and see if the arrangement makes sense.

The psychologist's argument is structured as follows:

Premise: However much society may have changed over the centuries, human psychology is still driven primarily by personal interaction.

Subconclusion/ Premise: Thus, the important social function of positively reinforcing those behaviors [of expressing gratitude] that have beneficial consequences for others can be served only if the benefactor knows the source of the gratitude.

Main conclusion: The obligation to express gratitude cannot be fulfilled anonymously.

The statement referenced in the question stem is the main conclusion of the argument, and as the answer choice correctly describes, the conclusion that the *argument* is designed to support.

The argument, when considered in terms of order, is "out of order":

First sentence = main conclusion
Second sentence = basic premise
Third sentence = subconclusion

The last sentence is a subconclusion, and in a Method-AP answer choice the author can describe a subconclusion in a variety of ways:

subsidiary conclusion
secondary conclusion
intermediate conclusion
supporting conclusion

Note that as predicted, the main conclusion is not modified by a conclusion indicator but the subconclusion is.

Answer choice (A): The statement in question is not an example of an idea raised in a premise.

Answer choice (B): The answer choice describes a premise that is used to defend the argument from attack. This would better describe the second sentence of the argument.

Answer choice (C): This answer choice describes a premise supporting a subconclusion. Again, this would better describe the second sentence of the argument.

Answer choice (D): This answer choice better describes the last sentence.

Often, the identifiers used before the subsidiary conclusion are dramatic and somewhat misleading, such as "clearly" and "obviously." In these cases, the conclusion is neither clear nor obvious, and those words are used to lead the reader into thinking that the conclusion should simply be accepted without further analysis.

Answer choice (E): This is the correct answer.

By consistently breaking down the structure of the argument before reading the answer choices, these problems become very easy to solve.

A Common Wrong Answer

One trick used by the test makers in Method-AP questions is to create wrong answers that describe parts of the argument other than the part named in the question stem. These answers are particularly attractive because they do describe a part of the argument, just not the part referenced in the question stem. Before proceeding to the answer choices, make sure you know exactly what part of the argument you are being asked about.

This trick was used in several answer choices in the previous problem.

Final Note

This chapter is the first of three successive chapters that focus on questions that are primarily structural in nature. In the next chapter we will continue to discuss methods of reasoning, and in Chapter Fourteen (which covers Parallel Reasoning), we will use these methods of reasoning to help identify correct and incorrect answers.

Method of Reasoning Question Type Review

Method of Reasoning questions require you to select the answer choice that best describes the method used by the author to make the argument. Structurally, Method of Reasoning questions are simply abstract Must Be True questions: instead of identifying the facts of the argument, you must identify the logical organization of the argument.

As part of the First Family of Questions, Method of Reasoning questions feature the following information structure:

1. You can use only the information in the stimulus to prove the correct answer choice.

2. Any answer choice that describes information or a situation that does not occur in the stimulus is incorrect.

The stimulus for a Method Reasoning question will contain an argument, and the argument can contain either valid or invalid reasoning.

You must watch for the presence of the premise and conclusion indicators discussed in Chapter Two.

Use the Fact Test to eliminate answers in a Method Reasoning question:

> If an answer choice describes an event that did not occur in the stimulus, then that answer is incorrect.

Several types of incorrect answers regularly appear in Method of Reasoning questions:

1. "New" Element Answers

2. Half Right, Half Wrong Answers

3. Exaggerated Answers

4. The Opposite Answer

5. The Reverse Answer

Method of Reasoning Argument Part Question Type Review

Argument Part (AP) questions are a specific subset of Method of Reasoning questions. In Method-AP questions, the question stem cites a specific portion of the stimulus and then asks you to identify the role that the cited portion plays in the structure of the argument.

The stimuli that accompany Method-AP questions tend to be more complex than the average LSAT stimulus.

Method-AP questions often feature two conclusions—a main conclusion and subsidiary conclusion—where the main conclusion is typically placed in the first or second sentence, and the last sentence contains the subsidiary conclusion. In addition, the subsidiary conclusion is often preceded by a conclusion indicator such as "thus" or "therefore" while the main conclusion is not prefaced by an indicator.

One trick used by the test makers in Method-AP questions is to create wrong answers that describe parts of the argument other than the part named in the question stem.

Method of Reasoning Problem Set

The following questions are drawn from actual LSATs. Please complete the problem set and review the answer key and explanations. *Answers on Page 363*

1. Jorge: You won't be able to write well about the rock music of the 1960s, since you were just an infant then. Rock music of the 1960s was created by and for people who were then in their teens and early twenties.

    Ruth: Your reasoning is absurd. There are living writers who write well about ancient Roman culture, even though those writers are obviously not a part of ancient Roman culture. Why should my youth alone prevent me from writing well about the music of a period as recent as the 1960s?

    Ruth responds to Jorge's criticism by

    (A)   challenging his claim that she was not in her teens or early twenties during the 1960s
    (B)   clarifying a definition of popular culture that is left implicit in Jorge's argument
    (C)   using the example of classical culture in order to legitimize contemporary culture as an object worthy of serious consideration
    (D)   offering an analogy to counter an unstated assumption of Jorge's argument
    (E)   casting doubt on her opponent's qualification to make judgments about popular culture

2. Anne: Halley's Comet, now in a part of its orbit relatively far from the Sun, recently flared brightly enough to be seen by telescope. No comet has ever been observed to flare so far from the Sun before, so such a flare must be highly unusual.

    Sue: Nonsense. Usually no one bothers to try to observe comets when they are so far from the Sun. This flare was observed only because an observatory was tracking Halley's Comet very carefully.

    Sue challenges Anne's reasoning by

    (A)   pointing out that Anne's use of the term "observed" is excessively vague
    (B)   drawing attention to an inconsistency between two of Anne's claims
    (C)   presenting evidence that directly contradicts Anne's evidence
    (D)   offering an alternative explanation for the evidence Anne cites
    (E)   undermining some of Anne's evidence while agreeing with her conclusion

3. Seemingly inconsequential changes in sea temperature due to global warming eventually result in declines in fish and seabird populations. A rise of just two degrees prevents the vertical mixing of seawater from different strata. This restricts the availability of upwelling nutrients to phytoplankton. Since zooplankton, which feed upon phytoplankton, feed the rest of the food chain, the declines are inevitable.

    Which one of the following most accurately describes the role played in the argument by the statement that zooplankton feed upon phytoplankton?

    (A) It is a hypothesis supported by the fact that phytoplankton feed on upwelling nutrients.
    (B) It is intended to provide an example of the ways in which the vertical mixing of seawater affects feeding habits.
    (C) It helps show how global temperature changes affect larger sea animals indirectly.
    (D) It is offered as one reason that global warming must be curtailed.
    (E) It is offered in support of the idea that global warming poses a threat to all organisms.

4. Nutritionist: Because humans have evolved very little since the development of agriculture, it is clear that humans are still biologically adapted to a diet of wild foods, consisting mainly of raw fruits and vegetables, nuts and seeds, lean meat, and seafood. Straying from this diet has often resulted in chronic illness and other physical problems. Thus, the more our diet consists of wild foods, the healthier we will be.

    The claim that humans are still biologically adapted to a diet of wild foods plays which one of the following roles in the nutritionist's argument?

    (A) It is a conclusion for which the only support offered is the claim that straying from a diet of wild foods has often resulted in chronic illness and other physical problems.
    (B) It is a premise for which no justification is provided, but which is used to support the argument's main conclusion.
    (C) It is a phenomenon for which the main conclusion of the nutritionist's argument is cited as an explanation.
    (D) It is an intermediate conclusion for which one claim is offered as support, and which is used in turn to support the argument's main conclusion.
    (E) It is a premise offered in support of the claim that humans have evolved very little since the development of agriculture.

5. Ingrid: Rock music has produced no songs as durable as the songs of the 1940s, which continue to be recorded by numerous performers.

    Jerome: True, rock songs are usually recorded only once. If the original recording continues to be popular, however, that fact can indicate durability, and the best rock songs will prove to be durable.

    Jerome responds to Ingrid's claim by

    (A) intentionally misinterpreting the claim
    (B) showing that the claim necessarily leads to a contradiction
    (C) undermining the truth of the evidence that Ingrid presents
    (D) suggesting an alternative standard for judging the point at issue
    (E) claiming that Ingrid's knowledge of the period under discussion is incomplete

6. Pedigreed dogs, including those officially classified as working dogs, must conform to standards set by organizations that issue pedigrees. Those standards generally specify the physical appearance necessary for a dog to be recognized as belonging to a breed but stipulate nothing about other genetic traits, such as those that enable breeds originally developed as working dogs to perform the work for which they were developed. Since dog breeders try to maintain only those traits specified by pedigree organizations, and traits that breeders do not try to maintain risk being lost, certain traits like herding ability risk being lost among pedigreed dogs. Therefore, pedigree organizations should set standards requiring working ability in pedigreed dogs classified as working dogs.

    The phrase "certain traits like herding ability risk being lost among pedigreed dogs" serves which one of the following functions in the argument?

    (A) It is a claim on which the argument depends but for which no support is given.
    (B) It is a subsidiary conclusion used in support of the main conclusion.
    (C) It acknowledges a possible objection to the proposal put forth in the argument.
    (D) It summarizes the position that the argument as a whole is directed toward discrediting.
    (E) It provides evidence necessary to support a claim stated earlier in the argument.

Method of Reasoning Problem Answer Key

All answer keys in this book indicate the source of the question by giving the month and year the LSAT was originally administered, the Logical Reasoning section number, and the question number within that section. Each LSAT has two Logical Reasoning sections, and so the Section 1 and Section 2 designators will refer to the first or second Logical Reasoning section in the test, not the physical section number of the booklet.

Question #1. Method. December 2002 LSAT, Section 2, #8. The correct answer choice is (D)

The arguments of Jorge and Ruth can be analyzed as follows:

Jorge's Argument

Premise:	Rock music of the 1960s was created by and for people who were then in their teens and early twenties.
Premise:	You were just an infant then [in the 1960s].
Conclusion:	You won't be able to write well about the rock music of the 1960s.

Ruth's Argument

Premise:	There are living writers who write well about ancient Roman culture, even though those writers are obviously not a part of ancient Roman culture.
Premise:	Why should my youth alone prevent me from writing well about the music of a period as recent as the 1960s?
Conclusion:	Your reasoning is absurd.

Note that the question stem asks you to identify how Ruth responded. When two-speaker stimuli are combined with Method of Reasoning questions, you are typically asked to identify the reasoning of only one of the speakers (often the second speaker). However, you must still understand the argument of the other speaker as the answer choices often refer to it.

Now let's use the answer choices to discuss the structure of the argument.

Answer choice (A): Ruth does not challenge Jorge's claim about her age. To the contrary, she seemingly admits he is correct when she says "Why should my youth alone..."

Answer choice (B): Although Ruth uses an example that cites culture, she does not clarify a definition of popular culture, and certainly not one left implicit in Jorge's argument.

Method of Reasoning Problem Answer Key

Answer choice (C): This is a Half Right, Half Wrong answer. The first part of the answer choice—"using the example of classical culture"—does occur in Ruth's response, but she does not use that example "in order to legitimize contemporary culture as an object worthy of serious consideration."

Answer choice (D): This is the correct answer. An analogy is a comparison between two items. In argumentation, analogies are often used to clarify the relationship between the items or reveal a fundamental truth about one of the items, as in "To better understand the operating system of your computer, think of it as the *brain* of your system." The use of "brain" in the preceding sentence is the analogy.

Analogies can be used to challenge a position or support a position, but their strength often rests on the relevant similarities between the two items or scenarios. In the next chapter we will discuss False Analogies, where an author uses an analogy that is dissimilar enough to be nonapplicable.

As referenced in this answer choice, Ruth analogizes writing about Roman culture to writing about the 1960s to show that it is not unreasonable that someone who was an infant can write about that time period. Jorge's assumption is that if a person was not a teen or older during the 1960s, then they cannot write well about the music of that period. Since all elements described in the answer choice occur and the answer describes the method used by Ruth, this is the correct answer.

Answer choice (E): Ruth does not attack Jorge's qualification to make his argument, just his pronouncement that she will not be able to write well about the rock music of the 1960s.

Question #2. Method-CE. June 2003 LSAT, Section 1, #4. The correct answer choice is (D)

The stimulus in this problem appeared in Chapter Two as an example of a stimulus with two separate speakers (however, no analysis was given at that time).

The arguments of Anne and Sue can be analyzed as follows:

Anne's Argument

Premise:	Halley's Comet, now in a part of its orbit relatively far from the Sun, recently flared brightly enough to be seen by telescope.
Premise:	No comet has ever been observed to flare so far from the Sun before.
Conclusion:	Such a flare must be highly unusual.

Method of Reasoning Problem Answer Key

<u>Sue's Argument</u>

Premise: Usually no one bothers to try to observe comets when they are so far from the Sun.

Premise: This flare was observed only because an observatory was tracking Halley's Comet very carefully.

Conclusion: [Your conclusion is] Nonsense.

As is often the case with two-speaker stimuli, the speakers disagree. In this case, Anne uses causal reasoning to indicate that the cause of the sighting is unusual activity with Halley's comet:

FU = the flare is highly unusual
NCO = no comet has ever been observed to flare so far from the sun

<u>C</u>   <u>E</u>

FU ——→ NCO

Sue counters by citing an alternate cause: no one has been looking for such a flare.

NO = no one bothers to try to observe comets when they are so far from the Sun
NCO = no comet has ever been observed to flare so far from the sun

<u>C</u>   <u>E</u>

NO ——→ NCO

The problem now becomes an exercise in figuring out how the test makers will describe the alternative cause cited by Sue.

Answer choice (A): This answer quickly fails the Fact Test. Sue does not comment on the *use* of the term "observed" (other than to explain why the flare was observed).

Answer choice (B): Although Sue cites an explanation that is inconsistent with Anne's claim, she does not point out an *inconsistency between* two of Anne's claims

Answer choice (C): Remember, evidence is the same as premises. Does Sue contradict Anne's premises? No, she only contradicts her conclusion. Do not be drawn in by the word "nonsense." That word is used to attack the conclusion, not the premises of the argument.

Method of Reasoning Problem Answer Key

Answer choice (D): This is the correct answer. In this answer, the alternate cause is described as an "alternative explanation." In most cases, a causal counterargument can be described as offering an alternative explanation.

Answer choice (E): This is a Reverse Answer. The answer appears as follows:

> "undermining *some of Anne's evidence* while agreeing with *her conclusion*"

If the answer choice was reversed in the following manner, it would be correct:

> "undermining *her [Anne's] conclusion* while agreeing with *some of Anne's evidence*"

The evidence she agrees with is the first sentence of Anne's argument (the premise in the second sentence is not directly addressed).

Question #3. Method-AP, CE. October 2000 LSAT, Section 1, #15. The correct answer choice is (C)

The argument is structured as follows:

Premise:	A rise of just two degrees prevents the vertical mixing of seawater from different strata.
Premise:	This restricts the availability of upwelling nutrients to phytoplankton.
Premise:	Zooplankton, which feed upon phytoplankton, feed the rest of the food chain.
Conclusion:	Seemingly inconsequential changes in sea temperature due to global warming eventually result in declines in fish and seabird populations.

The conclusion in the first line is echoed again in the final sentence. The argument part referenced in the question stem is a premise (note the use of the premise indicator "since" in the last line), and your answer must indicate that the role played by the argument part is that of a premise.

Answer choice (A): The portion referenced in the question stem is not a hypothesis, but rather a statement of fact.

Answer choice (B): The statement referenced in the question stem is not an *example* of the way the mixing of seawater affects feeding habits, but rather another premise that is then combined with the vertical mixing premise to help support the conclusion.

Answer choice (C): This is the correct answer. The phrase "it helps show" describes a premise, and in this case the premise is used to support a statement about the effect of temperature changes on fish and seabirds.

Method of Reasoning Problem Answer Key

Answer choice (D): The argument does not take a position that global warming should be curtailed. Instead, the argument shows how small changes in sea temperature lead to population declines, and no opinion of those effects is stated.

Answer choice (E): This is an Exaggerated Answer. The argument specifically indicates that fish and seabirds populations will decline. This answer choices states that *all* organisms are threatened.

Question #4. Method-AP. December 2003 LSAT, Section 2, #18. The correct answer choice is (D)

The nutritionist's argument can be deconstructed as follows:

Premise: Humans have evolved very little since the development of agriculture.

Subconclusion/
Premise: It is clear that humans are still biologically adapted to a diet of wild foods, consisting mainly of raw fruits and vegetables, nuts and seeds, lean meat, and seafood.

Premise: Straying from this diet has often resulted in chronic illness and other physical problems.

Conclusion: Thus, the more our diet consists of wild foods, the healthier we will be.

The statement referenced in the question stem is a subconclusion. Answer choice (D), the correct answer, describes this role using the phrase "intermediate conclusion." This is a great example of a question that allows you to *accelerate*: if you take the correct steps (fulfill the Primary Objectives) when analyzing the argument, you already know the correct answer and you simply need to scan the answer choices quickly for a match.

Answer choice (A): This is a Half Right, Half Wrong answer. The statement is a conclusion, but the only support offered for this conclusion is that humans have evolved very little since the development of agriculture. Since this fact contradicts what is stated in the answer choice, the answer choice is incorrect.

Answer choice (B): Since we know the statement is a subconclusion, there is justification provided and this answer choice is incorrect. Note that describing the statement as a premise is also accurate, since a subconclusion is a conclusion for one argument and a premise for another argument.

Answer choice (C): The main conclusion does not explain the statement referenced in the question stem, so this answer choice is incorrect. The answer would be much improved if it said: "It is a phenomenon *that helps explain* the main conclusion of the nutritionist's argument."

Answer choice (D): This is the correct answer, and the answer you should have been looking for after you analyzed the argument and read the question stem.

Answer choice (E): This is a Reverse answer. The claim that *humans have evolved very little since the development of agriculture* is a premise offered in support of the statement referenced in the question stem.

Method of Reasoning Problem Answer Key

Question #5. Method. October 1994 LSAT, Section 2, #14. The correct answer choice is (D)

The heart of Ingrid's argument is that durability is measured by how many times a song is recorded, and using this standard, rock music songs are not as durable as songs from the 1940s.

Jerome admits that rock music songs are not typically recorded multiple times, but he then introduces a new way of judging durability—one based on the continuing popularity of the original recording.

Answer choice (A): Jerome does not misinterpret the claim. He starts off by saying, "True, rock songs are usually recorded only once," and this a perfect characterization of part of Ingrid's statement.

Answer choice (B): This is a good example of an answer that might be kept as an initial Contender. However, as you further consider the answer, you must identify the "contradiction" mentioned in the answer choice. Does Jerome show that Ingrid's claim must lead to a contradiction? No.

Note that there is a difference between a speaker contradicting an argument (as Jerome does here) and a person making a statement that leads to an internal contradiction (known as a self-contradiction.) An example of a self-contradiction would be:

> "Everyone should join our country club. After all, it's an exclusive group that links many of the influential members of the community."

The self-contradiction occurs when the speaker says "Everyone should join" and then follows that by saying that it is "an exclusive group." *Exclusive*, by definition, means that some people are excluded.

Answer choice (C): As discussed in answer choice (A), Jerome accepts the evidence presented by Ingrid. Because he does not undermine the truth of the evidence used by Ingrid, this answer is incorrect. Again, evidence is another way to say "premise." We know that Jerome disagrees with Ingrid's conclusion, but that does not mean that he disagrees with her premise.

Answer choice (D): This is the correct answer. Jerome's standard for judging durability is the popularity of the original. This contrasts with Ingrid's standard, which is the re-recording of the song. The point at issue is the definition of durability.

Answer choice (E): Again, use the Fact Test on this answer. Where does Jerome claim that Ingrid's knowledge is incomplete? As we discussed previously, he has admitted that her premise is true.

Question #6. Method-AP. June 1995 LSAT, Section 1, #14. The correct answer choice is (B)

The argument has an interesting structure. Visually, the argument appears as follows:

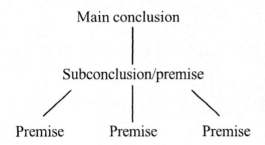

Premise:	Pedigreed dogs, including those officially classified as working dogs, must conform to standards set by organizations that issue pedigrees.
Premise:	Those standards generally specify the physical appearance necessary for a dog to be recognized as belonging to a breed but stipulate nothing about other genetic traits, such as those that enable breeds originally developed as working dogs to perform the work for which they were developed.
Premise:	Dog breeders try to maintain only those traits specified by pedigree organizations, and traits that breeders do not try to maintain risk being lost.
Subconclusion/ Premise:	Certain traits like herding ability risk being lost among pedigreed dogs.
Conclusion:	Therefore, pedigree organizations should set standards requiring working ability in pedigreed dogs classified as working dogs.

Given the size of the stimulus, this is a tough problem to analyze. The second to last sentence contains both a premise and a conclusion. The final sentence contains the main conclusion. Perhaps because of the size of the problem, the test makers kindly inserted the conclusion indicator "therefore" before the main conclusion.

Answer choice (A): This is a Half Right, Half Wrong answer. The phrase referenced in the question is a "claim on which the argument depends," but it is not one for which no support is given. In fact, several premises back up the statement.

Answer choice (B): This is the correct answer. The statement in question is a subconclusion, described in this answer as a subsidiary conclusion.

Method of Reasoning Problem Answer Key

Answer choice (C): The phrase in question is in agreement with the argument, and does not reference a possible objection. If you were to choose this answer, you would have to ask yourself, "What is the possible objection mentioned in this answer choice?"

Answer choice (D): The argument as a whole works towards supporting the recommendation that "pedigree organizations should set standards requiring working ability in pedigreed dogs classified as working dogs." The phrase in the question stem does not summarize the antithesis of that position.

Answer choice (E): This answer has the order of the argument backwards. The phrase referenced in the question stem provides evidence necessary to support a claim stated *later* in the argument.

CHAPTER THIRTEEN: FLAW IN THE REASONING QUESTIONS

Flaw in the Reasoning Questions ▮▮▮▮▮▮▮▮▮▮▮

First Family Information Model:

Flaw in the Reasoning questions are exactly the same as Method of Reasoning questions with the important exception that the question stem indicates that the reasoning in the stimulus is flawed. Because the question stem reveals that a flaw is present, you need not make a determination of the validity of the stimulus; the question stem makes the determination for you. This information provides you with a tremendous advantage because you can identify the error of reasoning in the stimulus *before* proceeding to the answer choices. And, if you did not realize there was an error of reasoning in the stimulus, the question stem gives you the opportunity to re-evaluate the argument and find the error of reasoning.

When indicating that a flaw is present in the argument, the test makers will use phrases such as "the reasoning is flawed" and "the argument is vulnerable," or synonymous phrases. Here are several example question stems:

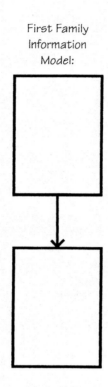

"Which one of the following most accurately describes a flaw in the argument's reasoning?"

"The reasoning in the argument is most vulnerable to criticism on the ground that the argument"

"The reasoning above is flawed because it fails to recognize that"

"A questionable aspect of the reasoning above is that it"

"The reasoning in the argument is fallacious because the argument"

To identify the right answer choice, carefully consider the reasoning used in the stimulus. The correct answer will identify the error in the author's reasoning and then describe that error in general terms. Beware of answers that describe a portion of the stimulus but fail to identify the error in the reasoning.

Because Flaw in the Reasoning questions are so similar to Method of Reasoning questions, the introduction to this chapter will be relatively brief.

The Value of Knowing Common Errors of Reasoning

In logic there are many more recognized forms of invalid argumentation than there are forms of valid argumentation. The test makers, being human (yes, it's true), tend to repeat certain forms when creating stimuli and answer choices, and you can gain a demonstrable advantage by learning the forms most often used by the test makers. Applying the knowledge you acquire in this chapter will take two avenues:

The paragraphs to the right help explain why test preparation works: the more you know about the exam before you walk in to take the test, the less time you have to waste during the exam thinking about these issues.

1. Identifying errors of reasoning made in the stimulus

    If you learn the mistakes that are often made by authors, then you will be able to quickly identify the error in the argument and accelerate through the answer choices to find the correct answer. Students without this knowledge will be forced to work more slowly and with less confidence.

2. Identifying answer choices that describe a common error of reasoning

    In Flaw in the Reasoning questions, the test makers tend to use certain types of answers again and again. Depending on the reasoning used in the stimulus, these answers can describe the correct answer, but more often than not they are used as "stock" wrong answers. Familiarizing yourself with these answer choices will give you an advantage when you encounter similar answer choices in the future. For example, "attacking the source of an argument, not the argument itself" has appeared as the correct answer in several LSAT questions. But, it has appeared in many more questions as a wrong answer choice. If you are familiar with a "source" argument, you can then make an immediate determination as to whether that answer is correct or incorrect.

Given the immense advantage you get by knowing the flawed reasoning that appear most frequently on the LSAT, the following section will detail a variety of errors of reasoning and provide examples of actual LSAT answer choices that describe the error under discussion. We strongly recommend that you spend a considerable amount of time learning these forms of flawed argumentation. It will definitely help you on the LSAT!

Common Errors of Reasoning Explained

The following classic errors of reasoning appear with some frequency. The review is given in layman's, not philosophical, terms:

In the last chapter you learned that studying the incorrect answer choices in any Method of Reasoning question assists you in preparing for future questions. The same advice holds true for Flaw in the Reasoning questions.

Uncertain Use of a Term or Concept

As an argument progresses, the author must use each term in a constant, coherent fashion. Using a term in different ways is inherently confusing and undermines the integrity of the argument. Here is an example:

> "Some people claim that the values that this country was built on are now being ignored by modern-day corporations. But this is incorrect. Corporations are purely profit-driven enterprises, beholden only to their shareholders, and as such they can only assess objects based on their value."

The term "value" is used in the example above in two different senses: first in a moral or ethical sense and then in a monetary sense. This shift in meaning undermines the author's position.

This type of answer choice appears more frequently as an incorrect answer than any other type. Here are examples of how this error of reasoning is described in LSAT answer choices:

> "depending on the ambiguous use of a key term"

> "it confuses two different meanings of the word 'solve' "

> "relies on interpreting a key term in two different ways"

> "equivocates with respect to a central concept"

> "allows a key term to shift in meaning from one use to the next"

> "fails to define the term"

Source Argument

Also known as an *ad hominem*, this type of flawed argument attacks the person (or source) instead of the argument they advance. Because the LSAT is concerned solely with argument forms, a speaker can never validly attack the character or motives of a person; instead, a speaker must always attack the *argument* advanced by a person. Here is an example:

> "The anti-smoking views expressed by Senator Smith should be ignored. After all, Smith himself is a smoker!"

A source argument can take different forms, including the following:

1. Focusing on the motives of the source.
2. Focusing on the actions of the source (as in the above example).

In the real world, you will often hear source arguments used by children and politicians (the two being alike in a number of ways, of course).

Here are examples of how this error of reasoning is described in LSAT answer choices:

> "makes an attack on the character of opponents"

> "it is directed against the proponent of a claim rather than against the claim itself"

> "he directs his criticism against the person making the argument rather than directing it against the argument itself"

> "it draws conclusions about the merit of a position and about the content of that position from evidence about the position's source"

> "assuming that a claim is false on the grounds that the person defending it is of questionable character"

Like Method of Reasoning questions, Flaw in the Reasoning questions are part of the First Family.

THE POWERSCORE LSAT LOGICAL REASONING BIBLE

Circular Reasoning

In circular reasoning the author assumes as true what is supposed to be proved. Consider the following example:

"This essay is the best because it is better than all the others."

In this example the premise and the conclusion are identical in meaning. As we know, the conclusion should always follow from the premise. In the example above, the premise supports the conclusion, but the conclusion equally supports the premise, creating a "circular" situation where you can move from premise to conclusion, and then back again to the premise, and so on. Here is another example: "I must be telling the truth because I'm not lying."

Here are examples of how this error of reasoning is described in LSAT answer choices:

"it assumes what it seeks to establish"

"argues circularly by assuming the conclusion is true in stating the premises"

"presupposes the truth of what it sets out to prove"

"the argument assumes what it is attempting to demonstrate"

"it takes for granted the very claim that it sets out to establish"

"it offers, in place of support for its conclusion, a mere restatement of that conclusion"

Unlike a college-level logic class, we will not waste time on classification distinctions, such as Formal versus Informal Fallacies.

Errors of Conditional Reasoning

In Chapter Six we discussed several mistakes LSAT authors make when using conditional reasoning, including Mistaken Negation and Mistaken Reversal. While you should now be comfortable recognizing those errors, Flaw in the Reasoning questions will ask you to describe those mistakes in logical terms. This often proves to be a more difficult task.

Remember, a Mistaken Negation and a Mistaken Reversal are contrapositives of each other, so the error behind both is identical.

When describing a Mistaken Negation or a Mistaken Reversal, the test makers must focus on the error common to both: confusing the sufficient condition with the necessary condition. As such, here are examples of how these errors of reasoning are described in LSAT answer choices:

> "taking the nonexistence of something as evidence that a necessary precondition for that thing also did not exist" (Mistaken Negation)

> "mistakes being sufficient to justify punishment for being required to justify it" (Mistaken Reversal)

Note that the authors can either mistake a necessary condition for a sufficient condition, or mistake a sufficient condition for a necessary condition:

Confuses a necessary condition for a sufficient condition

> "it treats something that is necessary for bringing about a state of affairs as something that is sufficient to bring about a state of affairs"

This discussion is not designed to include every possible error of reasoning, only those used most frequently by the makers of the LSAT.

> "from the assertion that something is necessary to a moral order, the argument concludes that that thing is sufficient for an element of the moral order to be realized"

Confuses a sufficient condition for a necessary condition

> "confuses a sufficient condition with a required condition"

It is interesting to note the frequency with which the words "sufficient" (or its synonym "assured") or "necessary" (or its synonym "required") are used when analyzing the answer choices used to describe conditional reasoning. This occurs because those words perfectly capture the idea and it is difficult to avoid using at least one of those words when describing conditionality. This is a huge advantage for you: if you identify a stimulus with conditional reasoning and are asked a Flaw question, you can quickly scan the answers for the one answer that contains "sufficient," "necessary," or both.

<u>Mistaken Cause and Effect</u>

As discussed in Chapter Eight, arguments that draw causal conclusions are inherently flawed because there may be another explanation for the stated relationship. Because of the extreme causal assumption made by LSAT authors (that there is only one cause), any of the following answer choice forms could be used to describe an error of causality. Underneath each item are examples of how the error of reasoning is described in LSAT answer choices.

1. Assuming a causal relationship on the basis of the sequence of events.

   "mistakes the observation that one thing happens after another for proof that the second thing is the result of the first"

   "mistakes a temporal relationship for a causal relationship"

2. Assuming a causal relationship when only a correlation exists.

   "confusing the coincidence of two events with a causal relation between the two"

   "assumes a causal relationship where only a correlation has been indicated"

3. Failure to consider an alternate cause for the effect, or an alternate cause for both the cause *and* the effect.

   "fails to exclude an alternative explanation for the observed effect"

   "overlooks the possibility that the same thing may causally contribute both to education and to good health"

4. Failure to consider that the events may be reversed.

   "the author mistakes an effect for a cause"

To determine the error of reasoning, focus on the connection between the premises and the conclusion. Remember, LSAT authors are allowed to put forth virtually any premise when making an argument; the key is how those premises are used, not whether they are factually true.

Note the frequency with which the words "cause" or "effect" are used. This occurs because there are few substitutes for those two words, and thus the test makers are often forced to use those words to describe an argument containing causality. If you identify a stimulus with causal reasoning and are asked a Flaw question, quickly scan the answers for one that contains "cause," "effect," or both.

This error occurs when an author attempts to attack an opponent's position by ignoring the actual statements made by the opposing speaker and instead distorts and refashions the argument, making it weaker in the process. In figurative terms, a "straw" argument is built up which is then easier for the author to knock down.

Often this error is accompanied by the phrase "what you're saying is" or "if I understand you correctly," which are used to preface the refashioned and weakened argument. Here is an example:

Politician A: "The platform proposed by my party calls for a moderate increase in taxes on those individuals making over $20,000 per year, and then taking that money and using it to rebuild the educational system."

Politician B: "But what you're saying is that everyone should pay higher taxes, and so your proposal is unfair."

In the example above, Politician B recasts Politician A's argument unfairly. Politician A indicated the tax increase would apply to those with incomes over $20,000 where Politician B distorts that to "everyone should pay higher taxes."

Here are examples of how this error of reasoning is described in LSAT answer choices:

"refutes a distorted version of an opposing position"

"misdescribing the student representative's position, thereby making it easier to challenge"

"portrays opponents' views as more extreme than they really are"

"distorts the proposal advocated by opponents"

General Lack of Relevant Evidence for the Conclusion

Some LSAT authors misuse information to such a degree that they fail to provide any information to support their conclusion or they provide information that is irrelevant to their conclusion. Here is an example:

> "Some critics claim that scientific progress has increased the polarization of society and alienated large segments of the population. But these critics are wrong because even a cursory glance at the past shows that society is always somewhat polarized and some groups are inevitably alienated."

Note the use of the construction "some critics claim..." As usual, the author's main point is that the claim that the critics are making is wrong.

The author provides irrelevant evidence in an attempt to refute the claim that "scientific progress has increased the polarization of society and alienated large segments of the population." Citing facts that such a situation has always existed does not help disprove that scientific progress has *increased* the severity of the situation.

Here are examples of how this error of reasoning is described in LSAT answer choices:

> "The author cites irrelevant data."

> "draws a conclusion that is broader in scope than is warranted by the evidence advanced"

> "It uses irrelevant facts to justify a claim about the quality of the disputed product."

> "It fails to give any reason for the judgment it reaches."

> "It introduces information unrelated to its conclusion as evidence in support of that conclusion."

Internal Contradiction

As discussed in the answer key to the previous chapter, an internal contradiction (also known as a self-contradiction) occurs when an author makes conflicting statements. The example used was:

> "Everyone should join our country club. After all, it's an exclusive group that links many of the influential members of the community."

The self-contradiction occurs when the speaker says "Everyone should join" and then follows that by saying that it is "an exclusive group." *Exclusive*, by definition, means that some people are excluded.

The following show how this error of reasoning is described in LSAT answer choices:

> "bases a conclusion on claims that are inconsistent with each other"

> "the author makes incompatible assumptions"

> "introduce information that actually contradicts the conclusion"

> "offers in support of its conclusion pieces of evidence that are mutually contradictory"

> "some of the evidence presented in support of the conclusion is inconsistent with other evidence provided"

> "assumes something that it later denies, resulting in a contradiction"

Appeal Fallacies

While there are a number of "appeal" fallacies that appear in traditional logic (Appeal to Fear, Appeal to Force, Appeal to Tradition, etc.), the following three are the most applicable to the LSAT:

1. Appeal to Authority

    An Appeal to Authority uses the opinion of an authority in an attempt to persuade the reader. The flaw in this form of reasoning is that the authority may not have relevant knowledge or all the information regarding a situation, or there may a difference of opinion among experts as to what is true in the case. Here is an example:

    > "World-renowned neurologist Dr. Samuel Langhorne says that EZBrite Tooth Strips are the best for whitening your teeth. So, you know if you buy EZBrite you will soon have the whitest teeth possible!"

    The primary defect in this argument is its use of a neurologist as an authority figure in an area of dentistry. While Dr. Langhorne can reasonably be appealed to in matters of the brain, dental care would be considered outside the scope of his expertise.

    Here are examples of how this error of reasoning is described in LSAT answer choices:

    > "the judgment of experts is applied to a matter in which their expertise is irrelevant"

    > "the argument inappropriately appeals to the authority of the mayor"

    > "it relies on the judgment of experts in a matter to which their expertise is irrelevant"

    > "accepts a claim on mere authority, without requiring sufficient justification"

2. Appeal to Popular Opinion/Appeal to Numbers

    This error states that a position is true because the majority believes it to be true. As you know, arguments are created by providing premises that support a conclusion. An appeal to popular opinion does not present a logical reason for accepting a position, just an appeal based on numbers. Here is an example:

"A recent poll states that 75% of Americans believe that Microsoft is a monopoly. Antitrust law states that monopolies have a deleterious effect on the marketplace (with the exception of utilities), and therefore Microsoft should be controlled or broken into smaller pieces."

The author uses the results of a poll that indicate many people *think* Microsoft is a monopoly to conclude that Microsoft is in fact a monopoly. This type of persuasion is often used in the arguments made by advertisements ("All the trend setters use EZBrite Tooth Strips"), politicians ("Everyone loves the environment. Vote for the Green Party!), and children ("C'mon, try this. Everyone does it.").

This type of reasoning most often appears as an incorrect answer. Here are examples of how this error of reasoning is described in LSAT answer choices:

"it treats popular opinion as if it constituted conclusive evidence for a claim"

"attempts to discredit legislation by appealing to public sentiment"

"a claim is inferred to be false merely because a majority of people believe it to be false"

"the argument, instead of providing adequate reasons in support of its conclusion, makes an appeal to popular opinion"

3. Appeal to Emotion

An Appeal to Emotion occurs when emotions or emotionally-charged language is used in an attempt to persuade the reader. Here is an example:

"Officer, please do not give me a ticket for speeding. In the last month I've been fired from my job, kicked out of my apartment, and my car broke down. I don't deserve this!

Here are examples of how this error of reasoning is described in LSAT answer choices:

"attempts to persuade by making an emotional appeal"

"uses emotive language in labeling the proposals"

"the argument appeals to emotion rather than reason"

Survey Errors

The makers of the LSAT believe that surveys, when conducted properly, produce reliable results. However, surveys can be invalidated when any of the following three scenarios arise:

1. The survey uses a biased sample.

    Perhaps the most famous example of a biased survey occurred in 1936. The *Literary Digest* weekly magazine sent out ballots to some 10 million voters (2.3 million were returned), and returns indicated that a solid majority would vote for Republican candidate Alf Landon in the upcoming presidential election. On the basis of these results (and the size of the sample), the *Literary Digest* predicted that Landon would win easily. Of course, when the election was held Franklin Roosevelt won in a landslide. The *Literary Digest* erred by sending the ballots to groups such as telephone owners and automobile owners, groups that in that era (late Depression) tended to be among the wealthiest individuals and overwhelmingly Republican. The *Literary Digest* ended up polling a large number of Republicans and on that basis declared that the Republican candidate would win.

    Note that a secondary error with the polling done by the *Literary Digest* is that the sample is self-selected; that is, the individuals being polled decided whether or not to respond. That opportunity introduces bias into the survey process because certain types of individuals tend to respond to surveys whereas others do not.

2. The survey questions are improperly constructed.

    If a survey question is confusing or misleading, the results of the poll can be inaccurate.

    Questions can be confusing, such as "Do you feel it is possible that none of the candidates would not vote to increase taxes?" (The question actually asks, "Do you feel it is possible that all of the candidates would vote to increase taxes?"). If a respondent cannot understand the question, how can they accurately answer the question?

    Questions can also be misleading, such as "How soon should the U.S. government withdraw from the United Nations?" The question presumes that the United States should withdraw from the United Nations—a course of action that the respondent may not agree with.

A similar type of sampling error occurred in 1948 when the Chicago Daily Tribune predicted Thomas Dewey would prevail over Harry Truman. The Tribune even went so far as to print the morning edition of the newspaper with that headline.

3. Respondents to the survey give inaccurate responses.

    People do not always tell the truth when responding to surveys. Two classic questions that often elicit false answers are "What is your age" and "how much money do you make each year?"

    If respondents give false answers to survey questions, the results of the survey are skewed and inaccurate.

Here are examples of how the errors of reasoning above are described in LSAT answer choices:

"uses evidence drawn from a small sample that may well be unrepresentative"

"generalizes from an unrepresentative sample"

"states a generalization based on a selection that is not representative of the group about which the generalization is supposed to hold true"

Exceptional Case/Overgeneralization

This error takes a small number of instances and treats those instances as if they support a broad, sweeping conclusion. Here is an example:

"Two of my friends were shortchanged at that store. Therefore, everyone gets shortchanged at that store."

This answer appears most frequently as an incorrect answer in Flaw questions, but as with any of the errors described in this chapter, occasionally it appears as a correct answer. Here are examples of how this error of reasoning is described in LSAT answer choices:

"supports a universal claim on the basis of a single example"

"The argument generalizes from too small a sample of cases"

"Too general a conclusion is made about investing on the basis of a single experiment"

"bases a general claim on a few exceptional instances"

Errors of Composition and Division

Composition and division errors involve judgments made about groups and parts of a group.

An error of composition occurs when the author attributes a characteristic of part of the group to the group as a whole or to each member of the group. Here is an example:

"Every party I attend is fun and exciting. Therefore, my life is fun and exciting."

Here are examples of how this error of reasoning is described in LSAT answer choices:

"assuming that because something is true of each of the parts of a whole it is true of the whole itself"

"improperly infers that each and every scientist has a certain characteristic from the premise that most scientists have that characteristic"

"takes the view of one lawyer to represent the views of all lawyers"

An error of division occurs when the author attributes a characteristic of the whole (or each member of the whole) to a part of the group. Here is an example:

"The United States is the wealthiest country in the world. Thus, every American is wealthy."

Here is an example of how this error of reasoning is described in LSAT answer choices:

"presumes, without providing justification, that what is true of a whole must also be true of its constituent parts"

False Analogy

As discussed in the answer key to the problem set in the previous chapter, an analogy is a comparison between two items. A False Analogy occurs when the author uses an analogy that too is dissimilar to the original situation to be applicable. Here is an example:

> "Just as a heavy rainfall can be cleansing, the best approach to maintain a healthy relationship is to store up all your petty grievances and then unload them all at one time on your partner."

The comparison in the example fails to consider that a heavy rainfall and an emotionally charged situation are fundamentally different.

Here are two examples of how a False analogy is described in LSAT answer choices:

> "treats as similar two cases that are different in a critical respect"

> "treats two kinds of things that differ in important respects as if they do not differ"

False Dilemma

A False Dilemma assumes that only two courses of action are available when there may be others. Here is an example:

> "Recent accidents within the oil industry have made safety of operation a critical public safety issue. Because the industry cannot be expected to police itself, the government must step in and take action."

The argument above falsely assumes that only two courses of action exist: industry self-policing or government action. But this ignores other courses of action, such as consumer watchdog groups.

Do not confuse a False Dilemma with a situation where the author legitimately establishes that only two possibilities exist. Phrases such as "either A or B will occur, but not both" can establish a limited set of possibilities, and certain real-world situations yield only two possibilities, such as "you are either dead or alive."

Here is an example of how a False Dilemma is described in LSAT answer choices:

> "fails to consider that some students may be neither fascinated by nor completely indifferent to the subject being taught"

Errors in the Use of Evidence

Mis-assessing the force of evidence is a frequent error committed by LSAT authors. Each of the following describes an error of reasoning involving the force of evidence:

1. Lack of evidence for a position is taken to prove that position is false.

    Just because no evidence proving a position has been introduced does not mean that the position is false. Here is an example:

    > "The White House has failed to offer any evidence that they have reached a trade agreement with China. Therefore, no such agreement has been reached."

    In the example above the White House may have valid reasons for withholding information about the trade agreement. The lack of confirming evidence does not undeniably prove that a trade agreement has *not* been reached.

    Here are two examples of how this error of reasoning is described in LSAT answer choices:

    > "treats failure to prove a claim as constituting denial of that claim"

    > "taking a lack of evidence for a claim as evidence undermining that claim"

2. Lack of evidence against a position is taken to prove that position is true.

    This error is the opposite of the previous error. Just because no evidence disproving a position has been introduced does not mean that the position is true. Here is a famous example:

    > "There has been no evidence given against the existence of God, so God must exist."

    The lack of evidence against a position does not undeniably prove a position. Here is an example of how this error of reasoning is described in LSAT answer choices:

    > "treating the failure to establish that a certain claim is false as equivalent to a demonstration that the claim is true"

3. Some evidence against a position is taken to prove that position is false.

The introduction of evidence against a position only weakens the position; it does not necessarily prove the position false. Here is an example:

> "Some historians claim that a lengthy drought preceded the fall of the Aztec empire. But we know from Aztec writings that in at least one year during the supposed drought there was minor flooding. Thus, the claim that there was a lengthy drought prior to the fall of the Aztec empire is false."

The evidence offered in the example above weakens the claim that there was a lengthy drought, but it does not disprove it. A drought by definition is a prolonged period of unusually low rainfall, and thus it would be possible for flooding to occur on occasion, but not enough flooding to overcome the general drought conditions.

Here is an example of how this error of reasoning is described in an LSAT answer choice:

> "it confuses undermining an argument in support of a given conclusion with showing that the conclusion itself is false"

4. Some evidence for a position is taken to prove that position is true.

The introduction of evidence for a position only provides support for the position; it does not prove the position to be undeniably true. Here is an example:

> "We know that the defendant was in the vicinity of the robbery when the robbery occurred. Therefore, the defendant is guilty of the robbery."

As the above example proves, partial support for a position does not make the position invincible (especially in LSAT arguments, which are relatively short). As you might expect, partial evidence for a position can be outweighed by evidence against that position.

Here is an example of how this error of reasoning is described in an LSAT answer choice:

> "the argument takes evidence showing merely that its conclusion could be true to constitute evidence showing that the conclusion is in fact true"

<u>Time Shift Errors</u>

Although this error has a rather futuristic name, the mistake involves assuming that conditions will remain constant over time, and that what was the case in the past will be the case in the present or future.

> "The company has always reimbursed me for meals when I'm on a business trip, so they will certainly reimburse me for meals on this business trip."

Clearly, what has occurred in the past is no guarantee that the future will be the same. Yet, many LSAT authors make this assumption, especially when hundreds or thousands of years are involved. Here are examples of how this error of reasoning is described in LSAT answer choices:

> "treats a claim about what is currently the case as if it were a claim about what has been the case for an extended period"

> "uncritically draws an inference from what has been true in the past to what will be true in the future"

<u>Numbers and Percentage Errors</u>

In Chapter Fifteen we will discuss numbers and percentages problems in detail. Meanwhile, consider that many errors in this category are committed when an author improperly equates a percentage with a definite quantity, or when an author uses quantity information to make a judgment about the percentage represented by that quantity.

Here is an example of how this error of reasoning is described in an LSAT answer choice:

> "the argument confuses the percentage of the budget spent on a program with the overall amount spent on that program"

Final Note

The errors discussed in this chapter represent the errors that appear most frequently in LSAT stimuli and answer choices. As mentioned previously, you should examine every answer choice in Flaw in the Reasoning questions because a familiarity with the language and terms used by the test makers is invaluable.

The following page begins a short problem set to help you identify errors of reasoning and understand how the test makers frequently use stock answers. Please read the explanations closely.

Flaw in the Reasoning Question Problem Set

The following questions are drawn from actual LSATs. Please complete the problem set and review the answer key and explanations. *Answers on Page 393*

1. Editorial: The premier's economic advisor assures her that with the elimination of wasteful spending the goal of reducing taxes while not significantly decreasing government services can be met. But the premier should not listen to this advisor, who in his youth was convicted of embezzlement. Surely his economic advice is as untrustworthy as he is himself, and so the premier should discard any hope of reducing taxes without a significant decrease in government services.

    Which one of the following is a questionable argumentative strategy employed in the editorial's argument?

    (A) rejecting a proposal on the grounds that a particular implementation of the proposal is likely to fail
    (B) trying to win support for a proposal by playing on people's fears of what could happen otherwise
    (C) criticizing the source of a claim rather than examining the claim itself
    (D) taking a lack of evidence for a claim as evidence undermining the claim
    (E) presupposing what it sets out to establish

2. Cotrell is, at best, able to write magazine articles of average quality. The most compelling pieces of evidence for this are those few of the numerous articles submitted by Cotrell that are superior, since Cotrell, who is incapable of writing an article that is better than average, must obviously have plagiarized superior ones.

    The argument is most vulnerable to criticism on which one of the following grounds?

    (A) It simply ignores the existence of potential counterevidence.
    (B) It generalizes from atypical occurrences.
    (C) It presupposes what it seeks to establish.
    (D) It relies on the judgment of experts in a matter to which their expertise is irrelevant.
    (E) It infers limits on ability from a few isolated lapses in performance.

Flaw in the Reasoning Problem Set

3. Activist: Food producers irradiate food in order to prolong its shelf life. Five animal studies were recently conducted to investigate whether this process alters food in a way that could be dangerous to people who eat it. The studies concluded that irradiated food is safe for humans to eat. However, because these studies were subsequently found by a panel of independent scientists to be seriously flawed in their methodology, it follows that irradiated food is not safe for human consumption.

The reasoning in the activist's argument is flawed because that argument

(A) treats a failure to prove a claim as constituting proof of the denial of that claim

(B) treats methodological flaws in past studies as proof that it is currently not possible to devise methodologically adequate alternatives

(C) fails to consider the possibility that even a study whose methodology has no serious flaws nonetheless might provide only weak support for its conclusion

(D) fails to consider the possibility that what is safe for animals might not always be safe for human beings

(E) fails to establish that the independent scientists know more about food irradiation than do the people who produced the five studies

4. Philosopher: Scientists talk about the pursuit of truth, but, like most people, they are self-interested. Accordingly, the professional activities of most scientists are directed toward personal career enhancement, and only incidentally toward the pursuit of truth. Hence, the activities of the scientific community are largely directed toward enhancing the status of that community as a whole, and only incidentally toward the pursuit of truth.

The reasoning in the philosopher's argument is flawed because the argument

(A) improperly infers that each and every scientist has a certain characteristic from the premise that most scientists have that characteristic

(B) improperly draws an inference about the scientific community as a whole from a premise about individual scientists

(C) presumes, without giving justification, that the aim of personal career enhancement never advances the pursuit of truth

(D) illicitly takes advantage of an ambiguity in the meaning of "self-interested"

(E) improperly draws an inference about a cause from premises about its effects

5. Several legislators claim that the public finds many current movies so violent as to be morally offensive. However, these legislators have misrepresented public opinion. In a survey conducted by a movie industry guild, only 17 percent of respondents thought that movies are overly violent, and only 3 percent found any recent movie morally offensive. These low percentages are telling, because the respondents see far more current movies than does the average moviegoer.

The reasoning in the argument is flawed in that the argument

(A) attempts to undermine the legislators' credibility instead of addressing their argument

(B) bases its conclusion on subjective judgments rather than on an objective criterion of moral offensiveness

(C) fails to consider the possibility that violent movies increase the prevalence of antisocial behavior

(D) generalizes from a sample that is unlikely to be representative of public sentiment

(E) presumes, without providing justification, that the people surveyed based their responses on a random sampling of movies

6. On some hot days the smog in Hillview reaches unsafe levels, and on some hot days the wind blows into Hillview from the east. Therefore, on some days when the wind blows into Hillview from the east, the smog in Hillview reaches unsafe levels.

The reasoning in the argument is flawed in that the argument

(A) mistakes a condition that sometimes accompanies unsafe levels of smog for a condition that necessarily accompanies unsafe levels of smog

(B) fails to recognize that one set might have some members in common with each of two others even though those two other sets have no members in common with each other

(C) uses the key term "unsafe" in one sense in a premise and in another sense in the conclusion

(D) contains a premise that is implausible unless the conclusion is presumed to be true

(E) infers a particular causal relation from a correlation that could be explained in a variety of other ways

7. Astronomer: I have asserted that our solar system does not contain enough meteoroids and other cosmic debris to have caused the extensive cratering on the far side of the moon. My opponents have repeatedly failed to demonstrate the falsity of this thesis. Their evidence is simply inconclusive; thus they should admit that my thesis is correct.

The reasoning in the astronomer's argument is flawed because this argument

(A) criticizes the astronomer's opponents rather than their arguments

(B) infers the truth of the astronomer's thesis from the mere claim that it has not been proven false

(C) ignores the possibility that alternative explanations may exist for the cratering

(D) presumes that the astronomer's thesis should not be subject to rational discussion and criticism

(E) fails to precisely define the key word "meteoroids"

8. Some people believe that good health is due to luck. However, studies from many countries indicate a strong correlation between good health and high educational levels. Thus research supports the view that good health is largely the result of making informed lifestyle choices.

The reasoning in the argument is most vulnerable to criticism on the grounds that the argument

(A) presumes, without providing justification, that only highly educated people make informed lifestyle choices

(B) overlooks the possibility that people who make informed lifestyle choices may nonetheless suffer from inherited diseases

(C) presumes, without providing justification, that informed lifestyle choices are available to everyone

(D) overlooks the possibility that the same thing may causally contribute both to education and to good health

(E) does not acknowledge that some people who fail to make informed lifestyle choices are in good health

Flaw in the Reasoning Question Problem Set Answer Key

All answer keys in this book indicate the source of the question by giving the month and year the LSAT was originally administered, the Logical Reasoning section number, and the question number within that section. Each LSAT has two Logical Reasoning sections, and so the Section 1 and Section 2 designators will refer to the first or second Logical Reasoning section in the test, not the physical section number of the booklet.

Question #1. Flaw. October 2000 LSAT, Section 2, #6. The correct answer choice is (C)

As with all Flaw in the Reasoning questions, you must closely examine the relationship between the premises and the conclusion. In this argument, the editorial concludes that the advice of the economic advisor is untrustworthy and "the premier should discard any hope of reducing taxes without a significant decrease in government services." What support is offered for this position? Is a discussion of taxation issued presented? Is a discussion of the cost of government service provided? Is the position of the economic advisor dissected? No. According to the editorial, the only reason for ignoring the economic advisor's advice is that the advisor was convicted in his youth of embezzlement. This fact has no bearing on the *argument* made by the advisor, and focuses instead on attacking the person making the argument. This is a classic Source or *ad hominem* argument, and you should immediately seek an answer choice that reflects this fact.

Answer choice (A): A proposal is not rejected in the stimulus; rather, a goal is advocated by the advisor and then the author questions whether that goal can be met by examining the background of the advisor. There is no discussion of a "particular implementation" that is likely to fail.

Answer choice (B): This answer fails the Fact Test because there is no discussion of "what could happen otherwise" and no discussion of people's fears.

Answer choice (C): This is the correct answer. The answer is a perfect description of a Source argument.

Answer choice (D): This answer describes an evidence error in which a lack of evidence for a position is considered to hurt the claim. In the argument, the author improperly used evidence about the advisor, and this mistake is the error in the argument. Even though this introduced a flaw into the argument, from the author's perspective this was an attempt to use evidence against a position to hurt the position. The editorial did not state or indicate that there was a *lack of* evidence when forming the conclusion. Put simply, the editor thought he had a reason that undermined the claim; no argument was made that there was a lack of evidence.

Answer choice (E): This answer describes Circular Reasoning. But, because the argument in the stimulus gives reasons for its position (albeit weak ones), the argument is not circular.

Flaw in the Reasoning Question Problem Set Answer Key

Question #2. Flaw. December 2001 LSAT, Section 1, #10. The correct answer choice is (C)

As always, look closely at the structure of the argument—specifically the relationships between the premises and conclusion. This breakdown presents the pieces in the order given in the argument:

Conclusion: Cotrell is, at best, able to write magazine articles of average quality.

Subconclusion/
Premise: The most compelling pieces of evidence for this are those few of the numerous articles submitted by Cotrell that are superior.

Premise: Cotrell, who is incapable of writing an article that is better than average, must obviously have plagiarized superior ones.

Examine the language in the conclusion ("Cotrell is, at best, able to write magazine articles of average quality") and the premise ("Cotrell, who is incapable of writing an article that is better than average"). The two are identical in meaning, and thus we have an argument with circular reasoning. Do not be distracted by the plagiarism argument in the middle of the text—that is a tool used to physically separate the conclusion and premise, making it harder to recognize that the two are identical.

Answer choice (A): The argument does not ignore the potential counterevidence to the conclusion. The potential counterevidence is the few articles submitted by Cotrell that are superior, and the author dismisses them by claiming they are plagiarized. Although the reasoning used to dismiss the good articles is flawed, it is an attempt to address the evidence, and thus the argument cannot be said to "simply ignore the existence of potential counterevidence."

Answer choice (B): This answer choice describes an Overgeneralization. The answer is wrong because the argument generalizes by dismissing the atypical occurrences (the superior articles), as opposed to generalizing *from* them.

Answer choice (C): This is the correct answer, and one of several different ways to describe Circular Reasoning (note that in the first problem in this set Circular Reasoning was an incorrect answer). More often than not, when you see Circular Reasoning it will be an incorrect answer choice, but you cannot be complacent and simply assume it will be wrong every time you see it. This problem proves that it does appear as the correct answer on occasion.

Answer choice (D): This answer describes an Appeal to Authority. The answer fails the Fact Test because there is no reference to the judgment of experts.

Answer choice (E): This answer is similar to answer choice (B). The answer starts out reasonably well—"it infers limits on ability." The argument does attempt this (depending on your definition of "infer"). But, does the argument make this inference based on a "few isolated lapses in performance?" No, the argument *dismisses* the few superior performances. In this sense the answer is Half Right, Half Wrong. Therefore, it is incorrect.

Flaw in the Reasoning Question Problem Set Answer Key

Question #3. Flaw. October 2002 LSAT, Section 1, #23. The correct answer choice is (A)

The structure of the argument is as follows:

Premise: Food producers irradiate food in order to prolong its shelf life.

Premise: Five animal studies were recently conducted to investigate whether this process alters food in a way that could be dangerous to people who eat it. The studies concluded that irradiated food is safe for humans to eat.

Premise: These studies were subsequently found by a panel of independent scientists to be seriously flawed in their methodology.

Conclusion: Irradiated food is not safe for human consumption.

The author uses the fact that the studies were flawed to conclude that irradiated food is not safe for human consumption. Is this a reasonable conclusion? No. The studies purported to prove that irradiated food is safe. The fact that the studies used flawed methodology should have been used to prove that the studies did not prove that irradiated food was safe. Instead, the activist takes the argument too far, believing that because the studies did not prove that irradiated food is safe, therefore irradiated food is not safe. This is the third error in the *Errors in the Use of Evidence* section, where "Some evidence against a position is taken to prove that position is false." Answer choice (A) perfectly describes this mistake.

Answer choice (B): Use the Fact Test to easily eliminate this answer. Although past studies were shown to have methodological flaws, this evidence is not used to prove that methodologically sound alternatives are impossible to achieve.

Answer choice (C): It's true, the argument does fail to consider the possibility that a non-flawed study might provide only weak support for its conclusion. But—and this is the critical question—is that a flaw in the reasoning of the activist? No, it is perfectly acceptable for the author to ignore an issue (non-flawed studies) that does not relate to his argument. Remember, the correct answer choice must describe a *flaw* in the reasoning of the argument, not just something that occurred in the argument.

Answer choice (D): As with answer choice (C), the author has failed to consider the statement in this answer choice. But is this a flaw? No. The fact that animal testing is widely done and the results are accepted as indicative of possible problems with humans falls under the "commonsense information" discussed back in Chapter Two. Testing products on animals is a current fact of life, and the author made a reasoning error by failing to consider the possibility that what is safe for animals might not always be safe for human beings.

Another way of looking at this answer is that it effectively states that the author has failed to consider that there is a False Analogy between animals and humans. He fails to consider it because the analogy between animals and humans is not false.

Answer choice (E): Again, the activist does fail to establish this, but it is not necessary since the independent scientists only commented on the methodology of the study, not the irradiated food itself.

Flaw in the Reasoning Question Problem Set Answer Key

Question #4. Flaw. October 2001 LSAT, Section 2, #18. The correct answer choice is (B)

This argument contains an error of composition, one where the status-enhancing activities of most scientists are said to prove that the *scientific community as a whole* acts to enhance its status.

Answer choice (A): This answer choice describes a compositional error, but not the one that occurs in the stimulus. The stimulus makes a judgment about the scientific community as a whole whereas this answer states that a judgment is made about *each and every scientist*. The community as a whole is different than each and every scientist, and thus this answer is incorrect.

If you are thinking about the difference between the community as a whole and each member within the community, consider this statement: "Our community is against stealing." While that may be true, there may also be individual members of the community who are thieves and have no qualm about stealing.

Answer choice (B): This is the correct answer, and the answer describes the correct compositional error made by the philosopher.

Answer choice (C): The answer is wrong—the author does not presume that the aim of personal career enhancement *never* advances the pursuit of truth. Consider the second sentence: "Accordingly, the professional activities of most scientists are directed toward personal career enhancement, and *only incidentally toward the pursuit of truth*. The portion that states "only incidentally toward the pursuit of truth" indicates that the author allows for the possibility that career-enhancement activities can result in activities that pursue truth, even if only a little bit. But, since that contradicts the force of *never*, this answer is incorrect.

This is the most frequently chosen wrong answer, as about 20% of test takers select this choice.

Answer choice (D): This answer choice describes the Uncertain Use of a Term. The term "self-interested" is used only once in the argument (at the end of the first sentence), and the remainder of the argument is consistent with the generally accepted meaning of "self-interested" and uses that meaning unambiguously.

Answer choice (E): The argument in the stimulus is about the relationships of parts and wholes, not about cause and effect. This answer, which describes reasoning from an effect in order to infer its cause, is therefore incorrect. An example of the reasoning described in this answer choice would be: "We know this window was broken this afternoon, and only one pane of the window was broken. We also know the pane was broken by a circular object. Therefore, a baseball was the cause of the broken window.

Question #5. Flaw. June 2003 LSAT, Section 1, #12. The correct answer choice is (D)

The argument opens with the classic "some people claim" construction. The legislators claim that the public finds many movies to be offensive, but the author rejects that position and concludes the legislators have misrepresented public opinion. The author uses the results of a survey as evidence. At first glance this argument looks very strong to most people, but then they encounter the question stem and realize there must be an error. This is a critical moment: when the question stem indicates an error is present but you did not realize one exists, you must go back to the stimulus and look for the error. Do not proceed to the answer choices thinking that the answers will clarify or reveal the error to you! The answer choices are designed to subtly draw your attention toward side issues, and it is far preferable that you find the error first and then find the answer that correctly describes the error.

In this argument, the error occurs with the people that were surveyed in the poll. The last sentence reveals that the survey did not use an unbiased sample: "the respondents see far more current movies than does the average movie goer." As you might imagine, individuals who attend a large number of movies are by definition interested in the movies that are being shown, and are more likely to be aware of the level of violence and accepting of it. These tendencies make the sample unrepresentative of the general population—an error correctly described in answer choice (D). To help spot this error, note that the last sentence of the argument indicates that the surveyed individuals saw more movies *than the average moviegoer*. In other words, the survey respondents were not average.

Answer choice (A): This answer describes a Source argument. The author uses survey data to attack the legislator's position and does not attack the credibility of the legislators.

Answer choice (B): The conclusion is based on the results of a survey about public opinion, not on subjective judgments of moral offensiveness.

Answer choice (C): The argument is not about what causes antisocial behavior, so it is not a flaw that the argument fails to consider that violent movies increase the prevalence of antisocial behavior.

Answer choice (D): This is the correct answer.

Answer choice (E): The argument gives no data to suspect that the responses were not based on a random sampling of *movies* seen. The error is instead that the *people* surveyed represented a biased sample.

Question #6. Flaw-FL. October 2003 LSAT, Section 2, #20. The correct answer choice is (B)

The premises of the argument contain a Formal Logic setup:

> HD = hot days in Hillview
> SUL = smog reaches unsafe levels
> WBE = wind blows in from the east

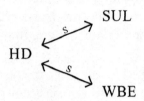

As you learned in Chapter Eleven, the combination of two "some" statements does not yield any inferences. Yet, the author draws a conclusion (SUL $\longleftrightarrow^{s}$ WBE) on the basis of the relationship and you must identify the answer that explains why this conclusion is incorrect.

Answer choice (A): There is no proof in the argument that the condition of WBE sometimes accompanies smog reaching unsafe levels—that is the mistake made by the author. The answer would be more attractive if it read as follows:

> "mistakes a condition (WBE) that sometimes accompanies hot days in Hillview for a condition that sometimes accompanies unsafe levels of smog"

Answer choice (B): This is the correct answer. When two "some" statements are joined, no inference can be drawn because the group common to both may be large enough that the two sub-elements do not overlap. For example, let's say there are 10 hot days in Hillview (HD), 1 day when the smog reaches unsafe levels (SUL), and 1 day when the wind blows in the east. Is it necessary that the 1 day when the smog reaches unsafe levels is the same day that the wind blows in from the east? No, but the argument concludes that is the case, and that error is described in this answer choice. For reference purposes, here is the answer choice with each abstract item identified in parentheses after the reference:

> "fails to recognize that *one set* (HD) might have some members in common with *each of two others* (SUL and WBE) even though those *two other sets* (SUL and WBE) have no members in common with each other"

Answer choice (C): This answer choice describes the Uncertain Use of a Term, but the argument is consistent in its use of "unsafe." Therefore, this answer is incorrect.

Answer choice (D): Each premise is plausible regardless of the truth of the conclusion.

Answer choice (E): The argument does not feature causal reasoning. The conclusion clearly states that the two events happen together, but there is no attempt to say that one caused the other. If you chose this answer, try to identify the causal indicators in the argument—there are none.

Question #7. Flaw. December 2003 LSAT, Section 1, #26. The correct answer choice is (B)

This is the second problem in this set to feature an Evidence error. In this problem, the astronomer falls into the second error from the *Errors in the Use of Evidence* section, where "Lack of evidence against a position is taken to prove that position is true." Answer choice (B) describes this mistake.

The astronomer's argument is structured as follows:

Premise: I have asserted that our solar system does not contain enough meteoroids and other cosmic debris to have caused the extensive cratering on the far side of the moon.

Premise: My opponents have repeatedly failed to demonstrate the falsity of this thesis. Their evidence is simply inconclusive.

Conclusion: They [my opponents] should admit that my thesis is correct.

Answer choice (A): The argument in the stimulus does not include a Source attack. There is a difference between stating that an opponent's argument is wrong (which is legitimate) and attacking the character of that opponent (a Source flaw). Always look to see if the author attacks the person or the position; a legitimate argument can sometimes appear questionable if the author uses weighted language such as, "My opponents are deluded in believing that my thesis is incorrect." Although that phrasing sounds like a personal attack, it is just a very strong way of stating that the author's opponents are incorrect, and it is not a Source attack.

Answer choice (B): This is the correct answer.

Answer choice (C): The astronomer's thesis asserts that meteoroids and other cosmic debris are *not* the cause of the cratering on the far side of the moon. By definition, therefore, the astronomer allows for alternate explanations of the cratering.

Answer choice (D): There is no presumption in the argument similar to the one described in this answer.

Answer choice (E): This answer describes the Uncertain Use of a Term, but the argument does not use "meteoroids" in an inconsistent way.

Flaw in the Reasoning Question Problem Set Answer Key

Question #8. Flaw-CE. December 2002 LSAT, Section 2, #20. The correct answer choice is (D)

The argument contains a causal conclusion that asserts that good health is primarily caused by informed lifestyle choices (education):

Premise:	Some people believe that good health is due to luck.
Premise:	However, studies from many countries indicate a strong correlation between good health and high educational levels.
Conclusion:	Thus research supports the view that good health is largely the result of making informed lifestyle choices.

The author errs in assuming that the correlation mentioned in the second premise supports a causal conclusion.

Answer choice (A): A disproportionate number of people (about one in three) select this answer. Does the argument presume that to make an informed lifestyle choice a person *must be* highly educated? The author certainly believes that high educational levels lead to informed choices, but the answer suggests that the author thinks that the highly educated are the *only* people able to make an informed choice. The wording is too strong and this answer is incorrect.

Answer choice (B): The author specifically notes that *good* health is largely the result of making informed lifestyle choices. There is no mention of *poor* health, nor need there be since the argument focuses on a correlation between good health and education. Thus, overlooking the possibility mentioned in this answer choice is not an error.

Answer choice (C): The author does not make the presumption that informed lifestyle choices are available to everyone, just that making good choices generally results in good health.

Answer choice (D): This is the correct answer. Remember, the error of causality is one with many facets, and one of those errors is assuming that no third element caused both the stated cause and the stated effect. This answer choice indicates that a third element (such as money) could cause both the conditions described in the argument. Remember, if you know an error of causality occurred in the stimulus, look for the answer that uses the words *cause* or *effect*! This is the only answer to do so, and it is correct.

Answer choice (E): Unlike many causal conclusions, the conclusion in this argument is not ironclad. The author specifically says that the effect *is largely the result* of the cause, and that statement implicitly allows other causes to lead to the effect, even if one does not make an informed lifestyle choice.

CHAPTER FOURTEEN: PARALLEL REASONING QUESTIONS

Parallel Reasoning Questions ████████████

Parallel Reasoning questions ask you to identify the answer choice that contains reasoning most similar in structure to the reasoning in the stimulus. Since this task requires you to first identify the method of argumentation used by the author and then to match that reasoning to the reasoning presented in each answer choice, these questions can be quite time consuming (a fact known to and exploited by the test makers).

Like Method of Reasoning and Flaw in the Reasoning questions, Parallel Reasoning questions are in the First Family and have the same information structure. However, because of the abstract nature of these questions, comparing the stimulus to the answer choices takes on a different dimension, and we will address this issue in a moment in the section entitled *Solving Parallel Reasoning Questions*.

Question stem examples:

> "Which one of the following is most closely parallel in its reasoning to the reasoning in the argument above?"

> "Which one of the following exhibits a pattern of reasoning most similar to that exhibited by the argument above?"

> "Which one of the following arguments is most similar in its logical features to the argument above?"

> "Which one of the following arguments is most similar in its pattern of reasoning to the argument above?"

> "The structure of the reasoning in the argument above is most parallel to that in which one of the following?"

Parallel Flaw Questions

The stimulus for a Parallel Reasoning question can contain either valid or invalid reasoning. Since the February 1992 LSAT, whenever a Parallel Reasoning question contains flawed reasoning, it is stated in the question stem. If there is no mention of flawed reasoning in the question stem, the reasoning in the stimulus is valid (and vice versa).

First Family
Information
Model:

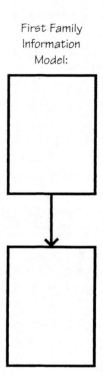

If the reasoning is flawed, the question stem will state that the reasoning is bad by using words such as "flawed" or "questionable." If the reasoning is not flawed, then the question stem will not refer to flawed reasoning.

When a Parallel Reasoning stimulus contains flawed reasoning, we identify it as a Parallel Flaw question. Like Flaw in the Reasoning questions, Parallel Flaw questions use many of the common forms of erroneous reasoning.

Here are two Parallel Flaw question stem examples. They are virtually identical to the previous Parallel Reasoning questions stems with the exception that they contain a term indicating that the reasoning in the stimulus is invalid:

"The flawed reasoning in which one of the following is most similar to the flawed reasoning in the argument above?"

"The questionable pattern of reasoning in the argument is most similar to that in which one of the following?"

The Peril of Abstraction

Parallel Reasoning questions force you to evaluate six different arguments.

Parallel Reasoning questions are challenging because they are the most abstract type of question on the LSAT. Not only must you understand the structure of the argument in the stimulus, you must also understand the structure of the arguments in each of the five answer choices. Juggling all this abstract information is difficult, and you will learn how to effectively approach Parallel Reasoning questions in the following pages.

We will address several effective ways to handle the abstract nature of these questions, but first you must understand what approach *not* to take. Some companies recommend that you make general abstract diagrams for the elements in each stimulus and do the same for each answer choice. This "general symbolization" approach involves representing the premises and conclusion as "A," "B," "C," etcetera, and writing them next to the stimulus. This approach, while well-meaning, is hopelessly flawed. Parallel Reasoning questions are difficult *because* they involve a great deal of abstraction. The use of non-specific symbols such as "A," "B," and "C" further abstracts the stimulus elements, increasing the difficulty instead of alleviating it.

Please note that the method described above is different from the symbolization described in the conditional reasoning and causal reasoning chapters of this book. In those chapters, we recommend diagramming in response to specific logical formations, and we strongly recommend using symbols that directly represent elements in the stimulus. That approach, when properly used, makes the questions easier to attack.

Solving Parallel Reasoning Questions

Because you must find the answer with a similar pattern of reasoning to that in the stimulus, using the details of the stimulus to attack the answer choices works differently in Parallel Reasoning question than in other First Family questions. For example, The Fact Test plays a minimal role in Parallel questions because the details (topic, etc.) of the stimulus and each answer choice are different. Instead, the structural basis of these questions forces you to compare the big-picture elements of the argument: intent of the conclusion, force and use of the premises, the relationship of the premises and the conclusion, and the soundness of the argument. Comparing these elements is like using an Abstract Fact Test—you must examine the general features of the argument in the answer choice and match them to the argument in the stimulus.

Parallel Reasoning questions are a continuation of Method of Reasoning questions: first you must identify the reasoning in the argument, and then you must find the answer with the same reasoning.

First, let us examine the elements of an argument that do *not* need to be paralleled in these questions:

1. Topic of the stimulus

    In Parallel Reasoning questions, the topic or subject matter in the stimulus and the answer choices is irrelevant because you are looking for the argument that has a similar pattern of *reasoning*. Often, same-subject answer choices are used to attract the student who fails to focus on the reasoning in the stimulus. For example, if the topic of the stimulus is banking, you need not have an answer choice that is also about banking.

2. The order of presentation of the premises and conclusion in the stimulus

    The order of presentation of the premises and conclusion in the stimulus is also irrelevant. As long as an answer choice contains the same general parts as the stimulus, they need not be in the same order because the order of presentation does not affect the logical relationship that underlies the pieces. So, for example, if the stimulus has an order of conclusion-premise-premise, you need not have the same order in the correct answer.

Neither of the elements above has any bearing on the correctness of an answer choice. Now, let's look at the elements that must be paralleled, and how to use these elements to eliminate wrong answer choices:

Answer choices with the same subject matter as the stimulus are almost always incorrect, and are generally used to lure students who fail to consider the reasoning in the stimulus. You should still consider answer choices with the same topic as the stimulus, but be wary.

1. The Method of Reasoning

It may sound obvious, but the type of reasoning used in the stimulus must be paralleled. When you see an identifiable form of reasoning present—for example, causal reasoning or conditional reasoning—you can proceed quickly and look for the answer that matches the form of the stimulus. Given the numerous forms of reasoning we have examined (both valid and invalid), you now have a powerful arsenal of knowledge that you can use to attack these questions. First and foremost, if you recognize the form of reasoning used in the stimulus, immediately attack the answers and search for the answer with similar reasoning.

2. The Validity of the Argument

The validity of the reasoning in the correct answer choice must match the validity of the reasoning in the stimulus.

Often, answer choices can be eliminated because they contain reasoning that has a different logical force than the stimulus. If the stimulus contains valid reasoning, eliminate any answer choice that contains invalid reasoning. If the stimulus contains invalid reasoning, eliminate any answer choice that contains valid reasoning.

3. The Conclusion

Every Parallel Reasoning stimulus contains an argument and therefore a conclusion. Because your job is to parallel the argument, you must parallel the subcomponents, including the premises and conclusion. You can use this knowledge to attack specific answer choices: if an answer has a conclusion that does not "match" the conclusion in the stimulus, then the answer is incorrect. Using this approach is especially helpful if you do not see an identifiable form of reasoning in the stimulus.

When matching conclusions, you must match the *certainty level* or *intent* of the conclusion in the stimulus, not necessarily the specific wording of the conclusion. For example, a stimulus conclusion containing absolutes ("must," "never," "always") will be matched by a conclusion in the correct answer choice using similar absolutes; a stimulus conclusion that gives an opinion ("should") will be matched by the same idea in the correct answer choice; a conditional conclusion in the stimulus will be matched by a conditional conclusion in the correct answer choice, and so on. This knowledge allows you to quickly narrow down the answer choices to the most likely candidates. This advice can initially be confusing, so let us discuss it in more detail.

Because Parallel Reasoning questions contain six different arguments, they are often lengthy. In fact, the longest LSAT Logical Reasoning question was a Parallel Reasoning question.

First, answers that have identical wording to the conclusion are Contenders (assuming there is no other reason to knock them out of contention). Identical wording for our purposes means answers where the controlling modifiers (such as "must," "could," "many," "some," "never," etcetera) are the same. For example, if the conclusion of the argument stated, "The reactor can supply the city power grid," an answer that had similar wording, such as "The bank can meet the needs of customers," would be a Contender. In brief, the advice in this paragraph is fairly simple: if the conclusion in the answer choice has similar wording to the conclusion in the stimulus, then the answer is *possibly* correct.

Second, because there are many synonyms available for the test makers to use, do not eliminate answers just because the wording is not identical. For example, an answer could state, "The majority of voters endorsed the amendment." The quantity indicator in the sentence— "majority"—has several synonyms, such as "most" and "more than half." Make sure that when you examine each sentence that you do not eliminate an answer that has wording that is functionally identical to the wording in the stimulus.

Third, remember that the English language has many pairs of natural opposites, so the presence of a negative term in the stimulus is *not* grounds for dismissing the answer when the stimulus has positive language (and vice versa). For example, a conclusion could state, "The councilmember must be present at the meeting." That conclusion could just as easily have been worded as, "The councilmember must not be absent from the meeting." In the same way, an answer choice can use opposite language (including negatives) but still have a meaning that is similar to the stimulus.

If the stimulus has a positive conclusion, then the presence of negative terms in the conclusion is not grounds for eliminating the answer; if the stimulus has a negative conclusion, then the lack of a negative term in the conclusion is not grounds for eliminating the answer.

4. The Premises

Like the conclusion, the premises in the correct answer choice must match the premises in the stimulus, and the same wording rules that were discussed in *The Conclusion* section apply to the premises.

Matching premises is a step to take after you have checked the conclusion, unless you notice that one (or more) of the premises has an unusual role in the argument. If so, you can immediately look at the answer choices and compare premises.

Because Parallel Reasoning questions are so long and time-consuming, they often appear toward the end of a section. This placement is the result of an old psychometric trick: just when a test taker is feeling pressured to work faster and finish the section, the test makers slip in a time-consuming question that slows students down and causes frustration.

Be wary of
Parallel Flaw
question stems
that ask you to
identify *both* the
logical flaws in
the stimulus.
When this occurs,
there is always an
incorrect answer
that contains
only one of the
flaws.

Because the four components above must be paralleled in the correct answer choice, the test makers have an array of options for making an answer *incorrect*. They can create answer choices that match several of the elements but not all of the elements, and to work through each answer choice in traditional fashion can be a painstaking process. However, since each element must be matched, you can analyze and attack the answer choices by testing whether the answer choice under consideration matches certain elements in the stimulus. If not, the answer is incorrect.

Upon hearing this advice, most students say, "Sounds good. In what order should I examine at the elements?" Although the process can be reduced to a step-by-step procedure, a better approach is to realize that examining the elements is like a waterfall and that everything will happen very quickly. Performing well on the LSAT is about flexibility and correctly responding to the clues provided. Rigidly applying the methods below will rob you of the opportunity to accelerate through the problem. Therefore, in Parallel Reasoning questions your job is to identify the features of the argument most likely to be "points of separation"—those features that can be used to divide answers into Losers and Contenders. Sometimes matching the conclusion will knock out several answer choices, other times matching the premises will achieve that same goal. The following list outlines the four tests you can use to evaluate answers, in rough order of their usefulness:

This section of
four tests for
Parallel Reasoning
questions
describes the
unique and
original Elemental
Attack™ used in
all of the
PowerScore LSAT
Courses.

1. Match the Method of Reasoning

   If you identify an obvious form of reasoning (use of analogy, circular reasoning, conditional reasoning, etc.), move quickly to the answer choices and look for the answer with an identical form of reasoning.

2. Match the Conclusion

   If you cannot identify the form of reasoning, or if you still have two or more answer choices in contention after matching the reasoning, or if the conclusion seems to have unusual language, examine the conclusion of each answer choice and match it against the conclusion in the stimulus. Matching the conclusion can be a critical time-saver because it often eliminates one or more answers. On occasion, all five conclusions in the answer choices will be identical to that in the stimulus. That is not a problem—it just means that the other elements must be used to knock out the wrong answers.

   The key to successfully matching the conclusion is that you must be able to quickly pick out the conclusion in each answer choice. This is where the conclusion identification skills discussed in Chapter Two come into play.

3. Match the Premises

If matching the method of reasoning and conclusion does not eliminate the four wrong answer choices, try matching the premises. The more complex the argument structure in the stimulus, the more likely you will have to match the premises to arrive at the correct answer. The less complex the argument, the more likely that matching the conclusion will be effective.

4. Match the Validity of the Argument

Always make sure to eliminate any answer choice that does not match the logical force (valid or invalid) of the argument. This test rarely eliminates all four answers, but it can often eliminate one or two answer choices.

Now practice applying these elements. Please take a moment to complete the following problem:

1. If the law punishes littering, then the city has an obligation to provide trash cans. But the law does not punish littering, so the city has no such obligation.

Which one of the following exhibits a flawed pattern of reasoning most similar to that in the argument above?

(A) If today is a holiday, then the bakery will not be open. The bakery is not open for business. Thus today is a holiday.

(B) Jenny will have lots of balloons at her birthday party. There are no balloons around yet, so today is not her birthday.

(C) The new regulations will be successful only if most of the students adhere to them. Since most of the students will adhere to those regulations, the new regulations will be successful.

(D) In the event that my flight had been late, I would have missed the committee meeting. Fortunately, my flight is on time. Therefore, I will make it to the meeting.

(E) When the law is enforced, some people are jailed. But no one is in jail. So clearly the law is not enforced.

Decision time:
suppose you
complete answer
choice (A) and you
are virtually
certain that you
have the correct
answer. Should
you read the
remaining answer
choices, or should
you skip to the
next problem? The
answer, in part,
depends on the
time remaining in
the section. If it
is late in the
section (say,
question #17 or
later), most
students are
pressed for time
and it would not
be unreasonable
to make a
calculated choice
to move on
without reviewing
answer choices
(B) through (E).
Before doing so,
you would be well-
advised to make
sure that you are
certain about the
reasoning in the
stimulus.

On the other
hand, if this
question were to
appear early in
the section, it
would be
worthwhile to
quickly check the
remaining answer
choices because
early in the
section one of
your goals is to
accumulate as
many correct
answers as
possible.

As you read the stimulus, you should recognize the conditional reasoning that pervades this argument. Remember, words such as "if" and "then" are conditional indicators, and you should pick them up on your LSAT radar and begin diagramming. In this argument, the first sentence contains a premise, and the second sentence contains a premise and the conclusion. The sentences are diagrammed as follows:

LPL = law punishes littering
OTC = city has an obligation to provide trash cans

First sentence: $LPL \longrightarrow OTC$

Second sentence: $\cancel{LPL} \longrightarrow \cancel{OTC}$

The argument is based on a Mistaken Negation. This is an easy form of argumentation to identify, and you should feel comfortable attempting to parallel this structure. Therefore, once you recognize a Mistaken Negation and read the question stem, immediately search for the answer that also contains a Mistaken Negation.

Answer choice (A): This answer choice contains a Mistaken Reversal.

Answer choice (B): This answer choice contains a contrapositive.

Answer choice (C): This answer choice contains a Mistaken Reversal.

Answer choice (D): This is the correct answer, and the relationship in the answer can be diagrammed as follows:

FL = flight late
MM = missed the committee meeting

First sentence: $FL \longrightarrow MM$

Second sentence: $\cancel{FL} \longrightarrow \cancel{MM}$

Please note that "my flight is on time" is equivalent to "flight is not late."

Answer choice (E): This answer choice contains a contrapositive.

This problem shows that if you can identify the reasoning structure in the argument, that gives you the best opportunity for moving quickly through the answer choices. If you quickly find the correct answer, you need not worry about checking conclusions, premises, etc. But sometimes you feel as if you understand the reasoning very well, but not perfectly. In those cases, supplement your attack with the other tests mentioned earlier in this chapter.

Please take a moment to complete the following problem:

2. People who are good at playing the game Drackedary are invariably skilled with their hands. Mary is a very competent watchmaker. Therefore, Mary would make a good Drackedary player.

    The flawed pattern of reasoning in the argument above is most similar to that in which one of the following?

    (A) People with long legs make good runners. Everyone in Daryl's family has long legs. Therefore, Daryl would make a good runner.
    (B) People who write for a living invariably enjoy reading. Julie has been a published novelist for many years. Therefore, Julie enjoys reading.
    (C) All race car drivers have good reflexes. Chris is a champion table tennis player. Therefore, Chris would make a good race car driver.
    (D) The role of Santa Claus in a shopping mall is often played by an experienced actor. Erwin has played Santa Claus in shopping malls for years. Therefore, Erwin must be an experienced actor.
    (E) Any good skier can learn to ice-skate eventually. Erica is a world-class skier. Therefore, Erica could learn to ice-skate in a day or two.

This problem also contains conditional reasoning ("people who" is a sufficient condition indicator), but the reasoning structure is not as clean as in the previous problem. In this argument the first and second sentences contain premises and the third sentence is the conclusion. We can diagram the argument as follows:

D = good at playing the game Drackedary
SH = skilled with their hands
M = Mary

Premise: $D \longrightarrow SH$

Premise: Mary is a competent watchmaker.

Conclusion: D_M

The argument makes the assumption that being a competent watchmaker is equivalent to being skilled with your hands, and then makes a Mistaken Reversal using that assumption.

The more complex the argument structure, the more important is to match the premises. The more simple the argument, the more important it is to match the conclusion.

Although this is an understandable form of reasoning, you may have difficulty quickly applying that form to five answer choices. Given that finding a duplicate of the reasoning may be time-consuming, how can you speed up the process? Consider the conclusion for a moment—the controlling element is that Mary "would make" a good player. That is a fairly specific statement, and one that must be reasonably matched in the correct answer choice. Thus, let's see if we can eliminate a few answer choices by attempting to match the conclusion. The process is made especially easy because the conclusion appears in the last sentence of each answer choice, conveniently prefaced by the word "therefore."

Answer choices (A) and (C) have conclusion components—"would make"—that are identical to the stimulus, so they both remain as Contenders.

Answer choice (B) contains a conclusion with no wording similar to "would make," so we eliminate this answer for now. We can always reconsider the answer if none of the others pan out.

Answer choice (D) contains an element—"must"—that is significantly different from "would make," so we also eliminate this answer.

Answer choice (E) can be eliminated since the operating element in the conclusion—"could—is not the same as "would make."

Thus, by comparing conclusions, three answers have been eliminated in nearly effortless fashion. Now focus on answer choices (A) and (C) and use the form of reasoning we identified in the stimulus to determine which answer is correct.

Answer choice (A): This answer contains valid reasoning, and since we are looking for an answer with flawed reasoning, the difference is sufficient to eliminate this answer.

Note that the term "family" in this answer is interpreted to include Daryl. If everyone in Daryl's family has long legs, then Daryl must also since he is in the family.

Answer choice (C): Because the other four answer choices have been eliminated, we can deduce that this is the correct answer. A glance at the structure of the argument confirms this:

RCD = race car drivers
GR = have good reflexes
C = Chris

Premise: $RCD \longrightarrow GR$

Premise: Chris is a champion table tennis player.

Conclusion: RCD_C

This argument equates two different terms (champion table tennis play = great reflexes) and then makes a Mistaken Reversal, and this is parallel to the argument in the stimulus.

The lesson to be learned from this problem is that different methods can be used to eliminate different answers, and the process should be fluid and based on the signals you derive from the stimulus. This question required a combination of checking the reasoning, the conclusion, and the validity of the argument. Other problems will require different combinations. Remember that you have four basic tests at your disposal, and be prepared to use them when you encounter a Parallel Reasoning problem.

Also, in case you were wondering, Drackedary is an imaginary game dreamed up by the jokers at Law Services.

Let's continue the discussion of the basic approach used to solve Parallel Reasoning questions. Please take a moment to complete the following problem:

3. No one in the French department to which Professor Alban belongs is allowed to teach more than one introductory level class in any one term. Moreover, the only language classes being taught next term are advanced ones. So it is untrue that both of the French classes Professor Alban will be teaching next term will be introductory level classes.

The pattern of reasoning displayed in the argument above is most closely paralleled by that in which one of the following arguments?

(A) The Morrison Building will be fully occupied by May and since if a building is occupied by May the new tax rates apply to it, the Morrison Building will be taxed according to the new rates.

(B) The revised tax code does not apply at all to buildings built before 1900, and only the first section of the revised code applies to buildings built between 1900 and 1920, so the revised code does not apply to the Norton Building, since it was built in 1873.

(C) All property on Overton Road will be reassessed for tax purposes by the end of the year and the Elnor Company headquarters is on Overton Road, so Elnor's property taxes will be higher next year.

(D) New buildings that include public space are exempt from city taxes for two years and all new buildings in the city's Alton district are exempt for five years, so the building with the large public space that was recently completed in Alton will not be subject to city taxes next year.

(E) Since according to recent statute, a building that is exempt from property taxes is charged for city water at a special rate, and hospitals are exempt from property taxes, Founder's Hospital will be charged for city water at the special rate.

The structure of the stimulus is as follows:

Premise: No one in the French department to which Professor Alban belongs is allowed to teach more than one introductory level class in any one term.

Premise: Moreover, the only language classes being taught next term are advanced ones.

Conclusion: So it is untrue that both of the French classes Professor Alban will be teaching next term will be introductory level classes.

First note that the reasoning is valid. If you are uncertain, check the question stem. Since no mention is made of flawed reasoning, you know that the reasoning is sound.

Most people find that there is no clearly identifiable (or easily described) form of reasoning used to draw the conclusion, and each of the answer choices except (B) contains a conclusion with similar language to the conclusion in the stimulus. Thus, you must look elsewhere for the factor that separates the answer choices. Take a moment to consider each premise and how it relates to the conclusion; the argument is unusual in that both premises independently prove the conclusion, and this structure must be paralleled in the correct answer.

Now examine each premise:

Premise: No one in the French department to which Professor Alban belongs is allowed to teach more than one introductory level class in any one term.

The premise contains two pieces of information: no one in the French department is allowed to teach more than one introductory level class and Professor Alban belongs to the French department. Combining those two pieces yields the conclusion that Professor Alban can teach at most one introductory level class in a term. This fact is reflected in the language of the conclusion.

Premise: Moreover, the only language classes being taught next term are advanced ones.

If only advanced language classes are being taught next term, then no person could teach an introductory level French class next term. That truth is encompassed in the conclusion when the author states that "it is untrue that both of the French classes Professor Alban will be teaching next term will be introductory level classes."

Turning to the answers, you should look for the answer that has two independent premises that both prove the conclusion. Because there are two premises, this "premise test" will take longer to apply and this is one reason we typically look at the conclusion in a Parallel Reasoning question before examining the premises.

Answer choice (A): This answer contains a conditional Repeat form, and as such, the two premises work together. Since the structure of the answer is different from that of the stimulus, the answer choice is incorrect.

Answer choice (B): Only the first premise in this answer choice proves the conclusion; the second premise is irrelevant to the conclusion. Therefore, this answer is incorrect.

As mentioned before, this answer choice is also suspect because the conclusion is different from that in the stimulus.

Answer choice (C): There are two excellent reasons to eliminate this answer choice:

1. The answer choice contains invalid reasoning.

2. The two premises work together and are not independent as in the stimulus.

Answer choice (D): This is the correct answer. As with the argument in the stimulus, each premise in this answer choice separately supports the conclusion.

Note that as mentioned previously, the negative term in the conclusion of the answer choice is not a factor that should be considered. For the purposes of matching the conclusion, "will be" and "will not be" are identical.

Answer choice (E): This answer is very similar to answer choice (A), and contains a valid form of reasoning based on the Repeat form. Since the two premises work together and neither proves the conclusion alone, this answer choice is incorrect.

This problem is more difficult than the previous two problems because you must go deeper in your analysis of the argument structure to find the point of separation. If you see that the reasoning is not easy to identify, and the conclusions in most of the answer choices are similar to the conclusion in the stimulus, carefully examine the premises as they are likely to be the part of the argument that will allow you to find the correct answer.

What To Do If All Else Fails

If none of the four tests of analysis reveals the answer, or if nothing stands out to you when you examine the argument, you can always fall back on describing the stimulus in abstract terms. Although less precise than the previous tests, abstracting the stimulus allows for one last shot at the problem.

To abstract the structure of the stimulus, create a short statement that summarizes the "action" in the argument without referring to the details of the argument. For example, if the argument states, "The bank teller had spotted a thief once before, so she was certain she could do it again," turn that argument into an abstract description such as "she had done it once, so she knew it could be done again." Then, take the abstraction and compare it to each argument. Does it match your generalized version of the stimulus? If not, the answer is incorrect. Your description should be a reasonable approximation of what occurred in the stimulus, but it does not have to be perfect.

In creating the abstraction above, the "it" in the short summary is purposely left indefinite so that when you attack the answer choices, you can plug in the "action" to the abstraction and see if it fits. Let's continue the discussion of the basic method we can use to solve Parallel Reasoning problems. Please take a moment to complete the following problem:

Here is another example of creating an abstract statement: if the argument states, "I nearly won the marathon several times so I have a good idea of how it feels to win the race," turn that argument into an abstract description such as "I was close, so I know what it is really like."

4. An independent audit found no indication of tax avoidance on the part of the firm in the firm's accounts; therefore, no such problem exists.

   The questionable reasoning in the argument above is most closely paralleled by that in which one of the following?

   (A) The plan for the introduction of the new product has been unmodified so far; therefore, it will not be modified in the future.
   (B) The overall budget for the projects has been exceeded by a large amount; therefore, at least one of the projects has exceeded its budget by a large amount.
   (C) A compilation of the best student essays of the year includes no essays on current events; therefore, students have become apathetic toward current events.
   (D) A survey of schools in the district found no school without a need for building repair; therefore, the education provided to students in the district is substandard.
   (E) An examination of the index of the book found no listing for the most prominent critic of the theory the book advocates; therefore, the book fails to refer to that critic.

The question above was selected to help you better understand how to create an abstraction of the argument and apply it to the answer choices. Approach the question from the following perspective:

> Imagine for a moment that when you first read the stimulus you were completely lost. Nothing in the argument stood out, and although you recognized the premise and conclusion, you did not feel that either was notable.

First, take the "action" of the stimulus and turn it into a generalized summary. Following is the stimulus and then an abstraction of that stimulus:

Stimulus: "An independent audit found no indication of tax avoidance on the part of the firm in the firm's accounts; therefore, no such problem exists."

Abstraction: "Since they looked and didn't find anything, it doesn't exist."

Remember, our abstraction does not have to be perfect—it simply needs to be a reasonable description of what occurred in the stimulus. If we can only eliminate three of the answer choices by applying the abstraction, then we can refine our description until one of the remaining answers is eliminated.

Answer choice (A): Does this answer match our short description of the stimulus? No, this answer is about "no changes from the past translate into no changes in the future." There is no element of "searching and not finding."

Answer choice (B): Again, quickly, does this answer match our short description of the stimulus? No, this answer is about cost overruns on projects.

Answer choice (C): This answer is superior to answers (A) and (B). The first lines indicate that essays on current events are missing from a compilation of the best essays. This knowledge implies a search has taken place and no essay fitting the description was found. So far, so good. The conclusion, however, fails to match what we are seeking. Based on the premise in this answer choice, we need a conclusion that states something to the effect of, "therefore no such student essay on current events exists." Instead, we get an entirely different type of conclusion: "therefore, students have become apathetic toward current events." Since this conclusion fails to match our abstract description of the stimulus, this answer is incorrect.

Answer choice (D): This answer has an element that is similar to the stimulus, but in the final analysis it fails to match our abstract description. First, just like the stimulus, the answer contains a search (the "survey"). However, the search in the stimulus did not turn up anything whereas the search in answer choice (D) turns up results ("no school without a need" is the same as "every school has a need"). Most damning, however, is that the conclusion of the answer choice does not have the same abstract form as the conclusion in the stimulus. Since the general intent and execution of this answer does not match our abstraction, this answer is incorrect.

Answer choice (E): This is the correct answer choice. First, let's revisit our general description of the stimulus:

"Since they looked and didn't find anything, it doesn't exist."

Now, compare that to the answer choice:

"An examination of the index of the book found no listing for the most prominent critic of the theory the book advocates; therefore, the book fails to refer to that critic."

A search was conducted but no results were found, and on that basis a conclusion is drawn that no such thing exists. This perfectly matches our description, and this answer is correct.

Creating an abstract description of the stimulus is just one more weapon in your arsenal. As with the previous four tests in this section, you should use it when you feel it is most applicable. Thinking on your feet is important when attacking any LSAT question, but no more so than with Parallel Reasoning questions. You have a variety of techniques at your disposal; you just need to logically think through each stimulus to decide which ones are most applicable.

Parallel Reasoning Question Review

Parallel Reasoning questions ask you to identify the answer choice that contains reasoning most similar in structure to the reasoning in the stimulus.

Parallel Flaw questions are Parallel Reasoning questions where the stimulus contains flawed reasoning.

The question stem for any Parallel question reveals whether the stimulus contains valid or invalid reasoning. If the question stem mentions a flaw, then the reasoning is invalid. If the question stem does not mention a flaw, then the reasoning is valid.

The following elements do *not* need to be paralleled:

1. Topic of the stimulus

2. The order of presentation of the premises and conclusion in the stimulus

Instead, you must parallel *all* of these elements:

1. The Method of Reasoning

2. The Validity of the Argument

3. The Conclusion

4. The Premises

Because each element must be matched, you can analyze and attack the answer choices by testing whether the answer choice under consideration matches certain elements in the stimulus. If not, the answer is incorrect. The following list outlines the four tests you can use to evaluate answers, in rough order of how useful they are:

1. Match the Method of Reasoning

2. Match the Conclusion

3. Match the Premises

4. Match the Validity of the Argument

If all else fails, create a short statement that summarizes the "action" in the argument. Then, take the abstraction and compare it to each argument. Does it match your generalized version of the stimulus? If not, the answer is incorrect.

Parallel Reasoning Question Problem Set

The following questions are drawn from actual LSATs. Please complete the problem set and review the answer key and explanations. *Answers on Page 421*

1. The student body at this university takes courses in a wide range of disciplines. Miriam is a student at this university, so she takes courses in a wide range of disciplines.

    Which one of the following arguments exhibits flawed reasoning most similar to that exhibited by the argument above?

    (A) The students at this school take mathematics. Miguel is a student at this school, so he takes mathematics.
    (B) The editorial board of this law journal has written on many legal issues. Louise is on the editorial board, so she has written on many legal issues.
    (C) The component parts of bulldozers are heavy. This machine is a bulldozer, so it is heavy.
    (D) All older automobiles need frequent oil changes. This car is new, so its oil need not be changed as frequently.
    (E) The individual cells of the brain are incapable of thinking. Therefore, the brain as a whole is incapable of thinking.

2. Commentator: Because of teacher hiring freezes, the quality of education in that country will not improve. Thus, it will surely deteriorate.

    The flawed reasoning in which one of the following is most similar to that in the commentator's argument?

    (A) Because Raoul is a vegetarian, he will not have the pepperoni pizza for lunch. It follows that he will have the cheese pizza.
    (B) Given that over 250 years of attempts to prove the Goldbach conjecture have failed, it will probably never be proved. Hence, it is more likely to be disproved than proved.
    (C) Since funding levels for social programs are being frozen, our society will not become more harmonious. Thus, it may become more discordant.
    (D) Since there is a storm moving in, the outside temperature cannot rise this afternoon. Therefore, it must fall.
    (E) The starter in Mary's car gave out weeks ago, and so it is impossible for the car to start. Therefore, it will not start.

3. Most people who shop for groceries no more than three times a month buy prepared frozen dinners regularly. In Hallstown most people shop for groceries no more than three times a month. Therefore, in Hallstown most people buy prepared frozen dinners regularly.

Which one of the following arguments has a flawed pattern of reasoning most like the flawed reasoning in the argument above?

(A) It is clear that most drivers in West Ansland are safe drivers since there are very few driving accidents in West Ansland and most accidents there are not serious.

(B) It is clear that John cannot drive, since he does not own a car and no one in his family who does not own a car can drive.

(C) It is clear that Fernando's friends usually drive to school, since all of his friends can drive and all of his friends go to school.

(D) It is clear that most people in Highland County drive sedans, since most people who commute to work drive sedans and most people in Highland County commute to work.

(E) It is clear that most of Janine's friends are good drivers, since she accepts rides only from good drivers and she accepts rides from most of her friends.

4. Bank deposits are credited on the date of the transaction only when they are made before 3 P.M. Alicia knows that the bank deposit was made before 3 P.M. So, Alicia knows that the bank deposit was credited on the date of the transaction.

Which one of the following exhibits both of the logical flaws exhibited by the argument above?

(A) Journalists are the only ones who will be permitted to ask questions at the press conference. Since Marjorie is a journalist, she will be permitted to ask questions.

(B) We know that Patrice works only on Thursday. Today is Thursday, so it follows that Patrice is working today.

(C) It is clear that George knows he will be promoted to shift supervisor, because George will be promoted to shift supervisor only if Helen resigns, and George knows Helen will resign.

(D) John believes that 4 is a prime number and that 4 is divisible by 2. Hence John believes that there is a prime number divisible by 2.

(E) Pat wants to become a social worker. It is well known that social workers are poorly paid. Pat apparently wants to be poorly paid.

Parallel Reasoning Question Problem Set Answer Key

All answer keys in this book indicate the source of the question by giving the month and year the LSAT was originally administered, the Logical Reasoning section number, and the question number within that section. Each LSAT has two Logical Reasoning sections, and so the Section 1 and Section 2 designators will refer to the first or second Logical Reasoning section in the test, not the physical section number of the booklet.

Question #1. Parallel Flaw. December 1999 LSAT, Section 1, #6. The correct answer choice is (B)

The stimulus in this problem exhibits an error of division, where the attributes of the whole are taken to apply to each part of the whole. In this case, the whole is the university student body, and the part is Miriam. You must find an answer that contains a similar whole-to-part error of division.

As you attack the answers, it becomes apparent that answer choices (A) and (B) are Contenders and answer choices (C), (D), and (E) are Losers. We will first analyze (C), (D), and (E):

Answer choice (C): Unlike the stimulus, this answer choice contains valid reasoning and is therefore incorrect. If that fact escaped you during your analysis, this answer choice also reverses the relationship, moving from part to whole (the stimulus moves from whole to part).

Answer choice (D): This answer contains a Mistaken Negation, not an error of division.

Answer choice (E): This answer choice contains an error of composition, where the attributes of the parts are mistaken for the attributes of the whole. This part-to-whole error is the reverse of the error in the stimulus.

Most students mark answer choice (A) as a definite possibility. Answer choice (B) also looks attractive, so look more closely at both in order to decide between them.

Answer choice (A): There are several points that differentiate the argument in this answer from the argument in the stimulus. First, the reasoning in this answer choice is valid, and that alone makes the answer incorrect. However, most students do not realize that the argument is valid; they are too caught up in analyzing the part-to-whole mechanics in the answer. Second, this answer has the same subject as the stimulus, always a red flag. Third, although it is similar in some ways to the argument in the stimulus, this answer choice focuses on a group where each member performs a single activity: the students take mathematics. If the students take mathematics and Miguel is a student, then he too would take mathematics. In the stimulus, the focus is on a group that *collectively* performs many activities—the students at the university "take courses in a wide range of disciplines." Obviously, as a student at the school, Miriam does not have to take courses in different fields and she could stick to a narrow range of disciplines.

Answer choice (B): This is the correct answer. Like the stimulus, the focus is on a group that *collectively* performs many activities: the editorial board of the law journal has "written on many legal issues." As a member of the editorial board, Louise need not write on many legal issues. Since the error is identical to that in the stimulus, this answer is correct.

Parallel Reasoning Question Problem Set Answer Key

Question #2. Parallel Flaw-CE. December 2002 LSAT, Section 2, #26. The correct answer choice is (D)

The commentator's argument is short and simple:

Premise:	[There are] teacher hiring freezes.
Subconclusion/ Premise:	The quality of education in that country will not improve.
Conclusion:	Thus, it will surely deteriorate.

The argument has several notable elements:

The error in the argument occurs in the leap from subconclusion to conclusion: just because the quality of education will not improve does not necessarily mean it will deteriorate (it could stay the same). This mistake occurs because the author believes in the False Dilemma of two possible outcomes (that quality of education must either rise or fall) when there are actually three possible outcomes.

The argument also features a causal relationship in the first sentence: teacher hiring freezes are the cause of a lack of improvement in the quality of education.

The conclusion features strong and definite language—"will surely." An answer choice that deviates from this level of certainty will be incorrect.

With three distinct elements to worth with, this problem should be easy to solve. The challenge is in deciding which element to attack first. Try to match the conclusion first because it will be the easiest (and therefore fastest) element to identify in each answer choice:

Answer choice (B) and (C) can be eliminated because they contain conclusions—"more likely" and "may," respectively—that are different than "will." Answer choice (A) has the same conclusion and remains a Contender. Be careful with answer choice (D) because the conclusion—"must"—is similar in certainty to "will surely." The conclusion of answer choice (E), "will not," remains in contention because the negative has no effect.

With only three remaining answer choices, let's next match the False Dilemma that underlies the conclusion:

Answer choice (A) seemingly relies on a similar assumption to that in the stimulus (that if one outcome does not occur then it must be the opposite outcome), but answer choice (A) is different from the stimulus because there are many different options for pizza, not just three.

Answer choice (D) is the correct answer. Each element is matched, and a False Dilemma is used that assumes that temperatures cannot stay the same.

Answer choice (E) is incorrect because the conclusion is identical to the premise: "impossible for the car to start" is the same as "it will not start."

Question #3. Parallel Flaw. October 2000 LSAT, Section 1, #22. The correct answer choice is (D)

The structure of the argument is very distinct: the two premises and conclusion each contain the quantity indicator "most." That structure must be paralleled in the correct answer choice, and you would be wise to immediately check the answers upon recognizing the triple "most" formation. Let us do so now:

Answer choice (A): The second line of the answer choice contains the phrase "very few." Since this is different from "most," this answer is incorrect.

Answer choice (B): The answer choice contains the phrases "cannot" and "no one," both of which are different than "most."

Answer choice (C): The phrase "usually" is a synonym for "most," but the two "all" statements are different enough to make this answer choice suspect.

Answer choice (D): This is the correct answer, and the only one with three "mosts."

Answer choice (E): The second line contains a conditional premise (introduced by "only"). Since the argument does not contain a similar premise, this answer is incorrect.

Amazingly, the application of this basic structural element solves the problem very quickly. The question itself represents a perfect example of how you should attack Parallel Reasoning questions: search for the most distinctive element, then use that element to eliminate as many answer choices as possible. You will not always be lucky enough to eliminate all four incorrect answer choices at once, but any answer you eliminate puts you one step closer to your goal.

For the record, the argument makes an error of division in assuming that a general proposition about "most people" will apply to any subset of that group. In this case, "most people who shop for groceries" could be about the entire United States, and within this group there could be town and cities such as Hallstown that do not conform to the general truth that applies to the whole.

Question #4. Parallel Flaw-SN. June 2001 LSAT, Section 1, #21. The correct answer choice is (C)

This tricky problem is a good example of why you can never simply glance at a question stem and assume that you know what it says. The stem in this problem specifically indicates that the correct answer must parallel *both* the logical flaws in the stimulus. As you might expect, before you reach the correct answer the makers of the test have placed answers that display only one of the flaws.

The most obvious error in the stimulus is a Mistaken Reversal (remember, "only when" introduces a necessary condition):

> CD = bank deposits credited on the day of the transaction
> 3 = deposit made before 3 P.M. on that day
> A = Alicia knows

> First premise: $\quad\quad\quad\quad\quad\quad\quad$ CD $\longrightarrow$ 3

> Second premise and conclusion: $\quad$ 3_A $\longrightarrow$ CD_A

Although most students recognize the Mistaken Reversal, they make the error of quickly glancing at the question stem, and when they see the word "exhibits" they move to the answers without realizing there is a second flaw. Although this action is not problematic because the correct answer will contain a Mistaken Reversal, the danger is that a student will select the first Mistaken Reversal that appears without examining the second flaw, and indeed, about half of the test takers erroneously choose answer choice (A) or (B), with answer choice (B) being the more popular of the two. A student considering each answer would recognize that answer choices (A), (B), and (C) contain Mistaken Reversals and thus there must be an additional differentiating factor.

We will dispense with answer choices (D) and (E) because they both contain the Repeat conditional form. In order to decide between answer choices (A), (B), and (C), we must re-examine the stimulus and discover the second error, or at least discover a factor that will allow us to choose one of the remaining three answers. Look carefully at the stimulus: did Alicia make the deposit herself or does she just *know* that the deposit was made and the transaction credited? As stated in the stimulus, she only "knows" the events occurred, not that they actually happened for certain. This is the second error, and a quick examination of the three remaining answers reveals that only answer choice (C) contains the same flaw of "knowing." Answer choice (C) is therefore correct.

Although the "double error" language appears infrequently in Parallel Reasoning questions, you can use the knowledge that such questions exist to implement a valuable safeguard strategy: if you find an attractive answer choice early on and you are contemplating skipping the remaining answer choices, before you exit the problem check to make sure the question stem does not contain a twist like the one in this problem. Doing so could save you from missing a question.

CHAPTER FIFTEEN: NUMBERS AND PERCENTAGES

Numbers and Percentages

Similar to Cause and Effect Reasoning, Conditional Reasoning, and Formal Logic, the concept of Numbers and Percentages is featured in many LSAT stimuli. Although most people are comfortable working with numbers or percentages because they come up so frequently in daily life (for example in balancing a checking account, dividing a bar tab, or adding up a grocery bill), the makers of the LSAT often prey upon several widely-held misconceptions:

> Misconception #1:   Increasing percentages automatically lead to increasing numbers.

Most people assume that if a percentage becomes larger, the number that corresponds to that percentage must also get larger. This is not necessarily true because the overall size of the group under discussion could get smaller. For example, consider the following argument: "Auto manufacturer X increased their United States market share from 10% last year to 25% this year. Therefore, Company X sold more cars in the United States this year than last." This is true if the size of the U.S. car market stayed the same or became larger. But if the size of the U.S. car market decreased by enough, the argument would not be true, as in the following example:

	Last Year	This Year
Total number of cars sold in the United States	1000	200
X's market share	10%	25%
X's total car sales in the United States	100	50

Thus, even though auto manufacturer X's market share increased to 25%, because the size of the entire market decreased significantly, X actually sold fewer cars in the United States.

When identifying problems that contain numbers or percentages as part of the reasoning, we use a "#%" notation, as in "Must-#%."

Of course, if the overall total remains constant, an increasing percentage does translate into a larger number. But on the LSAT the size of the total is usually not given.

If the percentage increases but the corresponding number decreases, then the overall total must have decreased.

If the percentage decreases but the corresponding number increases, then the overall total must have increased.

If the number increases but the corresponding percentage decreases, then the overall total must have increased.

In each of the first four misconceptions the makers of the test attempt to lure you into making an assumption about the size of the overall total.

If the number decreases but the corresponding percentage increases, then the overall total must have decreased.

Misconception #2:   Decreasing percentages automatically lead to decreasing numbers.

This misconception is the opposite of Misconception #1. Just because a percentage decreases does not necessarily mean that the corresponding number must become smaller. Reversing the years in the previous example proves this point.

Misconception #3:   Increasing numbers automatically lead to increasing percentages.

Just as increasing percentages do not automatically translate into increasing numbers, the reverse is also true. Consider the following example: "The number of bicycle-related accidents rose dramatically from last month to this month. Therefore, bicycle-related accidents must make up a greater percentage of all road accidents this month." This conclusion can be true, but it does not have to be true, as shown by the following example:

	Last Month	This Month
Number of bicycle-related accidents	10	30
Total number of road accidents	100	600
Percentage of total accidents that are bicycle-related	10%	5%

Thus, even though the number of bicycle-related accidents tripled, the percentage of total road accidents that were bicycle-related dropped because the *total number* of road accidents rose so dramatically.

Misconception #4:   Decreasing numbers automatically lead to decreasing percentages.

This misconception is the opposite of Misconception #3. Just because a number decreases does not necessarily mean that the corresponding percentage must become smaller. Reversing the months in the previous example proves this point.

Misconception #5:   Large numbers automatically mean large percentages, and small numbers automatically mean small percentages.

In 2003, Porsche sold just over 18,000 cars in the United States. While 18,000 is certainly a large number, it represented only about 1/5 of 1% of total U.S. car sales in 2003. Remember, the size of a number does not reveal anything about the percentage that number represents unless you know something about the size of the overall total that number is drawn from.

Misconception #6:   Large percentages automatically mean large numbers, and small percentages automatically mean small numbers.

This misconception is the reverse of Misconception #5. A figure such as 90% sounds impressively large, but if you have 90% of $5, that really isn't too impressive, is it?

Numerical situations normally hinge on three elements: an overall total, a number within that total, and a percentage within the total. LSAT problems will often give you one of the elements, but without at least two elements present, you cannot make a definitive judgment about what is occurring with another element. When you are given just percentage information, you cannot make a judgment about numbers. Likewise, when you are given just numerical information you cannot make a judgment about percentages.

In a moment, we will explore this idea by examining several LSAT questions. But first, you must be able to recognize number and percentage ideas when they appear on the LSAT:

Words used to introduce numerical ideas:

> Amount
> Quantity
> Sum
> Total
> Count
> Tally

Knowledge of a percentage is insufficient to allow you to make a determination about the size of the number because the exact size of the overall total is unknown, and changes in the overall total will directly affect the internal numbers and percentages.

Words used to introduce percentage ideas:

Percent
Proportion
Fraction
Ratio
Incidence
Likelihood
Probability
Segment
Share

Three words on the percentage list—"incidence," "likelihood," and "probability"—bear further discussion. Each of these words relates to the chances that an event will occur, and when the LSAT makers uses phrases such as "more likely" or "less likely" they are telling you that the percentage chances are greater than 50% or less than 50%, respectively. In fact, a wide variety of phrases can be used to introduce percentage ideas, including such disparate phrases as "more prone to" or "occurs with a high frequency."

With these indicators in mind, please take a moment to complete the following question:

1. From 1973 to 1989 total energy use in this country increased less than 10 percent. However, the use of electrical energy in this country during this same period grew by more than 50 percent, as did the gross national product—the total value of all goods and services produced in the nation.

    If the statements above are true, then which one of the following must also be true?

    (A) Most of the energy used in this country in 1989 was electrical energy.
    (B) From 1973 to 1989 there was a decline in the use of energy other than electrical energy in this country.
    (C) From 1973 to 1989 there was an increase in the proportion of energy use in this country that consisted of electrical energy use.
    (D) In 1989 electrical energy constituted a larger proportion of the energy used to produce the gross national product than did any other form of energy.
    (E) In 1973 the electrical energy that was produced constituted a smaller proportion of the gross national product than did all other forms of energy combined.

Like the vast majority of Must Be True problems, the stimulus does not contain a conclusion. We are given the following facts, however:

From 1973 to 1989 total energy use increased less than 10%.

During this same period, the use of electrical energy grew by more than 50%.

During this same period, the gross national product (GNP) grew by more than 50%.

A careful examination of the second sentence reveals that there is no stated connection between the growth of the GNP and the increase in the use of electrical energy. If you assume that the use of electrical energy somehow caused the growth of the GNP, you are guilty of making an unwarranted causal assumption. Because there is no stated connection between the two other than they both grew by more than 50%, any answer that attempts to connect the two is incorrect. Answer choices (D) and (E) can both be eliminated by this reasoning.

Now that we recognize that the GNP issue is only a red herring, let us examine the percentages that are given in the stimulus. The 50% increase in electrical energy gives the impression that the jump must have been substantial. But we know from Misconception #6 that a large percentage does not automatically mean a large number. For example, in this problem it is possible that the 50% increase in electrical energy use was a jump from 2 units to 3 units. The possibility that electrical energy use in 1973 was a relatively small percentage of overall energy use directly undermines answer choices (A), as shown by the following example:

	1973	1989
Total energy use (in units)	100	109
Electrical energy use (in units)	10	15
Percentage of total energy use that was electrical	10%	13+%

A close analysis of the chart also reveals that answer choice (B) can be eliminated. In the example, the use of energy other than electrical energy rose from 90 units to 94 units.

Although the example disproves both answer choice (A) and (B), obviously you do not have time to make a chart during the test to examine each possibility, so is there a faster way to eliminate the first two answers? Yes—consider the previous discussion point that information about percentages does not tell us about the numbers. With that idea in mind, because the stimulus contains only percentage information (even though there are two percentages), you should be very suspicious of answer choice (A) (which states that the number of electrical units used was greater) and answer choice (B) (which states that the use of non-electrical energy declined) since they both contain numerical information. At the same time, you should be attracted to an answer such as (C) because it contains only percentage information, and as it turns out, answer choice (C) is correct.

Because the misconceptions discussed earlier have a predictable effect when you try to make inferences, you can use the following general rules for Must Be True questions:

The rules to the right address the classic combination of a stimulus with numbers and percentages information and a Must Be True question.

1. If the stimulus contains percentage or proportion information only, avoid answers that contain hard numbers.

    Example Stimulus Sentence:

    The car market share of Company X declined this year.

    Avoid answers which say:

    Company X sold a smaller number of cars this year.

    Company X sold a greater amount of cars this year.

2. If the stimulus contains only numerical information, avoid answers that contain percentage or proportion information.

    Example Stimulus Sentence:

    Company Y sold fewer computers this year.

    Avoid answers which say:

    Company Y now has a lower share of the computer market.

    Company Y now possesses a greater proportion of the computer market.

3. If the stimulus contains both percentage and numerical information, any answer choice that contains numbers, percentages, or both *may* be true.

Please keep in mind that these rules are very general. You must read the stimulus closely and carefully to determine exactly what information is present because the makers of the LSAT are experts at camouflaging or obscuring important information in order to test your ability to understand complex argumentation.

Please take a moment to complete the following question:

2. The number of North American children who are obese—that is, who have more body fat than do 85 percent of North American children their age—is steadily increasing, according to four major studies conducted over the past 15 years.

    If the finding reported above is correct, it can be properly concluded that

    (A) when four major studies all produce similar results, those studies must be accurate
    (B) North American children have been progressively less physically active over the past 15 years
    (C) the number of North American children who are not obese increased over the past 15 years
    (D) over the past 15 years, the number of North American children who are underweight has declined
    (E) the incidence of obesity in North American children tends to increase as the children grow older

Like the previous question, this is a Must Be True question with a stimulus that does not contain a conclusion. But, this stimulus does provide information about both the numbers and percentages of obese children, and so you can end up with an answer that has either a number or a percentage (though a numerical answer is more likely since the percentage is fixed at a constant 15% in the stimulus).

The numerical information comes from the phrase, "The number of North American children who are obese...is steadily increasing." The percentage information comes from the phrase, "children who are obese—that is, who have more body fat than do 85 percent of North American children their age." The percentage information defines obese children as those who fall into the top 15% among all children their age in terms of body fat, and therefore the percentage is known to be constant. The numerical information tells us that the actual number of obese children is increasing (and since this is a Must Be True question we can accept that information as accurate).

Answer choice (A): This answer is incorrect because there is no evidence in the stimulus to support it. Although the stimulus mentioned four major studies that apparently agreed about the increase in the number of obese children, it would be an exaggeration to say that any time four major studies produce similar results they *must* be accurate.

Answer choice (B): This answer proposes a causal reason for why the number of obese children is growing. From the information in the stimulus we cannot determine the cause of the rise in obesity, so answer choice (B) is also wrong.

Answer choice (C): This is the correct answer. Consider the following example:

<u>15 years ago—100 total children of similar age</u>

Number of obese children	15	= 15%
Number of non-obese children	85	

Now, let us say that the number of obese children has risen to 150 children today:

<u>Today</u>

Number of obese children   150

So far we have conformed to the information given in the stimulus: the actual number of obese children is rising. However, although the number of obese children has now risen to 150, the definition of obesity ("more body fat than 85 percent of North American children") remains unchanged. Since this is the case, the 150 obese children today must still comprise the top 15% of the total child population. Consequently, the remaining 85% of non-obese children must now be 850:

<u>Today</u>

Number of non-obese children   850

(150 is 15% of 1000, and thus 85% of 1000 is 850)

Answer choice (C) is fully supported because the stimulus provides information about both the number and percentage of obese children. As stated earlier, if the stimulus provides information about both the numbers and percentages in a situation, then you can select any supported answer choice that contains either numbers or percentages. Note the emphasis on the word "supported." In the obesity problem, Law Services could easily have written an *incorrect* answer choice that says, "The number of North American children who are not obese *decreased* over the past 15 years."

Answer choice (D): This answer addresses "underweight" children, who are neither defined nor discussed in the stimulus.

Answer choice (E): This answer is directly contradicted by the information in the stimulus, which states that the incidence of obesity is definitionally set at a constant 15%.

Both of the previous questions were Must Be True questions, but of course the makers of the LSAT can also ask other questions about a stimulus that contains numbers and percentages. Please take a moment to consider the following problem:

3. Waste management companies, which collect waste for disposal in landfills and incineration plants, report that disposable plastics make up an ever-increasing percentage of the waste they handle. It is clear that attempts to decrease the amount of plastic that people throw away in the garbage are failing.

    Which one of the following, if true, most seriously weakens the argument?

    (A) Because plastics create harmful pollutants when burned, an increasing percentage of the plastics handled by waste management companies are being disposed of in landfills.
    (B) Although many plastics are recyclable, most of the plastics disposed of by waste management companies are not.
    (C) People are more likely to save and reuse plastic containers than containers made of heavier materials like glass or metal.
    (D) An increasing proportion of the paper, glass, and metal cans that waste management companies used to handle is now being recycled.
    (E) While the percentage of products using plastic packaging is increasing, the total amount of plastic being manufactured has remained unchanged.

The structure of the argument, in simplified form, is as follows:

Premise: Disposable plastics make up an ever-increasing percentage of the waste they handle.

Conclusion: Attempts to decrease the amount of plastic that people throw away in the garbage are failing.

Based on our discussion of numbers and percentages, it should be clear that the conclusion is flawed: a numbers conclusion ("amount") cannot be drawn solely from percentage information because the overall total could change dramatically. As you attack the answer choices, look for an answer that addresses this error.

Answer choice (A): The argument is about how people act when throwing away garbage, an issue that occurs before the waste management companies receive the trash. On the other hand, this answer discusses how the waste management companies dispose of plastics, an issue that occurs after they have received the waste. Because the two issues occur at different times in the cycle, this answer does not attack the argument and is incorrect.

Answer choice (B): Like answer choice (A), this answer raises an issue that occurs *after* the waste management companies have received the waste.

Answer choice (C): This answer addresses how people act prior to throwing away garbage, but it does not suggest that the amount of plastic that people throw away is not decreasing. The author would probably counter this statement by saying that regardless of the fact that people are more likely to save plastic containers, that tendency is only relative to glass and metal containers, and people are still throwing away plastics in an ever-increasing percentage (and thus amount).

Answer choice (D): This is the correct answer. The answer indicates that the waste management companies no longer receive as much paper, glass, and metal as they used to. Since this clearly affects the amount of trash that they process, this would also affect the percentages of each type of waste. If the amount of paper, glass, and metal drops by a large amount, the percentage of plastic in the waste would rise even if the actual amount of plastic waste was reduced. The following example shows how this is possible:

	Previously	Now
Total garbage (in units)	100	20
Plastic garbage (in units)	20 (20%)	10 (50%)
Other garbage (in units)	80 (80%)	10 (50%)

In the example, plastic garbage has risen from 20% to 50%, but the actual amount of plastic waste has decreased from 20 units to 10 units. Consequently, because this answer raises a scenario that could disprove the argument, it is the correct answer.

Answer choice (E): The amount of plastic being manufactured is not the issue in the stimulus; how much plastic is thrown away is the issue.

In all respects this is a classic numbers and percentages Weaken problem. Accordingly, we can use this discussion to highlight a general rule for handling Weaken and Strengthen questions paired with numbers and percentages stimuli:

> To weaken or strengthen an argument containing numbers and percentages, look carefully for information about the total amount(s)—does the argument make an assumption based on one of the misconceptions discussed earlier?

On the following page, another numbers and percentage problem is presented.

Please take a moment to complete the following question.

4. For next year, the Chefs' Union has requested a 10
    percent salary increase for each of its members,
    whereas the Hotel Managers' Union has requested
    only an 8 percent salary increase for each of its
    members. These facts demonstrate that the average
    dollar amount of the raises that the Chefs' Union has
    requested for next year is greater than that of the
    raises requested by the Hotel Managers' Union.

    Which one of the following, if true, most strengthens
    the argument?

    (A) The Chefs' Union has many more members than
         does the Hotel Managers' Union.
    (B) The Chefs' Union is a more powerful union
         than is the Hotel Managers' Union and is
         therefore more likely to obtain the salary
         increases it requests.
    (C) The current salaries of the members of the
         Chefs' Union are, on average, higher than the
         current salaries of the members of the Hotel
         Managers' Union.
    (D) The average dollar amount of the raises that the
         members of the Chefs' Union received last
         year was equal to the average dollar amount
         of the raises that the members of the Hotel
         Managers' Union received.
    (E) The members of the Chefs' Union received
         salary increases of 10 percent in each of the
         last two years, while the members of the
         Hotel Managers' Union received salary
         increases of only 8 percent in each of the last
         two years.

This problem makes the classic mistake of assuming that a larger percentage translates into a greater number (Misconception #6). According to the argument, because the Chef's Union requested a 10% raise and the Hotel Manager's Union requested only an 8% raise, the Chef's Union must have asked for more money than the Hotel Manager's Union. But, the argument never tells us how much the average member of each union makes, so the conclusion cannot be drawn with certainty, as shown by the following example:

Averages appear in a variety of LSAT questions. Just remember, an average is a composite number, and within the average there can be a significant degree of variation and no single entity need embody the exact characteristic of the average (for example, the average weight of a 1 pound rock and a 99 pound rock is 50 pounds).

	Chef	Hotel
Raise request	10%	8%
Average current salary	$1000	$10,000
Actual amount of raise requested	$100	$800

Even though the Chef's Union has asked for a greater percentage raise than the Hotel Manager's Union, it is still possible that the actual dollar amount of the Hotel Manager's Union request is greater. In this case, omitting the average current salary made by each member is tantamount to omitting the *total amount* made by the members, and thus, even though this problem uses averages, it trades on the mistake behind all the misconceptions discussed at the beginning of this chapter. To strengthen the argument, you must find an answer that indicates that the Chef's Union has a wage that is equal to or greater than the wage of the Hotel Manager's Union (the wage could also be very slightly below that of the Hotel Manager's Union).

Answer choice (A): Because the conclusion is specific about the average dollar amount requested, and an average can be calculated regardless of how many members are in the union, this answer is irrelevant to the argument.

Answer choice (B): The argument focuses on the size of each Union's raise request. Whether each union will receive the request is not at issue, and thus this answer is incorrect.

Answer choice (C): This is the correct answer. As discussed above, an answer that indicates that the Chef's Union has a wage that is equal to or greater than the wage of the Hotel Manager's Union would strengthen the argument. This is the answer you should look for when you read the question stem, and you should attempt to accelerate through the answer choices to find this answer.

Answer choice (D): This answer refers to the raises given out last year. Unfortunately, this fails to address the current salaries of the union members.

Both answer choice (D) and (E) attempt to lure you into the same mistake made by the author in the stimulus.

Answer choice (E): Like answer choice (D), this answer addresses previous raises, which does not tell us about current salaries.

Markets and Market Share

Entire books have been written about market operations, so a lengthy discussion of this topic is beyond the scope of this book.

The makers of the LSAT expect you to understand the operation of markets and the concept of market share. Market operation includes supply and demand, production, pricing, and profit. None of these concepts should be unfamiliar to you as they are a part of everyday life.

Market share is simply the portion of a market that a company controls. The market share can be measured either in terms of revenues (sales) or units sold. For example:

Heinz has a 60% market share of the $500 million ketchup market.

Jif brand peanut butter sold 80 million units last year, a 30% market share.

Like all numbers and percentages problems, market share is a comparative term, as opposed to an absolute term. Thus, many market share questions hinge on one of the Misconceptions discussed in this chapter.

Because market share is a numbers and percentages concept, market share can change when factors in the market change. For example, a company can gain market share (percentage) if the market shrinks and they maintain a constant size, or if they grow in an unchanging market. However, a company losing market share does not mean that their sales decreased, only that they became a smaller entity in the market relative to the whole (the market grew and they stayed the same size, for example). Similarly, a company could lose sales and still gain market share if the overall market became smaller.

Regardless of the size of a market and even though the total amount of the market can shift, the total market share must always add up to 100%.

Please take a moment to complete the following question:

5. Rumored declines in automobile-industry revenues are exaggerated. It is true that automobile manufacturers' share of the industry's revenues fell from 65 percent two years ago to 50 percent today, but over the same period suppliers of automobile parts had their share increase from 15 percent to 20 percent and service companies (for example, distributors, dealers, and repairers) had their share increase from 20 percent to 30 percent.

Which one of the following best indicates why the statistics given above provide by themselves no evidence for the conclusion they are intended to support?

(A) The possibility is left open that the statistics for manufacturers' share of revenues come from a different source than the other statistics.

(B) No matter what changes the automobile industry's overall revenues undergo, the total of all shares of these revenues must be 100 percent.

(C) No explanation is given for why the revenue shares of different sectors of the industry changed.

(D) Manufacturers and parts companies depend for their revenue on dealers' success in selling cars.

(E) Revenues are an important factor but are not the only factor in determining profits.

The conclusion of the argument states that the rumored declines in automobile-industry revenues are exaggerated (a numerical statement), but the premises provided in support of this argument only address the market share percentages of the three groups that have automobile-industry revenues (percentage statements). The percentage statements used by the author only indicates that the percentages have changed, not whether overall revenue has changed:

	2 Years Ago	Today
Manufacturers share	65%	50%
Suppliers share	15%	20%
Service company share	20%	30%
Total market size in %	100%	100%

Although the composition of the market has changed in terms of the market share of each group, this fact tells us nothing about industry revenues because market shares will always add up to 100% regardless of the actual dollars involved. Thus, automobile-industry revenues could have risen dramatically and the percentages above could still be accurate.

Answer choice (A): Although it is true that the possibility is left open that the statistics for the manufacturers share may come from a different source, this does not address the fundamental percentage-to-number error in the argument.

Answer choice (B): This is the correct answer. The answer reveals the error of the author: the changing market shares of different groups have no impact on the actual amount of revenues. In all instances, the market shares will add up to 100%, so a discussion of shifts within this 100% is meaningless as far as making a determination of whether revenues declined.

Answer choice (C): This is not a flaw of the argument. The author is allowed to simply note that the shares changed and use those facts to draw a conclusion. In the argument the conclusion is faulty, but not for the reason cited in this answer.

Answer choice (D): The interrelationship of the groups named in the stimulus is not an issue in determining whether the conclusion is in error.

Answer choice (E): The argument is about revenues, and information about profits will not reveal the error in the reasoning.

Numbers and Percentages Review

The makers of the LSAT often prey upon several widely-held misconceptions:

Misconception #1:	Increasing percentages automatically lead to increasing numbers.
Misconception #2:	Decreasing percentages automatically lead to decreasing numbers.
Misconception #3:	Increasing numbers automatically lead to increasing percentages.
Misconception #4:	Decreasing numbers automatically lead to decreasing percentages.
Misconception #5:	Large numbers automatically mean large percentages, and small numbers automatically mean small percentages.
Misconception #6:	Large percentages automatically mean large numbers, and small percentages automatically mean small numbers.

Words that introduce numerical ideas:

Amount
Quantity
Sum
Total
Count
Tally

Words that introduce percentage ideas:

Percent
Proportion
Fraction
Ratio
Incidence
Likelihood
Probability
Segment
Share

Use the following general rules for Must Be True questions:

1. If the stimulus contains percentage or proportion information only, avoid answers that contain hard numbers.

2. If the stimulus contains only numerical information, avoid answers that contain percentage or proportion information.

3. If the stimulus contains both percentage and numerical information, any answer choice that contains numbers, percentages, or both *may* be true.

Use the following general rules for Weaken and Strengthen questions:

To weaken or strengthen an argument containing numbers and percentages, look carefully for information about the total amount(s)—does the argument make an assumption based on one of the misconceptions discussed earlier?

Market share is simply the portion of a market that a company controls. Market share can be measured either in terms of revenues (sales) or units sold. Regardless of the size of a market, total market share must always add up to 100%.

The following questions are drawn from actual LSATs. Please complete the problem set and review the answer key and explanations. *Answers on Page 445*

1. Politician: Those economists who claim that consumer price increases have averaged less than 3 percent over the last year are mistaken. They clearly have not shopped anywhere recently. Gasoline is up 10 percent over the last year; my auto insurance, 12 percent; newspapers, 15 percent; propane, 13%; bread, 50 percent.

   The reasoning in the politician's argument is most vulnerable to criticism on the grounds that the argument

   (A) impugns the character of the economists rather than addressing their arguments
   (B) fails to show that the economists mentioned are not experts in the area of consumer prices
   (C) mistakenly infers that something is not true from the claim that it has not been shown to be so
   (D) uses evidence drawn from a small sample that may well be unrepresentative
   (E) attempts to persuade by making an emotional appeal

2. Ditrama is a federation made up of three autonomous regions: Korva, Mitro, and Guadar. Under the federal revenue-sharing plan, each region receives a share of federal revenues equal to the share of the total population of Ditrama residing in that region, as shown by a yearly population survey. Last year, the percentage of federal revenues Korva received for its share decreased somewhat even though the population survey on which the revenue-sharing was based showed that Korva's population had increased.

   If the statements above are true, which one of the following must also have been shown by the population survey on which last year's revenue-sharing in Ditrama was based?

   (A) Of the three regions, Korva had the smallest number of residents.
   (B) The population of Korva grew by a smaller percentage than it did in previous years.
   (C) The populations of Mitro and Guadar each increased by a percentage that exceeded the percentage by which the population of Korva increased.
   (D) Of the three regions, Korva's numerical increase in population was the smallest.
   (E) Korva's population grew by a smaller percentage than did the population of at least one of the other two autonomous regions.

3. In 1980, Country A had a per capita gross domestic product (GDP) that was $5,000 higher than that of the European Economic Community. By 1990, the difference, when adjusted for inflation, had increased to $6,000. Since a rising per capita GDP indicates a rising average standard of living, the average standard of living in Country A must have risen between 1980 and 1990.

    Which one of the following is an assumption on which the argument depends?

    (A) Between 1980 and 1990, Country A and the European Economic Community experienced the same percentage increase in population.
    (B) Between 1980 and 1990, the average standard of living in the European Economic Community fell.
    (C) Some member countries of the European Economic Community had, during the 1980s, a higher average standard of living than Country A.
    (D) The per capita GDP of the European Economic Community was not lower by more than $1,000 in 1990 than it had been in 1980.
    (E) In 1990, no member country of the European Economic Community had a per capita GDP higher than that of Country A.

4. Students from outside the province of Markland, who in any given academic year pay twice as much tuition each as do students from Markland, had traditionally accounted for at least two-thirds of the enrollment at Central Markland College. Over the past 10 years academic standards at the college have risen, and the proportion of students who are not Marklanders has dropped to around 40 percent.

    Which one of the following can be properly inferred from the statements above?

    (A) If it had not been for the high tuition paid by students from outside Markland, the college could not have improved its academic standards over the past 10 years.
    (B) If academic standards had not risen over the past 10 years, students who are not Marklanders would still account for at least two-thirds of the college's enrollment.
    (C) Over the past 10 years, the number of students from Markland increased and the number of students from outside Markland decreased.
    (D) Over the past 10 years, academic standards at Central Markland College have risen by more than academic standards at any other college in Markland.
    (E) If the college's per capita revenue from tuition has remained the same, tuition fees have increased over the past 10 years.

Numbers and Percentages Problem Set Answer Key

All answer keys in this book indicate the source of the question by giving the month and year the LSAT was originally administered, the Logical Reasoning section number, and the question number within that section. Each LSAT has two Logical Reasoning sections, and so the Section 1 and Section 2 designators will refer to the first or second Logical Reasoning section in the test, not the physical section number of the booklet.

Question #1. Flaw-#%. December 2003 LSAT, Section 1, #12. The correct answer choice is (D)

The politician's argument is that the claims that price increases have averaged less than 3 percent are wrong, and in support of that position the politician cites several examples of price increases, each of which is greater than 3 percent. As mentioned in one of the chapter sidebars, "an average is a composite number, and within the average there can be a significant degree of variation and no single entity need embody the exact characteristic of the average (for example, the average weight of a 1 pound rock and a 99 pound rock is 50 pounds)." In making the argument, the politician has focused in on several individual examples while ignoring the fact that an average is a compilation of many different numbers. Answer choice (D) perfectly captures the essence of this sampling error.

Answer choice (A): The argument does not contain a source or *ad hominem* attack. Simply stating that a position is wrong is different from criticizing the character of that person.

Answer choice (B): To properly claim that the economists are wrong does not require showing that they are not pricing experts, and hence this answer is incorrect

Answer choice (C): The politician attempts to refute the position by providing evidence about large price increases for certain products. This process, which involves facts, is different from inferring that a claim is false because it has not been shown to be true. This answer choice would better describe an argument such as the following: "you have not proven that God exists, so there must be no God."

Answer choice (D): This is the correct answer. Citing several examples to refute an average is a doomed strategy.

Answer choice (E): There is no appeal to emotion present; percentages are used to make the argument.

Question #2. Must-#%. December 1995 LSAT, Section 2, #24. The correct answer choice is (E)

The situation in Ditrama is as follows:

> Under the federal revenue-sharing plan, each region receives a share of federal revenues equal to the *share of the total population* of Ditrama residing in that region, as shown by a yearly population survey.

> Last year, the *percentage* of federal revenues Korva received for its share *decreased* somewhat even though the population survey on which the revenue-sharing was based showed that Korva's *population had increased.*

If the total population of Korva increased but at the same time they experienced a decrease in revenue allocation, the only possible solution is that the total population of Ditrama increased by more than the Korva increase. Thus, you must seek an answer that indicates that the total population increased more than Korva's population increased. But be careful: this question is one of high difficulty, and the test makers do not make it easy to spot the correct answer.

Answer choice (A): Either Mitro or Guadar could have a smaller number of residents than Korva.

Answer choice (B): This answer is impossible to prove because we do not have information about the population growth of Korva in the years prior to the last one.

Answer choice (C): This is the most popular wrong answer choice. The key error is the claim that "Mitro and Guadar *each* increased by a percentage that exceeded" Korva's increase. Although it must be true that at least one exceeded Korva's increase, it does not have to be true that both exceeded Korva, as shown by the following example:

	Before	After (Last Year)
Total Population of Ditrama	30 (100%)	100 (100%)
Population of Korva (people/percent of total)	10 (33%)	15 (15%)
Population of Mitro (people/percent of total)	10 (33%)	10 (10%)
Population of Guadar (people/percent of total)	10 (33%)	75 (75%)

In the example above, only one of the other regions had a population increase that exceeded Korva; the other did not. Hence this answer choice is incorrect. Note also that this example disproves answer choice (A) as well.

Numbers and Percentages Problem Set Answer Key

Answer choice (D): As shown by the previous example, this answer is incorrect.

Answer choice (E): This is the correct answer. From the stimulus we know that Korva had a population increase, but a revenue drop. So, the total population of Ditrama must have increased by more than Korva's increase, and for this to happen, at least one other country must have had an increase in population that exceeded Korva's.

Note that the scenario in answer choice (C) would force answer choice (E) to be correct, and based on the Uniqueness Rule of Answer Choices, answer (C) is incorrect for that reason alone.

Question #3. Assumption-#%. September 1995 LSAT, Section 1, #14. The correct answer choice is (D)

This is a challenging question. The author makes the following argument:

Premise:	In 1980, Country A had a per capita gross domestic product (GDP) that was $5,000 higher than that of the European Economic Community.
Premise:	By 1990, the difference, when adjusted for inflation, had increased to $6,000.
Premise:	A rising per capita GDP indicates a rising average standard of living.
Conclusion:	The average standard of living in Country A must have risen between 1980 and 1990.

The author has fallen into the trap of believing that an increase in the difference between GDP's means that the *actual* GDP of Country A has increased. Since that is not necessarily the case based on the number, you should look for the answer that assumes the total GDP of country A has not decreased.

Answer choice (A): The stimulus is clear that the GDP is a "per capita" (per person) figure. Hence, the author does not need to make an assumption regarding actual population increases.

Answer choice (B): The author does need to assume this is true because a bigger GDP gap does not prove that either must have fallen; the actual GDP of both Country A and the European Economic Community (EEC) could rise and the author's argument would still be valid.

Answer choice (C): In the argument the author uses the GDP of the entire EEC. Since the figure for the EEC would necessarily be an average drawn from the numbers of multiple countries, the author does not need to make any assumptions about figures for individual countries within the EEC.

Numbers and Percentages Problem Set Answer Key

Answer choice (D): This is the correct answer. In order to conclude that an increasing difference in GDP translates to an actual increase in GDP, the author must assume that the GDP of the point of comparison, the EEC, did not fall dramatically. Consider the following example, which assigns actual numbers to the GDP of each group in 1980, and then shows a variety of possibilities for the numbers in 1990:

	1980	#1: 1990	#2: 1990	#3: 1990	#4: 1990
GDP of Country A	105	107	156	96	105
GDP of the EEC	100	101	150	90	99
Difference	+5	+6	+6	+6	+6

Each of the four examples for 1990 is consistent with the claim that there is a $6000 difference between the GDP of Country A and the GDP of the EEC. The first two examples for 1990, #1 and #2, show that the total GDP of Country A, and therefore the standard of living as defined in the stimulus, has risen. Example #3, shows that even though the gap has increased between the two groups, the actual GDP of Country A has *decreased*, and therefore the standard of living in Country A has decreased. This is inconsistent with the author's conclusion, so the author must be assuming that this type of scenario cannot occur. In example #4, we see a second example that is incompatible with the author's conclusion, one where the gap remains at $600, but the GDP of Country A remains the same. The author must assume that the fourth scenario also cannot occur, and that the GDP of the EEC cannot drop by the $1000 that is the amount of the increase in the gap. Hence, the author must assume that if the GDP of the EEC drops, it drops by less than $1000, and therefore answer choice (D) is correct.

This is clearly a confusing answer, but do not forget that you can always apply the Assumption Negation Technique to any answer choice in an Assumption question. Answer choice (D), when negated, reads: "The per capita GDP of the European Economic Community was lower by more than $1,000 in 1990 than it had been in 1980." This negation would definitely weaken the argument because it would create a scenario like #3 or one even worse than #4. Because the answer choice weakens the argument when negated, it must be the correct answer.

Answer choice (E): This answer is incorrect for the same reason cited in answer choice (C): since the figure for the EEC would necessarily be an average drawn from the numbers of multiple countries, the author does not need to make any assumptions about the figures for individual countries within the EEC, regardless of year.

448

Numbers and Percentages Problem Set Answer Key

Question #4. Must-#%. September 1995 LSAT, Section 1, #20. The correct answer choice is (E)

The stimulus does not contain a conclusion, but it does contain an interesting fact set:

> "Students from outside the province of Markland, who in any given academic year pay twice as much tuition each as do students from Markland, had traditionally accounted for at least two-thirds of the enrollment at Central Markland College."

This sentence indicates that the non-Marklanders are paying a greater amount of tuition, and they previously accounted for at least 66% of the enrollment. This statement is followed by:

> "Over the past 10 years academic standards at the college have risen, and the proportion of students who are not Marklanders has dropped to around 40 percent."

This sentence can be deceptive because it contains two ideas that are unrelated and many people assume that the proportion of non-Marklanders has dropped because the academic standards rose. The sentence only states that the non-Marklanders have dropped, not that they dropped *because of* the raised standards.

As you learned from our discussion in this chapter, the fact that the non-Marklanders have dropped in percent does not mean that their actual number has decreased (Misconception #2). The following is an example of how the percent could decrease while numbers could increase:

	10 years ago	Today
Total number of students at Central Markland	100	200
Number of non-Markland students (people/percent of total)	66 (66%)	80 (40%)
Number of Markland students (people/percent of total)	34 (34%)	120 (60%)

Answer choice (A): The stimulus does not cite any reason for why or how the academic standards were increased, so this answer is incorrect.

Answer choice (B): This answer tests your ability to understand the last sentence of the stimulus. As discussed above, the last sentence does *not* provide a reason for the decline in non-Markland students, so removing the stipulation about the rise in academic standards would not tell us whether non-Marklanders would still be enrolled in the college.

Numbers and Percentages Problem Set Answer Key

Answer choice (C): This is a difficult answer. If the size of the college stayed the same, then this answer would be correct. But, as shown by the example above, the statement in this answer does not have to be true when the total size of the college changes. In the example, both Markland students and non-Markland student numbers grew.

Answer choice (D): Remember, this is a Must Be True question, so every answer must pass the Fact Test. No information was given about other Markland colleges, so this answer is incorrect.

Answer choice (E): This is the correct answer. If the college's *per capita* revenue from tuition remains constant while at the same time the high-tuition paying non-Marklanders have decreased in percentage, the college must have derived new tuition revenue by raising tuition. In other words, when the percentage of non-Marklanders drops, the average tuition per person must also drop because they pay twice as much as the Markland students. In order to keep the per person revenue the same, fees would have to be raised.

CHAPTER SIXTEEN: EVALUATE THE ARGUMENT QUESTIONS

Evaluate the Argument Questions

Evaluate the Argument questions ask you to consider the question, statistic, or piece of information that would best help determine the logical validity of the argument presented in the stimulus. In other words, you must select the answer choice that decides whether the argument is good or bad.

To better understand this question type, imagine that you are examining an argument and you have to ask one question that—depending on the answer to the question—will reveal whether the argument is strong or weak. By this definition, there must be a flaw in each argument, and your question, if posed correctly, can reveal that flaw or eliminate the flaw. Please note that you are not being asked to prove with finality whether the argument is good or bad—rather, you must simply ask the question that will help best analyze the validity of the argument. For this reason, Evaluate the Argument questions can be seen as a combination of a Strengthen and Weaken question: if you ask the best question, depending on the answer to the question the argument could be seen as strong or weak.

As mentioned in Chapter Three, this unusual question type is the only question that does not fall into one of the four question families. Evaluate the Argument questions are actually a combination of the Second and Third Families, and as such you should keep the following considerations in mind:

1. In all Second and Third Family questions the information in the stimulus is suspect, so you should search for the reasoning error present.

2. The answer choices are accepted as given, even if they include "new" information. Your task is to determine which answer choice best helps determine the validity of the argument.

Evaluate the Argument question stems almost always use the word "evaluate" or a synonym such as "judge" or "assess," but the intent is always identical: the question stem asks you to identify the piece of information that would be most helpful in assessing the argument. Question stem examples:

"The answer to which one of the following questions would contribute most to an evaluation of the argument?"

"Clarification of which one of the following issues would be most important to an evaluation of the skeptics' position?"

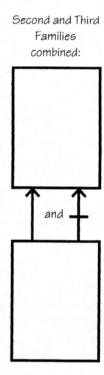

Second and Third Families combined:

"Which one of the following would be most important to know in evaluating the hypothesis in the passage?"

"Which one of the following would it be most relevant to investigate in evaluating the conclusion of George's argument?"

"Which one of the following would it be most helpful to know in order to judge whether what the scientist subsequently learned calls into question the hypothesis?"

Evaluate the Argument questions (and Cannot Be True questions, which are covered in the next chapter) appear infrequently on the LSAT, but the uniqueness of the question type forces students to take a moment to adjust when they do appear. Some question types, such as Must Be True and Weaken, recur so frequently that students become used to seeing them and are comfortable with the process of selecting the correct answer. When a question type appears rarely, test-takers are often thrown off-balance and lose time and energy reacting to the question. The makers of the LSAT are well aware of this, and this is the reason they intersperse different question types in each section (again, imagine how much easier the LSAT would be if the Logical Reasoning section was composed of 25 Must Be True questions). One reason we study each type of question is to help you become as comfortable as possible with the questions you will encounter on the test, making your reaction time as fast as possible.

The Variance Test™

Solving Evaluate questions can be difficult. The nature of the answer choices allow for separate interpretations, and deciding on a single answer can be challenging. In order to determine the correct answer choice on a Evaluate the Argument question, apply the Variance Test™.

The Variance Test consists of supplying two polar opposite responses to the question posed *in the answer choice* and then analyzing how the varying responses affect the conclusion in the stimulus. If different responses produce different effects on the conclusion, then the answer choice is correct. If different responses do not produce different effects, then the answer choice is incorrect. For example, if an Evaluate the Argument answer choice states "What is the percentage of people who live near a nuclear plant?" look to test the two most extreme possibilities: first test the response "0%" for its effect on the conclusion and then test the response "100%" for its effect on the conclusion. If the answer choice is correct, one of the percentages should strengthen the argument and one of the percentages should weaken the argument. If the answer choice is incorrect, neither response will have an effect on the argument.

Of course, the answer choice does not have to be about percentages for the technique to work; the Variance Test will work regardless of the nature of the answer choice. Here are some more example answer choices and Variance Test responses:

If an answer choice asks "Is the pattern permanent?" first test "Yes" as a response and then test "No" as a response (remember, you *must* test opposite answers). If the answer choice is correct, one response should strengthen the argument and one response should weaken the argument. If the answer choice is incorrect, neither response will have an effect on the argument.

If an answer choice asks "Are corporate or environmental interests more important?" first test "Corporate interests are more important" as a response and then test "Environmental interests are more important" as a response. If the answer choice is correct, one response should strengthen the argument and one response should weaken the argument. If the answer choice is incorrect, neither response will have an effect on the argument.

After you have narrowed your answer choices to the Contenders, or to the one answer choice you believe is correct, then apply the Variance Test. Do not apply the Test to all five answers!

Now we will use an LSAT question to more fully explore how the question type works and how the correct answer can be determined by the Variance Test. Please take a moment to complete the following question:

1. Advertisement: Most power hedge trimmers on the market do an adequate job of trimming hedges, but many power hedge trimmers are dangerous to operate and can cause serious injury when used by untrained operators. Bolter Industries' hedge trimmer has been tested by National Laboratories, the most trusted name in safety testing. So you know, if you buy a Bolter's, you are buying a power hedge trimmer whose safety is assured.

The answer to which one of the following questions would be most useful in evaluating the truth of the conclusion drawn in the advertisement?

(A) Has National Laboratories performed safety tests on other machines made by Bolter Industries?

(B) How important to the average buyer of a power hedge trimmer is safety of operation?

(C) What were the results of National Laboratories' tests of Bolter Industries' hedge trimmer?

(D) Are there safer ways of trimming a hedge than using a power hedge trimmer?

(E) Does any other power hedge trimmer on the market do a better job of trimming hedges than does Bolter Industries' hedge trimmer?

As with all questions, you must identify the conclusion of the argument. The conclusion states that if you buy a Bolter's power hedge trimmer, you know the trimmer is safe. In the question stem, we are asked to evaluate the truth of this conclusion. Each answer choice is then posed in the form of a question. The answer choice that is correct will contain the question that, when answered, will reveal whether the conclusion is strong or weak.

In order to understand the application of the Variance Test, we will look at each answer choice in succession and thus we will not perform an initial analysis of the argument (on the LSAT we would analyze the stimulus closely). Also note that on the test we would *not* apply the Variance Test to each answer choice, only to the Contenders. For teaching purposes, we will apply the Variance Test to each answer in an effort to give you the best possible understanding of how the technique works.

Answer choice (A) asks if National Laboratories has performed tests on other machines from Bolter Industries. To apply the Variance Test, we should supply different and opposing answers to the question posed by the answer choice. First, try the answer "No." With this answer, would the fact that National Laboratories did not perform safety test on other Bolters machines affect the safety of the Bolter's hedge trimmer? No—this does not help us evaluate the safety of the hedge trimmer. What if the answer was "Yes" ? Would the fact that National Laboratories performed safety tests on other Bolters machines affect the safety of the Bolter's hedge trimmer? Not at all. So, regardless of how we respond to the question posed in answer choice (A), our view of the conclusion is the same—we do not know whether the claim that the hedge trimmer is safe is good or bad. According to the Variance Test, if the answer is correct, then supplying opposite answers should yield different views of the conclusion. Since our assessment of the conclusion did not change, the Variance Test tells us that this answer is incorrect.

The question in answer choice (B) is, "How important to the average buyer of a power hedge is safety of operation?" Again, apply the Variance Test and supply opposite answers to the question in the answer choice. In this case, try "Very Important" and "Not Important." If safety of operation is very important to a buyer of hedge trimmers, would that affect whether the Bolter's hedge trimmer itself is safe? No. Let's look at the opposite side: if safety of operation is not important at all to a buyer of hedge trimmers, would that affect whether the Bolter's hedge trimmer itself is safe? No. Because our view of the validity of the conclusion does not change when we consider different responses to the question posed in answer choice (B), the Variance Test tells us that answer choice (B) is incorrect.

The question in answer choice (C) is, what were the results of the tests of Bolter's hedge trimmer? Using the Variance Test, supply one response that says, "Bolter's hedge trimmer *failed* the safety test." If this is true, then the conclusion is unquestionably weakened. Now supply a response that says, "Bolter's hedge trimmer *passed* the safety test." If this is true, then the conclusion is strengthened. So, depending on the answer supplied to the question posed in answer choice (C), our view of the validity of the argument changes: sometimes we view the conclusion as stronger and other times as weaker. Therefore, according to the Variance Test, this is the correct answer. In this instance, the Variance Test reveals the flaw in the argument: the author simply assumed that being tested means safety is assured. Nowhere in the argument did the author mention that the hedge trimmer passed the tests, and the Variance Test reveals this flaw.

In answer choice (D), "Yes" and "No" responses do not change our view of the argument, and answer choice (D) is incorrect.

In answer choice (E), "Yes" and "No" responses do not change our view of the argument, and answer choice (E) is incorrect.

The key thing to note is that the Variance Test is applied according to the nature of each answer choice. Thus, with some answer choices we might supply responses of "Yes" and "No," and other answer choices might require responses of "0%" and "100%," or "Very Important" and "Not Important." But, in each case, the answers we supply are opposites, and the correct answer is always the one that changes your view of the validity of the conclusion when those different responses are supplied. If your view of the argument does not change, then the answer choice is incorrect.

Keep in mind that the Variance Test should only be applied to the contending answer choices. In the discussion above we applied it to every answer choice, but we did this simply to show how to effectively apply the Variance Test. During the actual test you would only want to apply the Variance Test to two or three answer choices at most.

Final Note

Because this chapter and the next chapter address question types that appear infrequently, these chapters are shorter than other chapters and contain fewer problems in the problem set. On the next page is a review of this question type.

All flawed arguments contain an error of assumption. The correct answer in an Evaluate the Argument question reveals that error.

Evaluate the Argument Question Type Review

Evaluate the Argument questions ask you to consider the question, statistic, or piece of information that would best help determine the logical validity of the argument presented in the stimulus.

Evaluate the Argument questions are a combination of the Second and Third Families, and as such you should keep the following considerations in mind:

1. In all Second and Third Family questions the information in the stimulus is suspect, so you should search for the reasoning error present.

2. The answer choices are accepted as given, even if they include "new" information.

Evaluate the Argument question stems almost always use the word "evaluate" or a synonym such as "judge" or "assess."

To determine the correct answer choice on a Evaluate the Argument question, apply the Variance Test™ by supplying two opposite responses to the question posed *in the answer choice* and then analyze how the varying responses affect the conclusion in the stimulus. If different responses produce different effects on the conclusion, the answer choice is correct. If different responses do not produce different effects, the answer choice is incorrect.

The Variance Test should only be applied to Contenders (to determine which one is correct) or to the answer choice you believe is correct (to confirm your selection).

Evaluate the Argument Question Problem Set

The following questions are drawn from actual LSATs. Please complete the problem set and review the answer key and explanations. *Answers on Page 458*

1. Columnist: George Orwell's book *1984* has exercised much influence on a great number of this newspaper's readers. One thousand readers were surveyed and asked to name the one book that had the most influence on their lives. The book chosen most often was the Bible; *1984* was second.

The answer to which one of the following questions would most help in evaluating the columnist's argument?

(A) How many books had each person surveyed read?

(B) How many people chose books other than *1984*?

(C) How many people read the columnist's newspaper?

(D) How many books by George Orwell other than *1984* were chosen?

(E) How many of those surveyed had actually read the books they chose?

2. Anders: The physical structure of the brain plays an important role in thinking. So researchers developing "thinking machines"—computers that can make decisions based on both common sense and factual knowledge—should closely model those machines on the structure of the brain.

Yang: Important does not mean essential. After all, no flying machine closely modeled on birds has worked; workable aircraft are structurally very different from birds. So thinking machines closely modeled on the brain are also likely to fail. In developing a workable thinking machine, researchers would therefore increase their chances of success if they focus on the brain's function and simply ignore its physical structure.

In evaluating Yang's argument it would be most helpful to know whether

(A) studies of the physical structure of birds provided information crucial to the development of workable aircraft

(B) researchers currently working on thinking machines take all thinking to involve both common sense and factual knowledge

(C) as much time has been spent trying to develop a workable thinking machine as had been spent in developing the first workable aircraft

(D) researchers who specialize in the structure of the brain are among those who are trying to develop thinking machines

(E) some flying machines that were not closely modeled on birds failed to work

All answer keys in this book indicate the source of the question by giving the month and year the LSAT was originally administered, the Logical Reasoning section number, and the question number within that section. Each LSAT has two Logical Reasoning sections, and so the Section 1 and Section 2 designators will refer to the first or second Logical Reasoning section in the test, not the physical section number of the booklet.

Question #1. Evaluate. December 2001 LSAT, Section 1, #24. The correct answer choice is (B)

The conclusion of the argument is the first sentence: "George Orwell's book *1984* has exercised much influence on a great number of this newspaper's readers." The basis for this conclusion is that *1984* was the second most named book in a survey about influential books. The argument contains a serious error: just because 1984 came in second in the survey does not mean that "a great number" of readers selected it as influential. To illustrate this proposition, consider the following example:

Number of people surveyed = 1000

Number of people naming the Bible as the most influential book = 999
Number of people naming *1984* as the most influential book = 1

In this example, 1984 has come in second, but no one would say this second place finish supports a conclusion that "*1984* has exercised much influence *on a great number* of this newspaper's readers." You can expect the correct answer to address this issue.

Answer choice (A): The survey in the argument asks readers to name the one book with the most influence in their lives; the number of books read does not affect this answer. To apply the Variance Test, try opposite answers of "1" and a large number, say "10,000." These numbers will not alter the evaluation of the argument, and thus this answer is incorrect.

Answer choice (B): This is the correct answer, but it can be difficult since the wording is a bit unusual. The question is intended to reveal how many people selected *1984* relative to the other choices, and this addresses the issue raised in the analysis of the stimulus. Consider how the variance test works for this answer choice:

First try the response, "999." In this case, only one person selected *1984* as the most influential book, and the argument is greatly weakened.

Next try the response, "501." In this instance, 499 people selected *1984* as the most influential book and the conclusion is strengthened (the other 501 people would have selected the Bible). Note that you cannot try a number larger than 501 because that would mean that the Bible was not named most often.

Because the varied responses produce different evaluations of the argument, this answer is correct.

Answer choice (C): This answer is not relevant to the columnist's argument. Apply the Variance Test to disprove this answer by using opposite answers of "0" and a very large number, such as "1 million."

458

Evaluate the Argument Question Problem Set Answer Key

Answer choice (D): Because the argument is about Orwell's *1984*, other Orwell books chosen by the readers have no impact on the argument. Apply the Variance Test, using opposite answers of "0" and a small number such as "10" (Orwell wrote dozens of essays, but not dozens of books).

Answer choice (E): The survey in the argument addresses influence, not the actual reading of the book. A person might be influenced by a book like the Bible through church teachings, etc. without actually having read the book. To apply the Variance Test, try opposite answers of "0" and "1000."

Question #2. Evaluate. October 2002 LSAT, Section 2, #19. The correct answer choice is (A)

Yang's argument is as follows:

Premise: Important does not mean essential.

Premise: No flying machine closely modeled on birds has worked; workable aircraft are structurally very different from birds.

Premise/   So thinking machines closely modeled on the brain are also likely to fail.
Subconclusion:

Conclusion: In developing a workable thinking machine, researchers would therefore increase their chances of success if they focus on the brain's function and simply ignore its physical structure."

Yang's conclusion is very strong: "simply ignore the physical structure of the brain" when developing a thinking machine. As you might expect, this extreme conclusion and the relatively weak supporting evidence plays a role in the correct answer. Also note that the question stem uses the word "whether" to turn each answer choice into a question.

Answer choice (A): This is the correct answer. The Variance Test proves the answer:

> If the answer is "Yes, they did provide crucial information" then developers should not ignore the physical structure of the brain because the reasoning used to make that judgment (via the flying machine analogy) is faulty.

> If the answer is "No, they did not provide crucial information" then the argument is strengthened because the analogy suggests it would be acceptable to ignore the physical structure of the brain.

Because the varied responses produce different evaluations of the argument, this answer is correct.

Answer choice (B): The conclusion is about ignoring the physical structure of the brain, and information about what constitutes thinking will not help evaluate the argument. Apply the Variance Test to disprove this answer by using opposite answers of "Yes" and "No."

Answer choice (C): The relative amount of time spent on each project is not an issue in the stimulus. Apply the Variance Test to disprove this answer, using opposite answers of "Yes, as much time was spent" and "No, not as much time was spent."

Answer choice (D): The argument does not involve the background of the researchers and the projects they work on, only what they should focus on when trying to succeed. Hence, this answer is incorrect. Apply the Variance Test, using opposite answers of "Yes, they are among those trying to develop thinking machines" and "No, they are not among those trying to develop thinking machines."

Answer choice (E): The analogy in the argument is about flying machines that *were* modeled on birds. The possibility that some flying machines failed that were not modeled on birds has no place in the argument. Apply the Variance Test, using opposite answers of "Yes, some failed" and "No, none failed."

CHAPTER SEVENTEEN: CANNOT BE TRUE QUESTIONS

Cannot Be True Questions ████████████████

In Cannot Be True questions your task is to identify the answer choice that cannot be true or is most weakened by the information in the argument.

As discussed in Chapter Three, Cannot Be True questions are the sole member of the Fourth Question Family. The Fourth Family is very similar to the First Family with the exception of the bar on the arrow. This bar signifies a negative—instead of using the information in the stimulus to prove that one of the answer choices must be true, you must instead prove that one of the answer choices cannot occur, or that it disagrees with the information in the stimulus.

The following rules apply to the Fourth Question Family:

1. Accept the stimulus information and use only it to prove that one of the answer choices cannot occur.

2. If an answer choice contains information that does not appear directly in the stimulus or as a combination of items in the stimulus, then that answer choice could be true, and it is incorrect. The correct answer choice will directly disagree with the stimulus or a consequence of the stimulus.

From an abstract standpoint, Cannot Be True questions can be viewed in two ways:

1. Polar Opposite Must Be True Questions

    Cannot Be True questions are the polar opposite of Must Be True questions: instead of proving an answer choice, you disprove an answer choice.

2. Reverse Weaken Questions

    The information model of the Third Question Family (Weaken) is an arrow with a negative pointing up to the stimulus. The Fourth Family model is the same except that the arrow points down at the answer choices. From this perspective, Cannot Be True questions are reverse Weaken questions: use the information in the stimulus to attack one of the answers.

Fourth Family
Information
Model:

The First and Fourth Family information models are identical except for the negative bar on the Fourth Family.

Question types
that appear
infrequently, such
as Evaluate the
Argument and
Cannot Be True,
tend to consume
more time
because students
are not used to
seeing those
types of
questions.

Both question descriptions are similar, and neither sounds very difficult. In practice, however, Cannot Be True questions are tricky because the concept of an answer choice being possibly true and therefore wrong is counterintuitive. This type of question appears infrequently, but the test makers are savvy and they know Cannot questions can catch test takers off-guard and consume more time than the average question. When you encounter a Cannot Be True question, you must mentally prepare yourself to eliminate answers that could be true or that are possible, and select the one answer choice that cannot be true or that is impossible.

Fortunately, the stimuli in Cannot Be True questions rarely contain a conclusion (just as in Must Be True and Resolve the Paradox questions). Therefore, you will not need to assess an argument and you can instead focus on the facts at hand.

Cannot Be True questions are worded in a variety of ways. The gist of the question type is to show that an answer cannot follow, and this tasks tends to be expressed in three separate ways:

1. Stating that the answer cannot be true or does not follow.

    Question stem examples:

    > "If the statements above are true, which one of the following CANNOT be true?"

    > "The argument can most reasonably be interpreted as an objection to which one of the following claims?"

    > "The statements above, if true, most seriously undermine which one of the following assertions?"

    > "The information above, if accurate, can best be used as evidence against which one of the following hypotheses?"

When the word
"cannot" is used
in question stems,
it is capitalized.

2. Stating that the answer could be true EXCEPT.

    This construction is frequently used to convey the Cannot Be True concept. If the four incorrect answers could be true, then the one remaining answer must be the opposite, or cannot be true.

    Question stem example:

    > "If all of the claims made above are true, then each of the following could be true EXCEPT: "

3. Stating that the answer choice must be false.

    The phrase "must be false" is functionally identical to "cannot be true." The use of this wording is just one more way for the test makers to present you with unusual phrasing.

    Question stem example:

    > "If the statements above are true, then which one of the following must be false?"

The following LSAT question will be used to fully explore how the question type works. Please take a moment to complete the following question:

1. Sharks have a higher ratio of cartilage mass to body mass than any other organism. They also have a greater resistance to cancer than any other organism. Shark cartilage contains a substance that inhibits tumor growth by stopping the development of a new blood network. In the past 20 years, none of the responses among terminal cancer patients to various therapeutic measures has been more positive than the response among those who consumed shark cartilage.

    If the claims made above are true, then each of the following could be true EXCEPT:

    (A) No organism resists cancer better than sharks
         do, but some resist cancer as well as sharks.
    (B) The organism most susceptible to cancer has a
         higher percentage of cartilage than some
         organisms that are less susceptible to cancer.
    (C) The substance in shark cartilage that inhibits
         tumor growth is found in most organisms.
    (D) In the past 20 years many terminal cancer
         patients have improved dramatically
         following many sorts of therapy
    (E) Some organisms have immune systems more
         efficient than a shark's immune system.

As with most Cannot Be True questions, the stimulus does not contain an argument. Instead, a fact pattern is presented and you are tested on your knowledge of those facts. Let's review each statement, sentence-by-sentence, keeping in mind that in Cannot questions you accept the statements in the stimulus as true:

> Statement: Sharks have a higher ratio of cartilage mass to body mass than any other organism.
>
> This is a very broad, global statement indicating that *no other organism* has a higher ratio of cartilage mass to body mass than sharks.

> Statement: They [sharks] also have a greater resistance to cancer than any other organism.
>
> This is another very broad, global statement indicating that *no other organism* has a greater resistance to cancer than sharks.

> Statement: Shark cartilage contains a substance that inhibits tumor growth by stopping the development of a new blood network.
>
> This statement is narrower, and focuses only on shark cartilage. Since no information is given about the cartilage of other organisms, it is possible that other organisms contain the tumor-inhibiting substance mentioned in this statement.

> Statement: In the past 20 years, none of the responses among terminal cancer patients to various therapeutic measures has been more positive than the response among those who consumed shark cartilage.
>
> This statement is also narrower than the first two, but broader than the last statement. While it is specific in stating that no therapeutic measures have received more positive response than shark cartilage, the statement is limited to the past 20 years and to terminal cancer patients. Note also that just because shark cartilage has received a more positive response than any other therapy does not mean that other therapies were unsuccessful—they could have worked very well but not quite as well as shark cartilage.

Of the four statements above, the first two are global and can never be violated. The last two are possible sources of wrong answers as they are specific enough to eliminate certain statements, but open enough to allow for a variety of others.

The makers of the test love to play with these "edges," and you should make sure that the answer you select directly violates a statement in the stimulus.

Answer choice (A): This is the correct answer. The answer violates the second sentence of the stimulus, where the author indicates that sharks have a "greater resistance to cancer than any other organism." This statement means that no other organisms matches or exceeds the cancer resistance of a shark.

Answer choice (B): This answer focuses on the susceptibility of an organism to cancer. Other than stating that sharks are the least susceptible to cancer (greatest resistance = least susceptibility), we know nothing about cancer susceptibility of any other organism. Hence, this answer is possibly true and therefore incorrect.

Answer choice (C): The third statement in the stimulus notes that shark cartilage contains the inhibiting substance. There is no mention that other organisms do *not* have the substance or that the substance is the primary reason that sharks are cancer resistant. Thus, this answer choice could be true and is incorrect.

Answer choice (D): From the discussion of the fourth statement you know this answer choice could be true. Accordingly, it is incorrect.

Answer choice (E): The stimulus addresses sharks and cancer resistance. Although cancer resistance would logically have some connection to the immune system, cancer resistance is only one aspect of the immune system and therefore other organisms could have an immune system that is overall more efficient than the shark's immune system. Consequently, this answer choice is possibly true and therefore incorrect.

Two Notable Stimulus Scenarios

Although Cannot Be True questions are not associated with any particular type of stimulus scenario, two concepts we have discussed appear with some frequency: numbers and percentages, and conditional relationships. Both areas can cause confusion, so let's examine each in more detail:

1. Numbers and Percentages

   As detailed in Chapter Fifteen, numbers and percentages can be confusing when they appear on the LSAT, and the test makers know how to exploit certain preconceived notions that students bring with them to the test. In Cannot Be True questions, the stimulus will often supply enough information for you to determine that certain outcomes must occur (for example, increasing market share while the overall market size remains constant results in greater sales). The correct answer then violates this outcome.

2. Conditional Statements

   Many different scenarios can occur in Cannot Be True questions featuring conditional statements, except the following:

   > The sufficient condition occurs, and the necessary condition does not occur.

   Thus, when a conditional statement is made in a Cannot Be True question stimulus, you should actively seek the answer that matches the scenario above.

   Incorrect answers often play upon the possibility that the necessary condition occurs but the sufficient condition does not occur. Those scenarios could occur and are thus incorrect.

Take a look at another Cannot Be True question. Please take a moment to complete the following question:

2. Good students learn more than what their parents and teachers compel them to learn. This requires that these students derive pleasure from the satisfaction of their curiosity, and one cannot experience such pleasure unless one is capable of concentrating on a topic so intently that one loses track of one's own identity.

   If the statements above are true, each of the following could also be true EXCEPT:

   (A) Some people who are capable of becoming so absorbed in a topic that they lose track of their own identities are nevertheless incapable of deriving pleasure from the satisfaction of their curiosity.
   (B) Most good students do not derive pleasure from the satisfaction of their curiosity.
   (C) Many people who derive pleasure simply from the satisfaction of their curiosity are not good students.
   (D) Some people who are not good students derive pleasure from losing track of their own identities.
   (E) Most people who are capable of becoming so absorbed in a topic that they lose track of their own identities are not good students.

The stimulus in this problem contains a set of interrelated conditional statements:

GS = good student
LM = learn more than what their parents and teachers compel them to learn
DP = derive pleasure from the satisfaction of their curiosity
CC = capable of concentrating on a topic so intently that one loses track of one's own identity

1. First sentence: GS $\longrightarrow$ LM

2. Second sentence, first part: LM $\longrightarrow$ DP

3. Second sentence, second part: DP $\longrightarrow$ CC

Chain of all statements: GS $\longrightarrow$ LM $\longrightarrow$ DP $\longrightarrow$ CC

Remember, when you encounter Cannot Be True questions featuring conditional relationships, actively seek the answer that violates the precept that when the sufficient condition occurs the necessary condition must also occur. In this problem, that situation is found in answer choice (B).

Answer choice (A): This answer describes a situation where the necessary condition in the second part of the second sentence occurs and the sufficient condition does not. Since the occurrence of the necessary condition does not make the sufficient condition occur, this scenario could happen and this answer is therefore incorrect. This type of answer is a frequent wrong answer in Cannot Be True questions featuring conditional relationships.

Answer choice (B): This is the correct answer. The chain of statements in the stimulus shows that every good student derives pleasure from the satisfaction of their curiosity. Thus, it cannot be true that "Most good students do not derive pleasure from the satisfaction of their curiosity."

Answer choice (C): Like answer choice (A), this answer describes a situation where the necessary condition occurs and the sufficient condition does not. This time the scenario references the relationship in the first sentence.

Answer choice (D): The stimulus only offers information about good students; no information is given about people who are *not* good students. Accordingly, we can make no judgment about these individuals, and the answer is incorrect.

Answer choices that offer groups that do not meet the sufficient condition are also popular wrong answers in Cannot Be True questions featuring conditional reasoning.

Answer choice (E): Like answer choices (A) and (C), this answer describes a situation where the necessary condition occurs and the sufficient condition does not. Unlike those two answers, you must rely on your understanding of the chain of all statements in order to understand why this answer is possible. Because the "capable of becoming so absorbed in a topic that they lose track of their own identities" is the necessary condition for being a good student, it is possible that most people who meet this condition are still not good students. Again, avoid Mistaken Reversals!

Overall, Cannot Be True questions appear infrequently but they can be troublesome because of their unusual information structure. Whenever you encounter a Cannot question, focus on searching for the answer that does not follow or the answer that is disproved by the stimulus.

Cannot Be True Question Review

In Cannot Be True questions your task is to identify the answer choice that cannot be true or is most weakened by the information in the argument. Answers that could be true are incorrect. The stimulus in a Cannot Be True question rarely contains a conclusion.

For the Fourth Question Family, the following rules apply:

1. Accept the stimulus information and use only it to prove that one of the answer choices cannot occur.
2. If an answer choice contains information that does not appear directly in the stimulus or as a combination of items in the stimulus, then that answer choice could be true, and it is incorrect. The correct answer choice will directly disagree with the stimulus or a consequence of the stimulus.

Cannot Be True questions can be worded in a variety of ways, but the gist of the question type is to show that an answer cannot follow, and this tends to be executed in three separate ways:

1. Stating that the answer cannot be true or does not follow.
2. Stating that the answer could be true EXCEPT.
3. Stating that the answer choice must be false.

Cannot Be True questions are tricky because the concept of an answer choice being possibly true and therefore wrong is counterintuitive. When you encounter a Cannot Be True question, you must mentally prepare yourself to eliminate answers that could be true or are possible, and select the one answer choice that cannot be true or is impossible.

In problems that revolve around numbers and percentages, the stimulus will often supply enough information for you to determine that certain outcomes must occur. The correct answer then violates this outcome.

In problems featuring conditional statements, many different scenarios can occur, except the following:

> The sufficient condition occurs, and the necessary condition does not occur.

Thus, when a conditional statement is made in a Cannot Be True question stimulus, you should actively seek the answer that matches the scenario above.

The following questions are drawn from actual LSATs. Please complete the problem set and review the answer key and explanations. *Answers on Page 471*

1. For a ten-month period, the total monthly sales of new cars within the country of Calistan remained constant. During this period the monthly sales of new cars manufactured by Marvel Automobile Company doubled, and its share of the new car market within Calistan increased correspondingly. At the end of this period, emission standards were imposed on new cars sold within Calistan. During the three months following this imposition, Marvel Automobile Company's share of the Calistan market declined substantially even though its monthly sales within Calistan remained constant at the level reached in the last month of the ten-month period.

If the statements above are true, which one of the following CANNOT be true?

(A) The total monthly sales within Calistan of new cars by companies other than Marvel Automobile Company decreased over the three months following the imposition of the emission standards.

(B) Over the three months before the imposition of the emission standards, the combined market share of companies other than Marvel Automobile Company selling new cars in Calistan decreased.

(C) If the emission standards had not been imposed, Marvel Automobile Company would have lost an even larger share of the number of new cars sold in Calistan than, in fact, it did.

(D) A decrease in the total monthly sales of new cars within Calistan will occur if the emission standards remain in effect.

(E) Since the imposition of the emission standards, Marvel Automobile Company's average profit on each new car sold within Calistan has increased.

2. Two things are true of all immoral actions. First, if they are performed in public, they offend public sensibilities. Second, they are accompanied by feelings of guilt.

If all the statements above are true, then which one of the following must be false?

(A) Some immoral actions that are not performed in public are not accompanied by feelings of guilt.

(B) Immoral actions are wrong solely by virtue of being accompanied by feelings of guilt.

(C) Some actions that offend public sensibilities if they are performed in public are not accompanied by feelings of guilt.

(D) Some actions that are accompanied by feelings of guilt are not immoral, even if they frequently offend public sensibilities.

(E) Every action performed in public that is accompanied by feelings of guilt is immoral.

Cannot Be True Question Problem Set Answer Key

All answer keys in this book indicate the source of the question by giving the month and year the LSAT was originally administered, the Logical Reasoning section number, and the question number within that section. Each LSAT has two Logical Reasoning sections, and so the Section 1 and Section 2 designators will refer to the first or second Logical Reasoning section in the test, not the physical section number of the booklet.

Question #1. Cannot-#%. June 2000 LSAT, Section 1, #15. The correct answer choice is (A)

This question is a repeat of a question that appeared on the March 1985 LSAT (remember, on the LSAT past is prologue). The topic of the original question was also the car market, but the company in question was called Superb Automobile. Several of the answer choices, including the correct answer, were virtually identical to the answers in this problem.

Let us first review the facts given in the stimulus:

Statement: For a ten-month period, the total monthly sales of new cars within the country of Calistan remained constant.

The wording of this statement should alert you that numbers and percentages in the form of market share ("monthly sales...remained constant") may be an issue in this problem. Note that the statement is a simple fact; no explanation is given for why the total sales stayed constant.

Statement: During this period the monthly sales of new cars manufactured by Marvel Automobile Company doubled, and its share of the new car market within Calistan increased correspondingly.

If total monthly sales of new cars remains constant and Marvel's sales doubled, then Marvel's share of the new car market must also have doubled. Again, no explanation for Marvel's increase is given; the increase is just stated as a fact.

Statement: At the end of this period, emission standards were imposed on new cars sold within Calistan.

Imposing new emission standards serves as a chronology marker in this stimulus. Again, no explanation is given for why the new standards were imposed.

Statement: During the three months following this imposition, Marvel Automobile Company's share of the Calistan market declined substantially even though its monthly sales within Calistan remained constant at the level reached in the last month of the ten-month period.

This sentence is the key to the stimulus. From a numbers and percentages standpoint, we are given two pieces of related information: during the three months after the emissions standards were imposed, Marvel's monthly sales of new cars within Calistan remained constant at the pre-standards level, and at the same time Marvel's share of the market declined. From the discussion in Chapter Seventeen, we know that if sales remain constant but the share represented by those sales decreased, then the overall sales in the market *must* have increased. For example:

	pre-Standards	post-Standards
Marvel's Monthly New Car Sales	10	10
Total Monthly New Car Sales in Calistan	100	200
Marvel's Market Share	10%	5%

The other important part of this sentence is what is *not* said. No cause is given for Marvel's decline, and you cannot assume that the new emissions standards are the cause of the decline (causal indicators are needed to convey causality, and none are present in this stimulus). Remember, one error of causal reasoning is to assume that because two things occur in sequence that one caused the other. There could be many different explanations for Marvel's decline other than the new emission standards. For example, Marvel could have raised their car prices or perhaps Marvel received some negative publicity about the quality of their cars. Regardless, the problem is clearly designed to test whether you will fall into the trap of assuming that the new emission standards caused Marvel to lose market share, so read carefully and do not fill in the "spaces" in the stimulus.

Answer choice (A): This is the correct answer. As shown in the discussion of the last sentence of the stimulus, in the three months after the imposition of the emissions standards, the total monthly car sales in Calistan must have risen, and since Marvel's monthly car sales remained constant, we can conclude that the sales of other car makers must have *risen*. Since this answer claims they decreased, this answer cannot be true and is correct.

Answer choice (B): This answer is possibly true. The stimulus indicates that Marvel doubled sales and market share in the ten months prior to the imposition of the emissions standards, and it is possible that in the three months prior to the implementation of the new standards the market share of the other companies decreased.

Some students look at this answer and assume that it must be true based on the first two sentences of the stimulus. But that judgment assumes that Marvel's growth during the ten-month period was constant, a circumstance never stated by the author. It would be consistent with the stimulus if Marvel doubled sales in the first month and then remained constant for the remaining nine months.

Answer choice (C): No reason is given for Marvel's loss of market share (or alternately, the increased sales of other manufacturers), so it is possible that the new emission standards actually decreased Marvel's loss of market share (or alternately, the emission standards limited the increase in sales of the other manufacturers). Remember, no explanation is given for the situation after the imposition of the emission standards, so whatever happened in the absence of the standards could always be true.

Answer choice (D): This answer could occur because Calistan's future car sales could fall due to a variety of causes (including the emission standards). This is true regardless of whether the emissions standards remain in force because we know nothing of the effect of the standards.

Answer choice (E): No information is given about *profit* in the stimulus, so this answer choice could be true.

Question #2. Cannot-SN. October 2003 LSAT, Section 1, #7. The correct answer choice is (A)

At this point you should have memorized the Primary Objectives and know how to apply them to the problem. This question is an excellent example of Primary Objective #4: "Read closely and know precisely what the author said. Do not generalize!"

Most students make the mistake of thinking that both statements about immoral actions refer to actions performed in public, but this is incorrect. Instead, only the first statement refers to actions in public; the second statement refers to *all* immoral actions, public or not. Take a look at the two statements:

The first statement regarding immoral actions indicates that "if they are performed in public, they offend public sensibilities." The correct diagram for this statement is:

IP = immoral actions performed in public
O = offend public sensibilities

$$IP \longrightarrow O$$

The relationship above is restricted to public performances. No information is given about non-public performances.

The next statement in the stimulus is "second, they are accompanied by feelings of guilt." This statement can cause problems because most student assume that the "they" refers to immoral actions performed in public. But read the stimulus carefully—the first sentence states that two things are true of *immoral actions*, and the "they" in the last sentence refers to those actions in the first sentence. Because the last sentence does not reference actions in public, it is a broader statement that addresses *all* immoral actions:

I = immoral actions
G = accompanied by feelings of guilt

$$I \longrightarrow G$$

Thus, the two conditional statements in the stimulus do not have the same sufficient condition. Again, read carefully in order to avoid the error of assuming the two statements reference the same condition.

Answer choice (A): This is the correct answer. Answer choice (A) is correct because *any* immoral action is accompanied by feelings of guilt, and (A) improperly tries to assert that some immoral actions are not accompanied by feelings of guilt. Note how this answer plays off the second statement—the exact statement that many students are likely to misunderstand. If you interpret the second statement to apply to public actions, you will mistakenly think answer choice (A) could occur.

Answer choice (B): The stimulus does not address the "wrongness" of immoral actions. Thus, this answer could possibly be true and is therefore incorrect.

Answer choice (C): This answer is tricky. Look carefully at the wording of the answer—is immorality mentioned? No, it is not, and thus neither sufficient condition in the stimulus can apply. The statement in this answer choice is possible because a public action that offends public sensibilities does not have to be an immoral action, and so a public action that offends public sensibilities does not have to be accompanied by feelings of guilt.

For the purposes of discussion, say that the public action in question is flag burning. Such an action performed in public could offend the public, but since we do not know if it immoral according to the answer, the flag burner does not have to experience feelings of guilt. This conforms to the scenario described in answer choice (C).

Answer choice (D): This answer choice tests your knowledge a Mistaken Reversal. Remember, any Mistaken Reversal is an error because it is not *certain* that the sufficient condition must occur when the necessary condition occurs. So, if the necessary condition occurs, the sufficient condition may or may not occur. This answer states that the necessary condition of the second statement occurs and that the sufficient does not. This outcome is possible under any single-arrow conditional scenario. In concrete terms, just because some actions are accompanied by feelings of guilt does not mean they are immoral, so this answer choice could occur and hence is wrong.

Answer choice (E): This answer tests the flip side of possibilities that could occur under a conditional statement. In this situation, the necessary condition of the second statement occurs and the sufficient condition also occurs. Since a Mistaken Reversal *might* be true unless otherwise stated, this answer could occur and is incorrect.

Answer choices (D) and (E) present a dynamic one-two punch: answer choice (D) tests to see if you understand that the occurrence of the necessary condition does not automatically lead to the occurrence of the sufficient condition, and answer choice (E) tests to see if you understand that the occurrence of the necessary condition could lead to the occurrence of the sufficient condition.

CHAPTER EIGHTEEN: POINT AT ISSUE QUESTIONS

Point at Issue Questions

Last but not least, we arrive at Point at Issue questions, the thirteenth and final question type on the LSAT. Point at Issue stimuli are comprised of two speakers who disagree about an issue that is generally ethical or decision-oriented in nature, not factual. The question stem directs you to choose the answer that describes the point of disagreement between the two speakers, or to identify a statement that the two speakers would disagree is true.

Point at Issue questions are a variant of Must Be True questions and are part of the First Family Question type. Like all First Family questions, you can only use the information in the stimulus to evaluate the answer choices. Accordingly, the Fact Test applies to Point at Issue questions, with a modification accounting for the two speaker construction. We will discuss this idea in more detail momentarily.

The question stem of a Point at Issue question typically refers to a disagreement or the point at issue between the two speakers.

Question stem examples:

"Which one of the following most accurately expresses the point at issue between Tom and Mary?"

"Which one of the following most accurately represents what is at issue between Jorge and Ruth?"

"The dialogue above lends the most support to the claim that Sherrie and Fran disagree with each other about which one of the following statements?"

"On the basis of their statement, Logan and Mendez are committed to disagreeing over whether"

First Family
Information
Model:

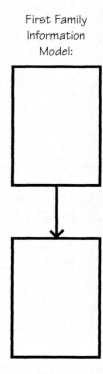

Although some companies claim that Point at Issue questions have appeared on the LSAT only recently, these questions can be traced all the way back to the beginning of the modern LSAT era in 1991.

Incorrect Answers in Point at Issue Questions

Finding the correct answer in most Point at Issue questions requires you to examine the conclusion of each speaker. But, because Point at Issue questions require you to select a specific type of statement, several unique forms of incorrect answers tend to appear in these problems.

Point at Issue stimuli almost always contain two separate arguments. Because you must assess more than one argument, these questions are generally difficult.

1. Ethical versus Factual Situations

    When a stimulus addresses an issue that is ethical in nature, answer choices that are factual in nature cannot be true. For example, imagine that two speakers are having a disagreement about whether doctors should inform their patients of a terminal illness. An answer such as the following would clearly be incorrect:

    > Every medical school includes ethics training in their curriculum.

    This answer, factual in nature, cannot address the underlying judgment issues that form an ethical or moral debate.

    The reverse is also true: when a stimulus addresses an issue that is factual in nature, answer choices that are ethical in nature cannot be true. However, disagreements over facts occur infrequently because they are generally easy for students to spot. For example, consider the following abbreviated example:

    > Damon: World War I began in 1910.
    >
    > Tania: No, World War I began in 1914.

    The gist of a disagreement is clear: did the war begin in 1910 or 1914? (1914 is correct). In a factual disagreement issue like this example, an answer choice that addresses an ethical issue (such as "should nations go to war?") would be incorrect.

2. Dual Agreement or Dual Disagreement

    Often, incorrect answer choices will supply statements that *both* speakers will agree with, or that both speakers will disagree with. These answer choices are typically quite attractive because they raise issues that are addressed in the stimulus and therefore they require some analysis. Remember, just because both speakers discuss the issue does not mean that it is an issue about which the two would disagree.

3. The View of One Speaker is Unknown

Another crafty trick used by the test makers is to create an answer where the view of only one of the speakers is known. In these instances the view of the speaker is unknown because the speaker's comments did not address the issue in the answer choice. Since the correct answer must contain a point of disagreement, these "one unknown" answers are always incorrect since there is no way to determine that the other speaker disagrees.

The Agree/Disagree Test™

Because of the specific nature of the correct answer choice, you can double-check answers by using the Agree/Disagree Test™:

> The correct answer must produce responses where one speaker would say "I agree, the statement is correct" and the other speaker would say, "I disagree, the statement is incorrect." If those two responses are not produced, then the answer is incorrect.

The Agree/Disagree Test crystallizes the essence of Point at Issue questions by forcing you to concretely identify the elements that determine the correct answer. Because the correct answer to a Point at Issue question can always be proven by referring to the viewpoints stated in the stimulus, the Agree/Disagree Test is actually a variation of the Fact Test expressly created for Point at Issue questions.

After trying the Agree/Disagree Test, some students become enamored of the technique and want to apply it to every answer choice. This is an overuse of the technique! Like other "litmus tests" for answer choices (such as the Assumption Negation Technique and the Variance Test), the Agree/Disagree Test is designed to either confirm you have selected the correct answer choice or to decide between two or three remaining answer choices. Applying the Agree/Disagree Test to every answer choice will produce the correct answer, but the process will take too much time. Use the Test judiciously.

Only four question types allow for a definitive confirmation once you have selected an answer:

Assumption questions—use the Assumption Negation Technique.

Justify questions—use the Justify Formula.

Evaluate the Argument questions—use the Variance Test.

Point at Issue questions—use the Agree/Disagree Test.

Consider the following problem:

1. Shanna: Owners of any work of art, simply by
    virtue of ownership, ethically have the right to
    destroy that artwork if they find it morally or
    aesthetically distasteful, or if caring for it
    becomes inconvenient.

    Jorge: Ownership of unique artworks, unlike
    ownership of other kinds of objects, carries
    the moral right to possess but not to destroy.
    A unique work of art with aesthetic or
    historical value belongs to posterity and so
    must be preserved, whatever the personal
    wishes of its legal owner.

    On the basis of their statements, Shanna and Jorge
    are committed to disagreeing about the truth of
    which one of the following statements?

    (A) Anyone who owns a portrait presenting his or
         her father in an unflattering light would for
         that reason alone be ethically justified in
         destroying it.
    (B) People who own aesthetically valuable works
         of art have no moral obligation to make
         them available for public viewing.
    (C) Valuable paintings by well-known artists are
         seldom intentionally damaged or destroyed
         by their owners.
    (D) If a piece of sculpture is not unique, its owner
         has no ethical obligation to preserve it if
         doing so proves burdensome.
    (E) It is legally permissible for a unique and
         historically valuable mural to be destroyed
         by its owner if he or she tires of it.

Shanna argues that ownership of art conveys absolute power to the owner, and such power includes and allows for the destruction of artwork for any reason. Jorge asserts that ownership of artwork carries certain restrictions when the art is unique, has aesthetic value, or has historical value, regardless of the wishes of the owner. This is clearly an ethical disagreement in which the speakers disagree on what rights ownership conveys to the owner. The question stem asks you to select a statement about which the two speakers will disagree, which is not necessarily the same as identifying the point at issue.

As mentioned in this chapter, certain types of incorrect answers tend to appear in Point at issue questions:

Because the argument revolves around an ethical issue, wrong answers will often bring up factual issues. Answer choices (C) and (E) are two such answers. Answer choice (C) states that valuable paintings are seldom destroyed by their owners. Whether or not this occurs is a factual issue that can be determined by examining records, etc. Answer choice (E) discusses the legal permissibility of destroying a valuable mural. Whether or not it is legally permissible to destroy the mural is also a factual issue, not a moral issue.

Other wrong answer choices will supply statements that both speakers would agree with, or that both speakers would disagree with. Answer choice (D) is incorrect because both speakers would agree with the statement. Shanna would agree because her ownership beliefs allow for the destruction of any owned artwork. Jorge would agree because the sculpture in question is not unique, and thus does not meet the qualifications Jorge imposed in his argument. If both speakers have the same opinion about an answer choice, then that answer choice must be wrong in a Point at Issue question.

Occasionally the LSAT contains a question that asks you to identify a statement that both speakers agree on. These are known as "Point of Agreement" questions.

With the elimination of answer choices (C), (D), and (E), only answers (A) and (B) remain.

Answer choice (A): This is the correct answer because Shanna would agree with the statement and Jorge would disagree with the statement. The key to answer choice (A) is the phrase "for that reason alone." According to Shanna, ownership of the portrait automatically allows the owner to destroy the artwork for any reason. Thus, disliking the portrait is sufficient justification for destruction. However, for Jorge the art would also have to be proven non-unique, non-aesthetically valuable, and non-historically valuable before he would justify its destruction. Thus, answer choice (A) passes the Agree/Disagree Test where one speaker says "I agree, the statement is correct" regarding the statement and the other speaker says, "I disagree, the statement is incorrect" regarding the answer choice.

Answer choice (B): This answer is incorrect because it discusses the obligation to make artworks available for public viewing, which is not mentioned in the stimulus.

Let us continue examining answer types in Point at Issue questions. Please take a moment to complete the following problem:

2. Consumer advocate: Tropical oils are high in saturated fats, which increase the risk of heart disease. Fortunately, in most prepared food tropical oils can be replaced by healthier alternatives without noticeably affecting taste. Therefore, intensive publicity about the disadvantage of tropical oils will be likely to result in dietary changes that will diminish many people's risk of developing heart disease.

Nutritionist: The major sources of saturated fat in the average North American diet are meat, poultry, and dairy products, not tropical oils. Thus, focusing attention on the health hazards of tropical oils would be counterproductive, because it would encourage people to believe that more substantial dietary changes are unnecessary.

Which one of the following is a point at issue between the nutritionist and the consumer advocate?

(A) whether a diet that regularly includes large quantities of tropical oil can increase the risk of heart disease

(B) whether intensive publicity campaigns can be effective as a means of changing people's eating habits

(C) whether more people in North America would benefit from reducing the amount of meat they consume than would benefit from eliminating tropical oils from their diets

(D) whether some people's diets could be made significantly healthier if they replaced all tropical oils with vegetable oils that are significantly lower in saturated fat

(E) whether conducting a publicity campaign that, by focusing on the health hazards of tropical oils, persuades people to replace such oils with healthier alternatives is a good public-health strategy

The consumer advocate argues that publicity about tropical oils would be beneficial since it would persuade people to reduce their use of tropical oils for the better. The nutritionist argues that since tropical oils are not the primary source of saturated fat in the average diet, focusing attention on the hazards of tropical oils would be counterproductive because it would lead people to believe that they had changed their diets sufficiently.

Again, several answer choices contain statements that both speakers would agree with. Answer choices (A), (B), and (D) contain statements where both speakers would say, "I agree, the statement is correct."

One type of wrong answer that you have not yet encountered involves statements where the opinion of one of the speakers is unknown. Answer choice (C) contains a statement that the nutritionist would agree with, but the consumer advocate's position is unknown. The consumer advocate did not address the subject of meat in the diet, and since we cannot determine that the two speakers would definitely disagree, answer choice (C) is incorrect.

At this point, having definitively eliminated answer choices (A) through (D), you could feel somewhat comfortable that answer choice (E) has merit. But, most students are caught off-guard because (E) appears to address a seemingly irrelevant issue.

In answer choice (E), the consumer advocate would agree with the statement and the nutritionist would disagree with the statement. Thus, answer choice (E) passes the Agree/Disagree Test and is correct. This answer surprises many students because they felt the disagreement was over fat in the diet. But let's re-examine the conclusion of each speaker, with italics indicating the real disagreement:

> The number of Point at Issue questions varies considerably from LSAT to LSAT. For example, the October 2003 LSAT did not contain any Point at Issue questions. The June 2004 LSAT contained three Point at Issue questions (plus a Point of Agreement question).

Consumer advocate's conclusion: Therefore, *intensive publicity* about the disadvantage of tropical oils will be likely to result in dietary changes that will diminish many people's risk of developing heart disease.

Nutritionist's conclusion: Thus, *focusing attention on the health hazards* of tropical oils would be counterproductive, because it would encourage people to believe that more substantial dietary changes are unnecessary.

Both conclusions address the focus of attention or publicity, and a glance through the answer choices shows that only answer choice (E) addresses a similar topic. Remember, when a conclusion is present you *must* identify it regardless of the type of question!

Point at Issue Question Review

Point at Issue stimuli are comprised of two speakers who disagree about an issue that is generally ethical or decision-oriented in nature, not factual. The question stem directs you to choose the answer that describes the point of disagreement between the two speakers, or to identify the statement that the two speakers would disagree is true.

Point at Issue questions are a variant of Must Be True questions and are part of the First Family Question type.

Because Point at Issue questions require you to select a specific type of statement, several unique forms of *incorrect* answer choices tend to appear in these problems.

1. Ethical versus Factual Situations

2. Dual Agreement or Dual Disagreement

3. The View of One Speaker is Unknown

Because of the specific nature of the correct answer choice, you can double-check answers by using the Agree/Disagree Test™:

> The correct answer must produce responses where one speaker would say "I agree, the statement is correct" and the other speaker would say, "I disagree, the statement is incorrect." If those two responses are not produced, then the answer is incorrect.

The Agree/Disagree Test crystallizes the essence of Point at Issue questions by forcing you to concretely identify the elements that determine the correct answer.

The following questions are drawn from actual LSATs. Please complete the problem set and review the answer key and explanations. *Answers on Page 485*

1. Hazel: Faster and more accurate order processing would help our business. To increase profits, we should process orders electronically rather than manually, because customers' orders will then go directly to all relevant parties.

    Max: We would lose money if we started processing orders electronically. Most people prefer to interact with human beings when placing orders. If we switch to electronic order processing, our business will appear cold and inhuman, and we will attract fewer customers.

    Hazel and Max disagree over whether

    (A) electronic order processing is faster and more accurate than is manual order processing
    (B) faster and more accurate order processing would be financially beneficial to their business
    (C) switching to electronic order processing would be financially beneficial to their business
    (D) their business has an obligation to be as profitable as possible
    (E) electronic order processing would appear cold and inhuman to most of their customers

2. Councilperson X: We have an obligation to help ensure that electricity rates are the lowest possible. Since the proposed design for a new generating station would clearly allow for the lowest rates, it must be the design we endorse if we agree that we have no choice but to approve construction of a new plant.

    Councilperson Y: Helping to ensure the lowest electricity rates is not the council's only job; we also have an obligation not to lower the quality of life of our community. A plant of the type specified by the design would damage our community's air quality to such an extent that the benefit of lower rates would be outweighed.

    Which one of the following is an issue about which the two councilpersons disagree?

    (A) The council should recommend the building of a new generating station.
    (B) It is the council's responsibility to improve the community's quality of life.
    (C) A plant of the type specified by the design in question would damage the air quality of the community.
    (D) If a new generating station is to be built, the council should endorse a plant of the type specified by the design in question.
    (E) A plant of the type specified by the design in question would allow for the lowest electricity rates.

3. Franklin: It is inconsistent to pay sports celebrities ten times what Nobel laureates are paid. Both have rare talents and work hard.

   Tomeka: What you've neglected to consider is that unlike Nobel laureates, sports celebrities earn millions of dollars for their employers in the form of gate receipts and TV rights.

   Franklin's and Tomeka's statements provide the most support for holding that they disagree about the truth of which one of the following?

   (A) Nobel laureates should be taken more seriously.
   (B) Nobel laureates should be paid more than sports celebrities.
   (C) Sports celebrities and Nobel laureates work equally hard for their employers.
   (D) There is no rational basis for the salary difference between sports celebrities and Nobel laureates.
   (E) The social contributions made by sports celebrities should be greater than they currently are.

4. Lea: Contemporary art has become big business. Nowadays art has less to do with self-expression than with making money. The work of contemporary artists is utterly bereft of spontaneity and creativity, as a visit to any art gallery demonstrates.

   Susan: I disagree. One can still find spontaneous, innovative new artwork in most of the smaller, independent galleries.

   Lea's and Susan's remarks provide the most support for holding that they disagree about whether

   (A) large galleries contain creative artwork
   (B) most galleries contain some artwork that lacks spontaneity and creativity
   (C) contemporary art has become big business
   (D) some smaller art galleries still exhibit creative new artwork
   (E) contemporary art, in general, is much less concerned with self-expression than older art is

Point at Issue Question Problem Set Answer Key

All answer keys in this book indicate the source of the question by giving the month and year the LSAT was originally administered, the Logical Reasoning section number, and the question number within that section. Each LSAT has two Logical Reasoning sections, and so the Section 1 and Section 2 designators will refer to the first or second Logical Reasoning section in the test, not the physical section number of the booklet.

Question #1. PI. June 2002 LSAT, Section 2, #7. The correct answer choice is (C)

Hazel argues that because electronically processed orders go directly to all relevant parties (as opposed to manual processing), profits will increase. Max argues that money will be lost if orders are processed electronically because the dehumanizing effect of electronic order-taking will lead to fewer customers. The conclusion of each speaker's argument illustrates the disagreement (italics added):

Hazel's conclusion: "To *increase profits*, we should process orders electronically rather than manually."

Max's conclusion: "We would *lose money* if we started processing orders electronically."

Although this question is considered relatively easy, you must read carefully to avoid being drawn to cleverly worded incorrect answers.

Answer choice (A): Hazel agrees with the statement since she compares electronic processing and manual processing in her argument. But Max's position is unknown—he does not directly address the issue, and instead focuses on the lack of customer service involved in electronic order-taking.

Answer choice (B): This answer is tricky, and the attractive nature of the answer works as a well-placed trap as this wrong answer appears just before the correct answer (remember—read all five answer choices!). Hazel clearly agrees with the statement since she makes virtually the same assertion in the first sentence of her argument. Max's position is unknown since he does not comment on the speed and accuracy of order processing. Since his position is unknown, this answer is automatically incorrect.

Answer choice (C): This is the correct answer. As highlighted in the two conclusions, the disagreement is about whether electronic order-taking would help the bottom line of the company.

Answer choice (D): Neither speaker addresses the topic of whether their business has an *obligation* to be profitable, only whether electronic ordering would help profitability.

Answer choice (E): Max would likely agree with this statement (it's not certain he would agree since he says the business would attract fewer customers and this answer choice uses the word "most," which is a bit strong). Regardless, Hazel does not mention the effect of the ordering system on customers, and since her viewpoint is unknown, this answer must be incorrect.

Question #2. PI. December 2002 LSAT, Section 1, #23. The correct answer choice is (D)

This question is more challenging than the previous question. Councilperson X's argument is that if a generating plant is to be built, the proposed design should be used since that design allows for the lowest rates. Councilperson Y's argument is that the proposed design would create such poor air quality that the benefits of the lower rates would be outweighed. Like the previous problem, the conclusion of each speaker's argument is critical:

> X's conclusion: "*It must be the design we endorse* if we agree that we have no choice but to approve construction of a new plant."

Y's argument is a bit more difficult to analyze because the conclusion is left unstated. Y's implicit conclusion is that *the proposed plant design should not be used* since the negatives of the proposed plant would outweigh the benefits.

Answer choice (A): This is the most attractive wrong answer, and about one in five students select this answer. Councilperson X's statement makes it clear that there is no certainty regarding the council's actions: "*if we agree that* we have no choice but to approve construction of a new plant." Hence, X's position on whether the council should recommend a new station is at best uncertain. The answer choice is also problematic because it does not specify the "proposed design." Both speakers refer specifically to the new design, whereas this answer choice refers to "a new generating station" and not necessarily a new station with the proposed design.

Answer choice (B): Councilperson Y agrees with this statement, as indicated in Y's second sentence. However, X's position on this statement is uncertain (no mention of quality of life is made), so this answer is incorrect.

Answer choice (C): Similar to answer choice (B), councilperson Y agrees with this statement, as indicated in the second half of Y's first sentence. However, X's position on this statement is uncertain (no mention of air quality is made), and thus this answer is incorrect.

Answer choice (D): This is the correct answer. Using the Agree/Disagree Test, Councilperson X would agree with the statement whereas Councilperson Y would disagree with the statement.

Answer choice (E): Councilperson X agrees with this statement, as indicated in X's second sentence. Councilperson Y's position on this statement is less certain. Y appears to agree with the statement, although a case can be made that Y's opening comments simply indicate that searching for low rates is not the only job the council has. Regardless, there is no disagreement present and this answer is incorrect.

Point at Issue Question Problem Set Answer Key

Question #3. PI. October 1999 LSAT, Section 2, #16. The correct answer choice is (D)

Franklin's argument is that since sports celebrities and Nobel laureates both have rare talents and work hard, sports celebrities should not be paid ten times as much. Tomeka responds that sports celebrities earn more for their employers than do Nobel laureates. Tomeka's statement is clearly meant to provide a reason for the salary difference, and from that we can infer that Tomeka disagrees with Franklin's conclusion.

The questions in this problem set get progressively harder, and the difficulty in this problem results from two challenging incorrect answer choices. Remember, just because the disagreement is easy to characterize does not mean that the question will be easy. The test makers always have the ability to create truly difficult answers.

Answer choice (A): Neither speaker addresses the issue of whether Nobel laureates should be "taken more seriously." In that same vein, it would be a mistake to equate salary with seriousness, as in a lesser salary means Nobel laureates are taken less seriously. Further, do not equate a *lower* salary with a *low* salary: Nobel laureates could make millions of dollars a year, but the sports celebrities simply make much more.

Answer choice (B): This is the most commonly selected wrong answer. The key word in the answer choice is "more." Franklin makes no assertion or implication that Nobel laureates should make *more* than celebrities. Instead, his argument makes the case that sports celebrities should not be paid ten times the pay of Nobel laureates.

Answer choice (C): Franklin would agree with this statement, but Tomeka makes no mention of working hard—instead, she only mentions that sports celebrities *earn* millions of dollars for their employers. Since Tomeka's view on the statement is unknown, this answer is incorrect.

Answer choice (D): This is the correct answer. Franklin notes that the salary disparity is inconsistent and both have talent and work hard. He would agree with the statement in this answer choice. On the other hand, Tomeka cites a reason for the pay disparity, and she would disagree with the statement. Because the two speakers disagree over the truth of the statement, this is the correct answer.

Answer choice (E): Neither speaker addresses the social contributions of celebrities, and you should not infer that a comparison is made simply because the other group in the discussion is composed of Nobel laureates.

Question #4. PI. June 2001 LSAT, Section 2, #15. The correct answer choice is (D)

Statistically, this is the most difficult question of the chapter, and only about one in three students selects the correct answer. In part, this difficulty rises from the fact that the disagreement identified in the correct answer does not arise from the conclusion, but from the premises of each speaker.

Lea argues that contemporary art is big business and that the work of contemporary artists lacks spontaneity and creativity, and this can be proven by visiting *any* art gallery. Susan counters by stating that spontaneous and creative work is present in most of the smaller, independent galleries, and on that basis she concludes that Lea is incorrect.

Answer choice (A): Both speakers would disagree with this statement, and dual disagreement is grounds for eliminating the answer.

Answer choice (B): This is a difficult answer choice, and one that most students reasonably hold as a Contender. Lea would obviously agree with this statement. Susan's position is less certain, and a large part of the uncertainty revolves around the phase "most galleries" in the answer choice. Susan states that "One can still find spontaneous, innovative new artwork in *most* of the *smaller, independent galleries.*" If smaller, independent galleries make up the vast majority of all galleries, then Susan would likely disagree with the statement in the answer choice. But there is no assurance that smaller, independent galleries make up the majority of all galleries (they could be outnumbered by the larger galleries), and under that circumstance Susan could agree with the statement. Since Susan's position is uncertain, this answer is incorrect.

There is a second issue underlying Susan's statement that has an impact on our assessment of this answer. Susan states that "one can still find" creative artwork in most small galleries. But finding such artwork in those galleries does not exclude the possibility that other artwork in the same gallery lacks spontaneity and creativity. If that were the case, both speakers would agree with the statement.

Answer choice (C): Apply the Agree/Disagree Test: Lea agrees with the statement, but Susan does not comment on whether contemporary art is big business. Her statement that there are smaller, independent galleries is not an implicit admission that the whole field has become overly commercialized. This answer is incorrect because there is no way to know Susan's position, and thus this answer fails the Test.

Answer choice (D): This is the correct answer. Again, the Agree/Disagree Test crystallizes the issue: Susan clearly agrees with the statement whereas Lea, who said that a visit to *any* art gallery shows that contemporary artists utterly lack creativity and spontaneity, disagrees with the statement.

Note that the reference to "new artwork" in the answer choice is important because it eliminates any discussion about older creative and spontaneous artwork that may be in galleries. The quantity indicator "some" also plays a role since it allows for a single example to suffice (see answer choice (B) for the impact a quantity indicator can have).

Answer choice (E): Lea would likely agree with the statement in this answer choice because she states that "nowadays art has less to do with self-expression." Susan's position is again uncertain. Although she states that innovative contemporary artwork is available in galleries, she does not make a comparison between the self-expression of contemporary art and the self-expression of older art. There is no assumption in her argument that spontaneous, innovative new artwork is *not* less concerned with self-expression, let alone "much less."

CHAPTER NINETEEN: PRINCIPLE QUESTIONS

Principle Questions

Principle questions (PR) are not a separate question type but are instead an "overlay" that appears in a variety of question types. For example, there are Strengthen Principle questions (Strengthen-PR), Justify Principle questions (Justify-PR), and Cannot Be True Principle questions (Cannot-PR), among others. In a question stem, the key indicator that the Principle concept is present is the word "principle." Here are several examples of Principle question stems:

> "Which one of the following judgments most closely conforms to the principle above?" (Must-PR)

> "Which one of the following judgments best illustrates the principle illustrated by the argument above?" (Must-PR)

> "The principle above, if established, would justify which one of the following judgments?" (Must-PR)

> "Which one of the following principles most helps to justify the reasoning above?" (Strengthen-PR)

> "The information above most closely conforms to which one of the following principles?" (Strengthen-PR)

> "Which one of the following most accurately expresses the principle underlying the argumentation above?" (Justify-PR)

> "Each of the following principles is logically consistent with the columnist's conclusion EXCEPT:" (Cannot-PR)

The word "proposition" or "precept" can be used in place of "principle."

Be careful of question stems using the word "conform." Sometimes they ask if the *stimulus* conforms (which is a Strengthen-PR question) but other times they ask if the *answer choice* conforms (which is generally a Must-PR question).

A principle is a broad rule that specifies what actions or judgments are correct in certain situations. For example, "Some companies are profitable" is not a principle because no rule is involved and no judgment can be drawn from the statement. "All companies should strive to be profitable" is a principle, and one that can be applied to any company.

The degree of generality of principles can vary considerably, and some are much narrower than others. For example, "Children at Smith Elementary School must wear uniforms" is a principle restricted to children attending Smith. The principle does not apply to a child attending a different school. On the other hand, the principle "Any person of voting age has an obligation to vote" applies to a large number of people regardless of background, education, wealth, etc.

Since a principle is by definition a broad rule (usually conditional in nature), the presence of the Principle indicator serves to broaden the scope of the question. The question becomes more abstract, and you must analyze the problem to identify the underlying relationships. Functionally, you must take a broad, global proposition and apply it in a specific manner, either to the answer choices (as in a Must or Parallel question) or to the stimulus (as in a Strengthen or Justify question). Here is a brief analysis of how this process affects the two question types most likely to appear with a Principle designation:

1. Must Be True Principle Questions

    In these questions you must use the principle presented in *the stimulus* and then apply it to the situation in each answer choice (one principle applied to five situations). Although these are Must Be True questions, the presence of the principle designation broadens the question, and the answer choice can address a scenario not specifically included in the stimulus; your job is to find the answer that follows from the application of the principle. If an answer does not match the principle, it is incorrect.

    Since many, if not all, of the principles in these stimuli are conditional, you will often be able to identify that reasoning and make a quick diagram. If you cannot clearly identify the conditional nature of the principle, create an abstraction of the stimulus similar to one you would create in a Parallel Reasoning question. This approach can be useful since it creates an accurate representation of the principle.

    The classification of these questions can sometimes be difficult for students since the relation of the stimulus to the answer choices is so similar to Parallel Reasoning questions (each answer often features a scenario and topic that is entirely different from that in the stimulus). Remember, both Parallel Reasoning and Must Be True questions are in the First Question Family, and they share many of the same characteristics. In the final analysis, when considering the answer choices, ask yourself, "Does this answer match the attributes of the principle in the stimulus?"

    Now, let us look at an example of this type of question and see how the addition of the Principle concept affects the problem.

Please take a moment to complete the following question:

1. To act responsibly in one's professional capacity, one must act on the basis of information that one has made a reasonable effort to make sure is accurate and complete.

Which one of the following judgments most closely conforms to the principle cited above?

(A) Peggy acted responsibly in ordering new computers for the school last year because they turned out to be needed due to an unexpected increase in enrollment this year.

(B) Mary acted responsibly in firing John, for she first examined the details of his work record and listened to negative reports from some of his supervisors and coworkers.

(C) Toril did not act responsibly in investing the company's money in Twicycled Ink, for, though the investment yielded a large return, she had not investigated the risks associated with that investment.

(D) Conchita did not act responsibly in hiring Helmer to do the company's bookkeeping because Helmer made a mistake that cost the company a lot of money, though he had never been known to make such a mistake in the past.

(E) Jennifer did not act responsibly in deciding where to go on her vacation because, instead of carefully weighing her options, she waited until the last minute and decided on impulse.

Some companies classify Principle questions as a stand-alone question type. This is incorrect; the addition of the principle concept to a question stem is simply a modification, and does not create an entirely new type of question.

The first thing students notice about this question is its length. Like Parallel reasoning questions, Principle questions are often quite lengthy, and this is part of the reason they are challenging.

In this instance the principle appears in the stimulus, and you are required to find the answer choice that most closely follows the principle. By comparing the principle with each answer choice, you can find the answer that best meets the stipulations of the principle.

As you read the stimulus, you should hone in on the conditional nature of the principle ("one *must* act..."):

AR = act responsibly in one's professional capacity
ABI = must act on the basis of information that one has made a reasonable effort to make sure is accurate and complete.

$$AR \longrightarrow ABI$$

Let's take a moment to review the conclusions that can be drawn when you are given a simple conditional statement and additional information:

What you can conclude

1. If the sufficient condition is met in one of the scenarios in the answer choice, then it can be concluded that the necessary condition has occurred.

    A simple conditional statement combined with a premise indicating that the sufficient condition has occurred allows the conclusion that the necessary condition will occur. This is the essence of the Repeat conditional argument form.

2. If the necessary condition is *not* met in one of the scenarios in the answer choice, then it can be concluded that the sufficient condition has not occurred.

    A simple conditional statement combined with a premise indicating that the necessary condition has not occurred allows the conclusion that the sufficient condition will not occur. This is the essence of the contrapositive argument form.

The two conclusions above are the most likely to appear in any given Principle question. The following two conclusions can also be drawn, but they appear less frequently than the conclusions above.

3. If the sufficient condition is *not* met in one of the scenarios in the answer choice, you can conclude that the necessary condition *may or may not* have occurred (to believe otherwise is a Mistaken Negation).

4. If the necessary condition is met in one of the scenarios in the answer choice, you can conclude that the sufficient condition *may or may not* have occurred (to believe otherwise is a Mistaken Reversal).

<u>What you cannot conclude</u>

1. If the sufficient condition is not met in one of the scenarios in the answer choice, you can conclude that the necessary condition has not occurred.

    A simple conditional statement in combination with a premise indicating that the sufficient condition has not occurred does not allows the conclusion that the necessary condition will not occur. This error is the essence of the Mistaken Negation argument form.

2. If the necessary condition is met in one of the scenarios in the answer choice, then you can conclude that the sufficient condition has occurred.

    Given a simple conditional relationship, there is no premise that can be used to conclude that the sufficient condition occurs. To make this error is to make a Mistaken Reversal.

The ideas presented in the discussion above are not new to you—this ground was thoroughly covered in Chapter Six: Conditional Reasoning. The ideas are reintroduced here because many Must-PR questions revolve around the conclusions that can and cannot be drawn from a conditional relationship, and the rate at which students miss these questions is astoundingly high. For example, this question is classified by Law Services as among the hardest of all Logical Reasoning questions.

Given that the first two conclusions described in the *What you can conclude* section are the most likely to appear, let's examine how they would be presented given the principle in this stimulus:

1. If one acts responsibly in one's professional capacity, then one must act on the basis of information that one has made a reasonable effort to make sure is accurate and complete.

2. If one acts on the basis of information that one has *not* made a reasonable effort to make sure is accurate and complete, then one has *not* acted responsibly in one's professional capacity,

Of the two, the second conclusion is the most likely to appear since it involves an extra step while taking the contrapositive (the test makers always want you to go the extra mile!).

Note also that although the principle is broad, it has specifications that must be met in order for the principle to apply:

- one must be acting in a professional capacity
- one must make a reasonable effort to ensure the information used is accurate and complete

Answer choice (A): Right out of the gate you are faced with a trap answer. From the discussion you know that you cannot draw a conclusion that a sufficient condition has occurred (there is no premise that can be used to force a sufficient condition to occur). Yet, this answer attempts to conclude that Peggy acted responsibly, which is the same as the sufficient condition. Therefore, the judgment (conclusion) in this answer does not conform to the principle in the stimulus and this answer is incorrect.

Answer choice (B): When creating incorrect answers, the test makers love to recycle difficult concepts and have them appear more than once in a problem. Structurally, this answer is identical to answer choice (A). Based on the principle in the stimulus, there is no way to conclude that anyone has acted responsibly, and once you recognize that fact, you can quickly eliminate the first two answer choices.

Answer choice (C): This is the correct answer. Applying the principle to this scenario, when Toril did not investigate the risks associated with investing in Twicycled Ink, he failed to make a reasonable effort to ensure the information used to make the decision was accurate and complete. On that basis, we know Toril did not meet the necessary condition in the principle, and therefore Toril did not act responsibly. Since the answer choice arrives at the same conclusion, this answer is correct. Note that, as you might expect, this answer requires the most work from the test taker.

Answer choice (D): This answer choice does not use the principle in the stimulus to arrive at its conclusion. Although Helmer made an error that cost the company money, the answer choice does not address the condition of the principle that states "one must act on the basis of information that one has made a reasonable effort to make sure is accurate and complete." More problematic, the conclusion addresses Conchita, not Helmer, and no information is given to indicate whether Conchita made a reasonable effort to assure the reliability of the information used to hire Helmer (since she hired Helmer, it is assumed she acted in a professional capacity). Since no information is given that proves Conchita did not fulfill the necessary condition, the principle cannot be used to arrive at the conclusion that Conchita did not act responsibly.

Although the conclusion is one that could be drawn from applying the principle, in this instance no premise is provided that calls for the application of the principle, and thus the answer choice is incorrect.

Answer choice (E): This answer choice indicates that Jennifer's decision involved a vacation, which is a personal decision, not a professional decision. Since the principle in the stimulus is clear that the requirements for acting responsibly address one's *professional capacity*, this situation does not conform to the principle.

This answer provides an excellent example of the intelligence used when LSAT questions are constructed. The stimulus is clear that professional capacity is part of the conditional relationship, but none of the first four answers test that fact. By the time most students reach this answer, they have forgotten the details of the principle, making this final answer a perfect place to test this element.

In Must-PR questions, the principle creates a broad rule that can then be applied to a variety of situations. The correct answer in these questions always features a scenario that addresses each part of the principle, and if an answer does not match part of the principle, it is incorrect.

Now take a look at the other type of Principle question that appears frequently on the LSAT.

2. Strengthen/Justify Principle Questions

In these questions each *answer choice* contains a principle that acts as an additional, broad premise that supports or proves the conclusion. Functionally, five different principles are applied to the situation in the stimulus. While reading the stimulus, you must think in abstract terms and identify an underlying idea or belief that can be used to draw the conclusion in the stimulus. Then, as you analyze the answer choices, tie this idea or belief to the structure of the author's argument and ask yourself, "If this answer is true, does it support or prove the conclusion?"

Now read an example of this type of question and get a better sense of how the inclusion of the Principle concept affects the problem. Please take a moment to complete the following question:

2. Jeff: Proposed regulations concerning the use of animals in scientific experimentation would prohibit experimentation on those species that humans empathize with: dogs and horses, for example. But extensive neurological research on mammals shows that they are all capable of feeling pain, just as dogs and horses are. Hence, this proposal should be extended to all experimentation on all mammals.

Miranda: Yet the issue of pain is not the crux of the matter. Experimentation on any nonhuman animal undermines respect for life itself because only humans are capable of consenting to an experiment. Since any activity that undermines respect for life diminishes the quality of all of our lives, the new regulations should ban all such experimentation.

Which one of the following is a principle that, if established, would best support Jeff's conclusion?

(A) Regulations on the use of animals in scientific experimentation should be primarily concerned with respecting the feelings of the humans who will perform those experiments.

(B) Whatever means are used to determine whether dogs and horses feel pain should also be used to determine whether other animals feel pain.

(C) Only those experiments on animals that are known to cause those animals pain should be prohibited.

(D) Scientists who perform experiments on animals should empathize with any mammal as much as they empathize with dogs or horses.

(E) Scientific experimentation should be prohibited on any creature that is capable of feeling pain.

Like the previous question, this is a lengthy and time-consuming problem. Regardless, do not be intimidated by the size of the question—some of the longest LSAT problems have been fairly easy.

The question stem in this problem asks for a principle that would support Jeff's conclusion. As such, this is a Strengthen-PR question, and *you can ignore Miranda's argument* since it appears after Jeff's argument.

Jeff's argument can be analyzed as follows:

Premise:	Proposed regulations concerning the use of animals in scientific experimentation would prohibit experimentation on those species that humans empathize with: dogs and horses, for example.
Premise:	But extensive neurological research on mammals shows that they are all capable of feeling pain, just as dogs and horses are.
Conclusion:	Hence, this proposal should be extended to all experimentation on all mammals.

On the basis that all mammals can feel pain, Jeff concludes that the experimentation prohibition should be extended to all mammals. In drawing this conclusion, Jeff goes beyond the parameters of the first premise, which indicates that empathy was the basis for the proposed experimentation prohibition. Jeff's conclusion ignores the empathy factor, and uses just the pain element to arrive at the conclusion. Most students find the argument relatively easy to understand, but it is important to separate out the exact reason that underlies Jeff's position before moving on to the answer choices.

In Strengthen-PR questions, the correct answer provides a broad premise that can be added to the argument to help prove the conclusion. In this problem, you must select the principle that, when applied to the specific situation in the stimulus, helps prove that scientific experimentation on all mammals should be banned.

Answer choice (A): While this principle provides minor support for the prohibition discussed in the first premise, this principle would not apply to Jeff's conclusion since Jeff did not use empathy as the basis for his conclusion.

Answer choice (B): Jeff's argument is not focused on the "means used to determine whether dogs and horses feel pain." From his second premise he knows that all mammals feel pain; they way in which that is

Do not eliminate an answer simply because you disagree with the principle in the answer choice. As with all Strengthen questions, the question stem indicates that the answers should be taken as true.

determined is not relevant to his conclusion. Thus, this answer choice does not help support Jeff's conclusion.

Answer choice (C): This answer attempts to draw you into a Mistaken Reversal. The principle in the answer choice states:

EP = experiment should be prohibited
KP = experiment known to cause pain to animals

$$EP \longrightarrow KP$$

The assumption in the argument is that scientific experimentation on animals causes pain, which meets the necessary condition in the relationship above:

KP

However, the combination of the principle in the answer choice and the necessary condition from the stimulus does not yield any conclusion. Hence, this answer does not support Jeff's conclusion.

Answer choice (D): This is the most frequently selected incorrect answer choice, with about one in four students selecting (D). As previously discussed, Jeff's conclusion is not based on empathizing with animals. Adding this principle to the argument does not help support the conclusion that the proposal should be extended to all mammals; instead, this principle would support the conclusion that researchers should *empathize* with all mammals. Since this is a different conclusion than the one in the argument, this answer choice is incorrect.

Answer choice (E): This is the correct answer. The principle in the answer, when combined with the premise, provides overwhelming support for the conclusion. As with many principles, the one in this answer choice is conditional:

KP = experiment known to cause pain to any creature
EP = experiment should be prohibited

$$KP \longrightarrow EP$$

From the premise we know that all mammals are capable of feeling pain, so the sufficient condition is met with respect to mammals (M):

KP_M

By applying the Repeat conditional form, we have support for Jeff's conclusion that experimentation on all mammals should be prohibited:

$$EP_M$$

Thus, if this principle is established, it would provide a great deal of support for Jeff's position.

Note the general nature of the principle in the correct answer. Although animals are addressed, it is in the broadest fashion possible ("any creature"). This generality is typical of Strengthen-PR and Justify-PR answer choices.

Some students are concerned that the answer choice does not mention mammals. By mentioning "any creature" (which of course includes all mammals), the answer subsumes the group of mammals and therefore the principle is still usable. For example, suppose you try to draw a conclusion that no person should hurt a black cat. A principle stating that "no cats should be hurt" would apply since "cats" naturally includes "black cats." The same type of reasoning is involved in this problem.

When you encounter a Principle designator in the question stem, prepare to apply the principle to a situation that falls under the purview of the principle but is not necessarily directly addressed by the principle. This process of abstraction consumes more time that the average question and contributes to lengthening the problem completion time. Regardless, if you use the skills you developed while examining other question types (such as Must Be True and Strengthen), you can successfully navigate Principle questions.

Principle Question Review

Principle questions (PR) are not a separate question type but are instead an "overlay" that appears in a variety of question types.

A principle is a broad rule that specifies what actions or judgments are correct in certain situations. The degree of generality of principles can vary considerably, and some are much narrower than others.

Since a principle is by definition a broad rule (usually conditional in nature), the presence of the Principle indicator serves to broaden the scope of the question. The question becomes more abstract, and you must analyze the problem to identify the underlying relationships. Functionally, you must take a broad, global proposition and apply it in a specific manner, either to the answer choices (as in a Must or Parallel question) or to the stimulus (as in a Strengthen or Justify question).

In Must-PR questions you must use the principle presented in *the stimulus* and then apply it to the situation in each answer choice (one principle applied to five situations). The presence of the principle designation broadens the question, and the answer choice can address a scenario not included in the stimulus.

In Strengthen-PR questions each *answer choice* contains a principle that acts as an additional, broad premise that supports or proves the conclusion (functionally, five different principles are applied to the situation in the stimulus).

When you encounter a Principle designator in the question stem, prepare to apply the principle to a situation that falls under the purview of the principle but is not necessarily directly addressed by the principle. This process of abstraction consumes more time that the average question and contributes to lengthening the problem.

Principle Question Problem Set

The following questions are drawn from actual LSATs. Please complete the problem set and review the answer key and explanations. *Answers on Page 503*

1. Because people are generally better at detecting mistakes in others' work than in their own, a prudent principle is that one should always have one's own work checked by someone else.

   Which one of the following provides the best illustration of the principle above?

   (A) The best elementary school math teachers are not those for whom math was always easy. Teachers who had to struggle through math themselves are better able to explain math to students.
   (B) One must make a special effort to clearly explain one's views to someone else; people normally find it easier to understand their own views than to understand others' views.
   (C) Juries composed of legal novices, rather than panels of lawyers, should be the final arbiters in legal proceedings. People who are not legal experts are in a better position to detect good legal arguments by lawyers than are other lawyers.
   (D) People should always have their writing proofread by someone else. Someone who does not know in advance what is meant to be said is in a better position to spot typographical errors.
   (E) Two people going out for dinner will have a more enjoyable meal if they order for each other. By allowing someone else to choose, one opens oneself up to new and exciting dining experiences.

2. Sharon, a noted collector of fine glass, found a rare glass vase in a secondhand store in a small town she was visiting. The vase was priced at $10, but Sharon knew that it was worth at least $1,000. Saying nothing to the storekeeper about the value of the vase, Sharon bought the vase for $10. Weeks later the storekeeper read a newspaper article about Sharon's collection, which mentioned the vase and how she had acquired it. When the irate storekeeper later accused Sharon of taking advantage of him, Sharon replied that she had done nothing wrong.

   Which one of the following principles, if established, most helps to justify Sharon's position?

   (A) A seller is not obligated to inform a buyer of anything about the merchandise that the seller offers for sale except for the demanded price.
   (B) It is the responsibility of the seller, not the buyer, to make sure that the amount of money a buyer gives a seller in exchange for merchandise matches the amount that the seller demands for that merchandise.
   (C) A buyer's sole obligation to a seller is to pay in full the price that the seller demands for a piece of merchandise that the buyer acquires from the seller.
   (D) It is the responsibility of the buyer, not the seller, to ascertain that the quality of a piece of merchandise satisfies the buyer's standards.
   (E) The obligations that follow from any social relationship between two people who are well acquainted override any obligations that follow from an economic relationship between the two.

3. A gift is not generous unless it is intended to benefit the recipient and is worth more than what is expected or customary in the situation; a gift is selfish if it is given to benefit the giver or is less valuable than is customary.

Which one of the following judgments most closely conforms to the principle above?

(A) Charles, who hates opera, was given two expensive tickets to the opera. He in turn gave them to his cousin, who loves opera, as a birthday gift. Charles's gift was selfish because he paid nothing for the tickets.

(B) Emily gives her brother a year's membership in a health club. She thinks that this will allow her brother to get the exercise he needs. However, the gift is selfish because Emily's brother is hurt and offended by it.

(C) Amanda gives each of her clients an expensive bottle of wine every year. Amanda's gifts are generous, since they cause the clients to continue giving Amanda business.

(D) Olga gives her daughter a computer as a graduation gift. Since this is the gift that all children in Olga's family receive for graduation, it is not generous.

(E) Michael gave his nephew $50 as a birthday gift, more than he had ever given before. Michael's nephew, however, lost the money. Therefore, Michael's gift was not generous because it did not benefit the recipient.

4. Some scientists have expressed reservations about quantum theory because of its counterintuitive consequences. But despite rigorous attempts to show that quantum theory's predictions were inaccurate, they were shown to be accurate within the generally accepted statistical margin of error. These results, which have not been equaled by quantum theory's competitors, warrant acceptance of quantum theory.

Which one of the following principles most helps to justify the reasoning above?

(A) A scientific theory should be accepted if it has fewer counterintuitive consequences than do its competitors.

(B) A scientific theory should be accepted if it has been subjected to serious attempts to disprove it and has withstood all of them.

(C) The consequences of a scientific theory should not be considered counterintuitive if the theory's predictions have been found to be accurate.

(D) A theory should not be rejected until it has been subjected to serious attempts to disprove it.

(E) A theory should be accepted only if its predictions have not been disproved by experiment.

Principle Question Problem Set Answer Key

All answer keys in this book indicate the source of the question by giving the month and year the LSAT was originally administered, the Logical Reasoning section number, and the question number within that section. Each LSAT has two Logical Reasoning sections, and so the Section 1 and Section 2 designators will refer to the first or second Logical Reasoning section in the test, not the physical section number of the booklet.

Question #1. Must-PR. October 2002 LSAT, Section 1, #7. The correct answer choice is (D)

The principle in the stimulus is clearly stated: "one should always have one's own work checked by someone else." Your task is to find the answer that most closely follows that guideline.

Answer choice (A): This answer choice does not contain any work to be checked, and therefore it cannot illustrate the principle in the stimulus.

Answer choice (B): Although this answer discusses "one's view," a view is not the same as "one's own work" and therefore the principle cannot be applied to this answer.

Answer choice (C): Although this answer involves the checking of work (juries "check" the work of lawyers), the heart of this answer is not that one should have one's own worked checked by others. Rather, this answer focuses on who is in the best position to do the checking: experts or novices.

Answer choice (D): This is the correct answer. The answer matches the principle by stating that a writer should have his or her work proofread by others, and then further provides a justification that matches the premise in the stimulus (that other people are better at detecting errors).

Answer choice (E): Ordering a meal does not qualify as "one's own work," nor does eating the meal qualify as checking the work. Hence, this answer has no attribute that illustrates the principle.

Overall, this question is classified as relatively easy.

Question #2. Strengthen-PR. October 2003 LSAT, Section 1, #17. The correct answer choice is (C)

The stimulus presents a clear and easy-to-understand situation, and Sharon's actions can be described as follows: Sharon paid the asking price for an item even though she was fully aware the asking price was far too low, and she feels her actions are not inappropriate.

The question stem requires you to identify the answer that contains a principle that would most strengthen Sharon's position regarding her actions. The principle that supports Sharon's position must address, in some way, the discrepancy between what Sharon paid for the item and what she knew to be the value of the item.

Please note that your personal view of the ethics of Sharon's actions have no place in this question. The stimulus describes what she did, and the nature of the question forces you to identify the answer that best justifies her decision.

Answer choice (A): This answer focuses on the obligations of the *seller*, not the buyer. Since Sharon is the buyer and it is her actions that are under scrutiny, this answer choice does not apply to the scenario in the stimulus. Remember, read carefully! This is a Reverse answer, and if you switch *buyer* and *seller* in the answer it will be correct.

Answer choice (B): The issue in the stimulus is not whether Sharon paid the storekeeper the asking price—she did. The issue is whether she took advantage of him by not disclosing the fact that the item was worth more than the asking price. Since this answer focuses on the whether the amount of money paid matches the asking price, it is incorrect.

Answer choice (C): This is the correct answer. The principle in this answer makes it clear that a buyer has no obligation beyond paying the asking price for an item. If this is true, then Sharon is justified in not disclosing the true value of the item to the storekeeper.

Answer choice (D): Sharon's position revolves around the discrepancy between what Sharon paid for the item and what she knew to be the value of the item. This answer choice addresses the buyer's responsibility regarding the *quality* of the item, and does not touch on the issue of the discrepancy.

Note that it appears Sharon did ascertain that the quality of the item met her standards. Regardless, since the principle fails to address the defensibility of her position, the answer is incorrect.

Answer choice (E): There is no indication that Sharon and the storekeeper were "well acquainted," so this principle cannot be applied to the situation in the stimulus. If they were well acquainted, then Sharon's position would be weakened.

Question #3. Must-PR, SN. December 2002 LSAT, Section 1, #11. The correct answer choice is (D)

Statistically, this question is considerably more difficult than either of the previous two questions. The difficulty occurs because many students mis-diagram one or both of the conditional statements in the stimulus. Although the question stems asks you to identify the answer that follows from the principle, the principle contains two similar but distinct conditional statements, you must be aware that either could figure in the correct answer. We will now examine both of the statements (the conditional indicators are italicized):

1. "A gift is not generous *unless* it is intended to benefit the recipient and is worth more than what is expected or customary in the situation."

   Applying the Unless Equation, the phrase modified by "unless" becomes the necessary condition and the remainder is negated and becomes the sufficient condition:

   G = a gift is generous
   B = the gift is intended to benefit the recipient
   WM = the gift is worth more than what is expected or customary in the situation

$$G \longrightarrow \begin{matrix} B \\ + \\ WM \end{matrix}$$

   As discussed in the chapter, the application of a conditional principle similar to this one does not allow a conclusion to be drawn that someone is generous (however, a conclusion could be made via the contrapositive that someone is *not* generous).

2. "A gift is selfish *if* it is given to benefit the giver or is less valuable than is customary."

   Remember, "if" introduces a sufficient condition.

   S = a gift is selfish
   BG = the gift is given to benefit the giver
   LV = the gift is less valuable than is customary

$$\begin{matrix} BG \\ or \\ LV \end{matrix} \longrightarrow S$$

Some students compare the two statements in the stimulus and conclude that the second is the contrapositive of the first. While the second relationship is very similar to the contrapositive of the first relationship, it is not an exact contrapositive because the logical opposite of "generous" is not "selfish" (it is "not generous"), the logical opposite of "benefit the recipient" is not "benefit the giver" (it is "not benefit the recipient"), and the logical opposite of "worth more than customary" is not "worth less than customary" (it is "not worth more than customary").

As you examine the answer choices, keep in mind that the test makers will try to devise answer choices that are similar to the guidelines in the principle, but that do not match exactly. These answers will be incorrect. Remember also that the contrapositive of either conditional statement can be used to arrive at the correct answer.

Answer choice (A): This is a very attractive wrong answer choice.

To draw the conclusion that one's gift is selfish, one must either give a gift that is given to benefit the giver *or* give a gift that is less valuable than is customary. Let us examine the answer choice and determine whether Charles's gift meets either condition:

1. Was the gift given to benefit the giver?

    No. Even though Charles hates opera, giving the tickets to his cousin did not benefit Charles (Charles was under no apparent obligation to attend the opera and could have left the tickets unused). In fact, they clearly benefitted his cousin, who loves opera.

2. Was the gift less valuable than is customary?

    Unknown. Even though Charles paid nothing for the tickets, they still had value (they could have been resold, for example). Whether they were less valuable than customary for a birthday gift is unknown (although common sense suggests they were not less valuable).

Since neither sufficient condition has been met with certainty, it cannot be concluded that Charles's gift was selfish.

Answer choice (B): Again, does the answer choice meet either sufficient condition?

1. Was the gift given to benefit the giver?

    No, the gift was given in order to help keep Emily's brother healthy.

2. Was the gift less valuable than is customary?

    No, the gift was apparently given for no special occasion.

In any scenario under this principle, the consequences of the gift (in this case that Emily's brother was hurt and offended) do not play a role in determining whether the gift was a selfish one.

Answer choice (C): This answer concludes that Amanda is generous on the basis of her actions. As discussed previously, there is no way to use the principle to conclude that an individual is generous.

Once you see the answer concluding that a sufficient condition ("generous") occurred, you can eliminate the answer with speed and confidence. Simply put, structurally an answer of this type could never be correct in a problem such as this one.

Answer choice (D): This is the correct answer. In order to arrive at the judgment that a gift is not generous, one or both of the necessary conditions from the first conditional relationship must *not* be met. Does that occur in this answer?

1. Was the gift intended to benefit the recipient?

    Yes. This gift was intended to benefit the recipient, and so this necessary condition was met.

2. Was the gift worth more than what is expected or customary in the situation?

    No. The answer choice indicates that all the children in Olga's family receive a computer for graduation. Since the gift of a computer is not worth more than is customary in the situation, this condition is not met and via the contrapositive we can conclude that Olga's gift was not generous.

Since one of the necessary conditions in the principle was not met, we can conclude that the sufficient condition was not met, and Olga's gift was not a generous one. As this matches the judgment in the answer choice, this is the correct answer.

Answer choice (E): Since the judgment in this answer ("not generous") is the same as in answer choice (D), we can analyze this answer in the same way:

1. Was the gift intended to benefit the recipient?

    Yes. Michael gave his nephew $50 dollars, and in doing so the intention was to benefit the nephew. The fact that the nephew subsequently lost the money does not show that Michael's intention was not to benefit his nephew. To some extent, this situation is like the one in answer choice (B) because in the principle the consequences of the gift do not play a role in determining the intentions of the giver.

2. Was the gift worth more than what is expected or customary in the situation?

    Yes, the first line spells out that the gift of $50 was more than Michael had ever given his nephew before.

Since both necessary conditions of the principle are met, the gift could be a generous one, a conclusion that does not conform to the judgment in the answer choice. Hence, the answer is incorrect.

A final note on this question: make sure you are comfortable with how the conditional relationship in this Must-PR problem (and in the one in the chapter text) is used to affect the answer choices (whether you can determine if someone is generous or not generous, selfish or not selfish). This form of Principle question has proven to be hard enough that the test makers will surely continue to place this type of question on the exam.

Question #4. Strengthen-PR. December 2003 LSAT, Section 2, #15. The correct answer choice is (B)

The argument in the stimulus is composed as follows:

Premise:	Some scientists have expressed reservations about quantum theory because of its counterintuitive consequences.
Premise:	But despite rigorous attempts to show that quantum theory's predictions were inaccurate, they were shown to be accurate within the generally accepted statistical margin of error.
Conclusion:	These results, which have not been equaled by quantum theory's competitors, warrant acceptance of quantum theory.

The argument uses the "some people say" construction discussed in Chapter Two. As some scientists are said to have reservations about quantum theory, you can predict that the author will conclude that they should not have these reservations, and indeed this occurs in the last sentence of the stimulus.

The author's reason for concluding that quantum theory should be accepted is that all attempts to disprove the theory have failed. From the Flaw in the Reasoning section we know this is an error in the use of evidence: lack of evidence against a position is mistakenly taken to prove that position is true. The question stem asks you to identify a principle that could help to justify this form of erroneous reasoning.

Answer choice (A): The author's reasoning is not based on "fewer counterintuitive consequences," but on the fact that the consequences have not been disproven. Hence, this principle would not help the reasoning and this answer is incorrect.

Answer choice (B): This is the correct answer choice. If this principle is accepted, then the argument in the stimulus is strengthened. The principle, when slightly restated, asserts that "if a scientific theory has been subjected to serious attempts to disprove it and has withstood all of them, then it should be accepted." We know from the stimulus that the theory has been subject to serious attempts to disprove it and it has withstood them. According to the principle, this justifies the conclusion that the theory should be accepted.

Answer choice (C): The conclusion of the argument in the stimulus is that the theory should be accepted. Using the principle in this answer choice would lead one to conclude that the consequences of the theory should not be considered counterintuitive. Since this result differs from the conclusion, this answer choice is incorrect.

Answer choice (D): This answer, when rephrased using the Unless Equation, reads "if a theory should be rejected, then it has been subjected to serious attempts to disprove it." The scenario in the stimulus meets the necessary condition, but that has no impact on whether the sufficient occurs or does not occur.

Answer choice (E): This is the Mistaken Reversal of answer choice (B). Applying this principle fails to justify the argument since only the necessary condition is met, and that does not prove the sufficient condition (in this case, that the theory should be accepted) will occur. Hence, this answer choice is incorrect.

CHAPTER TWENTY: SECTION STRATEGY AND TIME MANAGEMENT

Approaching the Section Strategically

The Logical Reasoning sections are the most important on the LSAT because combined they account for 50% of your score. While everyone should strive to complete all of the questions in each section, this is not always possible. This chapter will address issues of timing and section management in an effort to help maximize your score.

Section Structure

Many students believe that the questions in the Logical Reasoning section are presented in order of difficulty, and that each question is more difficult than the previous question. This is false. The difficulty of individual questions varies greatly, and the last question in a section may be easier than, say, the fourteenth question in the same section. That said, there is a rough order of difficulty to the section:

- On average, the first ten questions are considerably easier than the last ten questions.

- Within the first ten questions there are usually no more than two or three questions of above average difficulty.

- As the section moves into the teens, the difficulty begins to rise, and several questions in the ten through twenty range will be very difficult.

- Most, but not necessarily all, of the questions in the twenties will be medium to very difficult.

There can still be very difficult questions in the first ten, so do not let your guard down. However, you will see fewer difficult questions in the first ten questions of a section than in the last ten.

Given the information above, it is paramount that you capitalize on the relative ease of the first ten questions and answer them all correctly. Peak performance in any Logical Reasoning section is based on a solid start, and understanding that early questions are generally easier gives you the opportunity to focus and get as many correct as possible.

For more information on question difficulty, please visit our exclusive *PowerScore Logical Reasoning Bible* website at www.powerscore.com/lrbible. The site contains a more detailed look at difficulty and provides a statistical basis for the claims above.

Time Management: The Nexus of Speed and Accuracy

Strong performance on the LSAT depends on two factors: speed and accuracy. If you rush to complete every question but miss most of them, you will not receive a high score. On the other hand, if you increase your accuracy by slowing down, you may be able to increase your score despite doing fewer questions. The key to finding the correct pace is practice. As you work through LSAT sections, use a timer (more on this later) and keep track of how well you perform on each section, including how many questions you complete and where you were at important time markers during the section.

Of course, our preference is for you to complete each section, and that should be your initial goal.

If early in your studies you find yourself struggling to complete all of the questions, do not worry. It takes time to become comfortable with the types of questions presented on the LSAT, and it takes time for the techniques you have learned to become second nature. Once you become comfortable with the test and begin to apply the techniques without stopping to think about them, you will see your accuracy rise *and* your speed increase.

One of the crucial factors in a solid performance is good decision-making. You must maintain your composure as you work through each section, even if you feel as if you have missed a few questions. From the discussion throughout this book you know that the test makers employ a variety of psychological tricks to keep you off balance, and how you react to those traps has a tremendous effect on your score. Half the battle is understanding the way the questions are constructed, but you must also be smart in how you handle your emotions and reactions to each question. In particular, keep these ideas in mind:

- Do not get caught up in trying to answer one question. You cannot spend an exorbitant amount of time on a single question and still hope to complete the section. For instance, if you spend four minutes on one question, then you have lost the opportunity to complete at least two other questions. Remember, the goal is to win the war, and it is acceptable to lose a battle now and then.

  If you do accidentally get caught up in one question, do not let the frustration carry over to the next question. Once you have completed a question, put it out of your mind and move on.

- Know when to say when. If you have spent a minute and a half on a question, ask yourself how much more time you will need to solve the question. You want to maximize your return on the time you spend on each question, so if you think you can solve the question in relatively short order, go ahead and finish off the problem. On the other hand, if you do not see a clear path to solving the question, cut your losses and move to the next question without remorse. As they say, don't throw good money after bad.

Let's talk in more detail about the amount of time you have to complete each question. Each section of the LSAT is 35 minutes in length, and since there are always 24, 25, or 26 questions in a Logical Reasoning section, you have just less than 1 minute and 30 seconds to complete each question and transfer your answers:

Number of Questions	Time per Question
24	1 minute, 27 seconds
25	1 minute, 24 seconds
26	1 minute, 20 seconds

The amount of time listed includes time for transferring answers. You cannot transfer your answers after the test has ended.

However, no matter how hard you try, you will not complete each question in the exact amount of time allotted! Instead, completing a Logical Reasoning section is like riding a roller coaster: sometimes you will go very fast and other times you will slow down to a crawl. This is to be expected because some questions are much harder than others and naturally take more time to complete. As you practice, one of your tasks is to determine a reliable guideline for where you should be during certain points in the section (more on this in a moment).

The table above also assumes you will complete every question. For some students that is neither possible nor advisable. Consider the following comparison:

	Student #1	Student #2	Student #3
Questions completed in section	24	20	16
Accuracy Rate	50%	75%	100%
Total Correct Answers	12	15	16

Practice doing as many questions as possible with a timer so that you develop a comfortable and familiar pace.

Obviously, actual performance in a section depends on a variety of factors, and each student must assess their own strengths and weaknesses. Regardless, the message is the same: you *might* benefit from slowing down and attempting fewer questions. The way to determine this? Create your own Pacing Guideline.

Pacing Guidelines

Every test taker must have a plan of action before they start a section. As you practice, you should strive to determine your personal Pacing Guideline. For example, how many questions do you plan to complete in the first ten minutes? The first twenty minutes? How much time do you expect will have elapsed when you reach question #10? Question #20? Before you pick up a pencil and take the actual test, you should be able to answer these questions.

First off, we are not advocating that you create a strict timeline that controls where you are every moment in the section or that dictates when you quit working on a question. Instead, you must create a loose blueprint for completing the section—one that uses your particular strengths to create an achievable set of goals. To give you a better sense of how the idea works, here is an example of a Pacing Guideline for a high scorer:

> First ten minutes of the section: complete one question per minute. Accordingly, when ten minutes are up I should have completed question #10.

> Next twenty minutes of section: complete the remainder of the questions.

> Last five minutes of the section: double-check my work; return to any question I noted as especially challenging.

Clearly, this Guideline is an aggressive one that assumes that the test taker is good enough to complete all the questions accurately and still have time remaining. Your personal Guideline does not have to be the same! Take a moment, however, to review the above Guideline:

• The test taker assumes that he or she can work faster in the first ten questions, when the questions are typically easier.

• After the first ten questions, the test taker slows down in response to the expected increase in difficulty.

• Despite being good enough to expect to finish all the questions, the test taker doesn't just sit back and relax for the last five minutes. Instead, he or she uses that time to re-check troublesome problems.

• The Guideline is relatively loose and contains a minimum of components.

Here is how to create and use your own Pacing Guideline:

1. During your practice sessions, focus on determining how fast you can do a typical Logical Reasoning question while retaining a high degree of accuracy. To do this, you will need to time yourself religiously.

2. Make a benchmark for where you should be after either the first ten minutes *or* the first ten questions. Use easy to remember markers (such as 5, 10, 15, 20) so you won't forget your plan during the test or have to stop to think about it. If your Guideline is too complex to remember without writing down, it is too complex to use!

3. Consider making a second benchmark for where you should be after either the first twenty minutes *or* the first fifteen questions.

4. Try to take into account the difficulty level of the first ten questions versus the last ten questions.

5. Do not make your Pacing Guideline too detailed. The difficulty of the questions (and entire sections) varies, so you do not want to create a rigid Guideline that cannot account for these differences. For example, do not make a Guideline that specifies where you will be at questions #8, #10, #12, #14, etc. That is too specific and will be unusable if you run into a few hard (or very easy) questions early in the section. Try to make your Guideline broad enough to characterize several different points in the section. If you have more than four or five sections in your Guideline, it is getting too detailed!

6. Make sure you are comfortable with your plan and that your goals are achievable. This is not a plan of what you *hope* will happen, but rather what your practice has proven you can do.

7. Use the Guideline to help monitor your performance during the test. If you end up working faster than expected and you are beating your goals, then you will know that things are going exceedingly well and that should bolster your confidence. On the other hand, if you find yourself falling behind the marking points, then you will know that you must bear down and work a bit more quickly.

Implementing the steps above should not be too difficult, but you would be surprised at how many people fail to prepare even the most basic plan of action for each section. In many ways, it is as if they have been asked to run a triathlon but they practice only infrequently and do not keep track of how fast they can go without burning out. Athletes at all levels measure their performance frequently, and the LSAT is just a triathlon for the mind.

Some books and courses continue to include time-consuming "Triple True-False" questions (also known as "Roman Numeral" questions) in their materials. These questions have not appeared in the modern era of the LSAT and you should not worry about encountering this type of question on the test.

Let's take a look at some other Pacing Guidelines to help you get a better sense of the range of possibilities:

Can almost finish the section, paces by question number

First ten questions: complete in 14 minutes.

Next ten questions: complete in 18 minutes (32 total minutes elapsed/ 3 minutes remaining).

Last three minutes of the section: pick the shortest questions and try to complete as many as possible. Guess on any questions I cannot complete.

Can reliably reach question #20, paces by time

First fifteen minutes of the section: complete the first ten questions.

Next twenty minutes of section: complete the next ten questions.

Just as section ends: Guess on remaining questions.

Can often reach the end of the section, paces by time

First ten minutes of the section: complete the first eight questions.

Next ten minutes of section: complete the next seven questions.

Next ten minutes of section: complete the next six questions.

Last five minutes of the section: gauge the situation and finish the section if possible. If not, pick the shortest questions and try to complete as many as possible. Guess on any questions I cannot complete.

The examples above represent just a few of the possibilities. Your Pacing Guideline could look similar or it could be very different. The important thing is that you find a Guideline that works for you and that you have confidence in. Then, follow it on test day and always remember that you might have to be flexible to account for the unexpected.

Within each Pacing Guideline there is room to make decisions during the test. With practice you will discover your strengths and weaknesses, and you can alter your approach during the test to maximize your abilities. Here are some strategy decisions that might benefit certain test takers:

- If you have difficulty managing the large amount of information in lengthy questions, skip questions that appear overly long to you. The length of the question does not determine difficulty, but some students know through practice that long stimuli give them difficulty. If so, avoid those questions. Just make sure you guess on those questions if you do not have a chance to return to them.

  Apply this strategy if you have proven that you cannot accurately complete large questions.

- If you read a stimulus and are completely confused by what you have read, you can choose to simply guess and move to the next question. If you do not understand the stimulus, it will be very difficult to answer a question about that stimulus and sort through answer choices designed to test your knowledge.

- The topic of LSAT questions should not be of concern to you since you are reading for structure and relationship. However, we are also realists—if the topic of an LSAT question is one you really dislike (for example, science), then skip it. Word of warning: it is much better for you to adapt to the topics and get used to them. If a section has eight science questions, you can't skip all of them!

- As time winds down, you can make allowances in your approach to the questions. For example, if you are on question #24 (of 25 total) with only one minute remaining in the section and you find that answer choice (A) is extremely attractive, you can choose it and move on to the final question. Normally you would read all the answer choices, but when time is low, you can alter that approach if it is expedient to do so. Another example of "endgame" management would be if you only have one minute left but two questions to complete, and you choose the shorter of the two problems.

To help you more accurately calculate your Pacing Guideline, the following table correlates the number of questions completed to the average amount of time per question if all 35 minutes in the section are used:

Total Questions Completed	Average Time per Question
10	3:30 per question
12	2:55 per question
14	2:30 per question
16	2:11 per question
18	1:56 per question
20	1:45 per question
22	1:35 per question
24	1:27 per question
26	1:20 per question

This table assumes that your problem-solving rate is constant, but it shows that the typical student can actually spend a fair amount of time per question and still complete a respectable number of questions. For example, if you use just under two minutes per question you will still complete approximately 18 questions.

Second, note that as you complete more questions, the amount of time you need to cut off of your performance decreases. For example, if you complete exactly 22 questions you have an average of 1 minute and 35 seconds per question. To complete 24 questions, you only need to cut 8 seconds off your per-question performance (1 minute and 27 seconds per question). This explains why little adjustments have such a big effect on performance and it also explains why we are such strong believers in practicing with the techniques until they are second nature. Most students think that taking a few extra seconds to apply a technique is no big deal. But those seconds—when multiplied over 20 or more questions—quickly add up and are the difference between a very good score and an amazing score. To achieve an amazing score you must be very efficient and your application of the techniques must be effortless and transparent.

The header at the beginning of every Logical Reasoning section tells you how many questions are in the section.

The Answer Choices

As you know, every LSAT question has five answer choices. After you complete the problem, you are still not finished! You must properly transfer your answers from the test booklet to your answer sheet. This is one of the most important tasks that you must perform during the LSAT, so please take a moment to review the two answer transferring methods discussed in Chapter Three:

Once you have answered a question, it is critical that you correctly transfer that answer choice selection.

1. Logical Grouping

   This method involves transferring several answer choices at once, at logical break points throughout each section. This method generally allows for faster transferring of answers, but some students find they are more likely to make errors in their transcription.

2. Question By Question

   As the name implies, this method involves filling in the answer ovals on your answer sheet after you complete each individual question. This method generally consumes more time than the Logical Grouping method, but it usually produces a higher transfer accuracy rate. If you use the Logical Grouping method and find yourself making errors, use this method instead.

Either method is acceptable—practice using each so you can decide which one works best for you.

Three in a row?

Unlike some standardized tests, the LSAT often has three identical answer choices to consecutive questions (such as three D's), and on several occasions, four identical answer choices in a row have appeared. On the June 1996 LSAT, six of seven consecutive answer choices in one section were (C). The use of multiple answer choices in a row is one of the psychological weapons employed by the test makers to unnerve test takers. Any test taker seeing four (D)'s in a row on their answer sheet understandably thinks they have made some type of error, primarily because most tests avoid repetition in correct answer choices. If you see three or four answer choices in a row, do not become alarmed, especially if you feel you have been performing well on the section. We are still waiting for the day that the LSAT has five identical correct answers in a row, but we will not be surprised when it happens.

The test takers have many tricks to keep you psychologically off-balance.

Guessing Strategy

Never leave an answer blank on the LSAT! There is no penalty for wrong answers so it is in your best interest to guess on any problem you cannot complete.

Because the LSAT does not assess a scoring penalty for incorrect answer choices, you should always guess on any question that you cannot complete during the allotted time. However, because some answer choices are more likely to occur than others, you should not guess randomly. The following tables indicate the frequency of appearance of Logical Reasoning answer choices over the years.

All Logical Reasoning Answer Choices June 1991 - June 2004*

	A%	B%	C%	D%	E%
% appearance of each answer choice throughout the entire section	18.3	20.8	20.4	21.6	18.8

*These statistics do not include the unreleased February 1998, February 1999, February 2001, February 2002, February 2003, and February 2004 LSAT administrations.

The table above documents the percentage each answer choice appeared as a percentage of all Logical Reasoning answer choices between June 1991 and June 2004 inclusive. If history holds, when guessing on the LSAT Logical Reasoning section, you would be best served by always guessing answer choice (D). Do not choose random answer choices; do not put in a pattern such as A-B-C-D-E etcetera. Although guessing answer choice (D) does not guarantee you will get the questions correct, if history is an indicator then guessing answer choice (D) gives you a better chance than guessing randomly. Consider the following comparison of students guessing on five consecutive answer choices:

Correct Answer Choice	Student #1 Answer Choices (Pattern)	Student #2 Answer Choices (Random)	Student #3 Answer Choices (All D's)
B	A	D	D
D	B	C	D
E	C	A	D
A	D	E	D
C	E	B	D
# Correct =	0	0	1

Guessing randomly reduces each question to an independent event with a 1 in 5 chance of success.

Although one question may not seem significant, it adds up over four sections, and depending on where you are in the scoring scale, it can increase your score several points. And every point counts! By guessing answer choice (D), you increase your chances of getting extra answers correct.

The next table summarizes the percentage appearance of answer choices in just the last five answer choices of the Logical Reasoning section.

Last Five Answer Choices Per Logical Reasoning Section June 1991 - June 2004*

	A%	B%	C%	D%	E%
% appearance of each answer choice in the last five answer choices of the Logical Reasoning section	14.9	19.2	18.3	24.3	23.4

*These statistics do not include the unreleased February 1998, February 1999, February 2001, February 2002, February 2003, and February 2004 LSAT administrations.

Within the last five questions, the guessing strategy is still the same: answer choice (D). Notice the significant statistical deviation of answer choice (A). Answer choice (A) is not a good answer choice to choose within the last five answer choices!

The statistics in this second table have a greater variation because the sample (470 total questions) is smaller.

Please keep in mind that the advice above holds only for pure guessing. If you are attempting to choose between two answer choices, do not choose on the basis of statistics alone!

On a related note, if you are a strong test taker who correctly answers most questions but occasionally does not finish a section, quickly review the answer choices you have previously selected and use the answer that appears least as your guessing answer choice. For example, if you have completed twenty questions in a section, and your answers contain a large number of (A)'s, (C)'s, (D)'s, and (E)'s, guess answer choice (B) for all of the remaining questions.

In the last five questions per section, note that over 45% of the time the correct answer is either (D) or (E). Why would that be? Because those answers are the last two, so you have to work to get to them. The test makers want you to lose valuable time at a point when time is running out.

Using a Timer ■■■■■■■■■■■■■■■■

One of the most important tools for test success is a timer. Your timer should be a constant companion during your LSAT preparation, and, as discussed earlier, you should use your timer to help construct an accurate Pacing Guideline.

Although not all of your practice needs to be timed, you should attempt to do as many questions (and sections) as possible under timed conditions. Time pressure is the top concern cited by test takers, and practicing with a timer will help acquaint you with the challenges of the test. After all, if the LSAT was a take-home test, no one would be too worried about it.

Keep in mind the Law Services test center regulations concerning time: "Supervisors will keep official time. You may take a noiseless watch to the test center. Alarm, calculator, and beeping watches are not permitted. The supervisor will announce a five-minutes-remaining warning for each test section" (from the LSAT & LSDAS Registration & Information Book).

Excellent silent countdown timers can be purchased through our website at powerscore.com.

Your timer must be noiseless. Although this rule is randomly enforced, you do not want to find yourself in a position of having your timer taken away when you depend on it. Second, the supervisors will call a warning when there are five minutes remaining. Since you have a timer this warning announcement should come as no surprise to you. As you progress through the section, check your timer every 4-5 minutes for tracking purposes. There is no need to check it every minute!

When practicing with a timer, keep notes about how many questions you complete in a given amount of time. You should vary your approach so that practice does not become boring. For example, you could track how long it takes to complete 3, 5, or 10 questions. Or you could see how many questions you can complete in 10 or 15 minutes. Trying different approaches will help you get the best sense of how fast you can go while still maintaining a high degree of accuracy.

A timer is invaluable because it is both an odometer and speedometer for the section. With sufficient practice you will begin to establish a comfortable test-taking speed and the timer allows you to make sure you are maintaining this pace. Whether you use a watch, stopwatch, or a kitchen timer is irrelevant; just make sure you time yourself and that your timer is silent so you can use it on test day.

The day before the test

Be sure you have received or printed out your LSAT admission ticket from Law Services. Double-check the information on the admission ticket for accuracy.

If you are not familiar with your test center, drive by the test center and examine the testing room and parking situation. This will alleviate anxiety or confusion on the day of the test.

On the day before the LSAT, we recommend that you study very little, if at all. The best approach for most students is to simply relax as much as possible. Read a book, go see a movie, or play a round of golf. If you feel you must study, we recommend that you only briefly review each of the concepts covered in the course.

Eat only bland or neutral foods the night before the test and try to get the best sleep possible.

The morning of the test

Attempt to follow your normal routine on the morning of the test. For example, if you read the paper every morning, do so on the day of the test. If you do not regularly drink coffee, do not start on test day. Constancy in your routine will allow you to focus on your primary objective: performing well on the test.

Dress in layers, so you will be warm if the test center is cold, but also able to shed clothes if the test center is hot.

Take along a backpack with all your pencils, etc., and food and drink for the break.

For the September/October, December, and February LSAT administrations, all students must arrive at the test center no later than 8:30 AM. For the June LSAT administration, all students must arrive at the test center no later than 12:30 PM.

We strongly believe that performing well requires confidence and a belief that you can perform well. As you prepare to leave for the test, run though the test in your head, visualizing an exceptional performance. Imagine how you'll react to each game, reading passage, and logical reasoning question. Many athletes use this same technique to achieve optimal performance.

The following pages contain general notes on preparing for the day of the LSAT.

Do not study hard the day before the test. If you haven't learned it by then, that final day won't make much difference.

Even though test regulations require you to be at the center at a certain hour, the test will not begin immediately. Bring a newspaper or other reading material so that you have something to do while waiting.

At the test center

Yes, you read that correctly. You will be thumbprinted at the test center. This is done for test security purposes.

Upon check-in, test supervisors will ask you to present your admission ticket, one form of acceptable personal identification, and they will also take a thumbprint. Supervisors are instructed to deny admission to anyone who does not present a photo ID with signature.

The test supervisors will assign each examinee a seat. You are generally not permitted to choose your own seat.

Once you are seated, the test supervisors will read you the rules and regulations of the test, and have you write a certifying statement that attests that the person taking the test is the person whose name appears on the answer sheet and that you are taking the test for the sole purpose of admission to law school. Typically, the actual test will not begin until thirty to forty-five minutes after you are seated.

You are allowed only the following items on your testing desk:

> Number 2 pencils
> Erasers
> A noiseless timer
> A highlighter pen
> A non-automatic pencil sharpener

Food and drink are not allowed on your testing desk, nor are you allowed to consume them in the testing room. However, you may bring these items to the testing center to be consumed during the break.

Be sure to ask the test supervisors how they will keep time. There have been many problems with sections being mis-timed.

The test supervisors keep the official time, but they are not obligated to use a digital timer. They will announce a five-minutes-remaining warning for each test section.

You may only work on the assigned section. Testing supervisors may circulate throughout the testing room to ensure that all examinees are working in the appropriate section. Blackening of answer spaces on your answer sheet must be done before time is called for any given section. You will not be permitted time after the test to clean up your answer sheet or transfer answers from your test book to your answer sheet.

If you find it necessary to leave the room during the test, you must obtain permission from the supervisor. You will not be permitted to make up any missed time.

All test materials, including test books and answer sheets, are the property of Law Services and must be returned to Law Services by test supervisors after every administration. Legal action may be taken against an examinee who removes a test book and/or reproduces it.

If you engage in any misconduct or irregularity during the test, you may be dismissed from the test center and may be subject to other penalties for misconduct or irregularity. Actions that could warrant such consequences are creating a disturbance; giving or receiving help; working on or reading the test during a time not authorized by the supervisor; removing test materials or notes from the testing room; taking part in an act of impersonation or other forms of cheating; or using books, calculators, ear plugs, headsets, rulers, papers of any kind, or other aids. The penalties for misconduct are high: you may be precluded from attending law school and becoming a lawyer.

If you encounter a problem with the test supervision or test center itself, report it to a test supervisor. Reportable problems include: power outages, mis-timing of test sections, and any unusual disturbances caused by an individual.
If you feel anxious or panicked for any reason before or during the test, close your eyes for a few seconds and relax. Think of other situations where you performed with confidence and skill.

After the test

Test results will be emailed to you approximately three to four weeks after the test. A paper copy will be mailed approximately four to five weeks after the test. If you do not have an email account and you would like to know your LSAT score in advance of receiving your report in the mail, you may use LSAT TelScore, the early score reporting service. With a touch-tone phone, you can call (215) 968-1200 and receive your LSAT score approximately one to two weeks earlier than the paper copy will arrive. The fee is $10. TelScore is available approximately three to four weeks after your LSAT administration date. Before you call you will need the following information: your Social Security number, your Law Services Personal Identification number (PIN), and your credit card account number and expiration date.

Thank you for choosing to purchase the *PowerScore LSAT Logical Reasoning Bible*. We hope you have found this book useful and enjoyable, but most importantly we hope this book helps raise your LSAT score.

In all of our publications we strive to present the material in the clearest and most informative manner. If you have any questions, comments, or suggestions, please do not hesitate to email us at *lrbible@powerscore.com*. We love to receive feedback and we do read every email that comes in!

Also, if you haven't done so already, we strongly suggest you visit the website for this book at:

www.powerscore.com/lrbible

This free online resource area contains supplements to the book material, provides updates as needed, and answers questions posed by students. There is also an official evaluation form that we encourage you to use.

If we can assist you in any way in your LSAT preparation or in the law school admissions process, please do not hesitate to contact us. We would be happy to help.

Thank you and best of luck on the LSAT!

COMPLETE CHAPTER ANSWER KEY AND QUESTION USE TRACKER

Notes ███████████████████████████████████████

Answers to every LSAT question used in this book are found in the text of the chapter or in the chapter explanations. The consolidated answer key in this section contains four parts: the first part provides a question description legend, the second part provides an identification of the Four Question Families, the third part provides a quick chapter-by-chapter answer key for students who need to find the answers quickly, and the fourth part provides a comprehensive listing of the source of all LSAT questions used in this book. The fourth part is especially helpful for students who are taking practice LSATs and want to know ahead of time which questions we have used in this book. They can then skip those questions ahead of taking the test, or avoid taking certain tests until later.

Question Description Legend ████████████████████████████████████

Question Type Designations

Must = Must Be True
MP = Main Point
PI = Point at Issue
Assumption = Assumption
Justify = Justify the Conclusion
Strengthen = Strengthen/Support
Resolve = Resolve the Paradox
Weaken = Weaken
Method = Method of Reasoning
Flaw = Flaw in the Reasoning
Parallel = Parallel Reasoning
Evaluate = Evaluate the Argument
Cannot = Cannot Be True

FITB = Fill in the blank
AP = Argument Part
PR = Principle
X = Except question

Problem Type Designations

SN = Sufficient and Necessary Conditions
CE = Cause and Effect
FL = Formal Logic
#% = Numbers and Percentages

Family #1, also known as the Must Be or Prove Family, consists of the following question types:

(1) Must Be True
(2) Main Point
(3) Point at Issue
(9) Method of Reasoning
(10) Flaw in the Reasoning
(11) Parallel Reasoning

Family #2, also known as the Help Family, consists of the following question types:

(4) Assumption
(5) Justify the Conclusion
(6) Strengthen/Support
(7) Resolve the Paradox

Family #3, also known as the Hurt Family, consists of the following question type:

(8) Weaken

Family #4, also known as the Disprove Family, consists of the following question type:

(13) Cannot Be True

Evaluate the Argument questions are a combination of the Second and Third Families.

COMPLETE CHAPTER ANSWER KEYS

Notes

The chapter-by-chapter answer key lists every problem in this book in chronological order and identifies the classification and source of the question. You can use this answer key as a quick reference when you are solving problems. Each problem is explained in more detail in the text of the chapter.

Chapter-by-Chapter Answer Key

Chapter 2: Logical Reasoning Basics Chapter Text

    1. Must-FL. October 2003, Section 2, #25   (B)

Chapter 4: Must Be True Chapter Text

    1. Must. June 1999, Section 2, #1   (D)
    2. Must. December 2000, Section 2, #10   (E)
    3. Must. February 1992, Section 1, #22   (B)
    4. Must. October 2000, Section 2, #24   (B)
    5. Must. June 1999, Section 2, #8   (B)

Chapter 4: Must Be True Problem Set

    1. Must. October 2003, Section 2, #6   (A)
    2. Must. June 2002, Section 1, #7   (B)
    3. Must. June 2002, Section 1, #2   (E)
    4. Must. October 2000, Section 2, #10   (C)
    5. Must. October 2002, Section 1, #15   (C)
    6. Must. December 2002, Section 2, #16   (C)
    7. Must. June 2001, Section 2, #19   (B)
    8. Must. June 2000, Section 1, #20   (B)

Chapter-by-Chapter Answer Key

Chapter 5: Main Point Chapter Text

    1. MP. June 2003, Section 1, #9   (C)
    2. MP. December 2001, Section 2, #9   (C)
    3. MP—FITB. June 2002, Section 1, #9   (E)

Chapter 5: Main Point Problem Set

    1. MP. October 2002, Section 1, #2   (C)
    2. MP. December 2003, Section 2, #10   (D)

Chapter 6: Conditional Reasoning Chapter Text

    1. Must-SN. December 1991, Section 1, #10   (E)
    2. Must-SN. June 2000, Section 2, #22   (E)
    3. Must-SN. October 2000, Section 1, #7   (C)
    4. Must-SN. June 1999, Section 1, #14   (B)

Chapter 6: Conditional Reasoning Problem Set

    1. Must-SN. June 1999, Section 1, #10   (D)
    2. Must-SN. October 1999, Section 2, #12   (A)
    3. MP-SN. December 2001, Section 2, #3   (C)
    4. Must-SN. December 1999, Section 1, #18   (A)
    5. Must-SN. December 2002, Section 2, #6   (A)
    6. Must-SN. February 1992, Section 1, #12   (E)

Chapter 7: Weaken Chapter Text

    1. Weaken. December 2003, Section 1, #1   (A)
    2. Weaken. December 1994, Section 2, #12   (B)
    3. Weaken-SN. February 1994, Section 2, #9 (D)
    4. Weaken-SN. June 1997, Section 2, #19   (B)
    5. Weaken-SN. October 2001, Section 2, #17 (E)

Chapter 7: Weaken Problem Set

    1. Weaken. June 1999, Section 2, #15   (B)
    2. Weaken. October 2002, Section 2, #15   (D)
    3. Weaken. December 2003, Section 1, #20   (B)
    4. Weaken. June 2001, Section 1, #12   (A)
    5. Weaken. October 2001, Section 2, #20   (A)
    6. Weaken. October 2001, Section 1, #8   (E)

Chapter-by-Chapter Answer Key

Chapter 8: Cause and Effect Chapter Text

    1. Flaw-CE. December 2003, Section 1, #3   (D)
    2. Weaken-CE. December 1999, Section 2, #11   (A)

Chapter 8: Cause and Effect Problem Set

    1. Weaken-CE. December 2000, Section 1, #25   (D)
    2. Must-CE. December 2001, Section 1, #4   (C)
    3. Weaken-CE. December 2003, Section 2, #6   (C)
    4. Weaken-CE. October 1999, Section 2, #24   (B)
    5. Flaw-CE. October 2003, Section 2, #13   (C)
    6. Weaken-CE. December 2000, Section 2, #7   (A)

Chapter 9: Strengthen, Justify, Assumption Chapter—Strengthen Text

    1. Strengthen. June 2002, Section 1, #6   (E)
    2. StrengthenX. October 2001, Section 1, #15   (E)
    3. StrengthenX-CE. June 1999, Section 1, #26   (E)
    4. StrengthenX-CE. October 1999, Section 2, #20 (A)

Chapter 9: Strengthen, Justify, Assumption Chapter—Strengthen Problem Set

    1. Strengthen. June 2003, Section 1, #11   (A)
    2. Strengthen. December 2001, Section 2, #7   (B)
    3. StrengthenX-CE. October 2002, Section 2, #5   (B)
    4. Strengthen-CE. December 2000, Section 2, #20 (D)

Chapter 9: Strengthen, Justify, Assumption Chapter—Justify Text

    1. Justify. December 2000, Section 2, #23   (C)
    2. Justify. June 2000, Section 2, #10   (D)

Chapter 9: Strengthen, Justify, Assumption Chapter—Justify Problem Set

    1. Justify. October 2000, Section 2, #4   (B)
    2. Justify. October 2001, Section 2, #14   (B)
    3. Justify. October 2001, Section 1, #20   (A)
    4. Justify. December 2001, Section 2, #12   (A)

Chapter-by-Chapter Answer Key

Chapter 9: Strengthen, Justify, Assumption Chapter—Assumption Text

    1. Assumption. December 2000, Section 1, #10   (D)
    2. Assumption. October 2003, Section 2, #7   (A)
    3. Assumption-SN. June 1994, Section 1, #13   (A)
    4. Assumption-CE. December 1992, Section 2, #22   (E)

Chapter 9: Strengthen, Justify, Assumption Chapter—Assumption Problem Set

    1. Assumption-SN. June 2001, Section 2, #5   (D)
    2. Assumption. October 1999, Section 1, #5   (C)
    3. Assumption. October 2001, Section 1, #18   (B)
    4. Assumption. October 2002, Section 2, #22   (D)
    5. Assumption. October 2001, Section 2, #16   (A)
    6. Assumption. June 2000, Section 1, #14   (E)

Chapter 10: Resolve Chapter Text

    1. Resolve. December 2003, Section 2, #24   (C)
    2. Resolve. June 1995, Section 2, #20   (B)

Chapter 10: Resolve Problem Set

    1. Resolve. October 2003, Section 1, #4   (B)
    2. Resolve. October 2000, Section 2, #5   (A)
    3. Resolve. December 2001, Section 1, #9   (B)
    4. Resolve. October 2003, Section 1, #8   (D)

Chapter 11: Formal Logic Problem Set

    1. Must-FL. October 1997, Section 1, #12   (B)
    2. MustX-FL. December 1994, Section 2, #14   (E)
    3. Must-FL. October 2003, Section 2, #25   (B)
    4. Justify-FL. October 2001, Section 1, #22   (B)

Chapter-by-Chapter Answer Key

Chapter 12: Method of Reasoning Chapter Text

    1. Method. December 1994, Section 1, #2   (C)
    2. Method. December 1992, Section 2, #21   (E)
    3. Method-AP. December 2003, Section 1, #2   (D)
    4. Method-AP. December 2003, Section 2, #16 (E)

Chapter 12: Method of Reasoning Problem Set

    1. Method. December 2002, Section 2, #8   (D)
    2. Method-CE. June 2003, Section 1, #4   (D)
    3. Method-AP, CE. October 2000, Section 1, #15 (C)
    4. Method-AP. December 2003, Section 2, #18   (D)
    5. Method. October 1994, Section 2, #14   (D)
    6. Method-AP. June 1995, Section 1, #14   (B)

Chapter 13: Flaw in the Reasoning Problem Set

    1. Flaw. October 2000, Section 2, #6   (C)
    2. Flaw. December 2001, Section 1, #10   (C)
    3. Flaw. October 2002, Section 1, #23   (A)
    4. Flaw. October 2001, Section 2, #18   (B)
    5. Flaw. June 2003, Section 1, #12   (D)
    6. Flaw-FL. October 2003, Section 2, #20   (B)
    7. Flaw. December 2003, Section 1, #26   (B)
    8. Flaw-CE. December 2002, Section 2, #20   (D)

Chapter 14: Parallel Reasoning Chapter Text

    1. Parallel Flaw-SN. June 1999, Section 2, #21   (D)
    2. Parallel Flaw-SN. December 2000, Section 2, #15 (C)
    3. Parallel Flaw. October 1996, Section 1, #19   (D)
    4. Parallel Flaw. October 1997, Section 1, #23   (E)

Chapter 14: Parallel Reasoning Problem Set

    1. Parallel Flaw. December 1999, Section 1, #6   (B)
    2. Parallel Flaw-CE. December 2002, Section 2, #26 (D)
    3. Parallel Flaw. October 2000, Section 1, #22   (D)
    4. Parallel Flaw-SN. June 2000, Section 1, #21   (C)

Chapter 15: Numbers and Percentages Chapter Text

      1. Must-#%. September 1995, Section 1, #9   (C)
      2. Must-#%. June 1992, Section 2, #12   (C)
      3. Weaken-#%. October 1993, Section 1, #7   (D)
      4. Strengthen-#%. December 1999, Section 1, #4   (C)
      5. Flaw-#%. October 1992, Section 2, #24   (B)

Chapter 15: Numbers and Percentages Problem Set

      1. Flaw-#%. December 2003, Section 1, #12   (D)
      2. Must-#%. December 1995, Section 2, #24   (E)
      3. Assumption-#%. September 1995, Section 1, #14   (D)
      4. Must-#%. September 1995, Section 1, #20   (E)

Chapter 16: Evaluate the Argument Chapter Text

      1. Evaluate. February 1994, Section 1, #6   (C)

Chapter 16: Evaluate the Argument Problem Set

      1. Evaluate-#%. December 2001, Section 1, #24   (B)
      2. Evaluate. October 2002, Section 2, #19   (A)

Chapter 17: Cannot Be True Chapter Text

      1. Cannot. June 1999, Section 1, #11   (A)
      2. Cannot-SN. December 2002, Section 1, #24   (B)

Chapter 17: Cannot Be True Problem Set

      1. Cannot-#%. June 2000, Section 1, #15   (A)
      2. Cannot-SN. October 2003, Section 1, #7   (A)

Chapter-by-Chapter Answer Key

Chapter 18: Point at Issue Chapter Text

    1. PI. June 1991, Section 1, #25   (A)
    2. PI. February 1992, Section 2, #14   (E)

Chapter 18: Point at Issue Problem Set

    1. PI. June 2002, Section 2, #7   (C)
    2. PI. December 2002, Section 1, #23   (D)
    3. PI. October 1999, Section 2, #16   (D)
    4. PI. June 2001, Section 2, #15   (D)

Chapter 19: Principle Chapter Text

    1. Must-PR. February 14th, 2000, Section 2, #16   (C)
    2. Strengthen-PR. December 2002, Section 1, #19 (E)

Chapter 19: Principle Problem Set

    1. Must-PR. October 2002, Section 1, #7   (D)
    2. Strengthen-PR. October 2003, Section 1, #17 (C)
    3. Must-PR. December 2002, Section 1, #11   (D)
    4. Strengthen-PR. December 2003, Section 2, #15 (B)

This section contains a reverse lookup that cross references each question according to the source LSAT. The tests are listed in order of the PrepTest number (if any). The date of administration is also listed to make the process easier. If a test is not listed, then no questions from that exam were used in this book.

Questions listed under each test begin by listing the *Logical Reasoning Bible* chapter the question appears in, whether the problem appears in the chapter text or problem set, and then the question number.

For information on obtaining the publications that contain the LSATs listed below, please visit our Free LSAT Help area at www.powerscore.com/lsat/help/pub_ident.htm

PrepTest 1—June 1991 LSAT

> Chapter 18, Text, #1. PI. June 1991, Section 1, #25

PrepTest 3—December 1991 LSAT

> Chapter 6, Text, #1. Must-SN. December 1991, Section 1, #10

PrepTest 4—February 1992 LSAT

> Chapter 6, Problem, #6. Must-SN. February 1992, Section 1, #12
> Chapter 4, Text, #3. Must. February 1992, Section 1, #22
>
> Chapter 18, Text, #2. PI. February 1992, Section 2, #14

PrepTest 5—June 1992 LSAT

> Chapter 15, Text, #2. Must-#%. June 1992, Section 2, #12

PrepTest 6—October 1992 LSAT

> Chapter 15, Text, #5. Flaw-#%. October 1992, Section 2, #24

PrepTest 9—October 1993 LSAT

> Chapter 15, Text, #3. Weaken-#%. October 1993, Section 1, #7

Test-by-Test Question Use Tracker

PrepTest 10—February 1994 LSAT

Chapter 16, Text, #1. Evaluate. February 1994, Section 1, #6

Chapter 7, Text, #3. Weaken-SN. February 1994, Section 2, #9

PrepTest 11—June 1994 LSAT

Chapter 9, Text, #3. Assumption-SN. June 1994, Section 1, #13

PrepTest 12—October 1994 LSAT

Chapter 12, Problem, #5. Method. October 1994, Section 2, #14

PrepTest 13—December 1994 LSAT

Chapter 12, Text, #1. Method. December 1994, Section 1, #2

Chapter 7, Text, #2. Weaken. December 1994, Section 2, #12
Chapter 11, Problem, #2. MustX-FL. December 1994, Section 2, #14

PrepTest 15—June 1995 LSAT

Chapter 12, Problem, #6. Method-AP. June 1995, Section 1, #14

Chapter 10, Text, #2. Resolve. June 1995, Section 2, #20

PrepTest 16—September 1995 LSAT

Chapter 15, Text, #1. Must-#%. September 1995, Section 1, #9
Chapter 15, Problem, #3. Assumption-#%. September 1995, Section 1, #14
Chapter 15, Problem, #4. Must-#%. September 1995, Section 1, #20

PrepTest 17—December 1995 LSAT

Chapter 15, Problem, #2. Must-#%. December 1995, Section 2, #24

Test-by-Test Question Use Tracker

PrepTest 18—December 1992 LSAT

    Chapter 12, Text, #2. Method. December 1992, Section 2, #21
    Chapter 9, Text, #4. Assumption-CE. December 1992, Section 2, #22

PrepTest 20—October 1996 LSAT

    Chapter 14, Text, #3. Parallel Flaw. October 1996, Section 1, #19

PrepTest 22—June 1997 LSAT

    Chapter 7, Text, #4. Weaken-SN. June 1997, Section 2, #19

PrepTest 23—October 1997 LSAT

    Chapter 11, Problem, #1. Must-FL. October 1997, Section 1, #12
    Chapter 14, Text, #4. Parallel Flaw. October 1997, Section 1, #23

PrepTest 28—June 1999 LSAT

    Chapter 6, Problem, #1. Must-SN. June 1999, Section 1, #10
    Chapter 17, Text, #1. Cannot. June 1999, Section 1, #11
    Chapter 6, Text, #4. Must-SN. June 1999, Section 1, #14
    Chapter 9, Text, #3. StrengthenX-CE. June 1999, Section 1, #26

    Chapter 4, Text, #1. Must. June 1999, Section 2, #1
    Chapter 4, Text, #5. Must. June 1999, Section 2, #8
    Chapter 7, Problem, #1. Weaken. June 1999, Section 2, #15
    Chapter 14, Text, #1. Parallel Flaw-SN. June 1999, Section 2, #21

PrepTest 29—October 1999 LSAT

    Chapter 9, Problem, #2. Assumption. October 1999, Section 1, #5
    Chapter 3, Text, #8. October 1999, Section 1, #11-12   (stimulus only)

    Chapter 6, Problem, #2. Must-SN. October 1999, Section 2, #12
    Chapter 18, Problem, #3. PI. October 1999, Section 2, #16
    Chapter 9, Text, #4. StrengthenX-CE. October 1999, Section 2, #20
    Chapter 8, Problem, #4. Weaken-CE. October 1999, Section 2, #24

Test-by-Test Question Use Tracker

PrepTest 30—December 1999 LSAT

Chapter 15, Text, #4. Strengthen-#%. December 1999, Section 1, #4
Chapter 14, Problem, #1. Parallel Flaw. December 1999, Section 1, #6
Chapter 6, Problem, #4. Must-SN. December 1999, Section 1, #18

Chapter 8, Text, #2. Weaken-CE. December 1999, Section 2, #11

PrepTest 31—June 2000 LSAT

Chapter 9, Problem, #6. Assumption. June 2000, Section 1, #14
Chapter 17, Problem, #1. Cannot-#%. June 2000, Section 1, #15
Chapter 4, Problem, #8. Must. June 2000, Section 1, #20
Chapter 14, Problem, #4. Parallel Flaw-SN. June 2000, Section 1, #21

Chapter 9, Text, #2. Justify. June 2000, Section 2, #10
Chapter 6, Text, #2. Must-SN. June 2000, Section 2, #22

PrepTest 32—October 2000 LSAT

Chapter 6, Text, #3. Must-SN. October 2000, Section 1, #7
Chapter 12, Problem, #3. Method-AP, CE. October 2000, Section 1, #15
Chapter 14, Problem, #3. Parallel Flaw. October 2000, Section 1, #22

Chapter 9, Problem, #1. Justify. October 2000, Section 2, #4
Chapter 10, Problem, #2. Resolve. October 2000, Section 2, #5
Chapter 13, Problem, #1. Flaw. October 2000, Section 2, #6
Chapter 4, Text, #4. Must. October 2000, Section 2, #24

PrepTest 33—December 2000 LSAT

Chapter 9, Text, #1. Assumption. December 2000, Section 1, #10
Chapter 8, Problem, #1. Weaken-CE. December 2000, Section 1, #25

Chapter 8, Problem, #6. Weaken-CE. December 2000, Section 2, #7
Chapter 4, Text, #2. Must. December 2000, Section 2, #10
Chapter 14, Text, #2. Parallel Flaw-SN. December 2000, Section 2, #15
Chapter 9, Problem, #4. Strengthen-CE. December 2000, Section 2, #20
Chapter 3, Text, #6. December 2000, Section 2, #22 (stimulus only)
Chapter 9, Text, #1. Justify. December 2000, Section 2, #23

Test-by-Test Question Use Tracker

PrepTest 34—June 2001 LSAT

Chapter 7, Problem, #4. Weaken. June 2001, Section 1, #12

Chapter 9, Problem, #1. Assumption-SN. June 2001, Section 2, #5
Chapter 18, Problem, #4. PI. June 2001, Section 2, #15
Chapter 4, Problem, #7. Must. June 2001, Section 2, #19

PrepTest 35—October 2001 LSAT

Chapter 7, Problem, #6. Weaken. October 2001, Section 1, #8
Chapter 9, Text, #2. StrengthenX. October 2001, Section 1, #15
Chapter 9, Problem, #3. Assumption. October 2001, Section 1, #18
Chapter 9, Problem, #3. Justify. October 2001, Section 1, #20
Chapter 11, Problem, #4. Justify-FL. October 2001, Section 1, #22

Chapter 9, Problem, #2. Justify. October 2001, Section 2, #14
Chapter 9, Problem, #5. Assumption. October 2001, Section 2, #16
Chapter 7, Text, #5. Weaken-SN. October 2001, Section 2, #17
Chapter 13, Problem, #4. Flaw. October 2001, Section 2, #18
Chapter 7, Problem, #5. Weaken. October 2001, Section 2, #20

PrepTest 36—December 2001 LSAT

Chapter 8, Problem, #2. Must-CE. December 2001, Section 1, #4
Chapter 10, Problem, #3. Resolve. December 2001, Section 1, #9
Chapter 13, Problem, #2. Flaw. December 2001, Section 1, #10
Chapter 16, Problem, #1. Evaluate-#%. December 2001, Section 1, #24

Chapter 6, Problem, #3. MP-SN. December 2001, Section 2, #3
Chapter 9, Problem, #2. Strengthen. December 2001, Section 2, #7
Chapter 5, Text, #2. MP. December 2001, Section 2, #9
Chapter 9, Problem, #4. Justify. December 2001, Section 2, #12
Chapter 3, Text, #5. December 2001, Section 2, #13 (stimulus only)

Test-by-Test Question Use Tracker

PrepTest 37—June 2002 LSAT

Chapter 4, Problem, #3. Must. June 2002, Section 1, #2
Chapter 9, Text, #1. Strengthen. June 2002, Section 1, #6
Chapter 4, Problem, #2. Must. June 2002, Section 1, #7
Chapter 5, Text, #3. MP—FITB. June 2002, Section 1, #9

Chapter 3, Text, #4. June 2002, Section 2, #6   (stimulus only)
Chapter 18, Problem, #1. PI. June 2002, Section 2, #7

PrepTest 38—October 2002 LSAT

Chapter 5, Problem, #1. MP. October 2002, Section 1, #2
Chapter 3, Text, #1. October 2002, Section 1, #6   (stimulus only)
Chapter 19, Problem, #1. Must-PR. October 2002, Section 1, #7
Chapter 3, Text, #2. October 2002, Section 1, #11   (stimulus only)
Chapter 4, Problem, #5. Must. October 2002, Section 1, #15
Chapter 3, Text, #3. October 2002, Section 1, #22   (stimulus only)
Chapter 13, Problem, #3. Flaw. October 2002, Section 1, #23

Chapter 9, Problem, #3. StrengthenX-CE. October 2002, Section 2, #5
Chapter 4, Problem, #4. Must. October 2000, Section 2, #10
Chapter 7, Problem, #2. Weaken. October 2002, Section 2, #15
Chapter 16, Problem, #2. Evaluate. October 2002, Section 2, #19
Chapter 9, Problem, #4. Assumption. October 2002, Section 2, #22

PrepTest 39—December 2002 LSAT

Chapter 3, Text, #7. December 2002, Section 1, #2   (stimulus only)
Chapter 19, Problem, #3. Must-PR. December 2002, Section 1, #11
Chapter 19, Text, #2. Strengthen-PR. December 2002, Section 1, #19
Chapter 18, Problem, #2. PI. December 2002, Section 1, #23
Chapter 17, Text, #2. Cannot-SN. December 2002, Section 1, #24

Chapter 6, Problem, #5. Must-SN. December 2002, Section 2, #6
Chapter 12, Problem, #1. Method. December 2002, Section 2, #8
Chapter 4, Problem, #6. Must. December 2002, Section 2, #16
Chapter 13, Problem, #8. Flaw-CE. December 2002, Section 2, #20
Chapter 14, Problem, #2. Parallel Flaw-CE. December 2002, Section 2, #26

Test-by-Test Question Use Tracker

PrepTest 40—June 2003 LSAT

Chapter 2, Text, #3 (stimulus) and Chapter 12, Problem, #2. Method-CE. June 2003, Section 1, #4
Chapter 5, Text, #1. MP. June 2003, Section 1, #9
Chapter 9, Problem, #1. Strengthen. June 2003, Section 1, #11
Chapter 13, Problem, #5. Flaw. June 2003, Section 1, #12

PrepTest 41—October 2003 LSAT

Chapter 10, Problem, #1. Resolve. October 2003, Section 1, #4
Chapter 17, Problem, #2. Cannot-SN. October 2003, Section 1, #7
Chapter 10, Problem, #4. Resolve. October 2003, Section 1, #8
Chapter 19, Problem, #2. Strengthen-PR. October 2003, Section 1, #17

Chapter 4, Problem, #1. Must. October 2003, Section 2, #6
Chapter 9, Text, #2. Assumption. October 2003, Section 2, #7
Chapter 8, Problem, #5. Flaw-CE. October 2003, Section 2, #13
Chapter 2, Text, #4. October 2003, Section 2, #16   (partial stimulus)
Chapter 13, Problem, #6. Flaw-FL. October 2003, Section 2, #20
Chapter 2, Text, #1 and Chapter 11, Problem, #3. Must-FL. October 2003, Section 2, #25

PrepTest 42—December 2003 LSAT

Chapter 7, Text, #1. Weaken. December 2003, Section 1, #1
Chapter 12, Text, #3. Method-AP. December 2003, Section 1, #2
Chapter 8, Text, #1. Flaw-CE. December 2003, Section 1, #3
Chapter 2, Text, #6. December 2003, Section 1, #4   (partial stimulus)
Chapter 15, Problem, #1. Flaw-#%. December 2003, Section 1, #12
Chapter 7, Problem, #3. Weaken. December 2003, Section 1, #20
Chapter 13, Problem, #7. Flaw. December 2003, Section 1, #26

Chapter 8, Problem, #3. Weaken-CE. December 2003, Section 2, #6
Chapter 5, Problem, #2. MP. December 2003, Section 2, #10
Chapter 19, Problem, #4. Strengthen-PR. December 2003, Section 2, #15
Chapter 12, Text, #4. Method-AP. December 2003, Section 2, #16
Chapter 12, Problem, #4. Method-AP. December 2003, Section 2, #18
Chapter 2, Text, #2 and Chapter 2, Text, #5. December 2003, Section 2, #21 (partial stimulus)
Chapter 10, Text, #1. Resolve. December 2003, Section 2, #24

Official LSAT SuperPrep, Test #3—February 14th, 2000

Chapter 19, Text, #1. Must-PR. February 14th, 2000, Section 2, #16

CONTACTING POWERSCORE

Contact Information ████████████████████████

PowerScore LSAT Logical Reasoning Bible Information:

      Student Web Section: www.powerscore.com/lrbible
      Email: lrbible@powerscore.com

PowerScore Full-length LSAT Course Information:
      Complete preparation for the LSAT. Classes available nationwide.

      Web: www.powerscore.com/lsat/lsat.htm
      Request Information: www.powerscore.com/contact.htm

PowerScore Weekend LSAT Course Information:
      Fast and effective LSAT preparation: 16 hour courses, 99th percentile instructors,
      and real LSAT questions.

      Web: www.powerscore.com/lsat/weekend.htm
      Request Information: www.powerscore.com/contact.htm

PowerScore LSAT Tutoring Information:
      One-on-one meetings with a PowerScore LSAT expert.

      Web: www.powerscore.com/lsat/tutoring.htm
      Request Information: www.powerscore.com/contact.htm

PowerScore Law School Admissions Counseling Information:
      Personalized application and admission assistance.

      Web: www.powerscore.com/lsat/admissions.htm
      Request Information: www.powerscore.com/contact.htm

PowerScore International Headquarters:

      PowerScore
      37V New Orleans Road
      Hilton Head Island, SC 29928

      Toll-free information number: (800) 545-1750
      Facsimile: (843) 785-8203
      Website: www.powerscore.com
      Email: lsat@powerscore.com